D0402798

*f*P

The SCORECARD

ALWAYS LIES

A Year Behind the Scenes on the PGA Tour

CHRIS LEWIS

FREE PRESS

New York   London   Toronto   Sydney

FREE PRESS
A Division of Simon & Schuster Inc.
1230 Avenue of the Americas
New York, NY 10020

First Free Press hardcover edition May 2007

FREE PRESS and colophon are trademarks of Simon & Schuster, Inc.

For information about special discounts for bulk purchases,
please contact Simon & Schuster Special Sales:
1-800-456-6798 or business@simonandschuster.com

DESIGNED BY ERICH HOBBING

Manufactured in the United States of America

1   3   5   7   9   10   8   6   4   2

Library of Congress Cataloging-in-Publication
Data Control No. 1007005101

ISBN-13: 978-1-4165-3716-8
ISBN-10:   1-4165-3716-3

To everyone who helped,
especially Mom.

CONTENTS

CONTENTS

INTRODUCTION: GOLF 10 A.T.

The idea for this book came out of a clock radio one morning in a hotel room in Chicago. In town to cover the Western Open, I was sitting at my computer drinking coffee and checking my email, with the radio dial (thanks to the room's previous occupant) tuned to one of the city's innumerable sports talk radio stations. That morning's guest was a local baseball beat writer.

During the call-in portion of the show, the listeners were unconcerned about results, stats, and standings. Instead, they wanted to know about the reporter's close-quarters experiences with the players. Who, they asked, were the easiest to deal with? The toughest? Which were the nicest, and the nastiest? In essence, these were all variations on the same question: *What are these guys really like?*

It wasn't surprising. Sportswriters and our television colleagues are expected to supply such inside dope at every impromptu conversational occasion—in elevators, on airplanes, at cocktail parties. But hearing those questions often enough, it's hard not to notice in the subtext a subtle accusation—that we media types aren't doing our jobs. Fans want from us a sense for the personalities of their favorite athletes. But they evidently aren't getting it from standard TV, newspaper, and magazine coverage.

The athletes deserve part of the blame. Sports' new riches have made it unnecessary for them to use the press as a promotional tool. And why open up to strangers, when a stray unwise remark can result in brand-damaging embarrassment? But bland reporting is the media's fault, too. Publishers, editors, and TV execs—claiming that in the Internet age, immediacy is everything—care little about going behind the scenes, especially since it costs money to send reporters and camera crews to players' homes for in-depth profiles. And by keeping it short and sweet, they say, they're only giving their audience what it wants. Who cares if the voices on the hotel room clock radio argue otherwise?

This book aims to satisfy, if only a little, that lingering desire for up-close-and-personal reporting. A fan myself, I believe that spectator sports are far less interesting, even tedious, without a real feeling for the people playing the games—their backstories, habits, idiosyncracies, and their off-course preoccupations and behavior. Its goal, in other words, is to humanize at least a small group of professional athletes, and to provide a broader, richer, more personal context for the numbers they write on their scorecards.

It's ironic, in a way, that the book's subject is pro golfers. Traditionally, these athletes have been far better than others at sharing their private lives. Arnold Palmer set the modern standard, hanging in hotel bars with reporters until all hours of the night. Similarly, Jack Nicklaus spent interminable periods standing in front of the scribes, answering their every last question. As recently as the mid-nineties, John Feinstein, who was then a generalist (and whose book *A Good Walk Spoiled* was, in a sense, a model for this one) could alight on the PGA Tour and expect unlimited time with a dozen of golf's biggest names. The players—whose incomes, historically, lagged far behind those of their sporting peers—knew that courting the press was the best way for their little boutique sport to garner extra attention. They indulged sportswriters in order to show fans that there was more to them, and to the game, than was immediately apparent.

But that, along with everything else in the game, changed with the arrival of Tiger Woods.

Woods' first professional tee shot, in August 1996, had the socioeconomic exit velocity of a NASA rocket. It carried golf far beyond its usual demographics, growing its spectator base across lines of class, age, and race. And that meant more money. Between 1996 and 2001, the Tour's television revenue, its primary purse-feeder, nearly tripled, growing from about $85 million to $215 million per year.

Raw numbers, however, didn't describe Tiger's impact nearly as well as the way he altered the day-to-day business of the sport, and the lives of his peers. One summer evening in 2003, Woods, Ernie Els, Sergio Garcia, and Phil Mickelson found themselves standing on the 17th green of a golf course in the hills overlooking San Diego. They were bathed in temporary floodlights. The occasion was a Monday night prime-time telecast placed strategically where, in colder months, football would be. The match they'd just played, *The Battle at The Bridges,* was the fifth in a series of Tiger-centric made-for-TV affairs. Mickelson and Garcia, the winners, collected $600,000 apiece—more than was earned by the thirty-first highest player (Nick Price) on the 1995 Tour money list. The losers, Woods and Els, took home $250,000 each—not bad for a day's work.

Conducting the postgame interviews was Ian Baker-Finch. After trading a few words with Woods and Els, he turned to Mickelson, who had been playing a home game. He was a member at The Bridges.

"So," Baker-Finch asked, "do you think it was a little bit of local knowledge that helped you out tonight?"

Mickelson gave a brief, innocuous answer, and then took a detour. "You know, I'd just like to say one thing," he began. "On behalf of Ernie, myself, and Sergio, and all professional golfers, we want to thank Tiger for making this possible. Because, if it wasn't for him, we wouldn't be playing in prime time, and we just appreciate the opportunity to do that."

Mickelson's ring-kissing seemed weird, but he was dead right. Baker-Finch backed him up, remarking that Woods had made golf "a sexy sport." More seriously put, it was because of Tiger, as Tour commissioner Tim Finchem once said, that the game was now positioned "to become one of the premier mass sports."

As Tiger mainstreamed golf, the new cash influx remade the Tour from top to bottom. Foreign players flocked to the U.S., pushing aside the American-born sons of country clubbers who used to fill its ranks. The number of people who could make a living on the game's periphery—swing coaches, sports psychologists, trainers and the like—grew exponentially. Even the nature of the Tour caddie was transformed. Once, the men who carried the pros' bags were ordinary joes whose love of the game far outstripped their hopes of financial security. Now, more often than not, they were players' relatives or college buddies, who knew they might make more caddying than they would as bankers or lawyers.

The players themselves—even the moderately successful ones—now enjoyed lifestyles worthy of a Robin Leach voice-over, with private jets, multiple residences and multiple nannies, some of whom even took care of children. Indeed, their only headaches were the effects of raising their kids in such luxury. In a hotel room one day, Jim Furyk heard the son of a fellow pro say, "This room stinks—there's no mini-bar!" Lee Westwood's five-year-old son, Sam, once turned to his father during a rare commercial flight and said, "Daddy, what are these people doing on our airplane?"

Nothing, however, changed more than fan expectations. Before Tiger, golf had never (apart from two or three Sundays per year) been much of a spectator draw. And for good reason. True excitement was rare. The pace was slow, and the competion, even on television, was hard to follow. The subtleties of the game were elusive: while everyone recognizes how hard it is to dunk, few appreciate the difficulty of a 60-yard bunker shot. And there was little opportunity for casual sports fans to develop a feel for such nuances. Unless you lived at a country club, you couldn't just run out into the backyard on a Sunday afternoon after watching your heroes in action and try to imitate their feats.

Further, unknowns too often emerged from deep in the field to push familiar names out of the spotlight. In no other sport could a mystery guest like Craig Perks or Todd Hamilton win a marquee event, because in other sports, they weren't invited in the first place. When the Boston Celtics and Los Angeles Lakers met in the NBA finals, you could be reasonably sure the Buffalo Braves wouldn't storm out of the locker room and steal the trophy. But in golf, that sort of thing happened all the time.

Woods, however, rewrote most of those rules. The first six years of his career were one long highlight film, producing nonstop *SportsCenter* moments. The hole-outs and fist-pumps obviated any need for a deep understanding of the game. He also eliminated, to a fair extent, the problem of lesser-known winners. On Sundays he showed up as regularly as the Dallas Cowboys, and never seemed to lose. By way of explaining his own winlessness at major championships, Colin Montgomerie once said, "It's difficult to win majors in this era, because every year, Tiger takes two of them." Monty's accounting was exaggerated, but only slightly. And the ratio wasn't much different if you included regular-season Tour events. By the end of 2006, Woods had won a whopping fifty-four of his 200 Tour starts.

If Tiger turned golf into a one-ring circus, no one complained about it. Through most of his first decade as a pro, it was financially healthier than ever. The money was so good, in fact, that the game had to do virtually nothing to sell itself. The necessity for players like Palmer and Nicklaus to court the fans through the media had disappeared. Not even the lowliest players needed such attention. They too were getting rich, even though few fans knew their names.

But in late 2002—shortly before Mickelson's speech at *The Battle at The Bridges*—a certain downside to Woods' hegemony was coming into focus. His decision to undertake a swing change, leading to a stretch of substandard play, resulted in a steady decline of the Tour's television ratings. Each year, viewership for its Sunday broadcasts (including majors) slipped by about five percent. It became clear that interest fell through the floor when Tiger wasn't at the top of the game. And there were no second-tier stories to fall back on, since Woods had no real rivals. It didn't help that his dominance had stunted the development of young American pros. They rarely glimpsed the winner's circle, and faltered when they did, because they never had a chance to learn how to finish off a tournament.

Worse news came in 2005. Woods began to rebound (winning six tournaments, including two majors), but the ratings continued to fall. Compared to the previous year, the average Sunday viewership for events—not just any events, but those *in which he played*—dropped fifteen percent. When Woods won the British Open at St. Andrews, about as compelling a scene as the sport could muster, U.S. ratings were only marginally better (fewer than 100,000 households) than for little-known Todd Hamilton's victory at the previous year's Open.

The novelty, it appeared, had worn off. And the television executives noticed. Later that year, Disney, the parent company of ABC, owners of that Monday night prime-time franchise, pulled the plug on the series, declining to renew the $50 million, five-year deal that secured Woods' participation. The unthinkable had happened. Tiger got fired.

To be sure, the swoon in his and golf's popularity showed a volatility in the sport's new Tiger-curious golf audience. Excellence wasn't enough, especially for young male viewers increasingly distracted by the Internet, Grand Theft Auto, and next-door neighbors who looked and behaved like Britney Spears.

The Tour responded by revamping its product, announcing a schedule contraction that, beginning in 2007, would bring the top players together more often, and a new season-ending playoff series, the FedEx

Cup. Both were good ideas. But neither did much to optomize the sport's greatest resource, the players themselves.

Pro golfers are a special breed. The personality traits that they bring to the game, or are inculcated by the game, make them far more interesting than other athletes: they are at once fiercely analytical and creative, confident and humble, self-critical and good-humored. On top of that, they, like the game itself, tend to be relentlessly social. They usually make good use of their plentiful downtime, using off-weeks to indulge off-course interests, and, during tournament weeks, taking in ballgames, concerts, and dining out, all in the country's liveliest cities and toniest resort towns. That means they always have something outside of golf to talk about.

And despite all the Tiger Era's changes, they can still be remarkably open and candid. While they resist reporters they only see a few times a year, they are, with the beat writers who travel the Tour with them, more willing than the average athlete or even layman to let their guards down. Names as big as Vijay Singh and Ernie Els are still capable of giving cell phone numbers to reporters who cover the Tour on a weekly basis. In close company, even Tiger Woods and Phil Mickelson can come across with jokes, anecdotes, and well-placed pokes in the belly. Their behind-the-scenes stories, and those of their peers, never really went away. They just went underground and were still waiting to be told.

The Players

Chris Couch. A career grinder coming off a divorce and living in his RV. The Tour likes to say that any of its players, on a given week, is good enough to win, and he's about to prove it.

John Daly. No other fat man could balance so adeptly on the tightrope between excellence and laughability. With his wife facing jail time and his bad habits barely under control, no one knew what to expect from Long John in 2006.

Chris DiMarco. His rep was a long string of clichés, but they were all true: he was Gritty, fiery, and impossible not to love (unless you went to Florida State). The only mystery about the guy with the weird putting grip was why he hadn't won a tournament in four years.

David Duval. In twenty 2005 events, the former world number one made just one cut. Golf had seen slumps before, but never one this dramatic. His new family made him happy, but after 2006, the final year of eligibility from his 2001 British Open win, it might be the only thing he had left.

Jim Furyk. The Tour's Everyman didn't make many headlines, but no one got more respect from his peers. Injuries notwithstanding, he was always good for at least one win a year. Still, one wondered why he so often finished second (four times in 2005).

J. B. Holmes. The quiet kid from Kentucky won the previous year's qualifying tournament in a walk, but no one anticipated how much noise he and his driver would make in 2006.

Phil Mickelson. He still had his critics—oy, that smile!—but Lefty had completed a Janus-worthy career turnaround, going from perpetual underachiever to two-time major winner. He was now seemingly Tiger's most able challenger.

Sean O'Hair. Just 23, whispers were that the 2005 Rookie of the Year was the best American player of his generation. This was to be the year he emerged from the shadow of his troubled past.

Geoff Ogilvy. The latest in a line of fine Australian players had just notched his first Tour win in 2005. The press and his peers loved him, and no golfer this side of Tiger Woods would have a bigger 2006.

Adam Scott. The only young Aussie with more promise than Ogilvy (with whom he happened to be best friends). Still, it felt like forever since the 26-year-old won the Players Championship. Was there an expiration date on potential?

Vijay Singh. Not just the second-best player on the planet, but the only guy who had proven he could outplay Tiger when the chips were down. Big Daddy was coming off nine wins in 2004 and four more in 2005. The press, famously, wasn't on his side, and neither was time—he would turn 44 in 2006.

Camilo Villegas. The rookie from Colombia had star-quality looks, and game to match. Apart from Holmes, no new arrival would have a bigger impact in the coming year.

Michelle Wie. It was Year Three of the teen phenom's quest to make a cut on a men's tour. A season-opening straw poll would have shown more fans than skeptics among the Tour players. But that would soon change.

Tiger Woods. After two years in the swing-change wilderness, Tiggy (as some Tour brethren called him) bounced back with a two-major 2005. Going into 2006, he looked poised to return to dominating form. But golf was the last thing on his mind.

THE SUPPORTING CAST

Michael Allen. The likeable, perpetually upbeat 45-year-old epitomized the career grinder. He'd never finished higher than 73rd on the money list. What he did best was survive Q-school. Treating it like a revolving door, he'd come out the correct side eight out of twelve times. His goal for 2006, though, was qualifying for the U.S. Open: it would be held at Winged Foot, where he worked as a pro during a 1997 sabbatical from the game.

Stuart Appleby. The six-time Tour winner—now well into his second golfing life, following the tragic death of his first wife, Renay—was still the Aussie with most solid U.S. Tour résumé. The golf world awaited a breakthrough big-event victory. Meanwhile, he'd made the season-opening Mercedes Championships his own personal annuity: he'd won it twice in a row.

Mike Bennett and Andy Plummer. Not players but swing coaches, the teaching tandem, former disciples of legendary oddball Mac O'Grady, were steadily making a name for themselves on the Tour. They didn't know it yet, but their stock was about to go through the roof.

Mark Calcavecchia. Once one of the Tour's premier players, the achy but always competitive 45-year-old was busy adjusting to middle age. No one was better at cutting across Tour cliques: a Falstaffian FOT (Friend of Tiger), he was also a FOP (Friend of Phil).

Sergio Garcia. At 26, he was probably the best ballstriker in the game. But watching him putt was like watching Shaquille O'Neal shoot free throws. If he broke the hex—and found a way to avoid being intimidated by Tiger down the stretch—he was a shoo-in to displace one of the top five players in the world rankings.

Robert Garrigus. After turning pro at the tender age of 19, the 28-year-old rookie had finally reached the big time. His happy-go-lucky exterior was deceiving: his past had the makings of an *E! True Hollywood Story.* If he got his short game together, he could turn out to be the best player from the Pacific Northwest since Fred Couples.

Tom Lehman. Captain of the U.S. team in the upcoming Ryder Cup matches, he will regrettably spend more time this year hanging out with golf writers than Tour players. His desire to make his own team was stronger than he was willing to let on.

Retief Goosen. Starting the year as the fourth-ranked player in the world, the stoic South African, long thought to be the best tough-course player in the game, was still apparently reeling from his shocking meltdown at the 2005 U.S. Open, where he shot a final-round 84 to blow a three-stroke Saturday night lead.

Colin Montgomerie. No one's career had more ups and downs than Monty's. When he was the best player in Europe, the infamously major-less Scot was also the American galleries' favorite object of scorn. More recently, worldwide respect and sympathy arose from his Ryder Cup heroics and a long, trying divorce. Now, however, in the midst of a competitive rebirth, he was trying to live down cheating allegations.

The SCORECARD

ALWAYS LIES

1

THE MEN WHO WEREN'T THERE

Hawaii

Three Mondays before the start of the 2006 PGA Tour season, Mark Calcavecchia was in his living room at home in Scottsdale, Arizona, sitting in his well-worn La-Z-Boy recliner. The remote was in his hand, and on the TV in front of him was *Golf Central*, the Golf Channel's nightly news program. Filling the screen was the image of anchor Megan West, a perky young blonde with a toothpaste-commercial smile.

West was a new hire, but to Calc she was already a familiar face. The ever-amicable twenty-year veteran had gone out of his way to introduce himself to her two months earlier at the Disney in Orlando, a low-key tournament down the block from TGC headquarters. She had left the office to try to get a feel for an actual PGA Tour event and meet some of the players. It was natural for her to do so. The channel had a symbiotic relationship with the Tour, functioning as a de facto public relations arm.

Now, as she started reading her item, a headshot of Tiger Woods popped up in the corner of the screen. The world's best player, she reported, would be skipping the first tournament of the 2006 season, the Mercedes Championships in Maui, Hawaii. The reason? Good question. In most respects, the Golf Channel's access was unlimited. But no one could peer inside that head. Calc had guesses, but he didn't really know, either. True he was one of Woods' best friends on Tour. But Tiger didn't exactly provide daily updates on his personal life.

When West finished, Calcavecchia dropped the remote, picked up his cellphone, and found Tiger's name. He typed:

No Hawaii for you, more cash for me. Then he pressed "Send."

The line was funny enough. A purse untapped by Tiger was good news to an old pro who, by force of habit, counted every dollar.

But behind it was a little disappointment. Calcavecchia had been looking forward to seeing his buddy in Hawaii. Woods' two best Tour pals, veterans Mark O'Meara and John Cook, hadn't qualified for the event, so no one in the field was likelier than Calc to share Tiger's downtime. He figured they would play a couple of practice rounds, watch the Rose Bowl together, maybe have a meal or three.

If O'Meara and Cook were like big brothers to Woods, Calcavecchia was like a favorite cousin. Their relationship was easy-going, light-hearted. In 2005 at Augusta, the two had made a pact: whoever saw the other first was obliged to tell him to "do something unnatural to himself," as Calc would later say. On the range before the final round, Calcavecchia flipped at Woods, from fifty yards away, a practice ball inscribed with the message. But behind the levity was a terrific respect. At the 2000 British Open in St. Andrews, Calcavecchia, along with O'Meara, had come out and stood behind the 18th green to watch Tiger finish off his landmark victory, something pros, as a rule, never do.

Calc wasn't the only one who would miss him. For the tournament organizers, Woods' absence not only detracted from the glamor of the event, but also put a damper on ongoing sponsorship-renewal negotiations with Mercedes. Further, the Tour itself was at the tail end of negotiations with its television broadcast partners, and its inability to produce its top star for a marquee event only illustrated its inability to control the quality of its product.

Tiger wasn't the only no-show. Retief Goosen and Padraig Harrington were also skipping. So was Phil Mickelson, whose absenteeism was becoming chronic. Even before 2006, he had passed on both the Mercedes and the Tour Championship three of the previous four years.

Woods' absence, however, was symbolic. Not just the game's best player, he was the man who made such hooky-playing possible, in effect signing everyone's doctor's notes. Back in the day, a $5.5 million purse would have made Arnie, Jack, or Gary blink once, pack, and get on a plane. Now, the pros played for that kind of dough every week. And that was Tiger's fault. It was the new attention he brought to the game that ballooned television and sponsorship contracts, and consequently inflated purses. It was because of him that the best players' ancillary incomes could make a Rockefeller blush.

The trickle-down effect went all the way down the money list. In fact, it went well past it, even impacting teenage girls. Michelle Wie, the 16-year-old who would headline the following week's Sony Open in Honolulu, was the first true child of the Tiger Era: she grew up with the expectation of such riches, and had already begun to reap their benefits. She had turned professional the previous September, signing endorsement contracts with Nike and Sony worth a reported $10 million per year. Sure, she was talented. But that kind of money would never have been available if not for the attention Woods had drawn to the game.

Now, however, the sport was at a pivotal point. The TV negotiations were taking place under a cloud. Ratings, buoyed by Tiger during his early years, had started to dip. The feeling was that, for mass audiences, Tiger's novelty had worn off. That made the new television package a harder sell. At the same time, the stars—who, as Calcavecchia would bluntly say in Hawaii, simply "didn't need the money"—seemed uninterested in helping the Tour put its best fields forward. It couldn't help but create the impression that golf had grown too fat for its own good.

Not many right-minded humans would have passed up the trip to Maui. The 1,600-acre Kapalua resort—a former pineapple plantation on a peninsula on the northwest corner of the island, surrounded by the ocean on three sides—was one of the most beautiful places on earth.

The host Plantation Course, a miracle of a layout designed by Bill Coore and Ben Crenshaw, rolled in and around the resort's highest hills. Its expansive views made it virtually impossible to concentrate on golf. The 18th, and a few other holes on the back side, looked out toward the neighboring island of Molokai; a few tees on the front overlooked Lanai, to the west. At tournament time, every shot was accompanied by a humpback whale rising up, spouting water, and slapping the ocean with its tail.

Even without the whales, Kapalua would have been one of the coolest places anywhere to watch golf. Crowds were sparse, making for intimate pro-ogling. Instead of hot dogs and hamburgers, the concession stands served up ono and ahi on beds of sticky rice. But spectating came at a price. The course was hands-down the most taxing walk on Tour, enough to make anyone over 50 beg for a handful of ibuprofen. Even the players took carts up the steep fourth fairway, insuring that oldsters like Calcavecchia don't have coronaries, further thinning the field. One of the best pieces of tournament lore involved Steve Williams, Tiger Woods' ultrafit caddie. One year, Woods and his swing coach, Butch Harmon, bet him $500 each that he couldn't run the back nine, touching every tee and green, in less than thirty minutes. He did it, but wanted to spend his winnings on an ambulance.

No Tour event was as relentlessly player-friendly. In 2006, last-place prize money—what you were paid, in essence, for just showing up—was $70,000. Contestants all got free rooms at the on-site Ritz-Carlton. But they weren't just any rooms. Two-time defending champ Stuart Appleby's was, in his words, "big enough to play cricket in." Each came equipped with gift bags and baskets full of fruit, sunglasses, shirts, adult beverages, and macadamia nut candies—everything but a freshly caught tuna and a stack of bank notes.

Early in the week, the surroundings made it hard for the players to go to the golf course. Calcavecchia, his new wife, Brenda (whom he had married the previous May, at Lake Como, after the first round of the Italian Open), and his son Eric, who turned twelve on the first of the year, spent most of their week at the pool or in the ocean. One afternoon they went surfing at Lahaina, ten miles down the coast. Eric, a snowboarder from an early age, had caught his first wave on the same beach the last time his dad qualified for the Mercedes, in 2002. Yes, Calc surfed, too. "It's not pretty," he said, "but I can do it." Just the same, it took a certain toll on his 40-year-old body. "All that paddling is murder on your back and pecs. The next day, I really felt it."

Elsewhere, the other players—many of whom would play principal roles in the coming season—were settling in and getting used to the lush life on the Kapalua campus. No matter where they were or what they were doing, all the little scenes, because of the setting, were worthy of postcards home.

David Toms was running the same drill as Calcavecchia. Every day, sometimes twice a day, his son, Carter, 8, would drag the family down to nearby Honolua Bay, a five-minute walk from the hotel, intent on going boogie-boarding. Invariably the waves were too big, sending them back up to the hotel pool. Despite the to and fro, the week couldn't help but have a curative effect. Toms and his wife, Sonya, were still recovering from a chaotic 2005. In May, Toms filed a lawsuit against his agents, Links Sports, claiming mismanagement of his affairs. June brought the year's only good news, the birth of David and Sonya's second child, daughter Anna. In September, Katrina struck his home state; later that month, he collapsed on the golf course at the 84 Lumber Classic. In November he had surgery to repair the heart arrhythmia that caused it. In December, Adam Young, his manager and close friend, began tests that ultimately discovered he had Hodgkins lymphoma.

On Tuesday, while the Tomses were at the pool, Jim Furyk was standing behind the first tee, amid technicolor tropical flowers, having an informal conversation with a reporter about his holidays. He and his family, he said, had spent Christmas in Ponte Vedra, at his house just down the road from Tour headquarters. For New Year's, they adjourned to his second home here in Maui, on land his father had twisted his arm to buy back in 1999, early in his career, when a bank loan was still a necessity.

"The house is right near here, isn't it?" the reporter enquired.

"It's about 300 yards up the road," Furyk replied.

"So maybe tonight, I can check out of my hotel and come and stay in the guest house, right?"

"Uh, I don't know," Furyk said. "Actually, it's occupied."

(He wasn't lying. His mom and dad were staying there that week. Indeed, Mike and Linda Furyk spent about six months of every year at the house. Mike's regular golf game at Kapalua often included neighbor and New York Yankee manager Joe Torre.)

Sergio Garcia was about to start a practice round, but he too found time for a casual chat about the off-season. The high point, he said, was a charity soccer game in Düsseldorf, where he played alongside fellow Adidas-endorsers Ronaldo and Zinedine Zidane. "I had a couple of good passes and some good crosses, but no goals," he smiled. Otherwise, he hung out at his mountain home in Crans-sur-Sierre, Switzerland. "I just started cross-country skiing. It's not as dangerous as downhill, and it's definitely a better workout than golf."

Aussie Stuart Appleby, the two-time defending champion, was already out on the golf course, but his wife, Ashley, was browsing in the hotel gift shop, with one hand on daughter Ella's stroller. Mother and child were first-time attendees, but had nevertheless played a part in Stuey's win the previous year. After collecting his trophy and raising a celebratory glass, he literally sprinted to his car to make a flight to Australia, where Ashley was about to deliver their daughter after an uneasy pregnancy. Ella came into the world less than three days after his plane touched down.

Now, Ashley was checking out some ornately embroidered flip-flops, in the end settling on a pair whose big gold clusters covered the star tattoo on the top of one of her feet. Ella, sitting there with a little pink ribbon in her tawny hair, wasn't impressed. She looked a little bored.

That evening, Vaughn Taylor was getting into his courtesy Mercedes SUV, on his way to dinner, queuing up 50 Cent's new album on the CD player. To most fans he was an unknown, although he was a striking-looking guy. Blond, with a high hairline, thin, triangular face, and a little goatee, he looked like a pale version of the icon on the old Red Devil paint cans.

He was also golf's answer to Rodney Dangerfield. His consecutive-year wins at the Reno-Tahoe Open got little respect because it was a weak-field event, played opposite the high-profile WGC-Bridgestone Invitational in Akron. Beginning the season, he was one of very few players on Tour without a shirt manufacturer deal. In the back seat of the SUV, his caddie Adam Hayes was being insubordinate, complaining that Vaughn didn't let him run down to the pool that afternoon to catch a glimpse of sunbathing celebrity Jessica Alba. (Alba and Garcia had been out together a couple of times a few years back, but this week, she wasn't with him.) Even the restaurateurs were against Taylor. At dinner, he looked longingly at his lobster bisque, sighing, "Why isn't there any lobster in this?"

The following day Sean O'Hair was on the putting green working on his stroke. His $2.5 million rookie year had staked him, his wife, Jackie, and their daughter, Molly, to a new house in West Chester, Pennsylvania. He said he spent most of his winter helping Jackie shop for furniture and "hitting the gym pretty hard." The latter was hard to believe; he was still as thin as a celery stalk.

Another first-timer was Geoff Ogilvy. He was catching up with a friend just outside the locker room, in a hallway lined with photos of past Mercedes champions. The topics ranged from skin cancer fears to his new endorsement deal with Cobra to the week's no-shows. "What can you do?" he asked. "It's not like the Tour can start telling guys where and when to play.

"Think about it," he continued, glancing up at the photos on the wall. "Finchem tries telling that guy what to do, and he'll go play in Europe," he said, pointing at Sergio Garcia. "He'd go to Europe as well," he continued, moving over to Ernie Els. "Even he might go," he concluded, his finger on a picture of Tiger Woods.

That conversation took place on Wednesday morning. By the afternoon, word had leaked out that ABC, along with cable sister ESPN, had walked away from the PGA Tour TV-rights negotiating table. The network has just spent a ton of money on NFL football, the gossip said, and decided to invest much of the rest of its budget in NASCAR.

Other rumors, too, were starting to surface. Whispers said that Woods' absence wasn't cavalier, and that he was, in fact, in California at the bedside of his father, who was gravely ill. Earl Woods' health had been troubled since before Tiger turned pro—heart problems, and then prostate cancer, indicated that his time might be short. At the 2005 Masters, Tiger's emotional victory speech saluted his father, who hadn't been able to make it to the golf course to see him win. The following month, he indicated that the cancer was gone. Now, it seemed, it was back, and Earl was in bad shape.

The tournament itself turned out to be a grueling affair. Most of the time the trade winds blew a steady thirty-five miles per hour, with occasional forty-five m.p.h. gusts. The second round was especially wicked, with a stroke average of 75.5, the highest in eight years. At one point, second-year player Lucas Glover needed four full minutes to hit two putts—he stood over his ball for long stretches, with his pants legs flapping, waiting for his ball to stop quivering. Tailwinds, usually welcome, now introduced the possibility of disaster. On Thursday Stuart Appleby nearly drove the ball through the green on the 426-yard par-four 12th hole; it finished on the back fringe, just a few feet from a ravine.

It was Appleby, though, who best retained control of his ball. He had a one-shot lead after two rounds, and had widened it to two after the third. Through his first fifty-four holes he made only five bogeys, a remarkable achievement in such conditions.

It was impossible to deny he was playing superbly. And going into the final round, it was impossible not to root for him.

Appleby was one of the Tour's best wisecrackers and raconteurs. Savvy golf writers relied on him for a good, candid quote, but also to help while away deadly dull afternoons on driving ranges and practice greens. He and his equally well-liked caddie, Joe Damiano, were their own little *Seinfeld* episode, expertly making comedy out of nothing (the weather, Joe's granny glasses, Stuey's chest hair). When things really got slow, they could be relied on to produce a weird tale, culled from their rounds on foreign fairways, about the sexual habits of baboons or kangaroos.

Stuey was good company. But that was only half of what made him a sympathetic figure. The other, at the opposite of humor in the emotional spectrum, was his backstory.

During the summer of 1998, Appleby suffered a personal tragedy that led to years of almost unendurable grief. He had met Renay White, herself a gifted young player, in Australia in 1992. They were a dissimilar pair: he was a quiet kid who'd grown up on a dairy farm in Victoria, in Southeast Australia; she was an outspoken, animated young woman from Queensland, 500 miles north. They played mixed twosomes together for their country against college teams on a competitive tour of the U.S. Thereafter they were inseparable. When Stuart went abroad to play professionally, Renay traveled with him, usually caddying, at tournaments from Asia to Europe to America. When they weren't together, she was a prolific writer of love letters. He thought of her as the "first prize in the raffle of life." They married in December 1996, after Stuart's first year on the PGA Tour.

Appleby established himself quickly in the U.S., winning in early 1997, and again in early 1998. He and Renay bought a place at Isleworth, within walking distance of the homes of Mark O'Meara, Payne Stewart, Tiger Woods, and fellow Australian pro Craig Parry. Also nearby were Aussie tennis star Todd Woodbridge, and his wife, Natasha. While Stuart was off playing the Tour, spending countless hours alongside friend and fellow pro Robert Allenby, Renay fixed up the house and palled around with Natasha.

After the 1998 British Open, Stuart and Renay were set to embark on their second honeymoon, a trip to Paris. They were outside London's Waterloo train station, getting their luggage out of their double-parked cab, when a car closer to the curb inexplicably moved backward, crushing Renay between two vehicles. Appleby helplessly watched the entire incident.

"I was standing near the cab when I saw her pinned between two cars," he told *The Australian* years later. "I don't think there was a car in front of that car—there was no reason why he couldn't have just pulled forward—but he pulled back.

"Maybe he thought he was going forward when he went back. He kept his foot on the accelerator. I think he would have worked it out when I started banging on his window. I was yelling: 'Go forward! Go forward!' "

Renay, who was relatively short, suffered massive internal injuries. "If she'd been my height, it would have hit her legs," Appleby said. Stuart rode with Renay to the hospital, but she never regained consciousness.

"It was the worst feeling, walking out of that hospital, the worst feeling. My life had gone from being great, having everything, being extremely happy, in love, to nothing—all in fifteen minutes."

Appelby spent the next two years "glazed over," in the words of his friend and swing coach, Steve Bann. He wore his wedding ring for a long time afterward, through his win at the 1999 Houston Open. He didn't move out of their house in Orlando, but he was slowly becoming a different person. Much later, Appleby, describing a round in which he managed consistently to rebound from bogeys with birdies, declared, "Golf is all about the bounce-back stat." Quickly he caught himself, cocked his head, and added, "Actually, life is all about the bounce-back stat."

The way he overcame Renay's death proved it. In September 2000, in Akron, caddie Damiano introduced him, through a mutual friend, to a young local woman named Ashley Saleet. At first their relationship progressed slowly. Stuart would later express amazement at her "patience" with him. It was a very different raffle, but Appleby had won again: Ashley seemed to know intuitively how to handle the situation and how to put everyone at ease, from Renay's old friends to Stuart himself. His first wife would always be part of him, but his union with Ashley was proof that the heart expands according to need.

The last two of Appleby's six Tour wins had come at the Mercedes, and now he was in position to gain another. But three groups ahead of him, on yet another blowy day, Vijay Singh was shooting the round of the tournament. Singh's birdie on the 15th pushed him to seven-under on the day and gave him a two-stroke lead.

It wasn't a shock. All week Singh had been saying that he felt a low round coming on. Now—after two seasons that featured thirteen Tour wins and thirty-six top tens—he was picking up where he left off.

Appleby first noticed the change on the leaderboard a few minutes later, when he arrived on the 15th green. By then Singh had dropped a shot and was only one ahead. "I can't lose this tournament," Appleby said to himself, and promptly rolled in a tricky six-footer for birdie to move even with Singh. Walking to the 16th tee, Damiano intoned, "This is our party. He's not invited."

Both men birdied the par-five 18th, and they headed to a playoff. Replaying the home hole, Appleby played his third shot, from a bunker behind the green, to within two and a half feet of the hole, and rapped in the putt. For the third straight year, the tournament staff walked onto the green and draped Stuart's neck with leis.

During the champion's conference, Ella crawled up and down the center aisle, mewling with approval. Done talking, her father put down his trophy, a lidded loving cup, and picked her up. Detecting an odor, he asked Ashley for the diaper bag, plunked his daughter down on a tabletop, and changed her. Tournament director Gary Planos was standing by with the trophy. Jokingly Appleby picked up the lid and motioned as if he would put the dirty diaper inside.

"Great idea," Planos said. "Leave it in there to ferment, and it will be waiting for you when you pick up the trophy again next year."

This time, there was no hasty sprint to the airport. After dinner and celebratory drinks in the clubhouse bar, the family retired to the Ritz and put Ash and Ella to bed. He could never sleep after a win; he was always "just too wound up." He watched a little TV and answered e-mails. After a couple of hours he called it a night.

Early the next morning they departed for Honolulu. They weren't the only ones leaving Kapalua happy; it was hard not to, win or lose. Shortly before noon, Mark Calcavecchia and his wife, Brenda, perhaps the last to leave, walked down their corridor at the Ritz, on their way to check out. Outside each door was the detritus of the week—empty shopping bags, gift baskets, champagne buckets. Brenda—her hair by now salt-white—had some light luggage in her left hand and a unopened bottle of Veuve Clicquot in her right.

"You managed to go through the whole week without drinking that?" a passerby asked.

"No," Calcavecchia said. "We just found it lying out in the hallway. Pretty good stuff, for leftovers."

David Toms' birthday is January 4th. So is his wife, Sonya's. That was one coincidence. Another was that their drivers licenses both happen to expire the same day, January 4, 2006.

There was trouble as they boarded their Monday morning flight from Maui to Oahu, but they managed to talk their way on. At the airport car rental counter, they didn't do quite as well.

The Sony Open is the only tournament of the year that doesn't provide the players with courtesy cars. So after they arrived at the Honolulu airport, Toms left his wife, two kids, and their nanny—a recent LSU grad named Frances Meehan—on the curb and hopped aboard the Hertz shuttle. The agents looked at his license and suggested a taxi. He begged, pleaded, and argued, but to no avail. He returned to the terminal, retrieved everyone, and had Sonya try her luck, but to no avail. Good thing nannies can rent cars, too. (Later in the week, Toms' manager, Adam Young, would have to FedEx David and Sonya their passports so they wouldn't have any problems boarding the plane home.)

The ride from the airport to their hotel would have been interesting even without lingering memories of the drama. On Monday afternoon, on-again off-again showers produced big, vivid rainbows. The exit signs on the freeway mixed comedy and historical gravity: one was for Punchbowl Street, the next for Pearl Harbor. The traffic reminded them that the rest of Hawaii might be paradise, but Honolulu was a big city, with the usual big city problems. Even some of its beaches were urbanized: at Waikiki Beach, where most tourists lodge, the hotels are built right on top of the ocean, leaving only a sliver of sand. The main drag, Kalakaua Avenue, may as well be Rodeo Drive: it's packed with tony boutiques like Tiffany's, Bulgari, Fendi, and Ferragamo. Every day, it's jam-packed, mostly with honeymooning Japanese. A typical Waikiki hotel elevator conversation went something like this:

Anglo golf junketeer: "You look very happy."

New Japanese bride, holding Chanel shopping bag: "Yes." (Bows, and smiles.) "Very happy."

Most of the players, however, steered clear of Waikiki and stayed on the other side of Diamond Head, at the ultra-posh Kahala Mandarin Oriental. That hotel was tucked away in a secluded spot on the South Shore, across the street from Waialae Country Club. Its wooden lattice-work exoskeleton made it one of the most distinctive structures on the island. Its shaded, lagoonlike pool area was the ideal spot for an al fresco breakfast. After a day's golf, its private beach was perfect for a quick dip and a cold beer.

Nearly everyone who played the season-opening Mercedes had island-hopped over to play the Sony, too. (It was silly, after all, to come all the way to Hawaii for just one event.) But 116 other players were making their first starts of the year.

Among those milling around Waialae, breathing deep of the Tour atmosphere for the first time in over two months, was Tom Lehman, the Ryder Cup captain, looking fit and trim after an off-season thirty-pound weight loss. Shouldering up to him was the slumping David Duval, declaring his intention to make Lehman's team. Over on the practice range was Adam Scott, denied a place at the Mercedes because his win at the previous year's rain-shortened Nissan Open in L.A. went only two rounds and was therefore deemed "unofficial." An avid surfer who sometimes traveled with his board, he was miffed that his stay in Hawaii this year was one week, instead of two.

Lehman, Duval, and Scott were familiar faces. Yet the Sony, by and large, was about lesser-known players—rookies making their first-ever starts, and career grinders whose season-starting optimism resides, in their heads, just inches away from doubts about whether or not they belong.

The newbies, fresh from Q-school or the Nationwide Tour, numbered about two dozen. For them, the Sony was like the first week at a posh new private school. One of them, Robert Garrigus, a long-hitting 28-year-old from Portland, tried to arrange a practice round with one of his idols, Ernie Els. Somehow (surprise!) it didn't come off. It wasn't his only rookie mistake. On arrival, he had rented a high-style Cadillac, unaware that the bill would gut him for over $1,000. (Some neophyte mistakes were worse. One of Garrigus's playing partners, Australian rookie Steven Bowditch, would get himself disqualified in the second round for thinking he could play a provisional ball after hitting one in a hazard.)

One of the rookies was a recognizable name—kind of. The man who won Q-school the previous year was named John Holmes. In the media guide, however, he was John B. Holmes. When he arrived in Hawaii, he was J. B. Holmes.

"Why all the name changes?" a reporter asked.

"You know the answer to that one," he said.

The lesser-known veterans included Michael Allen, an engaging 46-year-old Northern Californian who, in the earlier years, had played just about every tour in the world. Making a living had never been easy: he had quit the game twice, putting in stints as a construction worker and then as a club pro at the venerable Winged Foot Country club, home of the upcoming U.S. Open. What he was really good at was Q-school. He had made it through, earning his card, eight of twelve times. Yet in those eight go-rounds on the big tour, he had never finished better than eighty-eighth on the money list.

Knowing how expensive Hawaii is, he took advantage of the opportunity to stay at the house of a friend, Dave Masters, who played minor league baseball in the eighties and nineties. Masters' house was five minutes from the golf course. Rather than renting a car, Allen rode Masters' bicycle back and forth to the golf course every day.

One of the two participants playing a home game was Dean Wilson. He had grown up on the other side of the island, in Kaneohe, in northeast Oahu. Wilson, 36, was also a career grinder. In college, attending Brigham Young University with Mike Weir, he had promised that the first time he won on Tour, he would do a backflip on the 18th green; his teammates thereupon nicknamed him "The Flyin' Hawaiian." But his chance never came. He spent most of his early years in the B-leagues, and in three full seasons on Tour had never finished higher than ninety-eighth in earnings. His only real notoriety came from being paired with Annika Sorenstam at Colonial in 2004.

Yet Wilson's game was starting to come around. During the second half of the 2005 season, he had posted four top tens. He credited the about-face to his new coaches, the teaching team of Andy Plummer and Mike Bennett. Bennett, in fact, was with Wilson this week, bunking in with him at his mom's house. His pupil was glad to be in the field: he had been passed over for a sponsor's exemption in 2005, the second year Michelle Wie got one. The backlash caused some controversy. "For him not to get in Sony is a bit embarrassing for the tournament," said Weir. That's how big Michelle Wie was in Hawaii—she made people forget the best male golfer the state had ever produced.

• • •

Indeed, Wies' presence produced a popular event-week riddle. Question: How do you make 143 male professional golfers disappear? Answer: make them play with a teenage girl from down the block.

Michelle Wie imposed a kind of stop-the-world feeling on the Sony Open, and indeed on the whole island. She was front page material in every daily paper, the lead story on every news broadcast.

That feeling, however, was oddly absent at the Punahou School, where she was a high school junior. Her fellow students were used to having a celebrity in their midst—they had been hearing about her exploits almost all their lives. They knew all about her becoming the youngest-ever participant in an LPGA event, at age 12; winning the U.S. Women's Amateur Public Links, at 13; and missing the cut at the Sony by just one stroke when she was 14. Here too the novelty had worn off. Besides, it was exam week: the school's schedule had all but one of the students buried in their books, preparing themselves for that week's semester-ending exams.

Punahou was a special place. Its old stone buildings gave it the feel of Northeastern prep schools like Andover and St. Paul's, though the flower beds were much prettier, and there was little opportunity for pond hockey. The curricula were also similar, with lots of student-tailored coursework and independent study. It also had its share (for a relatively young institution) of distinguished alumni: theirs included Steve Case and Barack Obama. The dress code, though, was quite different. There were no ties. Students, boys and girls, were required only to wear T-shirts that in one way or another bore the school name. Michelle loved to complain about it. From time to time she worked into her press conferences a little plea. "Punahou, please take away the uniform, please, if you hear this!" she once memorably cried.

For her classmates, Michelle's appearance at the Sony wasn't the only potential exam-week distraction. The school's surfers spent the week with their fingers crossed, waiting "for the Eddie to go off" over on the North Shore, at Waimea Bay. (In layman's terms, that meant they were hoping the waves would be big enough to stage the Eddie Aikau Invitational Surf Contest, possibly the biggest event in that sport. In twenty-two years, it had only taken place seven times: the prerequisite was waves of at least twenty feet high.) Also that week, on Tuesday, was a big boys' basketball game against arch-rival Iolani High School. A month earlier, at a pre-season tourney, Punahou had broken Iolani's 105-game intra-state winning streak; now they were looking to end its regular-season run of 57 consecutive wins.

Michelle took her exams early. Before the tournament she slogged through tests in Japanese, chemistry, and math (although the latter couldn't have been too hard for her: her father, a University of Hawaii professor from a family of academics, had started teaching her trigonometry when she was nine).

Her turning professional hadn't changed much about her life at school, apart from what she described as "the money jokes." She said, "Sometimes I forget to bring my lunch money and I have to ask my friends to buy my lunch. They're like, 'We're not going to buy your lunch anymore!'"

It certainly didn't magically transform her into a better golfer. Her first two outings as a pro were at best disappointments. In her first, the LPGA's Samsung Championship, in Palm Springs, she was disqualified because of an illegal drop during Saturday's third round. (That the penalty wasn't enforced until Sunday—and that it was precipitated by a reporter, *Sports Illustrated*'s Michael Bamberger—were causes of much controversy.)

Her second was a let-down in a very different way. In November, at the Japan Tour's Casio World Open, she went against a relatively small field of 102 men, sixty of whom would advance to weekend play. She was a shot inside the cut line with two holes to play, but then unraveled, going bogey-bogey to miss by one.

The Casio had been her sixth appearance in a men's professional event, and was the newest evidence of a disturbing trend: flirting with the cut, Wie would invariably fall victim to jangly nerves. It had also happened that past July, at the John Deere Classic. There too she was a shot inside the line late in her round. She then double-bogeyed her 15th hole and bogeyed the 16th to miss by two. Her coach, David Leadbetter, believed that once she got close, the prospect of making a cut was "changing her mindset. Instead of just playing golf, you get a little tight. You make mistakes."

Unlike most, the Wies saw every such outing as a success. Her skills, they believed, would improve in time. If she wanted to play against the men as an adult—which, of course, was the plan—her main objective now was getting used to the pressurized environments of men's tour events. The LPGA Tour didn't prepare her to compete in men's tournaments; only men's tournaments did. When asked whether she'd be better served by the Earl Woods model—letting a prodigy dominate his or her peers—their answer was always the same. She had to elevate her standards, and learn to deal with the stage on which she ultimately wanted to play.

Naturally, other female players found it insulting that she was looking past them. Fellow teenager Morgan Pressel pshawed Wie's skylarking as "going off to do her *woo-woo!* thing against the men."

Male tour players tended to support Wie, especially while they were standing on her home soil. David Toms said that her Sony appearance was "a great story, because she has the ability to compete with us."

Jim Furyk added, "She's a great talent. I can't think of a sixteen-year-old girl who can hit it like that. I'll go beyond that. I don't know too many sixteen-year-old boys that can go out there and play in a tour event, have that much composure, hit the ball that well. She's definitely one in a million, or one in a billion."

More than a handful of players, however, were convinced her PGA Tour appearances were pointless. And some of them even said so. Before the tournament began, a television reporter working the Wie angle cornered Vijay Singh. In a way, he was the worst person to ask. His critical remarks about Annika Sorenstam before her appearance at the 2003 Colonial had landed him in a heap of trouble, and was perhaps the primary reason for his frosty relationship with most of the media. In another way, however, he was precisely the man for the job.

"So, what do you think of Michelle Wie's chances to make the cut?" the reporter, a young woman, asked.

Singh rolled his eyes. "Can she win?" he asked.

"I don't know," the reporter replied. "But can she make the cut?"

"That's the wrong question," Singh repeated. "The right question is, 'Can she win?'"

Singh's objection was oblique because he now knew better than to criticize a media darling. As for its actual meaning—well, Singh couldn't help it if he was six months ahead of the popular opinion curve.

During Wie's practice round at Waialae on Tuesday, she was surrounded by familiar faces. She played with Sean O'Hair and Englishman Justin Rose, under the watchful eye of Leadbetter, who coached all three players. Unusually, her father, B.J., wasn't around: he had a class to teach that day over at the travel industry management school at the University of Hawaii, where he was a professor. The acting chaperone was her mother, Bo, a former Korean national amateur champion; her teaching B.J. the game had been part of their courtship. The other adult member of the group was a man named Ross Berlin.

Berlin was her agent, the man the William Morris Agency, her management firm, had hired to legitimize its presence in the sport. Until that point, its rich history had included clients from Marilyn Monroe and Elvis Presley to Eminem and Tom Hanks, but not a single golfer.

Berlin's path to the agency, and to the Wies, was a story in itself. The former entertainment industry lawyer had in 1994 taken a position with FIFA, overlooking U.S. stadium negotiations for that year's World Cup. He followed FIFA back to Switzerland and soon found himself running the 1997 Ryder Cup at Valderrama, in Spain. He was then hired by the PGA Tour, overseeing its World Golf Championships events, and liaising with its corporate title sponsors. He went to William Morris after it decided to compete with IMG for the Wie's affections.

B.J. Wie didn't like it that no one at William Morris agency had any experience in golf, and the agency hired Berlin expressly to solve that problem. It was his task to convince the Wies to sign on. Like Jerry Maguire, he went into the Wies' living room and did it alone. Well, almost alone. He carried an hour and fifteen minutes of William Morris's decisive two-hour presentation.

Now he rarely left Michelle's side. After her Tuesday practice round, Berlin shuttled her into her press conference, where she handled herself like the pro she now was. Thanks to the kind of courses that weren't taught at Punahou, she volleyed back every question like a world-class baseliner, with plenty of spin.

The structure of her four- or five-sentence responses was always the same. First was the direct but nondescript reply ("People have high expectations of me, but I have high expectations of myself"). Next was a little piece of personality-betraying teenage flair (practice rounds, being a pro, and the prospect of a first check were all either "awesome" or "pretty cool"). The finish was always an expression of humility (during that presser, she deployed the word "grateful" three times).

The only real break with form was her discussion of her new weightlifting regimen. She said that at first it was "pretty tough. I couldn't wash my hair in the shower. I couldn't lift my arms. It was way too painful." But it was working; she was getting stronger. To illustrate, she he held her arms out in front of her and flexed, like Hans and Franz from the old *Saturday Night Live* sketch.

The buzz surrounding Wie fell temporarily silent on Wednesday, when the Tour announced its new television package. NBC and CBS had renewed for six years each, but ABC and ESPN were out, as was everyone else—except The Golf Channel, which, astoundingly, had signed on for fifteen years, carrying every round of thirteen events, and providing Thursday-Friday coverage for thirty-one more. A year and a half earlier, at the 2005 Tour Championship, Commissioner Tim Finchem had expressed the desire for the Tour to have its own cable channel. Now it did.

The details of the deal were interesting, because there weren't any. The Tour said the contract would increase purses by thirty-five percent. But because it rolled together so many networks and so many years, there was no way to tell who paid how much for what. The silence was a break from standard practice. In past years numbers were purposely leaked to select media outlets, so that the Tour could be admired for a steady climb in broadcast fees. Now, the math looked fuzzy at best. There was simply no way to compare this package to the Tour's previous $850 million, five-year deal. Even the players were baffled. "I read the release," Peter Jacobsen shrugged. "It didn't say *anything*."

Those who tried to crunch the numbers figured that The Golf Channel was paying $220 million per year for their portion—a shriek-inducing sum for the shareholders of Comcast, its parent company, had the number been publicized. The only thing that was really clear was that TGC was going to have to get a lot better at what they did, and fast. It was going to take a lot more new hires than Megan West to carry all that airtime in a polished, engaging way.

David Toms' playing partners at Waialae weren't exactly contemporaries, but it seemed like he'd known them forever. Brad Faxon, 44, was a longtime running buddy: a few months earlier he and Toms had traveled together to Kennebunkport, Maine, to visit their mutual friend George H. W. Bush. At the time Fax was on crutches. He had just had ACL surgery, the result of a bizarre, knee-twisting accident with an exercise ball. He couldn't even play horseshoes.

David Duval was 34 but seemed older—golf had aged him fast. Once upon a time, he was the best player in the game, ranked number one in the world between March and June of 1999. He won his first major at the 2001 British Open. His game was then overtaken by physical problems (back and wrist injuries, and a bout of vertigo), along with a certain malaise. In the past three seasons he had made only eight of forty-nine cuts. Now his eligibility was in question: he about to start the last year of his five-year exemption from winning the British.

Standing on the first tee, Toms prepared himself for a brand of golf markedly different from Maui's. Wind notwitstanding, the Plantation Course was a fun, roller coaster of a course with big elevation changes, and sprawling fairways that granted considerable margins of error. Waialae, an old Seth Raynor layout, was absolutely flat. It wasn't exactly tight, but you had to be on the correct sides of the fairways to open up the optimal angles to the pins. This was precision golf, the kind Toms liked best.

Duval started his season badly, snap-hooking his first tee-shot into the driving range fencing on the left side of the hole. Toms prepared for the worst, immediately recalling something he once heard from Tommie Mudd, brother of former Tour player Jodie, when they were teammates back at LSU. One day, their coach asked Tommie who he wanted to play with. "You can put me with whomever you want," he said. "I play in a onesome every day."

Faxon, in contrast, was someone Toms wanted to watch. After all these years, he could still learn from him. Toms loved the placidity of his process—the way he started reading greens before setting foot on them, the way he eased into his putting routine. "I need to be doing that, too," Toms thought to himself.

Their gallery was thin, owing to the carnival over at the 10th tee.

There, Michelle Wie was making long, slow practice swings, getting ready to play her first hole of the day. She was surrounded on three sides by about 2,500 fans, and, inside the ropes, by perhaps three dozen media members and officials.

Standing a few yards from Wie, off to the side, were her playing partners, Camilo Villegas and Chris Couch. They were both University of Florida alums, but may as well have been from different planets. Villegas, a native of Medellín, Colombia, was a 24-year-old star on the rise. His arms, all popped veins and sinew, advertised his strength. But he was equally limber. In his signature putt-reading pose, he looked like Peter

Parker attending a yoga class, positioning his eyes as near as possible to the ground without dirtying the knees of his trousers. Even if he wasn't quite ready to beat Tiger, his Latin good looks promised future appearances on the cover of *Tiger Beat*.

Chris Couch was six-foot-four, with the belly and swagger of a small-town sheriff, and just as thin a résumé. An eleventh-year pro, he had a handful of wins on the Nationwide Tour, but in two previous years on the PGA Tour had never finished better than 181st on the money list. When he played the Sony Open in 2004, he shot 71–71 to miss the cut, finishing two strokes behind Wie. Back home, his buddies at Gainesville Country Club presented him with a white T-shirt with pink lettering. The front read: "I Got Beat by a 13-Year-Old Girl." On the back: "I Guess I Have to Practice a Wie Bit Harder." This week, his bag sported a new logo: Hilton Hotels had given him a one-week endorsement deal to capitalize on the TV exposure he'd get playing alongside Wie.

Couch and Villegas had a little history together. About seven months earlier, Chris dropped a final-round 60 on Camilo to overtake and beat him at the Nationwide Tour's Rheem Classic in Arkansas. When they saw each other off the course, Couch liked to wave at Villegas the watch that came the winner's check.

It wasn't surprising, then, that they were yukking it up, largely ignoring Wie. When it was finally time to play, the two boys went first. Couch hit a pull hook, and Villegas's ball bled right. Both wound up in the rough. Wie's tee shot split the fairway, never climbing higher than thirty feet off the ground. Growing up in Hawaii's winds made her favor a low ballflight.

Wie started steadily enough, parring her first two holes. While she was waiting to putt on the par-four 12th, she stood on a hillock behind the green, which borders Waiholo Place. Across the street, a bare-chested construction worker climbed atop the black lava-rock fence in front of the house and yelled, "We love you, Michelle!" Not satisfied with his volume, he did it a second time. It didn't help. She three-putted, yanking a four-footer left, for her first bogey of the day.

Things only got worse. Iffy ballstriking and bad decision-making led to doubles on her fourth, sixth, and eighth holes. She made the turn at seven-over. Already, she had dug herself a hole. Her chances of making the cut were already remote.

She made another bogey on the 1st hole, her tenth. Then something happened that seemed to loosen her up. Standing on the 2nd tee, waiting for the fairway to clear, Couch pulled a pouch from his pocket and started to reload his left cheek. As he did, he lectured Villegas on the pleasures and protocols of chewing tobacco. Wie looked on with horror. Then Couch turned to her and said, "This isn't the kind of thing you're supposed to talk about in front of a lady. Anyway, it's a habit I'd discourage you from ever picking up."

Michelle's chuckle was her first of the day. From that point she appeared to relax, and played her next eight holes in one over. Still there were mistakes. On her seventeenth hole she sailed her approach long and left of the green—and right at Ross Berlin. Her agent, reacting quickly, raised his ever-present brown leather portfolio out in front of him. When her ball hit it, it left a deep, dimpled imprint.

She finished the day tied for last, with John Cook, at nine over par. Afterward, she didn't own up to any nerves, saying instead that "the hard part" had been "not playing in a tournament since November." Getting up from her chair in the press room, she sighed and muttered, "I want some chocolate."

The following day Wie and Toms met on the practice green before the early afternoon start of their second rounds.

Toms said, "Not a great day yesterday, huh?"

"Not really."

"Well, don't let it get you down. Go out there today and show 'em what you're made of."

It wasn't Knute Rockne, but it worked. From the 8th to the 14th, she birdied five of six holes and finished with a 68. She still missed the cut by four strokes, but her Friday showing legitimized, at least to some extent, her being there in the first place.

On both Saturday and Sunday, Toms played with Chad Campbell. It was a good pairing. They were friends, and so were their caddies.

Judd Burkett, Campbell's sidekick since their boyhoods, was a distinctive figure: though fit, he was about twice as wide as anyone else on the golf course. If the Tour loopers had a football team, he would have been an offensive tackle. Scott Gneiser, Toms' man, was from Detroit: while Eminem was from 8 Mile, he was from 9 Mile. He now lived in Chicago—he had married the daughter of Blackhawks great Stan Makita—and was a member at Medinah, the site of August's PGA

Championship. In 2005, he and Burkett played together in the member-guest.

Toms and Campbell were close partly because they had the same representation—or at least used to, before Toms filed his lawsuit in May 2005. During the course of 2006, that same suit would join them together in the oddest of ways.

Toms' suit made four principal allegations against Texas-based Links Sports and its president, David Parker, who founded the firm in 1992. Toms claimed that Links, since their 2002 representation agreement, had failed to generate any new business; failed to follow up on opportunities Toms had initiated (not returning phone calls, missing meetings); "alienated" existing clients and associates; and taken percentages of his endorsement income not due to them. He further complained that Links was taking an "unconscionable" twenty percent from deals it brokered for him.

The issue of alienating existing partners was where Campbell came in. During discovery Toms learned that there had been a "disagreement" between Parker, representing Campbell, and equipment manufacturer Cleveland Golf, one of his sponsors. The rift, it seemed was part of the reason Campbell was no longer with Cleveland. Yet Cleveland was still Toms' brand. What worried him was that Parker had somehow poisoned the relationship between Toms and Cleveland as well.

To prove it, he and his attorneys spent the summer trying to depose Campbell, to hear his version of what had happened. Ultimately, the attempt wasn't successful; the court ruled the deposition was unnecessary. But it added a strange dimension to Toms' and Campbell's relationship.

On this day, however, legal actions were the furthest thing from their minds. They both played terrific golf, feeding off each other and swapping high-fives and fist bumps. Toms shot a 61 and Campbell a 62, distancing them from the field by seven shots.

The next day Campbell cooled, but Toms didn't. He shot a 65 to win by five. For Toms it was a landmark win, if only because it put the turmoil of 2005 behind him. Well, at least some of it.

Toms' victory party on Sunday was upstaged, in a way, by another affair taking place in one of the ballrooms at the Kahala Mandarin. That evening organizers of the Japan Tour's Casio World Open—another male professional tournament—were holding a press conference to announce that Michelle Wie would be playing the event. It was a bald-faced plea for attention: it wouldn't take place until eleven months from now, in late November. But that didn't affect the curiosity it inspired among golf writers, who rarely got a chance to talk with Wie away from the golf course.

The invitation to enter upon the grounds of the Mandarin was special in itself, a chance to observe the rich and famous at their leisurely best. Walking through the lobby on his way to the pool was Tom Lehman; below his grimy gray T-shirt, a huge, aqua-green towel was wrapped around his waist like a sarong. His ten-year-old son, Thomas, in a football jersey and shorts, was hanging off his arm, as if trying to do a chin-up.

The ballroom was downstairs. Outside, in the hall, there were appetizers and an open bar, although no alcoholic beverages were served, in deference to the age of the featured guest. Inside was a standard press-room setup: a lighted podium with a tournament-logoed backdrop, and rows of chairs bisected by a center aisle, with TV cameras at the back to record the proceedings.

Her entrance, when she finally made it, was grand. Up close and personal, she was prettier, smarter, and sixteenier than she ever seemed on the golf course. And taller. Lots taller. The layered colors on her blouse—orange, green, and white—seemed separated by yards of fabric; the chalk-stripes on her gray pants looked like they'd been borrowed from a football field.

She sat down to talk and brushed her long, henna-streaked hair out of her face. By her side, moderating, was Berlin. Wie said all the predictable things about the Casio World Open, but when the floor was opened for questions, she was light-years more candid than she'd been a few days earlier.

She knew from the start, she said, that her appearance at the Sony Open was bound to go wrong. "I knew it when I got out of bed on Thursday morning—you know, when you wake up and know that nothing's going to work." Here, finally, she confessed to being "really tense," much more so than the two previous years.

Most of the initial questions were asked by the Associated Press's Doug Ferguson, which was only appropriate. For one thing, he was the most-read golf writer in the country: his stories were reprinted by hundreds of newspapers and websites. For another, no other writer in the room had an easier rapport with Michelle. Plus, he always wore garish Hawaiian shirts, a ploy he had developed to catch the attention of speed-walking pros; the habit, in a way, made him something like an honorary citizen.

About the LPGA, he asked, "Do you get a sense that players out there think that you think their tour is too easy?"

"I'm not really sure what they think," she smiled. "I'm not really psychic."

"There's a class for that, too," Ferguson said, alluding to her schoolwork.

"Really?" Michelle shot back. "Mind-reading 101?"

After the formal questioning was over, Wie, in accordance with custom, presented the tournament organizers with a gift, a new Nike driver. She held it in front of her and smiled for the cameras. You could almost hear her say, "Suntory time," à la Bill Murray.

Then she said hello to individual writers, in effect giving each a little one-on-one.

At a certain point, she got a little impatient. You could tell: she started grinding the three-inch heel of her right shoe into the floor. The shoes themselves bore out something Berlin had mentioned just earlier to a few writers—that the kid was a fool for upmarket footwear. These looked pricey enough: the rear and sides were red and green, with little studs, and each of the toes—brown and extremely pointy—looked like the business end of a tortilla chip. The tops of her feet were tanned—no pasty golfer feet below the ankles. Evidently she managed to mix into her busy schedule a little beach time.

When she turned to face the next reporter, there was only one logical way to reawaken her interest: ask her about her shoes.

"Are these your favorites? That's what Ross was saying."

"Me? My favorite?" She sighed. "Oh, Ross. Yeah, I like these shoes."

"Where'd you get them?"

"I got them in Washington."

"They look expensive."

She smiled. "Oh, yeah. They put a hole in my pocket, definitely."

"Do you do that sometimes? Give yourself little presents?"

"Yeah. Actually, after Saturday I went shopping. I got some really cute stuff."

"But nothing as cute as those shoes."

"No."

"So, are they made by some big designer or something?"

"You know, I can't remember."

With that, she started taking off her shoe.

"No, no, that's okay! You don't have to take them off!"

She did it anyway. It didn't seem to matter to her that to some men, this would count as pornography. The reporter looked away, fearing arrest.

"Isabella Fiore," she reported. Then she put her shoe back on.

A few minutes later, she departed, her honor intact. It was time to go home and get some rest. She had a busy week ahead of her. On Tuesday she was taking the road test for her driver's license.

2

PHIL IN FULL

The Bob Hope Chrysler Classic

It wasn't the highest point in the Little San Bernardino Mountains, but the mesa Phil Mickelson had chosen for his Friday afternoon project launch made it clear he had come up in the world. Even halfway there, the views through the dark, tinted windows of his black Ford Explorer were expansive: Interstate 10 was visible in the distance, as were endless acres of Palm Springs wind farms. But as far as signs of civilization went, that was about it. Here, at the unpeopled, westernmost flank of the Coachella Valley, he was ten miles from the nearest highway, nine from the nearest building, and two or three from the nearest paved street. For Mickelson that was a kind of compliment. Someone thought he had the economic umph to plant a flag way up here, close to the precise geographic center of Nowhere.

Mickelson knew where he was going, but that couldn't be said for the people driving a few minutes behind him. Despite directions, they still felt lost. With their cars bouncing through ruts and rocky gravel, and scrub brush grazing their tires, some imagined they'd been tricked. It was like living a scene from Scorsese's *Casino*: when they got to the end of the road, Mickelson and Joe Pesci would certainly be waiting for them, holding guns and shovels.

As it turned out, Mickelson was standing in a clearing, empty-handed, with a dozen Desert Hot Springs city officials and a couple of silk-suited moneymen—the kind of guys who answer their cellphones when they ring in the middle of press conferences. Before long the featured speaker assumed his place at a beat-up wooden lectern that looked like it had been stolen from a high school auditorium. He talked proudly of what was to be built here: a two-course complex with 2,200 top-dollar homes and a five-star resort and spa boutique hotel. (The name on the hotel, someone whispered, would be Versace.) "I don't like to move a lot of dirt," he said about the process of building the courses. Good thing. The land was forbidding, the kind of barren, mountainside terrain that looked capable of refusing heavy industrial drill bits. How they were going to get an irrigation system into the brick-hard earth was anyone's guess.

Generally, though, the project's location, and the timing of the announcement, made sense. Inheriting Johnny Miller's old title, Mickelson was the new King of the Desert, with seven wins in Palm Springs, Phoenix, and Tucson. And this was the week of the 2006 Bob Hope Chrysler Classic. The Hope, close to Phil's native San Diego, was one of his showcase events, if only because Tiger Woods never played it. (When Woods was a teenager it had turned down his requests for exemptions, and Tiger, one of the all-time great bearers of grudges, never let them forget it.) More to the point, the time had come for Mickelson to exploit his résumé. The man formerly known as golf's greatest underachiever now had two majors under his belt, and was golf's second most bankable brand name. In mid-2005, *Sports Illustrated,* in its yearly survey of athlete incomes entitled "The Fortunate 50," listed Mickelson at number nine, with an off-course take of about $21 million. The figure was well short of the total of top earner Tiger Woods (whose endorsements were worth about $60 million), but it was also wildly incorrect, at least according to Steve Loy, Mickelson's agent. He claimed that his man's deals (with such companies as Callaway Golf, Ford, Bearing Point, ExxonMobil, and Rolex) were worth upwards of $50 million. "Phil Mickelson has one endorsement worth more money than they're reporting as his total," he told *Golfweek* magazine.

Mickelson's transformation was closely tied to the Hope not just because he had won it twice in the past three years, but because one of those two wins had been the most pivotal of his career—a better transitional marker, in certain ways, than his first major victory, at the Masters.

But to understand why, one had to go back down the mountain, head east to the Valley's more developed areas, and travel back in time to 2004. It was at that year's edition of the Hope that the Old Phil turned into the New Phil.

Once upon a time, the Hope was one of the PGA Tour's marquee events. One of the very first events on the yearly schedule, its telecasts filled the homes of snowbound northerners with Southern California sunshine. The golf itself was invariably fun to watch: there were always plenty of birdies, mostly because of the perpetually perfect weather. (As pro Joe Ogilvie said, the Hope was like playing in a dome.) It was also one of the Tour's two West Coast celebrity pro-ams (the other was Pebble Beach), and the host with the ski-jump nose always brought in big names. The high point came in 1995 when Gerald Ford, George H. W. Bush, and President Bill Clinton all played in the same foursome, with Scott Hoch cast in the role of Tim Russert.

Its galleries, however, had always been on the quiet side. One reason was logistics: the five-day event was played on four courses (until everyone finished up in the same place on Sunday), dispersing the early-week crowds. Further, the spectators were not of the boisterous kind. The retirees who make up the vast majority of the Valley's population were better known for raising highballs than voices. They weren't fond of walking, either. Indeed, one of the Hope's signature traits was that it was the only event on Tour without walking scorers. Instead there were scoreboards on every single hole. Other events had a teenager playing Sign Boy behind each threesome. The Hope had a wealthy old golf nut in a bucket hat getting in and out of his lawn chair to replace the red 8 next to Billy Mayfair's name with a red 9.

Whatever the physical capabilities of its fans, the years had not been kind to the tournament itself. Schedule changes had placed a pair of high-profile Hawaiian events before the nation's eyes, and the Hope's sunshine no longer made it must-see golf TV. Broadcast audiences were also hurt by Woods' absence: why watch a Tiger-less event when next week's tournament would feature the world's best player? There were still a lot of birdies, but maybe too many: because of equipment advances, the easier courses in its rotation were no longer really challenging enough to host a Tour event. Finally, with Mr. Hope ailing (he passed away in 2003), its celeb quality had started to wane. It still got the occasional visit from Hollywood A-listers like Justin Timberlake, Matthew McConaughey, and, yes, Joe Pesci. But too often it was forced to welcome career-declining actors like Andy Garcia or disgraced pill-popping demagogues like Rush Limbaugh. Gradually the event began to suffer from a well-deserved inferiority complex.

Yet Mickelson always showed up, and was always embraced. And he always played well: since 2000 he had never finished outside the top twenty. But it wasn't the Hope that had been keeping him down. Elsewhere, his career was like the golf version of the tale of Sisyphus: whenever he seemed to make a little progress toward the top of the mountain, his footing began to give way.

No one ever doubted his talent. Doubting his judgment and his nerve, however, had by 2003 become a national pastime. It wasn't just that he had never won a major. It was the way he squandered opportunities, at tournaments both large and small. In 2001 at Pebble Beach, for example, he stood in the middle of the fairway on the 72nd hole, 257 yards from the pin, needing a birdie to tie Davis Love for the lead. His chose the chanciest option, hitting driver off the deck, and flared the ball left, into Stillwater Cove.

Two months later, in the third round at the Masters, he was battling for the lead on Saturday when he reached the 14th hole. His ball was just off the green. Because the green sloped away from him, he tried a full-swing flop shot. He whiffed it and made double bogey. Despite that, he went into the final round just one shot behind Tiger Woods. Playing with Woods in the last group, he was undone by a poor drive on the 11th, and a three-putt on the 16th. But it was the previous day's mistake that haunted him. Afterward he said, "When I look back on this week, if I'm going to win with Tiger in the field, I cannot make the mistakes that I have been making. I just can't afford to keep throwing shot after shot away. I just think that mentally, I'm not there for all seventy-two shots. I feel like I'm just slacking off on two or three . . . and not really thinking through each shot, and it's cost me some vital strokes."

That speech looked like a promise that he would change his philosophy. But just the opposite happened. He instead recommitted to his risk-taking ways. The following year at Bay Hill, he was once again battling Woods down the stretch. On the par-five 16th, from deep in the trees, he tried to get home in two, attempting a 200-yard shot over a green-fronting pond. It didn't come off. "I had to catch it a little thin to get underneath the branches," he said. "But I caught it a little too thin." His ball didn't make it halfway across the hazard. After a similarly ill-advised play two weeks later, midway through the 2002 Players Championship, reporters again called him on the carpet. But he refused to second-guess himself. "I won't ever change my style of play," he growled. "I get criticized for it but the fact is that I play my best when I play aggressive, when I attack, when I create shots.

"If I were to change my style of play, I won't perform at the same level, nor would I enjoy the game as much. I have had a number of chances to win majors this year and in the past, and I wouldn't have had those chances had I played any other way. So I won't ever change. Not tomorrow, Sunday, or at Augusta or the U.S. Open or any tournament."

Lefty steadily became one of the media's favorite whipping boys. Jim Rome, for example, tagged him "Hefty" because of his perceivedly thick middle. But that wasn't the worst of it. Everyone had something to say about his perceived errors of judgment; *Sports Illustrated* ran a lengthy photo-analysis of malfunctions in his swing. Every major championship disappointment was punctuated not by celebrations of the champion's success—or astounding luck—but of Mickelson's failure to win his first major. After the 1999 U.S. Open, the ridiculousness of Payne Stewart's miracle 40-foot bomb on Sunday's 18th hole was less discussed than Mickelson's costly bogey at 16. After the 2001 Masters, the brilliance of Tiger Woods' play got only as much ink as Mickelson's course-management snafus and Sunday back-nine bogeys on the 11th and 16th. After the 2001 PGA, the focus wasn't David Toms' eye-popping hole-in-one on Saturday, nor his clutch championship-winning twelve-footer on the 72nd hole, but the fact Mickelson had made a silly go-for-broke play on the par-five 16th that resulted in another crippling bogey. Over the years it just got worse. Members of the Mickelson camp grew to hate what they believed was the media's fondness for the low road, especially when usually even-handed papers and magazines joined in on the abusiveness. In the words of one of them, it amounted to the Rome-ization of all Mickelson press coverage.

Then, in the course of a single week, everything changed.

When Mickelson arrived in Palm Springs for the 2004 Hope, reporters gathered for his Tuesday presser, ready to climb aboard the same old crazy train. But something about him was different. He seemed subdued. The guess was that he was a little humbled by his 2003 season, his first without a win since 1999. But as soon as he began talking, it was clear there was more to it than that.

The moderator asked Mickelson for some opening remarks. In the usual way, he wished everyone a happy new year, and said he felt like he was "in for a great year."

"Why do you think it's going to be a great year?" was the first question.

"Well, last year was a really difficult year for me," he began. "I didn't really get into it too much last year, but Amy, my wife, had a very dangerous delivery with the birth of Evan. He didn't breathe for seven minutes, and had the emergency nurses not been there with the equipment ready, he might have had some severe brain damage. Instead he's one hundred percent healthy.

"With Amy, we were two or three minutes away from losing her. Had the specialist not been driving to go see a friend and been two minutes away [from the hospital, she wouldn't have been able] to have an emergency procedure to stop a six-inch tear in a major artery, and I would have been without my wife."

The room was silent as the reporters picked their pens up off the floor. In less than two minutes, Mickelson had explained his poor 2003, but, more than that, radically altered the way the press related to him. The sympathy, of course, was tempered by a wonderment over why he "didn't get into it much" the prior year—the smallest leak to the press, after all, would have prevented reams of scathing criticism. Not tipping his hand was a public relations mistake. But those were quibbles. The near-tragedies generally transformed Mickelson from an object of derision to a player nearly everyone was pulling for.

Mickelson explained the circumstances more fully in his book *One Magical Sunday*, which appeared after his 2004 Masters win. Scar tissue from a previous birth had complicated Evan's delivery, and repairing the artery, in itself a highly complex procedure, was only made more difficult by excessive blood loss. Evan, meanwhile, had to have oxygen pumped into his body to ensure the health of his brain. Both mother and child wound up in intensive care, with Amy's stay lasting three days.

It took months for the family to return to normalcy. When they did, toward the end of 2003, Amy gave Phil a pep talk that seemed right out of a Hollywood screenplay, encouraging him to recommit to golf and lean more on Rick Smith and Dave Pelz to help him with his game.

There were other changes, too. Mickelson always had a taste for gambling. In 2000 Mickelson and some friends wagered $20,000 that the Baltimore Ravens would win that January's Super Bowl; it paid off to the tune of $486,000. Sitting in the clubhouse on Sunday afternoon at the 2001 NEC Invitational in Akron, he bet Mike Weir $20, at twenty-five-to-one odds, that Jim Furyk would hole out a bunker shot in his playoff against Tiger Woods (which Furyk promptly did). But in a late 2004 interview with *Golf Magazine*'s Cameron Morfit, Mickelson revealed that he had kicked the habit. He was vague about details, but it seemed that he had either made a deal with God, or decided that he didn't want to set a bad example for his son. He "did it for Evan," is all he would say.

The gambling that really mattered, though, was the kind he did on the course. When Rick Smith met Mickelson in Palm Springs for a five-day training camp in late December, they worked on increasing Phil's comfort level with hitting a cut, never his preferred shot shape. They also changed his strategy off the tee, ditching his usual going-hook in favor of a controlled fade. Distance, they thought, should be sacrificed for control.

With Dave Pelz, the noted short-game guru, the work similarly emphasized both broadening Phil's skill set, and changing on-course strategy. Mickelson and Pelz—an engineer by training, who had once worked for NASA— had known each other for years, although their early relationship was based on Pelz's fondness for Lefty's lob wedge parlor tricks. A staple of Pelz's Golf Channel shows was Mickelson standing just a few feet in front of him, taking a full swing, and sending a ball almost straight up in the air, over Pelz's head.

Now, meeting Mickelson in Palm Springs, just after Smith's visit, and right after New Year's (in fact, twice—once at the Hideaway, and then, after a break for the weekend, at Porcupine Creek), their relationship grew more serious. Pelz lectured Mickelson on the science of green-reading, with the specific aim of improving his success rate on left-to-right putts. But the bulk of their work focussed on Phil's wedge play. Pelz put him through the same battery of tests he devised for his first students (among them Tom Kite) and diagnosed his weaknesses from inside 130 yards. Mickelson adopted Pelz's system of abbreviated swings, each corresponding to a point on an imaginary clockface, that, with three wedges, produced a set of twelve go-to distances. Mickelson became so fond of the clockface system that it crept into the rest of his bag. For example, Phil and his caddie, Jim Mackay, were soon referring to a three-quarter (or nine o'clock) 9-iron as a "Pelz nine."

The course-management aspect to the sessions had Pelz stressing the value of playing higher-percentage shots around the greens. Going for the green in two, Pelz advised him, wasn't always the best move, especially if there was trouble in play. He showed him statistics that proved good wedge players could, on the average, score just as low by laying up as they could by flailing at every par-five green. "I don't care if you never make another eagle for the rest of your career," Pelz told him, "if you eliminate the possibility of making ten or fifteen double bogeys every year."

The change in Mickelson was clear to those who watched him closely at the 2004 Hope. On Sunday, he was leading Skip Kendall by two shots when he came to the par-five 14th hole. This was a tricky hole. A creek (overreachingly named the All-America Canal) bordered the fairway on the right side. It then crossed the hole in front of the green, making it a dicey proposition to go for the green in two.

That day Mickelson was playing with Kenny Perry and Kirk Triplett. All three hit perfect drives. Perry and Triplett then laid up. But there was Phil Mickelson, standing in the middle of the fairway, waiting for the green to clear. He had 243 in. Jim Mackay, his caddie, liked the 3-iron.

Minutes passed. Perry and Triplett were walking casually along, approaching their balls on the left side of the fairway, positioned for wedges into the green. Then, as if dropped from a spaceship, a golf ball suddenly landed just four or five yards to their right. The *thunk* snapped their heads around. Then they looked at each other and laughed. After waiting what seemed like an eternity, Mickelson too had decided to lay up.

The decision even surprised Bones. "He asked me for a lay-up yardage, and it totally caught me off guard," he later remembered.

Rick Smith, however, saw it coming. He had been walking Phil's round, and throughout saw the effects of his work with his pupil. Two holes earlier, he had watched Phil hit a cut to a back-right pin, in order to avoid trouble left of the green. It was testimony to their work together, and Mickelson's newfound faith in his ability to hit a cut under pressure.

When Mickelson laid up on the par-five, Smith saw it as evidence that Pelz's work too had paid off—that Phil now believed he didn't have to try to overpower every par-five, and could make just as many birdies by playing it safe. "It showed he had real confidence in his wedge play, and that he felt like his distance control was tremendous," he said.

As it turned out, Mickelson made a three-putt bogey on the 14th, and, when Kendall birdied ahead of him, fell back into a tie for the lead. But Phil kept his calm, stayed patient, and ultimately beat him on the first hole of their playoff.

While it didn't pay off, the decision was one of the most telling of his career. It was the first crunch-time reflection that he'd had a change of thinking about the way he played the game, and foreshadowed dozens of similar moments during the months that followed. Arguably the most important play of Mickelson's 2004 Masters, for example, was his choice, on the 18th hole of Saturday's third round, to employ his putter with his ball resting on a downslope just off the green. It was a departure from his usual Augusta MO, which was to chip every such shot. But it lead to an easy par, and preserved his spot atop the leaderboard heading into Sunday.

The New Phil could still make birdies in bunches, as he proved that Masters Sunday, when he shot 31 for his final nine to take the green jacket. But his restraint at key moments was the difference-maker in his magnificent run at 2004's majors. That year he came within five shots of winning the Grand Slam, losing by two at the U.S. Open, finishing one shot out of a playoff at the British, and two from a playoff at the PGA Championship.

Mickelson's 2004 ended badly. After an ill-timed equipment change, and an unseemly decision to practice alone rather than with his teammates, he went 1–3 at the Ryder Cup. His play alongside Tiger Woods was particularly embarrassing: they went 0–2 in team play, and Mickelson's blocked tee ball on the 17th hole of the Friday foursomes cost them that match.

But he rebounded with a strong 2005. In Phoenix, a second-round 60 propelled him to a win at the FBR Open. He took Pebble Beach on the strength of a course-record 62 at infamously difficult Spyglass Hill, and he earned a third early-season win in Atlanta. He underperformed at the first three majors, but then, at the PGA Championship at Baltusrol, he scored what was then his most impressive victory to date. During a miserable, sweltering week on an aggravatingly difficult golf course, he outlasted the field to win by a stroke. Mickelson couldn't have won that kind of grueling endurance test without the guts and patience of a fully mature player. The 2004 Masters had shown the New Phil had control and self-discipline. The 2005 PGA proved he had balls.

His 2006 began just like his previous two years, with mini-training camps with Smith and Pelz. This time they took place a little later—his sessions with Pelz ran right up until game time. But that was the only substantial difference leading into the Hope. Once again it would be Mickelson's first event, and the springboard to a big season.

At 9:00 a.m. on Monday morning, in Scottsdale, Arizona, Jim Mackay kissed his son, Oliver, and then his wife, Jennifer, who was eight-and-a-half months pregnant with their second child. He walked out of his house, and threw his gear into the back of a black Ford Explorer that in most ways resembled that of his employer. Then he got in, shut the door, and headed for Palm Springs.

Five hours later he arrived at the house he'd be sharing that week with Fred Couples and his caddie, Joe LaCava. LaCava was Mackay's best friend on Tour. The Hope was special for both of them, marking five different anniversaries. The 1990 edition was LaCava's first event with Couples. It was also Mackay's first as a Tour caddie, bagging for fellow Georgian Larry Mize. The final round that year's tournament, with Mize paired with Couples, was the first time Mackay and LaCava ever met. It was also the first time Mackay met Couples, and the day Couples hatched Mackay's nickname, "Bones."

Mackay and LaCava were the last of a dying breed. They were the youngest of a group of caddies that came out on Tour strictly because of their love for the game, with no previous attachments to any pros, and no guarantee of earning a living. In that respect they were just like their immediate forebears, men like Bruce Edwards, Andy Martinez and Mike Cowan. Newer Tour caddies, in contrast, were usually friends or relatives of the pros they came out with, and arrived on Tour safe in the knowledge that in the Tiger Era, life alongside a decent player would provide as good a wage as most any other profession.

When Mackay came through the door, the first thing he saw was Couples stretching out in his stocking feet in the middle of the living room. The TV was already on, and tuned to ESPN News. Freddie was getting ready to go hit balls at The Palms, a nearby private club. Mickelson, who would be staying elsewhere with his family, wouldn't be arriving until Tuesday.

Mackay and LaCava left the house almost immediately. They had work to do. For what seemed like the zillionth time, they climbed into LaCava's rented SUV (LaCava, a self-described "control freak," always drove) and headed off to the golf course. But the first order of business was lunch. Bypassing the local Subways, they pulled into a real delicatessen and grabbed a couple of heroes. After fifteen years of coming to the Valley, LaCava, who was born and lived in Connecticut, knew exactly where to find the places run by old, transplanted Italian guys from New York.

From there they headed to the Classic Club, a brand-new course that had just been introduced into the Hope rotation. Neither man had ever seen it before. Neither had their bosses, so it was important to get out and walk it before the tournament started.

As they drove, and ate, and drove some more, they were busy catching up. They hadn't seen each other since the previous September, so there was plenty to talk about. Jennifer's pregnancy was Topic One. They then discussed LaCava's New York Giants getting smoked a day earlier by the Carolina Panthers, and the surprisingly good play of his equally beloved New York Rangers. (Growing up, LaCava had season tickets for their games at the Garden.) Then it was back to family. Mackay's holiday season had been quiet. Oliver didn't yet know what Christmas was, and his second child (who would be a daughter) hadn't yet arrived. LaCava, who had a boy and a girl, wanted Bones to benefit from his experience, and told him what to expect. A girl, he said, will open her presents slowly, whereas a boy's technique is more rip-and-throw.

When that topic was exhausted, they traded a few words about Couples' ongoing divorce proceedings. Really, though, there wasn't much to say. LaCava had arrived late Sunday night and had only spent a couple of bleary-eyed morning hours with Fred. Since they hadn't yet talked about it, Joey couldn't offer Jim an update.

Finally they arrived at the course. It wasn't difficult to find: it was built so close to the Interstate that the big, white concessions, media, and corporate entertainment tents were visible from the highway. When they got out of the car they immediately registered a chill, and a good bit of wind.

They ducked into the pro shop and said hello to a friendly assistant pro. Clearly excited to meet them, he took pains to assure them that it wasn't always so windy. Mackay and LaCava nodded politely and asked for yardage books.

They had a choice of two. One was of the hand of George Lucas, a former caddie who had been charting Tour venues for decades, more or less living in his trailer, accompanied only by his golden retriever. His volumes were immediately recognizable. They were always bound in bright, Day-Glo colors. No matter the week, the cover always said, *The Book,* as if to confer biblical authority on the contents. Inside, however, they were little works of art. Although the distances were laser-measured, the diagrams were hand drawn. In the margins were quirky little notations that reflected the author's personality. Every week, for example, Lucas provided a few yardages for odd, out-of-the-way places, each bearing the small notation JICYFU—Just in Case You Fucked Up.

The other book was produced by Fred Funk's caddie, Mark Long. It was much cleaner-looking: the diagrams were computer drawn. Comparing a Long book to a Lucas book was like comparing a Bauhaus blueprint with a Goya painting. Some caddies preferred Long's no-frills approach. Others, like LaCava, favored Lucas's, which was full of both information and character. A few caddies, like Mackay, bought both, using one to check the other's accuracy.

As soon as they started walking the Classic Course, they realized it would be the oddest of all creatures: a Hope venue with teeth. The fairways were narrow and the bunkers were deep, with higher faces than anything they'd seen in the Valley. The greens were demanding, with plenty of awkward slopes. There were also thirty acres of water hazards. "This is the course they're replacing Indian Wells with?" Mackay asked in disbelief.

They also noticed they were turning blue. The wind had picked up, and was now blowing more than forty miles an hour. LaCava, just in from the east coast, had been looking forward to mild temperatures. Now he was starting to rethink the wisdom of wearing shorts. Mackay was wearing a rainsuit, as he's apt to do even in warm weather. But the gusts were going right through it.

"Are you kidding me?" Mackay cracked, deploying one of his favorite lines, as the pages of his yardage book flapped around in his hands.

"This place is going to be like a wind tunnel." LaCava remarked.

He was right. The reason so few courses were built alongside Interstate 10 was that the mountains on either side tended to funnel the winds. After a while, their new friend from the pro shop reappeared, once again attempting to convince them this was an unusual day. As he spoke, Mackay looked at the wind farm in the distance. The rotors, he thought to himself, must have been going about 300 miles per hour.

LaCava noticed where he was looking. "There's a reason those things are over there," he said.

"What we need to do," Mackay said, "is find someplace around here that sells turtlenecks."

As the week began, Mickelson was in good spirits. But the buzz around him was anything but pleasant. Hitting the newsstands that very week was the February issue of *GQ* magazine. Inside was a piece called "The Ten Most Hated Athletes in Sports." Terrell Owens topped the list. Barry Bonds, NASCAR's Kurt Busch, pitcher Curt Schilling, and Kobe Bryant were second through fifth. Mickelson was number eight.

The article didn't have a ton of credibility. *GQ,* after all, wasn't exactly *Golf Digest.* It hardly had its finger on the pulse of the Tour. Moreover, it was impossible to find a golf writer who'd talked to the magazine, even though reporters, along with players, were said to be the sources for the story.

It made sense, however, that some of Phil's peers, given the chance, would run him down. Mickelson's famous smile, the most scrutinized since the Mona Lisa's, was often disdained, sometimes even on the record. In August 2005 Paul Gow, a little-known Australian journeyman pro, said of Mickelson, "He's an arrogant person. What you see on television is totally different to what he is around the clubhouse. He has done some great acting classes in Hollywood, and they've worked out for him."

Gow wasn't the only critic. Vijay Singh had taken two different swipes at Mickelson. The first was in 2004, on Bryant Gumbel's HBO show *Real Sports.* Asked about Mickelson's image, he said, "Is that the true Phil? Is that the true person?" Then, at the 2005 PGA Championship, he said, "I'm not a fake, like many guys out there." There wasn't much question whom he was talking about.

The smile wasn't the only source of ire. During tournaments, Mickelson often preferred to hit balls off-site, which added to the perception of aloofness. On occasion, he could be less than kind about lesser players' importance to the Tour. A few years earlier, he had criticized the Tour's practice of staging secondary events opposite some of the majors and

World Golf Championships. The rank-and-file considered those tournaments invaluable opportunities to keep pace on the money list during what would otherwise be weeks at home. Yet Mickelson advised doing away with the events, since they "diluted the product."

He made similar remarks at the end of 2005 in an interview with Mark Rolfing for his show *Golf Hawaii*. Asked about the Tour's new FedEx Cup playoff system, he said it didn't go far enough, insisting there should be even more events that gathered the top players together, while excluding the others. "The reason it doesn't happen," he said, "is that the 150 guys on Tour who are fighting to keep their cards have such a strong voice that it stops anything like that from going through. So 150 guys control, and can stop, what would be ultimately good for the Tour."

Indeed, there was enough resentment around Mickelson that some players took pleasure in creating and perpetuating rumors about him. One, about an illegitimate child, was particularly tasteless. Another looked like a simple wisecrack gone out of control. After Mickelson signed with Callaway in late 2004, people began saying that the terms of his contract included the company's repayment of millions of dollars in gambling debts. Those, of course, had been the terms of John Daly's 1997 Callaway contract—it was pretty clear that someone simply dropped Mickelson's name into Daly's situation. But that didn't stop the rumor. Somewhere along the line, someone added a telling detail that lent it credibility, saying that *Sports Illustrated* was soon going to bear the rumor out in an exposé. It was a clever touch: *SI* had a reputation for that kind of player-indifferent ruthlessness. Things reached a breaking point a few months later, in Phoenix, when Steve Loy, Mickelson's agent, confronted an *SI* reporter and threatened legal action if the story was actually published. No such story, of course, had ever been in the works.

When Mickelson appeared before the press at the Hope, no one asked about any rumors or *GQ* articles. Neither were there any questions about his skipping the Tour Championship and the Mercedes, nor his remarks about the FedEx Cup. These, after all, were friendly Southern California golf reporters, who had watched Mickelson grow up. They weren't going to hit him with any heavy leather.

(It wasn't until two weeks later, in Phoenix, that Mickelson was asked about the *GQ* article. "It's part of being in the public eye," he shrugged. "It sucks sometimes, but I enjoy 99.9 percent of my life and my job and everything. I just don't worry about it.")

Mickelson's golf at the Hope showed no signs of bother. He opened with a 66 at La Quinta Country Club, followed by a 69 at the Palmer course at PGA West. He caught a relatively docile day at the Classic Club and shot a 68, moving him into a tie for fourth. (Couples wasn't as fortunate. He played the course on Thursday, at its windiest, and his 71 relegated him to the back of the pack.)

Mickelson's real standing in the tournament was hard to measure, because he hadn't yet played Bermuda Dunes, the easiest of that year's four courses. But when he finally did, on Saturday, he didn't play partic- ularly well. Coming to the 8th hole—his seventeenth of the day—he was only three under for the day. There, on the longish par-five, he pounded what was probably his best drive of the year, right down the middle and miles long. It was a pleasant surprise. His personal history on that partic- ular hole wasn't great, and he and Mackay knew it. As they walked to the ball, they laughed about how nice it would be to play from that fairway for a change, for maybe the first time ever. After a so-so approach, he found his ball on the back fringe, and chipped in for eagle.

His 67 looked good on paper, but it gained him no ground. Chad Campbell, the tournament leader, had shot the same number on the Classic Course. Now, going into Sunday, Mickelson was six back. He would play in the next-to-last group behind Campbell and fellow pur- suers Scott Verplank and John Senden. Mickelson knew that Campbell had finished second at the previous week's Sony Open and was playing well. "For me to catch him," he said, "he's going to have to make a cou- ple of mistakes."

Chad Campbell doesn't look like the kind of guy who rattles easily. His game face is a kind of blankness, a faraway gaze that suggests not just immunity to pressure, but a complete lack of concern about the out- come of any given shot.

But image isn't everything. Jitters at Q-school prevented the 31-year- old Texan him from reaching the Tour until he was 27. At the 2004 Ryder Cup, his first, he broke down in tears after losing both his Satur- day matches. His seventeen majors featured one great finish—he was a gritty runner-up to Shaun Micheel in the 2003 PGA Championship— and nine missed cuts.

Small stages never troubled him. He excelled in his student days at UNLV. (He played on the scholarship originally earmarked for Tiger

Woods, and roomed with Chris Riley.) In the bushes he was a super-hero, winning so often on the Hooters Tour (in 2000, eight of its first sixteen events) that the circuit started paying him a $5,000-per-event appearance fee. His peers, sure of his future success, nicknamed him "Big Money."

When he finally arrived on the PGA Tour (via the Nationwide Tour), he was splashed on the cover of *Sports Illustrated*'s *Golf Plus* as the sport's "Next Big Thing." He notched an early win at the 2003 Tour Championship and backed it up with a victory at March 2004's Bay Hill Classic. From there, however, problems invaded his game. After leaving Cleveland Golf for Nike, he spent months trying to find a driver that worked. More seriously, he underwent a prolonged crisis of putting confidence that lasted from mid 2004 through the end of 2005. He still managed to creep into contention from time to time, but the "Next Big Thing" hype wasn't panning out.

Even when he was playing well, he was easy to miss. His white-shirt-and-khakis wardrobe was as drab as a prison inmate's. Amiable enough in close company, he never had much to say when the spotlight shone on him. Interview requests were invariably refused (although it was hard to say whether that was his agents' doing, or because of the wishes of Campbell himself). There had always been players who couldn't, or didn't want to, sell themselves. The difference—now, in the Tiger Era—was that they weren't financially hurt by it. Prize money was so bountiful that there was no pronounced need for peripheral income. Campbell was a perfect example: between contracts with Cleveland and Nike, he was perfectly happy carrying around a blank bag.

His reticence—along with his Texas upbringing, flat swing, and ball-striking prowess—drew comparisons to a strong, silent type from the sport's past. "Campbell's been compared to Ben Hogan," *Golf World* once remarked. "Except he's not as outgoing."

The media's attention, therefore, gravitated toward his wife, Amy. They lived the first part of Campbell's golf career as an unassuming couple, the boy and girl next door whose distaff half taught grade school while hubby played the Tour. But her spitfire nature gradually emerged. Always a good singer, she tried in 2003 to get on *American Idol*; when it didn't happen she had her husband bankroll a music career. In 2005 a second *Sports Illustrated* profile—this time, more about Amy than Chad—labeled them golf's "Odd Couple," and leaned on her first album's independence-seeking lyrics (sample song title: "Love is a Compromise") to suggest that their marriage was something less than stable.

Campbell spent the 2005–2006 off-season the same way he always did—watching football, and drinking beers with his friends. He was part of a close-knit group of pros and caddies, who, for the most part, all lived in the same neighborhood in Hurst, Texas. The posse included his caddie and best childhood friend, Judd Burkett; fellow pro Ryan Palmer; Palmer's caddie, James Edmondson; and Ben Crane's caddie, Brett Waldman. When Campbell wasn't hanging out on the couch, he was over at Nike's Fort Worth facility working on his putting and his driver problem, or down at the lake, helping Burkett build a new house.

One evening Campbell and Burkett were sitting on the house's half completed porch, mapping out the coming season. Judd rubbed at his bloodied left leg (the two had just cut down a tree) and made some predictions for Campbell's early season success.

"There are four places you're going to play well," he said—"Sony, the Hope, TPC and the Masters." His reasoning was based, more than anything else, on his friend's talents as a wind player. Those four events usually saw more than a little breeze. So far Burkett was two for two: Campbell had finished second in Hawaii, and was now the Saturday night leader at the Hope.

Perhaps predictably, Campbell was unperturbed by playing in the Hope's celebrity draw, a circumstance a lot of players hate. (Mickelson, for one, always begged out of it, saying it prevented him from focusing on his game.) From Wednesday through Saturday his partners included Roger Clemens, Mike Eruzione, Matthew McConaughey, and Justin Timberlake. But Campbell barely said a word to any of them. After one round, a celeb-crazy reporter asked whether or not he had talked to Timberlake about his relationship with Cameron Diaz. Said Campbell: "I didn't feel like we were close enough to get into that." Timberlake probably appreciated it.

Sundays at the Hope are quite different from the rest of the week. With the amateurs gone, Tour officials move the pins from the middle of the greens to the edges, providing a tougher challenge. That, plus the usual Sunday nerves, brings to an end Wednesday through Saturday's how-low-can-you-go limbo contest. Players still have to make birdies, but now, for a change, pars actually mean something.

Mickelson, with a six-shot deficit to make up, had a tough time getting started. Rust, apparent only to a small extent earlier in the week, began to show on his driver, as he lost tee shots both left and right. He invariably recovered, and was bogey-free through fourteen holes, but had only made one birdie. Soon enough it was clear that this year, there would be no Hope.

The first part of Campbell's scorecard was as bland as his wardrobe. He opened with five straight pars. As he neared the turn, however, his play became erratic. After a bogey at the 6th, he birdied 8 and eagled 9, but then made double bogey at the 10th. Still, no one within striking distance was making a move behind him.

Until that point, it had been a typical January day in the desert. The sun was bright enough to make the players squint, and a dry breeze swept the course. But shortly after the leaders turned, the wind picked up dramatically. Pant legs now flapped so fast and so loudly that they sounded like baseball cards in bicycle spokes. Gusts and swirls made shot selection difficult.

Campbell fell prey to the wind on the 13th, a long, dogleg-left par-four whose left side was bordered by a lake. He took his tee shot over the water, trying to cut off a big chunk of the hole. But it started slightly left of his intended line, was blown further left by the wind, and never made it across the hazard. It finished about six feet short of dry land. As Campbell stuck another tee in the ground, his grip on the tournament suddenly looked precarious.

It got worse. His second drive also went left, and found a nasty fairway bunker with a ten-foot face. Stepping in and out of the bunker to size up his predicament, Campbell knew he was in trouble. He would have to get the ball up quickly, yet carry it far enough to reach the green. The wind didn't make it any easier. Double bogey seemed like the happiest possible outcome.

He had 143 yards to the flag, which was planted on a finger of green on the right side. Burkett gave him a six-iron, making sure Campbell had enough club to get to the hole. Now the trick was picking it clean enough, and launching it high enough, to clear the bunker face.

As he got over the ball, there wasn't a trace of emotion on his face. There it was again: that blessed blankness. He seemed as cool as Gary Cooper in an old western, just before he shot somebody. "I was a little upset right then," Campbell would later say. But you needed a brain scan to know it. Outwardly, he showed no sign.

He aimed a little right of the TV tower and swung away. When his ball came down it was four feet from the pin. He buried the putt for a miracle bogey, left the green with a one-shot lead, and never looked back, ultimately winning by three.

Apart from the tidbit about being "upset," Campbell, true to form, didn't have much to say about the shot that won him the tournament.

"What were you thinking when the ball was in the air?" a reporter asked.

"I really wasn't thinking anything," Campbell replied, a line that should probably be inscribed on his tombstone.

> Chad Campbell, 1974–2062.
> I Really Wasn't Thinking Anything

Two weeks after the tournament, there appeared alongside Interstate 10, just outside the Classic Club, a twenty-foot-tall wooden figure of Campbell, celebrating him as the winner of the 2006 Bob Hope Chrysler Classic. It wasn't as ambitious as the monument to Mickelson being built up in the hills. But for Campbell, it was more than enough.

3

TIGER, DISTRACTED

The Buick Invitational

While Phil Mickelson, Chad Campbell, and company were at the Hope, Tiger Woods was anything but idle. Out on the coast, in Orange County, California, he was running through the paces at a training camp of his own.

For weeks Woods had been holed up at his new home in Newport Beach, shuttling almost every day to be with his ailing father in the house he grew up in on Teakwood Street in Cypress, about thirty minutes up the 405. (The lone exception, confidants said, was December 30, his thirtieth birthday, when he went to Las Vegas to celebrate with friends.) Then, on the Tuesday of Hope week, his instructor, Hank Haney, arrived, and it was back to work. They spent long, ten-hour days at Shady Canyon, an exclusive club in Irvine that Woods had recently made his West Coast home base.

On Monday, after five days of knocking off rust, they went south to San Diego for the Buick Invitational. Joined by Steve Williams, just in from New Zealand, they checked into the Lodge at Torrey Pines, a pretty, craftsman-style hotel on the grounds of the fifty-year old, thirty-six-hole municipal facility. On Tuesday they woke up early: Woods always played his practice rounds at "zero-dark-thirty," as college pal and fellow pro Notah Begay liked to say. They arrived on North Course's first tee in the half-light, the air still heavy with the remnants of overnight fog.

They weren't alone. Woods' playing partner that day was twenty-five-year veteran Tommy Armour III, a Dallas resident who became chummy with Woods in 2003, during Tiger's first visits down to Vaquero Golf Club to work with Haney. With Armour was his brother-slash-caddie, Sandy. Also part of the retinue was Vencie Glenn, a 42-year-old longtime friend of Woods who played defensive back in the NFL for ten years, mostly with the Chargers; he still shared the league record of 103 yards for the longest-ever interception return. During Woods' younger, premarriage days, the pair were notorious for their can't-miss nights out in San Diego and Las Vegas. On the strength of their relationship Glenn had scored, in 2000, a six-figure deal with Upper Deck trading cards. He had little trouble completing the implicit task of signing his buddy to an endorsement deal.

The usual half dozen security men were also on hand to protect Woods' person. Two were inside the ropes, in plain clothes. Outside were a few local rent-a-cops in bright red jackets, gung-ho types whose rep preceded them: a couple of years earlier they had been seen handcuffing a mouthy caddie. Now, walking alongside Woods, they leaped into action again when, on the 8th hole, an apparent intruder ducked under the ropes. They only pulled up when Sandy Armour started waving his arms and shouting, "It's okay! It's okay!" The startled newcomer was Tommy's swing instructor, Andy Plummer.

It was the only moment of drama during what was otherwise a quiet morning. San Diego fans, some of the savviest on Tour, know that Tuesday is the best time to get an up-close look at Woods. But knowledge is only half the battle. At Torrey, fans can't park anywhere close to the course, and the remote parking shuttles don't run that early on Tuesdays. On this particular morning, only two dozen or so committed golf nuts—half of them adults, half waist-high kids—were present. Apart from one golf writer, that was the extent of Woods' audience.

Truth to tell, there was nothing much to see. Woods and Armour went about their usual business of hitting shots and worrying their swings and putting strokes. The incidental conversation was minimal; most of it revolved around the shaft of Armour's driver, which somehow enabled him to keep up with Woods off the tee. On the 18th hole Armour even nosed one by him.

By the time they reached the 18th green, a few more golf writers had appeared, looking to talk to Woods. They were all familiar faces, reporters who stood in front of Woods for ten to twenty weeks per year. But on this morning Woods didn't so much as make eye contact with them. Coming off the green he breezed right by them and headed to the driving range.

Woods knew what they wanted to talk about, and wanted no part of it.

The health of Tiger's father, Earl Woods, had been declining for longer than his son had been a pro. Earl had his first open-heart surgery before Tiger had reached his teens. He had another just months before Tiger's landmark win at the Masters in 1997, and was almost unable to make it to Augusta to deliver that year's storybook 18th-hole embrace. The following year he was diagnosed with prostate cancer. Radiation therapy seemed to eradicate it, but by 2004 the cancer had returned. That August Earl revealed that it had spread throughout his body, causing lesions in his back and a tumor behind his left eye. "My eye was literally pushed out of the socket," Woods, then 72, told the *Boston Herald*. "The pain was so bad. It was past being a headache; there's no such thing as a headache like that. Every beat of my heart, there was pain."

In the months that followed, the outlook alternated between hopeful and pessimistic. When Woods won the Masters in 2005, Earl once again made it to Augusta but this time was too ill to come to the golf course, and stayed behind in their rented house. After the victory Tiger, his voice thick with emotion, said, "Every year that I've been lucky enough to win this tournament, my dad's been there to give me a big hug. And today, he wasn't there. I can't wait to get home and see him."

Earl's condition subsequently improved. By May of 2005, at the Memorial, Tiger reported, "He's done with the radiation treatments. He's got no more cancer. But unfortunately he's one over par–73. He doesn't quite recover as fast as he did the last time.

"He doesn't exactly take care of himself," he continued. "He's still puffing away, and that's just the way it is. He's been real stubborn about everything. It's got him this far, so we'll just kind of leave him be."

Just before the start of the 2006 season, things took a turn for the worse. Tiger was with his wife, Elin, in Park City, Utah, for the first half of a planned two-week ski vacation. (It was supposed to conclude in Beaver Creek, Colorado.) But he was summoned home before they could start the second leg.

The situation, an intimate of Tiger's said, "was touch and go. It didn't look too good. I'd like to be able to tell you that Earl's getting better. But the truth is, he's not getting better." Between Tiger's last tournament of 2005 (the Dunlop Phoenix, in Japan) and that January mini-camp with Haney, Tiger spent twenty-four days without touching a club, the longest he'd ever gone.

When Tiger breezed past those reporters on Tuesday morning at Torrey Pines, the reason was plain—he didn't want to entertain questions about his father. The implicit message was that he would address such questions once and once only, at his formal press conference the following day.

But his mood wasn't morose. Indeed, he seemed to be the same Tiger as always, cracking jokes on the range and, eventually, with one or two of the pressmen who had followed him there. In between buckets, one of the reporters with whom Woods was friendliest made a second pass at him, asking for a short private audience.

"Tiger, got a minute for me?" he asked.

"I've got a foot for you," Woods replied.

"You don't have a foot. You're half-Asian."

"That's why it's only a foot."

The Buick Invitational was Tiger's tournament, in much the same way that the Hope was Mickelson's. He didn't always win (he was three for his last seven tries), but his appearances always carried a special sense of importance. In 2000, on his way to the best summer in golf history, he came in riding a six-event PGA Tour winning streak, the longest since Hogan's six straight in 1948, and Byron Nelson's epic eleven in 1945. In 2003 he was returning from a long layoff after knee surgery. In 2005 he was coming off the worst season of his career, and his victory brought an end to a fifteen-month, twenty-one-event stroke-play winless drought.

Now, in 2006, his father's health made him the focus of pre-tournament attention. It was fitting: Earl had spent many days walking Torrey Pines, and other San Diego courses, with his son. He began driving him down from Cypress for the Junior Worlds in the mid 'eighties, before Tiger had reached his teens.

One of those visits was a touchstone, illustrating the almost mystical connection that existed between father and son. In 1988 Tiger was playing the Mission Bay executive course in the final round of competition for the 11-to-12-year-old age group. After hitting his approach over the 18th green, he needed to get up and down to win. Earl was standing behind the green, out of Tiger's field of vision. He began muttering to himself, *Don't do anything stupid. Put the ball on the green and trust your putting.*

A pitch and a putt later, Tiger came running over to his father, shouting, "I heard you, Daddy! I heard you!"

"That's when we knew," Earl later told *Sports Illustrated.* "He knows where I am at all times."

Earl regarded his son's success as the culmination of a personal journey whose purpose, from the very beginning, was raising the world's greatest golfer.

Earl was born in 1932 in Manhattan, Kansas. He attended Kansas State, graduating in 1953 with a degree in sociology. He played catcher on the baseball team and was the first African-American to play baseball in the what is now the Big Eight Conference. When the team traveled he was forced to stay in blacks-only hotels. His teammates brought food out to him in the car while they dined in restaurants.

He married early, to a young woman from a nearby small town, and began a family. He and his wife had three children—two boys and a girl—but he was often away, serving in the Army. His first tour of duty in Vietnam began in 1962. In the late sixties, while in Thailand, he met Kultida Punsawad, who was then working as a secretary in Bangkok.

Following a divorce, he married Tida in Brooklyn in 1969, while stationed at Fort Hamilton, where he first discovered golf. He returned to Vietnam in 1970, after choosing to undergo Green Beret training at age 35. He spent most of his second tour as an adviser to the deputy chief of the Binh Thuan province, Colonel Vuong Dang Phong, whom Earl called "Tiger." Earl retired in 1971, as a lieutenant colonel, bought a two-bedroom tract house on a corner lot in Cypress, California, and took a job as a contracts administrator with McDonnell Douglas.

Earl and Tida's first and only child was born on December 30, 1975, seven months after the fall of Saigon. For the baby, Tida invented the name Eldrick—the "e" was for Earl, the "k" for Kultida, and the rest improvised.

Earl called the child "Tiger" from the start. He felt he was "destined for fame," and that one day, his old Vietnamese friend would hear about him, then say, "That must be Woody's kid," and get back in touch. Sadly, Phong died in September 1976, nine months after his namesake's birth, after surrendering to the occupying North Vietnamese.

Thousands of miles away, at about the same time (could it have been the same day?) Earl's nine-month old son, watching his father hit balls in the garage, crawled out of his high chair, picked up a sawed-off 9-iron, and flushed his first true golf shot into a net.

The legend of Tiger's younger years is filled with tales of his father molding his golf, especially its mental side. He created a "personal par" for the courses they played together, so his son wouldn't judge himself by adult standards. He jangled change in his pockets and shouted in his backswing so he would learn to block out distractions.

(Those years were filled with Earl's broad, hyperbolic predictions. "He's the bridge between the East and the West," Earl said in one of his more famous pronouncements. "He is the chosen one. He'll have the power to impact nations. Not people. Nations.")

Yet golf never had as much to do with the formation of Tiger's character as what happened on that corner lot in Cypress.

The house he grew up in was modest. It had a little backyard where Tida grew Thai apples, and peppers that were (as one friend remembered) "hot as lava rocks." Upstairs, the walls of Tiger's room were plastered with posters and photos of Luke Skywalker and members of the San Diego Chargers, along with the famous, faded *Los Angeles Times* newspaper clipping of Jack Nicklaus milestones. The entire house served as a short-game practice area. Visitors were often entertained by the sight of balls skittering through the hallways, or floating over the living room furniture.

Conventional wisdom is that Tida was the law inside those four walls—"You will never, never ruin my reputation as a parent, because I will beat you," she once said—and that it was she, not Earl, who instilled in Tiger his killer instinct, imploring him to "step on the throats" of his opponents, to "never let up." That may have been the case. But Tiger's respect for his father's authority was second to none. Even as a young adult, he responded to Earl's voice differently than anyone else's.

One afternoon in late 1997, the year Tiger won his first Masters, he was visiting the new Tiger Woods Foundation headquarters in Cypress, California, with *Golf Digest*'s Tom Callahan, who was with him that day for a story. At one point Tiger headed into a side office and got on the phone with his buddy Jerry Chang. Soon the magazine's photographer, down the hall with Tida and Earl, decided he needed another picture. Tida called to him once, then again, to come out of the office. Tiger kept right on talking. Then Earl uttered his name, in more or less his normal speaking voice. "Gotta go," Tiger said to Chang. He hung up the phone and quickly left the room.

Earl had a lot of time to be the architect of Tiger's game, and his personality. He was 50 by the time his son was eight, gearing down from the working life, able to take a more active role than most fathers.

That was a good thing, considering the contemporary social conditions in lily-white Orange County, California. The Woodses were miles away from the closest family of color. When they first moved in, neighbors threw rocks and eggs at the house. At school Tiger was once tied to a tree and beaten by his classmates. There were people on the block who, until he became a celebrity, refused to say hello.

Tiger grew up surrounded by unconditional love. Home was a safe haven, as was golf, but those other circumstances shrank his world, making him an introvert. If his own experience didn't teach him enough about racism, he had his father's stories, and those that were told by his father's friends. At an early age, he developed out of necessity a certain imperviousness to the way the outside world regarded him. "That kid is hard," Earl observed.

His sensitivity to unpleasant social realities wasn't just personal. It was political. It had to be, growing up with a father like Earl. Though a soldier, Earl's political consciousness was formed by the experiences of his youth, and by the civil rights movement. That the sixties had a profound effect on him was evident years later, when he presided over the Tiger Woods Foundation clinics that took place, often in urban areas, during the first few years of Tiger's career. Before his son appeared, Earl would address the audience of parents and children, speaking plainly and pointedly about how kids in the inner cities, particularly children of color, were "kept down," and "denied opportunities." Tiger himself rarely—make that never—dropped any hints about his own politics. Many assumed that he was a conservative Republican, like most of his fellow Tour players. That may have been the case. Still, Earl's influence had to be in there somewhere.

• • •

In light of Earl's health, Tiger's Wednesday press conference was one of the oddest in recent memory. It took place in a capacious, chandeliered ballroom at the La Jolla Hilton, the Lodge's next-door neighbor, which borders the South Course's 18th hole. Its first fifteen minutes, emceed by Buick marketing manager Larry Peck, was non-stop corporate ballyhoo—the screening of commercials Woods had filmed at Vaquero six weeks earlier; the unveiling of a silvery, corporate-logo'd golf bag; and the announcement of a new-car giveaway promotion.

All of it was contrary to the prevailing mood. So too was the start of the media question-and-answer period. Tiger was asked about relatively trivial matters like equipment changes, the possibility of his starting to design courses, and the expansive, $38 million property he had just bought in South Florida, on Jupiter Island, near Palm Beach. (The purchase of the new house in Newport Beach had happened under the radar).

There was a question about the 81-point game a few nights earlier by Kobe Bryant, the Laker star who, once upon a time, had claimed Woods as a friend.

A Norwegian reporter asked if Woods had ever heard of Henrik Bjornstad, the first player from that country ever to earn a PGA Tour card, and followed by asking, "Since you're married to a Swedish girl, would you ever consider going to Norway for vacation?"

By now twenty-five minutes had passed. All along, savvier reporters had held their tongues about Earl, for fear of seeming morbid. As the presser wore on, one leaned over to another and said, "Is anyone going to ask about his father?"

Eventually someone did.

Politely but tersely, Woods said that his dad was "doing better," and "hanging in there," and that he'd "spent the entire break with him."

The longest of his four or five sentences had an odd flow, showing how uncomfortable the topic was. "He's my best friend, and any time you can spend as much time with your parents that you truly love, especially when he wasn't feeling all that well, it meant the world to me."

His reticence was the best measure of his concern.

A question he couldn't answer was how Earl's health would affect his play. But most surmised it wouldn't. As Tiger's friend Charles Howell III put it, "He's pretty good at blocking things out." Yes, he was. It was one of the things Earl had taught him.

• • •

It only figured that the man who would yank the pre-tournament focus away from Woods would be John Daly.

Shortly after Tiger's press conference ended, Daly was walking down the South Course's 18th hole, finishing up his pro-am round. Out of the corner of his eye he spotted Golf Channel reporter Mike Ritz, who was riding along in a golf cart, just outside the ropes, with a cameraman and their equipment.

Daly waved him over, and the two exchanged greetings. Daly then told Ritz that he had news about his wife, Sherrie. He suggested that he might want to set up the camera.

Two and a half years earlier, in July 2003, the former Sherrie Miller had been indicted for her alleged role in a drug and money laundering conspiracy. Her father, Alvis, a Collierville, Tennessee used car dealer, had been involved with men charged with buying and selling cocaine, methamphetamine, and marijuana. Their profits, authorities said, were running through Alvis's dealership.

Between 1996 and 2002 Sherrie had been going to local banks for her father and making deposits of just below $10,000—the amount that banks are required by law to report to the authorities. What the Millers didn't know was that banks, at their discretion, can report any deposits they deem suspicious. That, in Alvis and Sherrie's case, is exactly what happened.

On the day Sherrie was indicted she was 27. She and John had been married about two years. Their first child together, son John Patrick (or "Little John") had been born just five days earlier. John said he knew nothing of his wife's activities. Sherrie herself claimed she knew nothing of where the money came from.

Sherrie's father was sent to prison for two and a half years. Her mother, Billie, also complicit, was sentenced to five months, plus five months of house arrest. Sherrie's path through the courts, however, was long and convoluted. Initially she arranged a plea bargain, but the judge struck down the deal, deeming it too lenient. She was eventually found guilty on December 14, 2004, and sentenced to five months in prison.

An appeals process ensued, but now, Daly told Ritz, it was over. Federal marshals had arrested her that morning and taken her to the county jail in Lexington, Kentucky.

The arrest, Daly said, caught everyone by surprise. "There wasn't much notice for us, and that's what hurts the most. We never got the sentencing on paper. I don't think I would be here in San Diego if I'd have known. Sherrie's mom's taking care of the kids"—not just Little John, but also Sherrie's older son, Austin—"and I'll probably get them out in Phoenix next week."

For any other Tour player, an episode like this would have been shocking. But for Daly, it was par for the course. His relationships with women had always been star-crossed.

Daly married his first wife, Dale, in 1987, when he was just 21. It was over as soon it began—she had no desire to live a life on the road with a golf pro. He met his second wife, Bettye, in 1990, the year before his Cinderella win at the PGA Championship. It was, he later said, "sex at first sight." They were married in May of 1992, in Las Vegas, and had a daughter, Shynah. Less than a year later, their union ended: Bettye served him with divorce papers at the 1993 Masters.

He had met his third wife, Paulette, in early 1992, just a few months before he married Bettye. Daly was playing the Hope alongside the tournament host, Gerald Ford, and Dan Quayle. She was one of the invariably buxom young women who followed Hope around, wearing shorts and T-shirts bearing the words "Hope," "Chrysler," and "Classic." (Paulette was "Classic," as Daly never tired of pointing out.) They too married in Las Vegas, in early 1995. During their honeymoon he bought her a Rolex, the seed for his later ditty, "All My Exes Wear Rolexes." Their daughter, Sierra, was born that June, and Paulette watched John win the British Open that July. But their marriage would only last two more years.

Running through those relationships—and indeed Daly's entire post-pubescent life— was a river of booze. It was likely the reason he tore up his and Bettye's home in Colorado in late 1992, a rampage that also resulted in assault charges. (They were later dropped.) It also precipitated the end of his relationship with Paulette. After shooting 76 in the first round of the 1997 Players Championship, he spent several hours drinking in a bar. That night their hotel room suffered physical damage worthy of a heavy-metal band, and the divorce papers arrived two weeks later.

In the wake of that episode Daly stayed sober for two years, a condition of a pact he signed with Callaway Golf. Company founder Ely Callaway had given him a five-year, $10 million endorsement contract, as well as paying off millions in gambling debts, on the condition he stop drinking. The deal was voided in September 1999, when Daly decided that the burden of staying dry was too much for him. Drinking, he told *Golf World*'s Tim Rosaforte, is "in my blood."

His marriage to Sherrie didn't exactly reform him. But it (along with the death of his beloved mother, Lou, in 2002) appeared to even him out. There were wholesale changes in his entourage. He was still drinking, but the room-wrecking, at least, was kept to a minimum. There was a divorce scare at the end of 2003, with both John and Sherrie telling their lawyers to file court papers, and then rescinding those instructions. But there was also some of Daly's best golf in years. The end of 2003 saw a win in Asia, and at two silly-season events. The run was capped by his victory at the 2004 Buick Invitational at Torrey Pines, his first official PGA Tour title in nine years.

Daly almost won again in late 2005, in a showdown with Tiger Woods at October's WGC American Express Championships in San Francisco. He wasn't contending regularly, but he still seemed capable of playing world class golf. And the length of his relationship with Sherrie—at the beginning of 2006, three and a half years—was a personal best.

It was hard to tell how her incarceration would affect him. But talking to Ritz, he seemed committed to riding out the storm. "I talked to Sherrie last night," he said, "and she was very emotional. But she said, 'Just play. Just get through it.'"

For maybe the first time ever, Tiger Woods and John Daly were going into a tournament thinking the same thing.

The North and South Courses at Torrey Pines had a lot in common. Both were among the most scenic places in the world to play golf, with dramatic ravines and gorges, and oceanfront holes that boasted expansive, picture-postcard views of the Pacific. Like Pebble Beach, they were the kind of courses one might walk just for recreational purposes, although a better way to enjoy them—for some local residents, at least—was to go up in a paraglider and swoop along the blufftop, taking in the beauty of the coastline and the crashing waves below.

Both were also city-owned municipal tracks, halves of a thirty-six-hole facility that annually generated for San Diego about $1.7 million.

The similarities ended there. The North was a short, birdie-friendly layout. The South, on the other hand, was a 7,600-yard monster that, for shorter hitters, was virtually unplayable. Every Thursday and Friday at the Buick Invitational the pros went one round on each of the two courses, and the scoring averages told the story: the South played about four shots harder than the North.

The South's difficulty, of course, had a purpose. It was rebuilt as a beast in 2001, in hopes of landing the 2008 U.S. Open. The architect charged with the task was the so-called "Open Doctor," Rees Jones. The $35 million for the renovations had been raised by local civic leaders: the efforts were spearheaded by Jay Rains, a local venture capitalist who was a past president and director of the Century Club, the organization that runs the Buick Invitational. (In 2004, less than two years after Torrey was awarded the Open, Rains became a member of the USGA executive committee.)

The upcoming U.S. Open would undoubtedly be a blessing. Its projected economic impact was $100 million. But it was also a curse. The city was expected to foot the bill for preperatory golf course maintenance. For that reason, area residents' greens fees were hiked, and their allotment of tee times was pared back to make room for higher-paying out-of-town-ers. The city was also supposed to pay for a new clubhouse, plus renovations to the North Course, not so much to enhance playability, but to make it more hospitable to Open infrastructure needs. Each part of the puzzle was the source of ongoing city council strife. The controversies collectively cast another curious shadow over the 2006 tournament.

At any rate, the disparity between the two courses imposed on the first two rounds a firm rule: Go low on the North, or go south on the leaderboard.

Tiger Woods began his 2006 Buick Invitational on the North Course and got off to a slow start, shooting a disappointing one-under 71. Considering the four-stroke differential, he was in effect spotting the rest of the field three or four shots. He had little success with the new driver shaft he put into play after his practice round, on Armour's recommendation. After the first round he led the 156-player field in distance off the tee (averaging 326 yards a pop), but was last in accuracy, finding only one of fourteen fairways. He had the shaft switched back almost as soon as he signed his scorecard, saying, "Hopefully tomorrow it'll be a little bit better."

It was. On Friday he played the South Course's first ten holes in a remarkable five-under. Phil Mickelson, for his part, was going about business in a more conventional way. After a first round 71 on the South, he was now having a field day on the North. Within five minutes of each other both Woods and Mickelson crashed the leaderboard top ten. Woods reached six-under with a 120-foot, cross-country bomb for eagle on the South's par-five 13th hole, and Mickelson got to the same number with a birdie on the North's 2nd (his tenth hole of the day). It was like someone finally rang an alarm clock to wake up the golf tournament. Each slipped a little coming in, but when they finished, their scores were nearly identical. Mickelson shot 71–67 for a share of twelfth place. Woods went 71–68 and was tied for twenty-second.

On Saturday both played solid rounds. Mickelson's 69 moved him into a tie for fifth, but Woods was two better. His 67 landed him in a tie for second. He would play Sunday's final round in a threesome with the co-leaders, Australian Rod Pampling and Sergio Garcia. Mickelson would play one group behind them.

Garcia's fine play was remarkable in at least one respect. He was putting unusually well, in stark contrast to his performance over the previous two or three seasons. "It's a new feeling for me," the 26-year-old joked, candidly acknowledging what everyone in golf already knew: that the only thing preventing him from breaking through as a top-five player was his iffiness on the greens. With six Tour victories, he was easily the best young player in the world (25-year-old Adam Scott, his nearest rival, had three). He was even being touted as the new Best Player Without a Major. A more fitting title, however, might have been the one then possessed by Vijay Singh: Best Ballstriker on Tour Who's Consistently Undone by His Putter.

It wouldn't be the first time Sergio played in a final group with Woods. The most recent had been the 2002 U.S. Open at Bethpage Black. Garcia, at the time still a prisoner of his pre-shot waggles, had a miserable day, flipping a heckler the bird and eventually getting run over by Woods. That week also saw a worsening of the already bad blood between the two. After a long, rain-soaked round on Friday afternoon, Garcia ill-manneredly said that the USGA would have stopped play had Woods been on the course. (Garcia had first rubbed Woods the wrong way after their 2000 prime-time *Battle at Bighorn* match: when Garcia won, he celebrated as if he had won a major.)

The Sunday pairing generated a festival atmosphere. On the first tee, under clear skies, everyone was primed for a great day, for one reason or another. Waiting near the first tee for the combatants to arrive, Buick's Larry Peck, the emcee at Wednesday's Woods presser, remarked, "It looks like it's raining in the East and Midwest, so the ratings should be pretty good."

Sergio was smiling broadly as he prepared to hit his opening drive, thanks to announcer Mike Perez (the father of Tour player Pat Perez) who generously rolled his *l*'s and *n*'s as he pronounced the name of Garcia's hometown, "Castellón, España!" Sergio's enthusiasm didn't last. He took himself out of the running almost immediately, bogeying four of his first six holes. Pampling's start was equally dismal. He played the 4th and 5th holes in three-over, scuttling his hopes.

Tiger wasn't much better, bogeying two of his first five. The day's best play was coming from the groups ahead. José María Olazábal shot three-under on the front to move into a tie for the lead; joining him, with a front nine of four-under, was none other than Norway's favorite son, Henrik Bjornstad.

It took forever for the leaderboard to sort itself out. The tournament was turning into a symphony of loose shots and missed putts, and as the leaders played the 12th hole, seven players were tied for the lead at nine under par. Even at this early juncture, a playoff looked inevitable.

It was the unlikeliest of players who broke the logjam. On 13, unheralded 30-year-old Australian rookie, Nathan Green—whose upbringing as the son of morticians had been the source of jokes all week—drained a wedge shot from the fairway to take a sudden two-shot lead. In the pressroom, in front of the television, Steve Elling of the *Orlando Sentinel* exclaimed, "Right in the bottom of the urn!"

Halfway through the back nine, Phil Mickelson still had a chance to win, but shot himself out of it with three consecutive bogeys beginning on the 14th hole. Tiger Woods wasn't playing particularly well either. His ballstriking was passable, but his putting was at best substandard. As he played the 14th, he hadn't made a putt of more than ten feet since Friday; on Sunday he would wind up missing three putts from inside seven feet. In the end, though, he made the one that counted most, a nine-foot slider on the 18th green to gain a share of a playoff with Olazábal and Green.

After holing out, Woods slipped his putter in his bag and walked through the tunnel under the grandstands toward the scoring trailer. His final round of 72 made him anything but happy. He knew he had played poorly.

Waiting there in the clearing near the trailer were dozens of people—reporters, marshals, Century Club members, and Buick execs—all of whom had expected Woods to end the tournament on the final hole. No one said a word. The silence was broken by a small woman who was just now approaching the trailer's entrance. "Where's Tiger?" she said to no one in particular, in a tone of voice that demanded an answer. It was his mother, Tida.

Her presence was not unexpected. Every year she drove down from Orange County for the Buick Invitational's finish, accompanied by the same pair of friends (female contemporaries of hers from the neighborhood). Her outfit never varied: she always wore the same red and black ensemble as her son, along with the kind of broad-visored sunbonnet favored by golf-loving Asian women of a certain age. She was already carrying the red roses that were also part of the drill. Every year, win or lose, a tournament official always presented her with the same bouquet of flowers.

When her son emerged, they embraced. Tiger then went back through the tunnel, and sat down in a golf cart. An official drove him back to the 18th tee for the playoff, with caddie Steve Williams piggybacking on the rear with Woods' clubs.

The mass of reporters, officials, and other inside-the-ropers followed Woods through the tunnel and took places behind the green.

"How are you?" someone asked Tida.

She held her hand up to her mouth. "I'm fighting a cold," she said.

"Is Earl hanging in there?"

She nodded, and said, "He's at home," not so much to explain that he wasn't on the premises, which no one expected, but to say that he wasn't in the hospital.

The questioner knew that Tida and Earl, although separated, were still close. She frequently drove from her new house, also in Newport Beach, over to the old place in Cypress to check in on Earl, have a look at the garden, and do a little cleaning up. She knew, as Tiger did, that Earl was watching on television. Tiger's parents, in a sense, were still together, doing what they'd always done: rooting hard for their son.

No one gave Nathan Green any chance in the playoff. Olazábal, however, was a different story. A 40-year-old veteran with twenty-three worldwide victories—including two wins at Augusta, and one, three years earlier, at Torrey Pines—Chima (as Olazábal's friends called him) was also a pal of Tiger's, dating back to their rounds together at Augusta in 1995, where Woods, the U.S. Amateur champ, was paired with Olazábal, the defending Masters champ. More important, however, Ollie figured not to be intimidated by Woods. He was, after all, one of the few players in the world—maybe the only player in the world—with a wedge game better than Tiger's, something that would surely come into play on the first hole of the playoff, that same long, par-5 18th.

Green, playing only his second event on Tour, imploded early, hitting a 3-wood from the fairway into the grandstands and effectively eliminating himself. After poor drives, both Olazábal and Woods had to lay up. Ollie, with 93 yards left, went first. He hit an uncharacteristically poor wedge, not carrying his ball far enough beyond the front left pin; its backspin pulled it into a dicey lie in the fringe, dooming him to par.

Now it was Woods' turn. He had only 80 yards left and was coming in at an angle, from the right side of the fairway. He talked the shot over with Steve Williams, tossed a little grass, and made one abbreviated practice swing, than another. Those with long memories knew what he was rehearsing. Long ago, during one of Tiger and Earl's early in-studio appearances on The Golf Channel, Tiger explained how his father had taught him to use a system identical to the one Dave Pelz taught Mickelson, using the points of an imaginary clockface to control one's distance on shots inside 100 yards. What Woods was now planning looked like eight o'clock. Finally he hit a low driving shot that landed thirty feet beyond the pin, sucked back hard, and wound up eight feet left of the hole, almost pin high. It was nearly perfect.

Then Tiger missed the putt, yanking it hard left. So much for storybook endings. He and Olazábal would move to a second playoff hole.

The two men got back in their golf carts, and rode to the 231-yard par-3 16th. Woods found the green and hit a nice, evenly paced lag from 38 feet to secure a tap-in par. Olazábal, meanwhile, was in a tough predictament—he was in a bunker, short-sided, with the green running away from him. He hit a marvelous shot that stopped four feet above the hole. But he missed his putt, giving Woods the win.

In Monday's papers, Olazábal's miss would be described as an awful whiff. But that wasn't really the case. It was a slippery putt, a downhiller with a fair amount of break. On the other hand, Olazábal never really gave it a chance. He couldn't summon the nerve that the putt required. It seemed to be one of those cases where an opponent of Tiger's, convinced of the perceived inevitability of the outcome, doesn't put his best effort into a tough but makeable putt. The same thing had happened to John Daly just three months earlier—in the playoff at the 2005 WGC-American Express Championship in Harding Park, in San Francisco—where he blew a three-footer to hand Woods a victory.

"I'm sorry," Woods told Olazábal, taking off his cap and extending his hand. Neither man wanted to see it end that way. Woods, in fact, could hardly believe that his so-so play had been good enough for a victory.

He acknowledged as much during his 18th-green victory speech. Picking up a trophy that looked like a cross between a hood ornament and the figure of Mercury on the FTD logo, he said, "This is a surprise. I didn't hit the ball very well, and didn't putt very well at all."

One putt he seemed pleased with was his lag on the last playoff hole. Describing it, he invoked the telepathic connection he always shared with his dad. "I could hear him telling me, just lag it up to the hole," he said. He didn't formally dedicate the victory to his father, but he didn't have to. From here on, every win was for Earl.

Still, he knew that for those wins to come, he would have to play better. Minutes after his speech, Woods was leaning against a Buick Lucerne that had been rolled out onto the front fringe of the green for the ceremony. A few feet away was one of his friends from the Century Club, a gray-haired, middle-aged local attorney named Bill Potter.

"Hey, Tiger," Potter said. "Maybe we should go hit some practice putts."

"Yeah, no shit, huh?" Woods replied.

4

Cinderella Stories

The FBR Open, Phoenix

Maurice Holmes was spending a long weekend at Auburn University in Alabama, trying his darnedest to relax. He had traveled down from Campbellsville, Kentucky, with his wife, Lisa, to visit their daughter, Amanda, a student at the veterinary school. On Thursday they had celebrated Amanda's 26th birthday. On Sunday, while most of the country was watching the Super Bowl, they would celebrate Lisa's.

But the family was distracted. J. B. Holmes, just 23, was in contention at the FBR Open in Phoenix, and Maurice, his dad, couldn't put it out of his mind. Friends from home weren't helping much. They kept calling him to talk about it. On Saturday he turned on the television at Amanda's place to have a look, but he couldn't find the golf. The telecast was being preempted, it seemed, by the Mississippi vs. Tennessee college basketball game. So he got back on the phone to get an update from Mike Kehoe, the head pro at their home course, Campbellsville Country Club. Kehoe was as excited as Maurice was. He was they guy who had given J.B. the only two or three lessons he'd ever had.

They talked, on and off, for the better part of the next ninety minutes.

"He's—shoot, he's in the bunker on eleven," Kehoe, said over the phone, doing the play-by-play.

"Nice sh—oh! He hit the pin!"

Finally, the basketball game ended, and Maurice got to see the action for himself. The third round ended with J.B. leading by one. Soon Kehoe was on the phone again, imploring Maurice (pronounced *Morris*) to get on a plane and go to Phoenix for the final round.

It took a little convincing. "I'll go out there and he'll have a bad round," Maurice said.

"Maurice, I've watched John play an awful lot." (At home, everyone still called J.B. "John.") "You know how it is when he's got that air of confidence about him. He's going to win, and you've got to be there."

"You're right," Maurice finally gave in. "I've got to go."

Holmes, a fit-and-trim 50-year-old insurance agent with square eyeglasses and Eugene Levy eyebrows, always thought this might happen. His son had always been ridiculously good at the game. Back in little Campbellsville, in central Kentucky—population 10,500—he made the high school golf team when he was in third grade, and won the club championship at 12. At 13, he was driving the greens on its short par-fours with first-generation metal woods and the old, wound Titleist Tour Balatas. "He used to eat those old balatas up," Maurice remembered. "He'd go through two sleeves of those things every round. He always hit the ball as hard as he could."

His dad tried to discourage him. Once, while they were on the course together, he said, "You're swinging so hard your feet are coming off the ground." It just so happened Maurice had a camera with him, and he took a picture of his son's next swing. Sure enough, they were.

Later, at the University of Kentucky, J.B. was a four-time All-America. In November 2005, in his first go-round at Q-school, he not only made it to the final stage, but finished first. So Maurice expected good things. But not this soon. The FBR Open was only J.B.'s fourth event as a pro.

Maurice sat down at his daughter's computer and logged on to an online travel service. For some reason, he bought a one-way ticket. ("I don't know why in the world I did that," he'd later say.) When he talked to his son that night, he told a little fib, promising, "We'll be watching you tomorrow on TV."

The next morning he woke up at 3:30 a.m. Lisa, Amanda, and her boyfriend shuttled him to Atlanta, an hour and a half away, to drop him off at the airport. On the plane, the in-flight movie was *The Greatest Game Ever Played,* the story of caddie Francis Ouimet's miracle win at the 1913 U.S. Open. Much of the film dealt with the 20-year-old's relationship with his father. Maurice took it as an omen. "Things are really lining up here," he thought to himself.

When he arrived, he hopped in a car with Sam McNaughton, part of his son's SFX Sports management team, who had also flown in that morning. Together they drove to the TPC of Scottsdale.

Oddly, Maurice had been there before, on a golf holiday. It was October of 2001, right after 9/11. As they drove up to the clubhouse, he suddenly remembered leaving the pro shop that day.

"Come back and visit us again," the pro had told him.

"Maybe someday I will," Maurice replied. He never dreamed it would be under these circumstances.

They got out of the car, raced through the credential process in one of the Tour trailers, and went out onto the golf course. J.B. was now on the 3rd hole. Almost as soon as Maurice spotted his son, he also saw three buddies from Campbellsville—J. Paul Newton (whose son, Austin, was J.B.'s best friend); his brother, David Allen Newton; and Robby Westbrook. They were on a golf vacation of their own. By chance, they had run into J.B. on Tuesday night in a Chinese restaurant, and decided to stay in town and watch him play for as long as his week lasted.

Once out on the course, Maurice immediately went into hiding. He spent most of the afternoon ducking behind his friends, explaining, "I don't want him to know I'm here." That didn't stop him from griping about how his son's putts wouldn't fall. "Somebody take that cellophane off the hole," he muttered.

Finally, on the 10th, J.B. made his first birdie of the day, and was off and running. Playing commanding golf, he was crushing his drives well over 300 yards and burning little wedges close to the hole. At the same time, his nearest competitor, Ryan Palmer, was faltering, rinsing a total of three balls on the 11th and 15th. When J.B. birdied the short par-four 17th—after hitting a three-wood 300 yards onto the front of the green—it extended his lead to seven strokes.

"He can just ease this one in," Maurice smiled to his friends. "I'm gonna let him know I'm here." With that, he found an empty spot along the roped-off path between the 17th green and 18th tee. When his son came through, he said, "Hey, bud, do you want me to play this last hole for you?" J.B. stopped, smiled wide, and threw his arms around his father, almost popping the eyeglasses off his head.

His son's performance turned out to be one of the most memorable of the year, all the more so because it was completely unexpected. But then, something wild always seemed to happen in Phoenix.

Sometimes it had to do with the quality of the golf. In 1996 Arizona State alum Phil Mickelson one-putted the last seven greens and made a unmakeable 20-footer on the second playoff hole to steal the tournament from Justin Leonard. In 2005 he shot a second-round 60, one away from golf's most magical number, on his way to a five-stroke victory. After his closing birdie on 18, Mickelson, dressed completely in black, leaned slightly backward, with his open hands extended at his sides, just like The Fonz. You could almost hear him say, "Ayyyyy!"

In 2001 Mark Calcavecchia set the PGA Tour scoring record by shooting an eye-popping 28-under for the tournament; his worst round that week was a 67. In 1997 Tiger Woods made the only hole-in-one of his Tour career on the 16th hole. The bedlam it inspired was one of the most enduring images of the first phase of Tigermania.

Most years, however, the most remarkable moments involved the crowds. Phoenix's are invariably the biggest of the year, despite the fact that Sunday's final round is played on Super Bowl Sunday. (In 2006, the final gate for the week would be a record 536,767.) They are also the loudest and rowdiest in all of golf. Their primary gathering point, the par-three 16th, isn't just a golf hole—it's the world's best-landscaped insane asylum. When Mickelson stepped onto the tee on Saturday, half the people in the grandstands were wearing gold and maroon T-shirts that read I ♥ PHIL; the shouts of "ASU! ASU!" were deafening. Yet when he missed the green long with his 7-iron, he was given the same treatment as anyone who failed to hit it close. He was roundly booed.

A specialized chant greeted every player. The all-time favorite, judging by the volume, was the one reserved for Fred Funk: "Funk You! Funk You!" The crowd had a special knack for ferreting out information on lesser-known players. On Saturday, they somehow learned that Holmes's hometown, Campbellsville, was located in Taylor County. Holmes heard "Taylor County! Taylor County!" all the way from the tee to the green. Maurice's friend J. Paul Newton was standing outside the ropes, taking it all in. "It gave me goose bumps," he said.

The 16th-hole crazies were sometimes too unruly. Tiger's hole-in-one sent more debris flying than an explosion on a garbage barge. On the way to his win in 2002, Chris DiMarco had "some jerk" removed from the course after he shouted "Noonan!" during the backswing of his par putt. Leonard had the very same experience—same insult, even—in 1996.

On other holes, the fans were alternatingly helpful and frightening. During one Tiger appearance, a clutch of spectators rolled a boulder aside to clear the way for his next shot. During another, a man following his group was found to be carrying a handgun, and left the course wearing handcuffs. In yet another incident a fan sent an orange flying past Woods' head. He too was led away in silver bracelets. It was no wonder that Tiger never played the tournament after 2001.

In other ways, too, the golf often seemed incidental. In the opinion of most pros, Phoenix (with the possible exception of Dallas) had "the best talent on Tour"—"talent" being Tour lingo for attractive women. Here, the practice green wasn't necessarily a place to work on your game. On Thursday, Jason Gore and his caddie, Lewis Pulley, were sizing up two rope-hopers (more Tour lingo), who were sizing them up in return. One had dark hair, the other light. Pulley seized the opportunity to launch into Owen Wilson's routine from the movie *Starsky and Hutch*.

"Which one do you want? The blonde or the brunette?"

Gore, who is married, smiled and shook his head. But he got the joke and dutifully delivered his line. "I don't know," he said.

"It doesn't matter," Pulley followed. "I'll take anything."

The tournament slogan was "The Greatest Show on Grass," but it may as well have been "The Busiest Beer Tents on Earth." The party often got out of control—whether outside during play, or afterward in the Bird's Nest, the tourney's infamous 19th hole. It wasn't uncommon to see fans who were, quite literally, falling down drunk. A Tour pro knew he was in Phoenix when he could hit a tee shot, turn around, and watch a big-haired fan in an overstuffed camisole take a long swig on a margarita and topple off her platform sandals, going from vertical to horizontal right before his eyes.

• • •

The week began quietly enough. The pros got their clubs tuned up at the equipment trailers, hit range balls, and played practice rounds. With no Michelle Wie, Hollywood celebs, or Tiger in the field (as in Honolulu, Palm Springs, or San Diego), it was the most typical Tour week they had seen since October.

Chris DiMarco arrived in town on Tuesday morning, put in a few minutes on the range, and then walked over to the first tee. Spying a group of three about to tee off, he shouted, "Got room?" They waved him over.

One was Kenny Perry, that good ol' Kentucky boy with the going hook and unlikely fondness for drag racing. (One of his best friends was ten-time NHRA pro stock champion Bob Glidden.)

The second was four-time Tour winner Duffy Waldorf. One of the game's most unassuming guys, his calling cards were his floral-print shirts and hats and his multicolored golf balls: before going off to a tournament, his children would work them over with a sixty-four-pack of Sharpies, so that they looked like Easter eggs. Duffy was not, however, without his refined side. He had a great wine cellar, and would, at the end of the year, be brought to the Ryder Cup in Ireland by captain Tom Lehman as the U.S. team's official sommelier.

The third was John Riegger, a tall, lanky native Midwesterner known to the world (if he was known at all) for offering to play Annika Sorenstam for a million dollars of his own money. His peers knew him as a good stick whose career had nearly been ruined by injury (he was coming off surgery for a mysterious wrist ailment), as well the Tour's best duck-caller and leading hunting purist. Riegger would often go into the wilderness for days at a time armed only with a longbow.

DiMarco, of course, was one of the most intriguing players in the game. Though not obviously talented, the 37-year-old was the game's consummate grinder—he had ridden his lazy fade, claw putting grip, and bulldog determination all the way to a world ranking of eleven.

He himself never expected to come this far. After his victory at the Phoenix Open in 2002, he had sat in the locker room, tears welling in his eyes, reflecting on what was then a twelve-year journey from obscurity to established star. He had already won twice, at late-season, diminished-field events, but this was something else. "This is big," he said. "Nobody believed this would happen, winning something like this. Heck, sometimes I didn't believe it would happen. The other two times were great, don't get me wrong. With this kind of field, and all these people. . . ." He stopped to shake his head. That it was his first win without his wife and children by his side only deepened the personal sense of accomplishment.

It took a while, however, for him to adjust to his new status. It wasn't until three years later that he stared down Tiger at the Masters. "I just got outchipped, so to speak," he said referring both to Woods' rousing chip-in on the 16th hole and one of his own, on the 18th, that rattled off the pin.

He was the hero of the 2005 Presidents Cup, lifting Phil Mickelson to an undefeated record in team play, and then holing a 15-foot birdie putt to end the competition. The image was unforgettable. He pumped his fist and let out a mighty howl that stretched his skin tight over his face, like Lord Valdemort in the Harry Potter movies.

Still, he hadn't notched an individual win since 2002 in Phoenix. The near-misses were numerous. In New Orleans in 2004, he coughed up a two-shot lead on the back nine, bogeying the last to miss a spot in a playoff. Later that year he lost the International, in Denver, after holding a big lead on Saturday night. In the very next event, the PGA Championship at Whistling Straits, he left a birdie putt short on the final hole, missing another playoff. It wasn't always his fault. In 2005 he played splendidly at the Match Play at La Costa, only to get run over in the final by David Toms, who was playing the best golf of his career. Toward the end of that summer, at the NEC in Akron, Tiger Woods drained an impossible birdie putt on the 16th to edge him by one.

Before the 2006 Masters, the Associated Press's Doug Ferguson would write a column asking whether DiMarco was an overachiever or overrated. It was an interesting question. Another way to see it, though, was that even at this level, there were players—DiMarco chief among them—who couldn't quite believe how good they were, and balked at letting themselves finish off winnable tournaments.

Now, however, DiMarco had the kind of look that only belonged to a recent winner. Two weeks earlier, he had earned a victory on the European Tour, in Abu Dhabi. The spring in his step was hard to miss.

The victory also made unavoidable some practice round ribbing. Since Perry was next-highest in the group's pecking order, it was his job to initiate it. Every time DiMarco hit a decent shot, he exclaimed, "another good ball by the Abu Dhabi champ!" When DiMarco rolled his eyes, Perry rejoined, "That's what The Golf Channel was calling you, so I'm going to call you that, too."

Country Kenny wouldn't let up. As he and DiMarco came off one tee box—DiMarco first, Perry a few steps behind—a clutch of kids was waiting for autographs. DiMarco stepped toward them, but they were focused on Perry. "What's the matter?" Kenny said to the kids, loud enough for everyone to hear. "You don't want the Abu Dhabi champ?"

Apart from the ritual abuse, the four pros passed the time with typical Tour talk.

They chatted, for example, about equipment and other sports. DiMarco was calling the new black, yellow, and white shaft in his driver his "Steeler shaft," honoring the previous year's Super Bowl champs. Someone protested that he was a front-runner, to which DiMarco replied, "I've been a Steeler fan all my life!"

They discussed injuries, with Riegger revealing the gory details of his surgery, and showing off the scar around his right thumb.

They talked about course conditions. Perry complained about the patchiness of the turf, which, to his mind, was well below Tour standards. Fellow Kentuckian Fred Saunders (his former caddie, now working for Riegger) chimed in, "There are a bunch of guys back in Paducah who can grow grass better than this."

Occasionally the conversation strayed far afield of sports. After a passing mention of New Orleans, Saunders, an expert poker player, idly inquired whether anyone knew whether the Harrah's in the Big Easy had reopened yet.

DiMarco later struck up a wine conversation with Waldorf. A relative novice, he described his new fondness for Silver Oak, saying that one evening he had light-fingered a couple of bottles from the Presidents Cup team room, sneaking them out in his backpack. He also mentioned that he had recently noticed what happens as a wine opens up—it "tastes good at the beginning," he said, "and then it gets better." Duffy nodded, agreeing that it made a big difference, and launched into a lecture, stopping just short of decanting procedures. Everything he said was spot-on, even if he looked odd saying it. Getting wine tips from a golfer—even a well-heeled PGA Tour player—was sort of like learning to make a soufflé from an auto mechanic.

But much of the conversation, predictably, had to do with DiMarco's adventures in the Middle East. None of the other players had the name recognition (or connection to IMG, which, in addition to repping players like DiMarco, also staged several European Tour events) to be invited over. The only reason pros went, really, was the appearance fees (in DiMarco's case, high six figures). Several things impressed him. One was the security surrounding the American players. "They drive you around everywhere," he said. Another was his digs at the seven-star Emirates Palace Hotel. "The ceilings in the room were twenty feet high. If I was in my bathroom brushing my teeth and the doorbell rang, it would have taken me twenty-five seconds to answer it. I tested it."

It was tough for his caddie, Pat O'Bryan, to hear such tales. He hadn't made the trip. Instead, Chris's wife, Amy, once his high school sweetheart, carried his bag. It was a great feeling, DiMarco said privately, out of O'Bryan's earshot, to walk up the 18th hole with her.

He was looking forward to the next time, no matter who was lugging the clubs. Golf, he said, was "like a big mountain. You scrape, and you climb, and you do everything you can to get to where you can see the top. And then, when you do see it, it's almost easier just to stop and look around, instead of actually going all the way up. Some guys just get comfortable, and they stay there. They get stuck." He was talking, of course, about himself. The victory, he felt, was an important next step. Now it was time to see how much further he could climb.

On Tour, Tuesday night is God Squad night.

That's the nickname (more Tour lingo) for the Christians who gather on that night each week for Bible study. Their get-together in Phoenix is usually one of the biggest of the year. In 2006 it took place at the home of Aaron and Richelle Baddeley. By Aaron's estimate, it drew "fifty-plus" people. Presiding was Les Hughey of Scottsdale's Highlands Church, who was Baddeley's pastor as well as Tom Lehman's. (Lehman himself wasn't hosting because he had held the previous week's study at his home near Torrey Pines, in Del Mar.)

Aaron said it was "definitely" the largest he had seen. "We didn't have nearly enough chairs. At the beginning, we were thinking, Where is everybody? But people just kept coming and coming. There were people on the couch, on the floor, and on the stairs."

"I thought we were going to have way too much food," Richelle added. "But by the end of the night we were scraping out the fridge trying to find enough for everyone to eat."

A notable absence, in a way, was rookie Robert Garrigus.

That evening, he was in his house about fifteen minutes from the TPC manning the barbeque, entertaining Chris Couch and Couch's caddie, Greg Bitterly, both friends from the Nationwide Tour. Bitterly was bunking in for the week, saving on expenses. Couch's RV was parked down the street. Garrigus himself wasn't in the field. In this, a relatively popular event amongst his fellow players, his ninth-place Q-school finish wasn't good enough to get him in.

Still, there was cause to celebrate. Now, eight years after turning pro, he was finally a full-fledged Tour member. And he was three years sober, having put behind him two habits that almost destroyed his career.

Garrigus's love affair with pot and booze began when he was in high school in Portland, Oregon. At first it was recreational, something to do after afternoons spent convincing the locals that this innocent, chubby-cheeked kid might be the best golfer out of the Pacific Northwest since Fred Couples, or at least Ben Crane.

He left home at 19, and enrolled at Scottsdale Community College. He immediately fell in with a group of friends who he would come to regard as "troubled." Soon his casual use became a kind of vocation. He began and ended each day smoking what contemporaries described as prodigious amounts of marijuana.

After three semesters he quit school and turned pro, convinced the fastest way to get better was to play against better competition. By now his mother, Linda, had divorced his father, Thomas (a silver medalist at the 1968 Mexico City Olympics and now the coach of the U.S. Olympic shooting team). She was remarried, to a man who had made a fortune in frozen fruit packaging. The allowance to which they staked him allowed him to travel and compete on the mini-tours, and to feed his vices.

Despite them, he made it through to the finals of the PGA Tour qualifying tournament in 1999, on his second try; that gave him partial eligibility on the Nationwide Tour for 2000. That year, he made no cuts and zero dollars. He went back to the mini-tours in 2001, and then regained a Nationwide spot in 2002. On his second go-round, he made eight of twenty-one cuts, earning about $15,000.

Throughout that period, Garrigus continued smoking and drinking. He later calculated that he was spending "fifty or sixty thousand dollars a year on that habit." Never, he said, did he use anything harder, although he had been around other drugs.

In 2002, he was driving with a friend who had a fondness for crack from Nashville to Hershey, Pennsylvania. "I stopped to party with one of my buddies in Lexington, Kentucky. It was a Friday night. I didn't hear from him again until Monday afternoon. He sold the car, and my golf clubs, and my clothes. I said, wow, that's pretty powerful stuff, to do that to a person."

During those years, Garrigus said, he played stoned "every day." On the rare occasion that he didn't, he "couldn't wait to get done and get high. I had no idea what I was doing." He never left home without a stash. "It was almost a mental thing with me. I always thought that I needed it, and I thought that I needed to have it with me and travel with it and do all that stuff."

It was almost a miracle that in 2002, he managed to shoot ten rounds in the 60s, on some fairly difficult golf courses. It sparked a curiosity about what he might be able to do playing straight. Still, nothing changed.

That fall, he washed out of Q-school in the first stage. "I hit it pretty hard for five or six weeks afterward. And then I just decided, that's it. It was just one of those situations where I'd be waking up in the middle of the night and partying and wouldn't stop for three days, and it just got to the point where I'd had enough.

"I knew what potential I had as a golfer, and, you know, I wanted to see that full potential come out. So I just decided drugs weren't doing it for me, and I needed to go somewhere and get my life straight."

Another little push came from his mother. By then well aware of what was going on, she cut off his funding.

At the same time an old friend reappeared—the same one who, on a crack binge, had sold Garrigus's car out from under him in Lexington. Now sober, he suggested that Robert check into the same place he'd gotten clean: Calvary Ranch, a Christian-run rehab center in Lakeside, California, twenty miles inland from San Diego.

The ranch provided support and discipline, in the form of a strict schedule. "You'd get up every day and have breakfast and do Bible study, and then go out and work on the horse farm they had there," he said. But otherwise, it was a lonely time. "On the weekend, when other people got visitors, I went up into the mountains." His favorite spot was in nearby Santee. It afforded big views of San Diego County and, in the distance, the Pacific Ocean. "I'd just go up there, chill out, just relax, and talk to God."

On the whole, the religious aspect of Calvary made for less of a conversion experience than the discovery of a stabilizing influence. (Over the course of 2006, Garrigus would attend the Tour Bible study, but only once in a while. "It seemed like every Tuesday I'd be sitting at dinner, and realize, 'Oh, this is Bible study night!'")

When he got out of rehab, he returned to Scottsdale and to his old apartment. He had left it in the care of his roommate, but that was a mistake. When he got back, the roommate had moved out, leaving behind "a whole bunch of stuff I didn't want to see—pipes and bongs and stuff." Garrigus gathered it all together, took it down to the trash bins, and threw it out. It was easier, he said, than he had expected. Harder to get rid of was the smell in the apartment. "The roommate was supposed to pay the electric bill, and he didn't tell me when he left, so I didn't pay it. At the time, I would always eat chicken breasts—there were a bunch of them in the freezer. The electricity had been turned off, and the entire place smelled like rotten chicken."

He slept there anyway. The following day, he was entered in local qualifying for the U.S. Open. He hadn't touched his clubs in two months, so it almost made sense that he forgot to take his putter with him. Racing back home and then back to the course, he almost incurred a two-stroke penalty for being late to the tee. Still, he shot two-under, failing to advance by just one shot.

Then he turned around, went back to San Diego, and took a place in Del Mar. He met a young woman named Ami on a blind date, and they fell in love. After a successful year on the Nationwide Tour (he made 12 of 19 cuts, earning $60,000), they moved to Scottsdale together, bought a house, and got married.

Now, starting the 2006 season, things were looking up. At the Hope, his second event, he was paired in the final round with his boyhood idol, Fred Couples, and beat him by a stroke. Garrigus's 66 was the low round of the day, and earned him his first PGA Tour top-twenty finish. He played well again at Torrey Pines, finishing twenty-eighth. Not getting into the tournament in Phoenix was his only complaint. By all indications, he'd completely turned his life around.

• • •

By Saturday night J.B. Holmes was the talk of the golf tournament. But it wasn't just because he finished the third round in the lead. It was what he was doing with his driver. That day, he hit the big stick seven times. The distances: 338, 343, 349, 341, 328, 353, and 343 yards. Yes, the air was thinner in the desert. But still.

The shot that popped everyone's eyeballs was his second on the 595-yard par-five 13th. After a drive of 353 yards, he had 198 left. He hit an 8-iron. As Geoff Shackelford (the best golf blogger in the business) later pointed out, the numbers uncannily replicated those from Bill Murray's "Cinderella story" scene in *Caddyshack*. When Carl Spackler pulled an 8-iron from "about 190 yards," it was laughable. When Holmes hit his, there was nothing funny about it.

Indeed, some found it alarming. However much Holmes' raw physical power had to do with it, the display couldn't help but send a shudder through a golf community already made anxious by the new, distance-obsessed direction of the game.

Ever since the advent of large, titanium-headed drivers—and, more importantly, two-piece solid-core balls like the Titleist Pro V1—Tour driving distances had been skyrocketing. In 2000, the Tour average was 273.2 yards; by 2005 it had risen to 288.9. In response, PGA Tour venues annually tacked on more yardage. Every year's major championships saw new, record-setting course lengths. At the same time, it became clear that venerable old tracks like Merion, Cherry Hills, Bellerive, and Inverness—all of which had held a U.S. Open in the past forty years—were no longer suitable for pro events.

Most of the top players, including Tiger Woods, agreed that the only way to halt the trend was to roll back the ball. But no one made the case more bluntly than Jack Nicklaus. "It is so simple to just restrict the golf ball," he said at the 2001 Masters. "If I had it my way, I would have done it twenty years ago, before every golf course in this country became obsolete."

The new technology's repercussions were farther-reaching than that. Fears were that the longer players were reaping larger benefits from the equipment than the shorter ones, nullifying the latter's ability to compete. (Most Tour pros figured that the higher one's swing speed, the more of an advantage you got from a livelier ball.) Also, because the new balls spun so little, it was no longer a challenge to hit it straight; that, along with a decreasing need to shape approach shots to tucked pin positions (why would you need to, when you were always hitting wedge?), diminished the importance of shotmaking.

They also extended beyond the pro game. Super-sizing the blueprints of every new course that hoped to host a pro event increased land costs, and therefore greens fees, making the game more expensive for recreational players.

To many minds, the USGA, America's writers of the Rules of Golf and those that govern equipment, had failed in their obligation to circumscribe such advances. Some restrictions had been put in place—notably 2004's revision of the "overall distance standard," which ostensibly limited the distance a ball could travel (carry plus roll), when struck by a 120 mile-per-hour swing, to 320 yards. Other than that, they seemed indifferent. At the organization's 2004 annual meeting, Walter Driver, then the body's president, attributed seventy-five percent of the distance increase to "player athleticism." In 2006, senior technical director Dick Rugge issued a list of ten "Distance Myths." It argued, among other things, that distance increases among the pros had now plateaued, increasing at a mere one yard per year, and that it was plainly false that longer hitters benefited more from technology advances than shorter hitters.

That latter point was debatable. Rugge's evidence pointed out that between 2000 and 2005, Corey Pavin's increase off the tee (7.4 yards) was almost as great as John Daly's (8.7). He probably figured that the increases for Phil Mickelson (11.3), Adam Scott (13.1), Vijay Singh (21.2), and Tiger Woods (18.1) were due to "athleticism."

It was still early in the season, but it was already clear that its first-year players would be inflating the Tour's average driving distance. Going into the Phoenix Open, four of the statistical leaders were rookies:

1. Bubba Watson, 324.9 yards
3. J.B. Holmes, 316,.0 yards
4. Camilo Villegas, 310.9 yards
6. Robert Garrigus, 308.6 yards

Whatever the data, it was inarguable that the distance developments had changed the way the pros played the game. Most of the long-hitters now chose to hit driver everywhere, knowing that even if they were in the rough, they would only have a wedge left to most par-fours. The lofts of the club—and, more important, their deep, sharp square grooves—usually enabled them to control the ball well enough to take dead aim at any flag. If a lie was particularly horrid, they would simply play to the middle of the green and two-putt for par, with no damage to their scorecards.

The new style even had a name. In fact, it had a few. The most colorful came from *Golf Digest,* which christened it "Bomb and Gouge," and Shackelford, who named it "Flog" (*golf* spelled backwards).

The movement's spiritual father was Vijay Singh. He more or less invented it in 2004 and rode it, that season, to nine Tour wins. (That year, he ranked 149th in driving accuracy.) Four more victories followed in 2005, despite Singh's worsening putting woes.

Other players took notice well before the nickname bestowers did. Early in 2005, Woods said that driving accuracy was "not as relevant as it has been in the past," so long as you weren't hitting the ball out of play. "If you're just in the rough, it's no big deal." He, like Singh, would much rather be hitting wedge from the rough than hitting "5-irons or 6-irons" from the fairway. He also gave Singh his props. "If you look at the way Vijay played last year, he drove it on every hole that he could. And there's a reason for that. If you're able to drive the ball far enough," hitting it in the rough "really doesn't matter."

The long-driving rookies were running the same playbook. In Phoenix, Holmes was in the midst of showing how adept he was at it. Camilo Villegas, Michelle Wie's playing partner in Hawaii, was right behind him. He finished his Saturday round tied for sixth. (His first true moment in the sun would come four weeks later, at Doral.)

Bubba Watson, the statistical king of the Baby Bashers, had already made plenty of waves. In Hawaii, at the Sony, his Sunday 65 was a sideshow unto itself. He concluded by belting one 366 yards on Waialae's 530-yard, par-five 18th. Because he had cut off most of the dogleg, he had only 142 yards left in.

At Torrey Pines, he would have been the talk of the tournament had it not been for Woods and Daly. Even so, the cognoscenti were watching him closely. One measure of his length was the problems he caused at Torrey's two-ended driving range. On Wednesday, hitting some drivers, he purposely bent his first few balls to avoid reaching the other end. Most often, he started huge left-handed cuts out over El Camino Real, the street bordering Torrey's range to the east. Only once did he truly let fly. That ball landed twenty yards short of the hitting line on the other end, and bounced forward, directly between Zach Johnson and rookie John Engler, until it reached the green temporary fencing behind them. "That's long. Real long," said Zach, eyebrows raised high for emphasis. The hard data was provided by the rangefinder of Brandt Jobe's caddie, Corby Segal. It was 353 to Bubba's hitting line, and about 20 yards to where his ball first landed, meaning that Watson's ball had carried— *carried*—approximately 335 yards. Upon hearing of the incident, PGA Tour official Mark Russell, sounding a little like Police Chief Brody in *Jaws,* deadpanned, "They're gonna need a bigger range."

Most of the other players already knew about Bubba. Phil Mickelson and Tiger Woods had seen him in action. Mickelson enjoyed a casual round with him at the Country Club of Athens when Watson was at the University of Georgia (Mickelson and his caddie, Jim Mackay, often played casual rounds there with friends). There, Watson gave Mickelson the needle when he hit it by him. "He'd say, 'Did you get all of that one?'—just little things like that," Mickelson related. "But it was well-warranted. I couldn't hang with him."

Woods got his first look in late 2005, during the Dunlop Phoenix in Japan. "The 13th hole," Tiger said, "is a driveable par-4. It's like 324 yards, or something like that. I have to rip a 3-wood, and I can bounce it in the front bunker. Well, he's two groups ahead of us, and we have a big logjam." That put Woods on the tee box watching him play. "He pulled out an iron. We had heard he was long, but come on! And he pumped it onto the green. I don't have that shot.

"On top of all that, he's a real character," Tiger added. He had that right. An ever-smiling Southern boy from Bagdad, Florida, he arrived on Tour with Elvis sideburns, a pink-shafted driver, and red tape spiraled around the white shaft of his putter, so that it looked like a candy cane. He happily referred to himself as "a redneck" and liked to laugh about how he got his name. "Ten seconds after I was born," he explained, "my dad took a look at me and said, 'Well, he's fat and ugly—let's name him Bubba.'"

The other side to the jocularity was what all this new length meant for the game. Watson, Holmes, and Villegas soon became media stars— whenever they played in the same event, someone wanted a picture of the three of them together. Yet they offered only a glimpse, some thought, of the years to come. They were relatively average-size guys; one could only imagine what would happen when larger players, who had chosen golf over football and basketball, arrived on the scene. "In all seriousness, this is the future of the game of golf," Woods said. "Pretty soon all the guys are going to be longer, bigger, more athletic. I'm only six-foot. Wait until guys who come out here are six-five and six-six, and have the skills to play the game. It'll be truly remarkable to see how far they can hit it."

Holmes, of course, wound up winning the tournament in a walk. Afterward, he was humble and gracious, and saying all the right things. So did Maurice. "He's a good boy," Papa Holmes said. "I always told him, 'Don't let your hat get too big.' And it hasn't."

Once they were done with media obligations, Maurice, J.B., and his agents, McNaughton and Terry Reilly, went out among the crowd that had gathered near the Jumbotron behind the 9th hole, and watched the first half of the Super Bowl. Then they went out to dinner, watching the second half at a restaurant. From there, they went back to J.B.'s hotel room.

After the evening news, the local CBS affiliate reaired the golf tournament. J.B. and Maurice stayed up and watched the whole thing, laughing together on the couch until two in the morning. Dissecting the scene on the 18th tee, J.B. explained to his father the conversation he was having with his caddie, Mike Carrick.

J.B. said, "See, right here, this is where I said to Mike, 'I'm going to hit this one real hard.' See those grandstands over on the left? Worst thing that happens is I hit it in there. If it goes way right, I'm clear of all those bunkers."

The next morning they got on a private plane ("a pretty neat way to travel," said first-timer Maurice) and flew back to Auburn. J.B. slept on his sister's air mattress. Maurice reclaimed his place next to Lisa on the fold-out couch. It was probably a good thing they didn't go straight back to Campbellsville. Back home, Mike Kehoe said, "it was bedlam. When I got to the shop on Monday morning, the first two phone calls I picked up were from young women. They both wanted to know whether or not John was single, and what his home address was."

5

COAST TO COAST

The West Coast and Florida Swings

The cliché is that all PGA Tour players travel in private planes. But it's not true. While the top forty or so fly the friendliest of skies more or less all the time, the rank-and-file usually fly commercial.

When lesser earners live above their station, their peers roll their eyes at their profligacy. As the Tour prepared to leave Phoenix for Pebble Beach, Joe Ogilvie—the 31-year-old, Duke-educated stock market maven who had finished thirty-seventh on the 2005 money list—said, "Those guys are nuts. You're making half a million dollars a year, and you're going to pay $2,500 for a one-way ticket? Round-trip, that's one percent of your annual income." (Ogilvie's math was based on double- or triple-occupancy: the going rate for a private plane at the time was about $6,000 to $7,000 per hour.)

The preference of some pros for commercial flights was one of the reasons America West Flight 6136 on February 5, 2006—Super Bowl Sunday, but also the final day of the FBR (Phoenix) Open—was sold out. Of the fifty people on the little Canadair regional jet, about a dozen were Tour players. Also on board were plenty of caddies, equipment reps, and peripheral circus-troupe members.

The scheduled departure of 4:25 p.m. was twenty-five minutes after the scheduled end of Sunday play. For some of the pros, making the flight was easy. Jay Williamson and Graeme McDowell had missed the cut, giving them about 48 hours to drive to the airport. David Gossett, the struggling former winner of the U.S. Amateur and John Deere Classic, hadn't even played in Phoenix—he was flying out of Sky Harbor simply because he lived in Scottsdale. Others—John Senden and Daniel Chopra, for example—had played on Sunday, but played early, and therefore had time to spare. But for a handful of late-starters, getting to Sky Harbor was a mad scramble. Ogilvie, Jerry Smith, and Tom Pernice boarded at what seemed like the last minute. When Hawaii's Dean Wilson arrived, the door almost spanked him on his way in. How he managed to get to the airport so quickly was a mystery, because he had played in the second-to-last group. He must have abandoned his courtesy car at the terminal curb, leaving the door and trunk open.

The lucky passengers had window seats. As the plane approached Monterey the view was spectacular: the sunset looked like molded Jell-O, with perfectly defined layers of orange, pink, and purple. That wasn't all. On its way out to the Pacific to circle back for landing, the plane flew directly over the ocean-flanked 16th hole at Cypress Point. If the course was the Sistine Chapel of golf, this was the best part, the section at which God and Adam touched fingers.

Claiming his luggage, Chopra was ecstatic. Born in Sweden and raised in India, he had played all around the world, and had a connoisseur's appreciation for the game's finer tracks. Since his marginal Tour status kept him out of most Wednesday pro-ams, he used those days to run off and play some of the host cities' finer layouts (National Golf Links in New York, Champions in Houston, Los Angeles Country Club in L.A., and so forth). Flying over perhaps the best par-three in the world, and easily the prettiest, had been a thrill.

"Did you see that?" he enthused, his eyes open wide, as he gathered his luggage. "That was amazing. Who would have believed that the flight path would take us right over that hole?"

So began a seven-week stretch that would bring the Tour to some of its most glamorous destinations—Pebble Beach, Riviera, and, heading to Florida at the end of February, Doral and the TPC at Sawgrass. It would also include two of its marquee events—the World Golf Championships-Accenture Match Play, and the Players Championship, pro golf's unofficial fifth major.

Hopes, as always, were that the weeks would produce great golf, great finishes, and advance some of the year's early storylines. In the end, that's not how things worked out. Except for two tournaments—Doral and the Match Play—the season went into a kind of two-month, midair stall. What kept things interesting, for the most part, were goings-on away from the course.

For some, one of the big attractions of the AT&T National Pro-Am at Pebble Beach is its celebrity field. The galleries relish the opportunity to see Hollywooders and retired sports idols with their hair down—or, in the case of Randy Quaid, sticking straight up. This year, the actor showed up looking like a pack of firecrackers had gone off on the top of his head. He was growing out his hair, one of his hangers-on explained, in preparation for an upcoming role. Still, some mousse would have helped.

To real golf nuts, of course, the celebs were a distraction. Watching actor James Woods play, for example, was a subtle form of torture. After his first round, at Spyglass Hill, he lingered for what seemed like forever on a practice green working on his putting stroke, a wristly, flippy motion that made him look like a kitten swatting a ball of yarn. It was too much even for his daughter—oops, make that girlfriend—to watch. She begged him to go home, protesting that his efforts wouldn't help him play any better the next day. She was right.

It was hard, however, to find anyone who didn't want to follow Bill Murray around for a few holes. The way he dressed for the event was in itself entertainment: on Thursday he showed up at Spyglass Hill wearing a lime-green shirt, brown shoes, black socks, beige cargo pants, and a hat that looked like like something your grandmother wore to church in 1940. The getup wasn't as provocative the bib overalls he wore in 1992, and he didn't throw a granny into a bunker, as he once did in the mid-nineties. Still, he was *resplendent* (as Carl Spackler would have said), and a pleasure to watch.

Among Pebble's amateurs the captains of industry far outnumbered the celebs. Some—like Charles Schwab, Donald Trump, and Scott McNealy—are recognizable names. But even the anonymous ones carried considerable weight. The presence of so many high-ranking execs from the Tour's corporate sponsors and partners was what made Pebble, in Peter Jacobsen's words, "the most important tournament of the year."

The pros' efforts to show them a good time was only enlightened self-interest—it helped ensure the future financial health of the Tour.

Ted Forstmann's relationship with the Tour was a little more complicated. Forstmann made his name doing leveraged buyouts. One of the higher-profile plays of his firm, Forstmann Little & Company, was for Nabisco—his role was commemorated in the book *Barbarians at the Gate*. Never married, he found time between raids to squire around women like Elizabeth Hurley and Lady Di. In 2004, Forstmann Little bought IMG, management firm to over half the world top twenty (including Tiger Woods and Vijay Singh), fifty other top professional golfers, and hundreds of other athletes. A regular at the AT&T, he was also one of the most powerful people in golf.

In 2006 Forstmann partnered, as usual, with Singh. As they made their way around Spyglass on Thursday, they were followed by Joey Diovisalvi. Joey D., as he was more commonly known, was Singh's longtime trainer, and the man the Fijian refered to as "my best friend." Indeed, he was a big part of Singh's life, by his side every day for their 5:30 a.m. workouts. Once, after Vijay said he had made some renovations to his weightroom, Steve Elling of the *Orlando Sentinel* cracked, "Does Joey still sleep underneath a bench?"

In a way, Diovisalvi was as interesting a character as Forstmann. Before finding his way to Singh in early 2000, he worked for Bruce Springsteen—indeed, he was the man responsible for the iconic rear end of the cover of *Born in the U.S.A.* Joey D. himself was so fit you could get tired just looking at him. In the summer of 2004, when Singh left him behind to go to Scotland for the British Open, Joey hopped a plane to California. On Tuesday he hiked Mount Dana, at 13,000 feet the second-highest peak in Yosemite National Park. On Wednesday and Thursday he trekked the park's treacherous Vogelsang Loop. Moving north to Washington State, he spent Friday and Saturday climbing Mount Rainier.

Recently, Diovisalvi had picked up two other big-name clients. One of them, unbelievably enough, was the 65-year-old Forstmann, who had decided his pro-am outings could be improved by a change in diet and a little exercise. The other, Chris DiMarco, was just as big a surprise. As Elling once put it, he was a guy "whose practice regimen best could be described as minimalist, and whose workout routine ranks a notch below that."

Even Joey D. was entertained by his marriage to DiMarco. A few years earlier, as Joey told it, Chris "actually pointed his finger at me and said, 'You stay away from me!'" DiMarco then pointed to his belly and bragged to Diovisalvi, "Most people have a six-pack. I have a keg."

On Thursday afternoon at Spyglass, DiMarco happened to be playing at the same time as Singh and Forstmann, on the opposite nine. After their rounds, they all came together at the scoring trailer. Singh and DiMarco headed upstairs into a trailer to sign their cards. Forstmann waited outside, and dipped his hand into a box of frosted donuts. (Spyglass volunteers always had donuts on hand for post-round pick-me-ups.) As Forstmann took his first healthy bite, DiMarco, at the top of the stairs, wheeled around and screamed, "Oh no! I'm telling Joey D.!"

Perhaps the best thing about 2006 Pebble week was the absence of the so-called "Crosby weather," the wind and rain that plagued the tournament even when the clambake bore Der Bingle's name.

An unhappier absence was Tiger Woods. He was a big part of Pebble Beach lore, due to his win in 2000, when he overtook leader Matt Gogel after being seven strokes down with seven holes to play. Yet he hadn't played Pebble since 2004. His pal Mark O'Meara explained that the cause was the AT&T's greens. The two were paired together that year at notoriously soggy Poppy Hills, the third course in the tournament rota. At one point, O'Meara said, "Tiger has a one-and-a-half-foot putt, straight in. He makes a perfect stroke, hits it right in the middle of the face. The ball goes sideways, and misses the hole. 'That's it,' he says. 'I'm not doing this anymore.'"

In a way, the most interesting happening this week was Friday's opening of the Tiger Woods Learning Center in Anaheim, near Woods' boyhood home in Cypress.

Woods called the launch of the $25 million, 35,000-square-foot facility "the greatest thing that's ever happened to me." And he meant it. As well as being the firmest evidence yet of his ever-elusive social conscience, it was also (not unrelatedly) a monument to his ailing father, Earl. But Tida, too, was part of its spirit, as featured speaker Bill Clinton hinted when he joked, "In the background of every great man is a boy who was terrified of his mother."

Tiger conceived the idea for the center in the days following 9/11. That week, he was in St. Louis for a Tour event. When it was canceled, flying home out was of the question. So he drove his courtesy car back home to Orlando. On the way he had plenty of time to think.

Woods had already more or less given up on the youth clinics that, until that point, were his largest contribution to the greater good. As his fame grew, they became nearly impossible to stage. More to the point, he probably realized that teaching minority kids to play golf wasn't going to help them pay for their greens fees when they grew up. Education was a smarter investment. Donors like Nike and Augusta National lined up to fund the project, and $5 million came from Tiger's own pocket.

Back up the coast, the AT&T turned out to be a two-man race. By the end of Saturday's play Mike Weir and Arron Oberholser were tied at seventeen-under, six clear of the rest of the field.

Oberholser, who had just turned 31, was a late-ripening Californian who went to school at nearby Santa Clara State. It didn't bode well for him that he was playing in his first final group. It also didn't help that it had a reputation as a hothead. The last similarly demeanored player in this position at the AT&T had been Pat Perez, back in 2002. He spent his final round swearing and slamming clubs on the way to a runner-up finish. A comparable performance from Oberholser wouldn't have been surprising.

More to the point, it was virtually impossible to bet against Weir, especially with Sunday's final round being played, as always, at Pebble Beach. Three days earlier he had torn the place up, shooting a 63. In his previous outing on the hallowed links, the final round of the tournament's 2005 edition, he had shot an amazing 67 on a day so windy and rainy that even the sea otters stayed indoors.

But Sunday didn't turn out as expected. On the second hole, an easy par-five, Weir pulled his second shot way right. It bounced off a cart path, onto a service road, and, finally, into a hedgerow fifty yards from the green. Oberholser made four, Weir made seven, and that was that.

When the Tour was in Southern California, much of the players' time was preoccupied with equipment-related business. Most paid visits to their sponsors' corporate facilities in Carlsbad and Oceanside, both about halfway between L.A. and San Diego; the headquarters of Callaway, TaylorMade, and Acushnet brands Titleist and Cobra were all located in the area. Scotty Cameron's putter studio was a few miles inland of Carlsbad, in San Marcos.

There were also dinners with sponsors and, sometimes, a photo or commercial shoot. This year was no different. One such occasion, the filming of television spots for Cobra, took place on the Monday and Tuesday following Pebble, a couple of days before the start of the Nissan Open in Los Angeles.

The shoot itself was in Palm Springs. Coming together over two days in the guaranteed sunshine were Phoenix winner J.B. Holmes; Camilo Villegas; colorfully-dressed, spiky-haired British Ryder Cupper Ian Poulter; Geoff Ogilvy; and rising Korean-American star Kevin Na. (Na would miss most of the rest of the season with a wrist injury.)

Poulter was only 30, but he was the eldest of the five. The group's kiddie corps quality was wholly intentional, as Ogilvy had explained back at Kapalua. And all the players hit the ball a long way, which jibed nicely with Cobra's long-time marketing strategy.

Holmes' driver-fueled victory had been brand magic. In fact, it was so good for Cobra that it caused certain spreadsheet problems. Todd Colburn, the company's marketing director, had what was called a win-ad contingency budget, and, after Holmes' win, he couldn't resist emptying it. The circumstances were ideal: the ads existed, almost ready-made, in the footage from CBS's broadcast. David Feherty's commentary was full of breathy superlatives ("This is as much fun as I've had watching golf in a long time!" he cried), making it perfect for repurposing. A further happy accident was that Feherty was already Cobra's lead spokesperson. The trouble was that if another of these kids won, or if Holmes won again, Colburn would have to call Acushnet chairman and CEO Wally Uihlein to ask for more money.

Feherty too was in on the Palm Springs shoot. Each of the ten-second ads Cobra was taping featured a little driving range exchange between the Irishman and one of the players. The shoot's grand finale, however, was a Feherty solo number, with him bouncing up and down on a trampoline in a cheerleader outfit.

During Monday's downtime, he told Geoff Ogilvy about it, without sounding particularly enthusiastic.

"I heard it was your idea," Ogilvy said.

"It was," Feherty replied. "But I never thought they would take me seriously."

Feherty discussed it again the following day with Villegas. While they were standing around, he looked over to the suit, resting on a table, and said, "Can you believe I'm going to have to put that thing on?"

"Why not?" Villegas said. "It will look good on you."

"Uh, *you*," Feherty shot back. "It would look good on *you*."

The funniest of the ads—apart from the cheerleader spot—was one featuring Villegas. Marketing director Colburn knew that one of his favorite movies was *Scarface*—which was interesting enough, considering that Camilo was from Medellín, Colombia. Colburn wasn't sure how he would react to the idea of reading one of Tony Montana's lines as part of a spot. But Villegas was all over it. "I'll have to watch the movie again to get back in character," he told him.

The spot began with Feherty watching Villegas hit drivers on the practice range.

Feherty: Wow, Camilo, you're crushing that out there past the 300-yard marker. What's the secret?

Villegas (pointing clubhead at Feherty and camera, aping Tony Montana's accent): Say hello to my not-so-little friend.

Coming down the stretch that Sunday at Riviera, the pace-setters were South Africa's Rory Sabbatini and old American hand Fred Couples. Giving chase was Australia's Adam Scott, the defending champion.

Of all the names on the leaderboard, it was Couples' that provoked the most interest. He was, of course, a fan favorite, especially here in L.A. In Tinseltown, the only thing that trumped good looks was good looks combined with cool, and that was Couples to a tee. Even in the wardrobe of an aging schlub—his usual ensemble of windshirt, visor, and baggy khakis—he was golf's answer to Cary Grant. The swing was still beautiful. Its effortless power invariably elicited comparisons to Sam Snead's, although the way he exploded at the ball at the bottom was more reminiscent of Bobby Jones. Even his walk set him apart. His slight backward lean and loose limbedness made him look like he was floating on air, like a flesh and blood hovercraft.

But as he strolled the fairways at Riviera—along with Augusta National, one of his two favorite courses in the world—insiders knew that he was in the midst of a painful divorce.

In Tour circles, breakups were anything but rare. In 2006 alone, plenty of pros (Couples, Chris Couch, Nick Faldo, Greg Norman, and

Billy Mayfair, to name a few) would find themselves embroiled in such proceedings. Hal Sutton alone had so many false starts—three in total—that peers took to calling him "Halimony." (Finding happiness with his fourth wife, Ashley, led to the career resurgence that culminated in his win at the 2001 Players Championship.) Tom Watson's 1997 divorce was much talked about, not only because he had been married for twenty-five years, but also because he was soon married again to the former wife of fellow pro Denis Watson.

Common sense suggests that Tour life—the pressure, the travel, the rope-hopers—makes it especially difficult to keep a marriage together. But that's not necessarily the case. In a lengthy 2005 piece on Tour marriages, *Golfweek*'s Jeff Rude approximated that about thirty-eight percent of the top 215 players had been through or were going through a divorce. That wasn't good, but it was somewhat better than the forty to fifty percent estimates for the U.S. general population.

If Tour marriages were healthier than normal it probably had something to do with money. But beyond that, it may have had to do with the edifice the Tour built around the institution. It kept a marriage counselor on call and did everything possible to provide on-the-road family stability, including on-site day care.

The news about Couples was particularly disappointing because he had seemed so happy with new wife, Thais, after a long period of being terribly unlucky in love.

His first wife, Deborah, was as sassy as they come. When Couples holed a two-footer to win the 1983 Kemper Open, she charged through a greenside bunker in an electric blue mini-dress, waving her white cowboy hat in her hand, and jumped into her husband's arms, throwing her legs luridly around his waist.

While living with Couples in La Quinta, the platinum blonde Texan fell in love with the Palm Springs resort lifestyle. She claimed a job as a tennis pro (she was on the tennis team at the University of Houston, where she and Fred went to college) but spent much of her time playing polo.

Couples left her in 1992, while he was in full ownership of the Tour, after an embarassing incident at the British Open: Deborah was spotted in a pub dancing on a table, singing along with the hit "I'm Too Sexy for My Shirt," while reportedly undoing her blouse buttons. (She denied that it ever happened; her friends claimed Fred was already in the middle of an affair.) Her initial alimony request was eye-popping: she asked for $168,000 a month, mostly because she anticipated about $300,00 a year in polo expenses. (Almost a decade later, Deborah would commit suicide, at age 43, jumping from the top of a chapel in Claremont, California, a town halfway between L.A. and Palm Springs.)

By 1995, Couples, now 35, was engaged to another woman, Tawnya Dowd, but broke it off in 1997, when he met 35-year-old Thais Bren. Bren, who herself was in the process of getting divorced, was a mother of two young children (daughter Gigi and son Oliver) who lived in Los Angeles. She and Fred met while he was in town for that month's Nissan Open.

Thais was your typical girl next door—if your door happens to be attached to beachfront property in Malibu. One of her childhood neighbors was her future first husband, Steven Michael Bren, son of Donald Bren, chairman and primary owner the Irvine Company, a real estate conglomerate whose holdings included an estimated one-sixth of the land in Orange County, California.

When Thais (pronounced *tha-EES*) was thirteen she wrote a letter to her neighbor declaring, "I'm going to marry you someday," her mother, Sandra, once told the *Los Angeles Times*. In 1988, at age 26, she did, in a posh ceremony in Santa Barbara. It was like marrying into royalty. Her new father-in-law, worth about $1.5 billion, was at the time literally richer than Donald Trump. If that wasn't glamorous enough, one of her new grandmothers-in-law was Claire Trevor Bren, winner of the 1948 best supporting actress Oscar for her role in *Key Largo*.

The golf world first heard Thais's name when Couples brought her to the 1997 PGA Championship in Louisville, Kentucky. "The relationship has been terrific for me," he told Peter Higgs of England's *Daily Mail*. But the news wasn't all good—Fred's new friend had breast cancer. "Thais told me about the cancer two weeks after we started seeing each other," he explained. "She said 'You don't need this—you can be with a healthy woman,' but I don't feel that way at all. I'm not going to spend the rest of my life playing golf and going back to my room alone."

Thais credited Couples with forcing her to get the second opinion that yielded the correct diagnosis of her condition. "I had been suspicious for a while that something might be wrong," she told *Sports Illustrated*'s Alan Shipnuck, "but I was told not to worry, that I was healthy.

Fred was the one who really encouraged me to get a proper diagnosis. He told me that I had to be sure."

If Thais was living through a tumultuous period in her life, so too was Couples. Two years earlier his mother, Violet, had died of cancer. His father, Tom, was battling leukemia. While spending as much time as possible with his father, he also accompanied Thais to Switzerland for her cancer surgery.

Fred's father passed away, but Thais got healthy. By 1998 they couldn't have seemed happier. That June's *Golf Digest* ran a photo of them at home in Santa Barbara, with Thais lying directly on top of her fiancé—the picture pretty much told the story. Gigi and Oliver were now seven and five, enrolled in the same school as Tom Hanks' kids. Couples was comfortably settling into a new life as a soccer dad. The wedding took place in September.

Then, in August 2005, Couples filed for divorce. The court papers said the grounds were "irreconcilable differences," but also showed Thais to be unhappy about it. When she was served, she refused the documents, saying "I am not taking them." (They were then tossed into her car.) His court-sanctioned visit to his former residence to pick up his belongings was in mid-January, just a few days before the start of the Hope. By that time he was already spending a lot of time in Scottsdale, playing golf at Phil Mickelson's club, Whisper Rock, and shopping around for a new place.

Throughout the Nissan Open, the media respectfully kept the divorce under wraps. (It was only after the Masters that any sign of it appeared in the press.) In the end he lost the Nissan, too, faltering down the stretch. Sabbatini held on for the win, becoming the surprise early-season leader of the Tour money list.

The Tour's next stop was the first World Golf Championships event of the year, the Accenture Match Play. It was played, for the last time, at La Costa, a sprawling Mission-style resort in Carlsbad that was among the oldest in California. It had its charms, but it also labored under a curse: at tournament time, it always seemed to rain. Poor drainage compounded the problem. Nicknamed "Lake La Costa," the course was often completely submerged by the time the players arrived. That was the principal reason the tournament was about to pick up and leave Carlsbad, and head to Tucson.

In one sense it was a shame. The Tour had a long history at La Costa. It started visiting the resort in 1969 for the old season-opening Tournament of Champions. In 1999 the event moved to Kapalua, but the Tour itself never left; that year also saw the birth of the Match Play.

Despite the rain, the players loved the resort. One of the tournament's all-time neatest scenes was Sergio Garcia rallying on a tennis court next to the clubhouse with then-girlfriend Martina Hingis after one year's Wednesday matches.

But no one enjoyed La Costa more than Tiger Woods. He first won there in 1997, in the next-to-last Tournament of Champions, coming out on Monday after a week of almost continuous rains to polish off Tom Lehman in a play-off with one swing of his eight-iron on the par-three 16th. He claimed victories at the Match Play in 2003 and 2004, largely because of his ability to control the spin on his wedges on the slopey, invariably soggy greens.

Woods' success in the new format wasn't surprising. In his younger days, he had been a match-play killer, taking three straight U.S. Junior titles, and then three straight U.S. Amateurs. He was not, however, immune to its perils. Playing poorly in his first match in 2002, he was bounced by anonymous Australian Peter O'Malley.

For some, first-round exits were all too common, and were especially painful when long trips were involved. Ernie Els's globetrotting schedule often had him flying in for the event from Europe or the Middle East. In 2002 he too exited on Wednesday, after falling in the first round. Now, in 2006, Els again lost his first match. Afterward, he walked back to his room in a little condo complex beside the tenth hole. He paused at the bottom of the stairs and tipped his white hat back on his head. It looked, in a way, like a dunce cap. Underneath it, he seemed to be saying to himself, "Why did I come all this way, again, for this?"

He wasn't the only one whose exit featured a tragicomic moment. After his 19th-hole Wednesday expulsion by Geoff Ogilvy, U.S. Open champ Michael Campbell stood in the clubhouse lobby doing some glad-handing with staffers from Callaway, his equipment sponsor. One of them, used to Thursday starts, finished his conversation with Campbell by saying, "Good luck this week."

The headline first-round pairing in 2006 pitted Tiger Woods against Stephen Ames, who was born in Trinidad and Tobago, but now lived in Canada, in (of all places) Calgary. The match came with a backstory. In

2000 Ames told the *Calgary Herald* that Woods was "a spoiled 24-year-old" who had "no consideration for the other players"; he was "coming across," in Ames' opinion, "as though he was bigger than the game." It was hard to imagine Tiger hadn't heard about Ames' comments, even if he hadn't actually read them. And for Woods, whose memory is famously elephantine, it no doubt still served as mental bulletin board material. In case Woods didn't remember those comments, Ames put his foot in his mouth again on the range on Monday afternoon. Discussing his chances against Woods with the Associated Press's Doug Ferguson, he said, "Anything can happen, especially where he's hitting the ball."

Woods responded with as close to a perfect round as he'd ever played as a pro. He birdied the first six holes, as well as the 8th. He won the 7th and 9th with pars, and closed out the match on the 10th with a halve in pars. The final score was Woods 9 and 8.

Afterward, in the press room, Woods was pricelessly glib.

Reporter: Were you aware of Stephen's comments yesterday that you weren't striking the ball well?
Woods: Yes.
Reporter: I assumed you were.
Woods: Yes.
Reporter: What was your reaction when you saw that?
Woods: 9 and 8.

Then, another try.

Reporter: Obviously you like challenges, the idea of someone saying you're not driving the ball well. It must have lit a fire under you.
Woods: You might say that.
Reporter: It would be better if you said it.
Woods: As I said, 9 and 8.

(It wasn't the first time Woods had issued payback at La Costa. Six years earlier, in 2000, Michael Campbell came into the event as the hottest player in golf, having won three of his previous four events. Asked if he was looking forward to his first-round matchup, he said, "Hell, yeah. I want Tiger. I'm not here to fill out the field." When they arrived on the first tee, Campbell said an innocent hello. Woods leaned in, and said, "I heard you want a piece of me. Well, now you've got me." Woods then shellacked him, winning 5 and 4.)

In Woods' 2006 second-round match he squeaked by Robert Allenby. But on Friday, in the third-round, he was beaten by Chad Campbell. It was a day of upsets, with Phil Mickelson and Vijay Singh also falling. But easily the most interesting match that day was the one between Geoff Ogilvy and Mike Weir.

Ogilvy, the fifty-second seed, was 4 down with four holes to play. On the 15th hole, Weir was in the middle of the fairway with a wedge in his hand, but pulled it into a bunker and missed his ten-foot par putt. Ogilvy won 16 with a birdie, and Weir made hash of the 17th. On the par-five 18th, Ogilvy made birdie, and Weir missed his birdie putt to finish the match. They replayed the 18th, and Ogilvy won it with an eagle.

The young Aussie was actually lucky to have made it to his match with Weir. His first-round opponent, Nick O'Hern, had let him off the hook with a missed five-footer on their second extra hole. In the second round Ogilvy had chipped in on the first extra hole to beat Michael Campbell. After the third round, the question was whether or not Ogilvy would fully take advantage of all this good fortune.

Ogilvy came into the week in an upbeat mood. The previous week, in L.A., was his first opportunity all year to hang with his best friend, Adam Scott. They'd get to spend time together again at La Costa. Following the Match Play, they were planning to head to Georgia for Ogilvy's first look at Augusta National. More important, he and his wife, Juli, had found out only three weeks earlier that she was expecting. Even the morning sickness ("actually, all-day sickness," Geoff said) couldn't dampen their happiness.

By Saturday, however, some of the Match Play's little peculiarities had begun to unsettle him. Almost ninety percent of the field, including Scott, had packed up and left La Costa. Never having played this event before (he owed his sudden jump in the world rankings to his first Tour win, at Tucson's opposite-field event, fifty-two weeks earlier) Ogilvy was put off by the ghost town feeling. And now, in the final eight of the year's biggest tournament so far, he couldn't help but notice that most observers believed he was out of his depth.

But he wasn't. Although a relative unknown in America (his picture was often mixed up in the local papers with that of fellow pro Joe Ogilvie), he had a solid golf pedigree. Growing up at Victoria Country Club (also the home course of four-time British Open champion Peter Thomson) he dominated Melbourne junior golf. In his teens he looked to be a future great, although he was overshadowed to some extent by two other Australian prodigies, Scott and Aaron Baddeley.

He turned pro at 21, and cut his teeth in Europe. Though he never won there, he found enough confidence to cross the Atlantic in 2000. Everyone who knew him was convinced he was destined for stardom. The first two to say so were probably Steve Bann and Dale Lynch, the directors of the Victorian Institute of Sport, which had already produced Tour winners Robert Allenby and Stuart Appleby. Bann, who frequently traveled in America as coach to Allenby and Appleby, was once asked which young Australian—Baddeley, Scott, Ogilvy, or any of a handful of others—would be the first to win a major. He unflinchingly named Ogilvy. Noted Australian player and commentator Mike Clayton presciently said that, like Retief Goosen, Ogilvy was "probably one player the masses will discover after a stunning result."

His talent was also plain to the people at his new home course. After moving to the States Ogilvy settled in Scottsdale and joined Whisper Rock, the club Phil Mickelson built in the late nineties, and whose membership was composed almost exclusively of Tour players, ex-jocks like Wayne Gretzky and John Elway, and Phil's old ASU buddies. One member, and a frequent playing partner, was CBS commentator and Scottsdale mafia don Gary McCord. During one 2005 broadcast he declared about Ogilvy, "This guy should win four times a year."

His game had no perceptible weaknesses. Lynch, his primary coach, had never messed with his natural swing, a simple repeating motion that, with his long limbs, produced plenty of distance, even if he wasn't always accurate with his driver. He was also a great long iron and fairway wood player. But his real genius was his short game. The combination of length and deftness around the greens perfectly matched the emphases of the Tour's current style of play.

What held him back was his tendency to be overly self-critical. On the course, he said, it was "pretty embarassing" what he said to himself. After bad shots, he often called himself "useless," and wondered, "What am I doing out here?" Summing his attitude up, he said, "If you talked to anyone the way I talked with myself, you wouldn't be friends with him."

The first step in overcoming it, Ogilvy said, was recognizing "that the great players don't berate themselves constantly." Tiger Woods, he noticed, "gets as angry as anyone," but "keeps it under control. It doesn't affect his next shot." Ogilvy's wallet helped impart the lesson. "Every time you walk off the golf course, and you finished twelfth or fifteenth, you look back, and two shots better would have made a lot of money and finished fourth or had a top ten. You look at how many shots you threw away, because your attitude wasn't there. It starts getting expensive. You start realizing it's just stupid."

Even during those struggles Ogilvy won people over with his personality. Unusually grounded and humble, he tended to see things just the way laymen saw them. Often he would say things like, "It's crazy. I made more money last year than my parents made in their whole lives, and they had good jobs."

What made him especially popular among golf writers was his willingness to stand around and chat about things other than himself, from politics to music and films. His favorite topics were golf course architecture and design. He had read just about every significant book on the subject, and expressed his views better than many of his conversation partners. His status as a long-hitter didn't stop him from expressing dismay at the effect technology was having on the game.

In a conversation with Scottish writer John Huggan, he said, "My mind keeps going back to the Road Hole," the 17th at St. Andrews. "It's the most fearsome hole in golf and yet they had to grow all that silly rough up the right hand side. If they hadn't we would have been hitting chip shots to the green. Symbolically, they could not allow that. So they had to do it. That golf hole is the reason the golf ball needs to be changed. It's no fun with the modern ball. I was hitting a 4-iron off the tee at the Road Hole! Are you kidding me?"

Saturday at the Match Play meant 36 holes of golf. Ogilvy's morning quarter-final was another marathon. He finally overtook Englishman David Howell by holing a 20-footer for birdie on the 19th hole. The afternoon semis were appreciably easier. He beat Tom Lehman 4 and 4.

Walking with him for most of the day were his wife, Juli, and Cobra's Todd Colburn. As Geoff wrapped up his match with Lehman, Colburn found himself thinking again about his win-ad budget. That call to Wally Uihlein was looking likelier by the minute.

Saturday night found Ogilvy back in his digs in the condo complex near the 10th hole. After room service, he puttered around on the internet, burning the usual circuits: he'd start at pgatour.com, and then move over to the Australian newspaper sites, checking the Aussie rules football, rugby, and cricket scores. He favored his hometown Melbourne papers, *The Age* and Rupert Murdoch's tabloid the *Herald Sun*. The latter was a boyhood habit. For short young arms, it was easier to handle than the broadsheet *Age*. That was Murdoch's secret: publish a paper small enough to hook 'em while they're young.

The following day, facing Davis Love in the final, Ogilvy was unflappable. He took the lead on the 16th hole and never relinquished it. The most difficult part of the day was waiting behind Zach Johnson and Tom Lehman's consolation match. At one point, Love and Ogilvy asked official Mark Russell if they could play through. It was out of the question—ABC, the event's network broadcasters, wouldn't have it. Oddly, on the broadcast itself, Paul Azinger relentlessly blasted the Tour for sending the matches out so close together. Finally, Mike Tirico had to interrupt him to say, "Paul, it probably has something to do with us."

In the end, Ogilvy won the final 3 and 2. The victory was easily the high point of his career. No one imagined how quickly it would be surpassed.

When the Tour arrived at Doral, Miami's golf fans were hoping for just one thing: a rematch between Tiger Woods and Phil Mickelson, who, a year earlier, had hooked up for one of the Tour's all-time epic final-round duels.

They got it. Sadly, it came one day too early and ended a hollow disappointment. But there were compensations. One was the coming-out party of a kid who hailed from a different continent but may as well have been from down the street. The other was Woods' second victory of the year.

The kid, of course, was Camilo Villegas. He had already lived through what for some would have been a season's worth of excitement—playing alongside Michelle Wie in Hawaii, and playing a prominent part in the Baby Basher ballyhoo that surrounded him, J.B. Holmes, and Bubba Watson.

Clearly, Villegas was a pop idol in the making. His second-place finish in Phoenix proved he had game. On top of that, he had the kind of good looks that could make Melanie Griffith think about dumping Antonio Banderas.

On the strength of that second-place finish, those looks, and the Spanish-speaking media's fascination with both, the tournament staff at Doral had already received plenty of calls about whether or not the young Colombian would be playing there.

By now, Villegas was used to getting the royal treament at Doral. During previous visits to the resort (mostly for college tournaments) he had become friendly with many of the numerous Colombians on its staff. There were countrymen working "everywhere," he said, "from the pro shop to valet parking." Even the head greenskeeper was from his native land.

At 4:50 a.m on Wednesday, just hours before his first-round tee time, fire alarms rang out at the resort's Building C. Camilo, lying in bed, thought to himself, What's going on here? When he realized what had woken him up, he decided, "I ain't getting up. I'll just throw two pillows on top of my head and stay here." His room was on the first floor, with a walk-out patio; if it wasn't a false alarm, he could be out on the driving range in about four seconds.

He tried to get back to sleep, but it didn't happen. He couldn't stop thinking about the audience that would greet him during his morning round. Dozens of Colombians had flown up for the occasion. Among them were his parents, an aunt, and a grandmother and grandfather.

But that wasn't the half of it. There were also plenty of Colombians who lived in and around Miami. And Brazilians. And Venezeulans. And, of course, Cubans. All told, thousands of people came out to see him play—on a Thursday morning. "It felt more like a soccer game than a golf tournament," Villegas said.

Early during the first round, he approached playing partner Mathias Grönberg and apologized for the noise.

"Don't worry about me," said Grönberg, an amiable Swede, who, although he hadn't seen much Tour success, had made a comfortable home in America, marrying a New Jersey native and hanging out at tony Hamptons clubs like Sebonack when the family wasn't at its other residence, in Monaco. "Just play your game and enjoy it," he smiled.

Eventually, Villegas did. One-over after seven holes, he rallied to play his last eleven in eight-under, finishing with a 65. He was leading the tournament after the morning wave.

It was heady stuff. Villegas was just six years removed from his arrival at the University of Florida. At the time he weighed 139 pounds. During the next four years added twenty more, while claiming first-team All-America honors three times. No Colombian (except perhaps for LPGA star Marisa Baena) had ever achieved so much in the game. He probably never would have discovered golf if his father, an architect, hadn't joined Campestre de Medellín, one of only four courses in the city, on a lark.

Coming into Doral, the buzz surrounding him was deafening. *Cigar Aficionado* magazine was already planning a cover story (although the eventual cover line—"Is This the Next Tiger Woods?"—made it seem like its staffers were moonlighting from jobs at *High Times*). On Tuesday of Doral week Colombia national television network purchased the rights to televise the last thirty PGA Tour events of the season. Their first broadcast would be Friday's second round.

So much had happened, and the headliners had yet to tee off.

Despite Villegas's presence, Woods and Mickelson dominated the tournament run-up. Memories of their showdown the previous year were still fresh in everyone's mind—above all, Mickelson's. He too was staying on campus at Doral, and the resort's dedicated cable channel was spooling highlights of the matchup, endlessly rerunning Mickelson's lipped-out chip on the 72nd hole, which would have sent the tournament to extra holes.

Mickelson saw the footage whenever he turned on his TV. "Every time," he said, "with three or four feet to go, it just looks like it's going to go right in the middle, and it just somehow snaps off at the end. I keep waiting for the video to change, but it never does."

A rematch wasn't hard to imagine. The Blue Monster played to both men's strengths. It was the Tour's consummate Bomb and Gouge venue—except that little gouging was needed, because the rough was so sparse. At Doral, bad lies were about as common as polar bears.

Predictably, both had their way with the course. Tiger opened 64–67, and Mickelson shot 65–66. That meant they would be paired together in the final group on Saturday. Villegas, too, continued his stellar play and finished his Friday tied with Tiger and Phil for the lead. Finishing later in the day, he would go off on Saturday in the next-to-last group.

Camilo's brother, Manuel, saw the first two rounds at home in Gainesville. The two lived together in an apartment near campus; Manuel, also a Gator golfer, was in his sophomore year. As he watched, he couldn't help but grow excited. "It looked like it was going to be special," he said. "It looked like he might play with Tiger." That wasn't the way it worked out. Nevertheless, on Friday night at 9:00 p.m. Manuel got in his car and drove to Miami, arriving at the door of his family's rented apartment, about twenty minutes from the golf course, at 3:00 a.m. They were still up waiting for him. They hadn't seen him since Christmas.

On Saturday morning Manuel went to Doral to visit his brother in his room. Since they had seen each other on Monday, before Camilo drove down, there wasn't much catching up to do. His room looked the same as it always did. Like many pros, Camilo was compulsively organized. His clothes and clubs were tidily spread out around the room. Soon the rest of the family joined them. Heading back outside, they greeted a couple of countrymen who played on the University of Miami golf team. When his brother went to hit balls, Manuel couldn't get over the size of the assembling galleries. It was something television hadn't quite prepared him for. He ran into Dudley Hart, a University of Florida alum, and asked, "Can you believe how crazy this is?"

By the time Camilo approached the first tee, the crowds around it were twenty deep. Thousands more were packed between the tee and the fairway landing area. It figured that they would watch Villegas hit, wait for Lefty and Tiger, and then walk the course with the two superstars. But that's not what happened. After Camilo teed off and began walking up the fairway, half the crowd—the most boisterous, noisy, interestingly dressed half—went with him. There were lots of flags and lots of cigar smoke. There were also lots of bare female shoulders and midriffs. From certain vantage points, it looked like Villegas had decided to play his golf that day on the home page of hotlatinas.com.

To Manuel, what was most impressive was the way his brother blocked everything out. There was no interaction with the gallery, not even any eye contact. He had all the purposeful indifference of a veteran pro.

Behind them, the Woods-Mickelson matchup was proving anticlimactic. Tiger eased ahead during the first few holes. Then, on the 9th, Mickelson made double, taking all remaining air out of the pairing. In the absence of drama, fans settled for low comedy. On the 10th, Mickelson's pulled approach sailed well right of the green and smashed into the Citizen wristwatch of a spectator named Noel Grullon. When Lefty came over and saw the damage—the face was hanging from the wristband—he produced a couple of C-notes and handed them to him.

Toward the end of the round, the group found itself on the 18th tee waiting out a long delay. Just ahead, Villegas had played well right of the fearsome lake to the left of the hole, which made for the only truly tough shot on the entire course. He wound up directly behind a banyan tree, had to chip out sideways, and after a three-putt, carded a double-bogey. Back on the tee, Woods, as he later said, "was joking with Stevie and Bones that maybe we could order pizza, and see if they could really be here in thirty minutes or less."

Woods himself wound up driving his ball behind the same tree, but his ball came to rest on a cart path, allowing him a free drop. He finished his round with a 68, two strokes clear of his nearest pursuers, 2002 PGA winner Rich Beem and Cypress Point admirer Daniel Chopra. Villegas was three back, tied for fourth with David Toms. Mickelson's lackluster 72 dropped him back into a tie for seventh.

It was the thirty-sixth time Woods had held a lead after the third round of a Tour event. He buckled so rarely that each time he did, it changed the answer to a trivia question. At this point, the only three men to overtake him on a Sunday were Ed Fiori (1996 Quad City Classic), Mickelson (2000 Tour Championship), and Retief Goosen (2004 Tour Championship). He looked pretty safe; in this position he wasn't due for another such loss until 2008.

On Sunday Woods played a respectable round, in what was now the usual fashion. As he made the turn, he had only hit 45 percent of his fairways on the week. But it didn't matter. As Johnny Miller said on NBC's broadcast, "He's getting it down there far enough that with those square grooves, he can dominate that grass." His only real challenge came from Toms. That was a surprise, considering that Toms hated this style of golf. He spent much of the week wondering why he'd made the trip. "My wife and kids went skiing this weekend at Beaver Creek," he said, "and I wouldn't have minded going with them." The reason, in the end, was probably sentiment. As a kid, he often came to Doral with his grandfather. Together they would play fifty-four holes a day.

Toms made his move with three birdies between the 8th and 11th holes, pulling to within one. But that was still the margin when he hit his final tee shot. A short hitter, Toms, unlike Woods and Villegas, couldn't bash his ball over the edge of the lake and somewhere up onto the right side. He had to carefully place his drive short of the hazard. His ball finished nearly 200 yards away from the pin on the 467-yard hole. Hitting a long-iron in, he three-putted, allowing Woods to coast in.

At first glance, it was a case of Woods' opponents once again wilting in the waning moments. It had happened, now, in each of his last four wins. The first instance was Daly's three-foot whiff at October's Amex. Then Olazábal had blown a three-footer at Torrey Pines. The third was the duck-hook the Ernie Els hit to begin, and effectively end, his playoff with Woods at February's Dubai Desert Classic.

But Toms didn't see it that way. Afterward, he issued a clarion call about the way the Tour, in his view, was setting up courses to favor the longer hitters. All week long he had begged Tour officials to move up the tees on the hole, in the interest of fairness.

"It has nothing to do with the superintendent, the tournament sponsor, or the designer," Toms said. "It's the guy who puts the frickin' tee markers down. I told them early in the week, if it comes down to a guy like me, or Verplank, or anyone like that, trying to beat Villegas or Tiger, it's unfair to be putting the tee box back there. And ultimately it did come down to that. It gives them too big an advantage. They said, 'What about the other holes? They're better for the shorter hitters.' And I'm like, it's the last hole, it's the hardest hole on the golf course, and it's the one everybody's watching. It's the only one you have to play well to win. Make it fair for everybody."

It sounded like sour grapes, but he had a point. It was highly unlikely, however, that anything was going to change.

The following two events were, for the most part, PGA Tour golf at its most unremarkable. At best, they turned out to be early-season European Team Ryder Cup auditions. Englishman Luke Donald passed his, stiffing a 6-iron on the final hole at the Honda Classic to edge Geoff Ogilvy for his second Tour win. Greg Owen, another Englishman, did not. His three-putt from three feet on the next-to-last hole at Bay Hill handed a win to Australia's Rod Pampling.

The next stop was the Players Championship, the Tour's showcase event. It had long been touted as golf's fifth major, and it was getting there. Due to its generously inclusive field, it had produced some head-scratcher winners (Jodie Mudd in 1990, Craig Perks in 2002). But it also boasted some great ones (Norman, Couples, Duval, Woods, and Love). It had a huge purse (the 2006 winner's check would be $1.44 million) and a uniquely challenging course, the TPC at Sawgrass, whose 17th hole was probably the most nerve-wracking in golf. Apart from Hal Sutton's ever-famous "Be the right club to*day*!" (uttered at the end of his 2000 Tiger Woods stare-down) just about every tournament highlight, or lowlight, was generated by the hole. There was Len Mattiace's epic meltdown in 1998; Tiger Woods' ridiculous "better than most!" 60-footer for birdie on the way to his win in 2001; and Bob Tway's unbelievable, windswept 12 in 2005. The hole even produced spectacular moments when it wasn't being used for the Players. Tiger Woods' dramatic birdie there in the finals of the 1994 U.S. Amateur propelled him to a magical comeback win over Trip Kuehne for the second of three U.S. Am titles.

What the tournament lacked—and what denied it major status—was 100 years worth of tradition, and, to a certain extent, a distinct personality. Yes, the course was unique, but in setting it up, the Tour seemed to channel the USGA, or at least try to: they grew plenty of rough and tried to get the fairways and greens hard and fast, although rains usually made that impossible. (That was why the Tour, for 2007, moved the event from April to May.)

Since so many of the contestants lived nearby, the Players was also— perhaps more than any other week on Tour—a big social week. Jim Furyk, for one, always had people over. On Wednesday night he and wife, Tabitha, hosted Brad Faxon, Justin Leonard, Phil Mickelson, and Davis Love, along with their wives and kids, serving up some slightly burnt but nevertheless tasty grilled beef tenderloin.

But the biggest party—hands-down the social event of the year—was Vijay Singh's annual Monday night bash, at his expansive oceanside spread a few miles south of the TPC. "Every year it gets bigger and better," opined Adam Scott, who estimated the number of attendees at well over 200.

The host himself had lost count. "At first it was just a handful of guys," Singh said, reflecting on the affair's ten-year history. "Then two handfuls. Once you get up near 200, it's like, what's another plate?"

The door policy, by and large, was indiscriminate. This year, even Dave Renwick, the caddie Singh abruptly fired at the end of 2005, was present. Rehiring Renwick, one Singh intimate said, was "never going to happen, because of what he said about Vijay in print." (There had been some bitter comments about day-to-day discourteousness and dressing-downs after perceivedly bad yardages.) "But yeah, he was there. Vijay knows how to bury the hatchet."

Just about the only Tour folk who didn't attend were members of the press. There was a good reason for that. Singh's relationship with the media had always been frosty, stemming, for the most part, from two specific articles.

The first—or, better, the one that ratified a long, scattered series of earlier rumor-filled pieces—appeared right after Singh's fifth-place finish at the 1996 PGA Championship at Valhalla. Late in that Sunday's broadcast, CBS's Jim Nantz had said, "They must be dancing in the streets in Fiji." The line reappeared as the epigraph of John Garrity's story in the following week's *Sports Illustrated,* which explored allegations that had dogged Singh for a decade: that he had signed for an incorrect score at the 1985 Malaysian Open in Jakarta, in order to make the cut; and that during his 1982 campaign on the Australian Tour he had left behind him a long string of big, unpaid phone bills. The incidents resulted in bans from tour golf in both Asia and Australia. (Singh has always maintained that the scorecard in question in Indonesia was kept by someone else, and that he simply didn't check it thoroughly enough before signing it. About the phone bills, he has said he repaid the money he owed as soon as he was able.)

The second piece involved remarks he made to the AP's Doug Ferguson during the run-up to Annika Sorenstam's appearance at the 2003 Colonial. The most pointed of them—the one that more or less led Ferguson's story the next day—was, "I hope she misses the cut." Singh always maintained he was misquoted and really said, "If I miss the cut, I hope she misses the cut," emphasizing he didn't want her to beat him. Ferguson, for his part, stuck by his notes. With the leading golf writer in the country now on his shit list, Singh retreated into a de facto media blackout.

Between and even before the articles, Singh had established himself as one of the finest players in the game. His first four years as a regular on the European Tour, from 1989 to 1992, produced four wins, and were accompanied by four other international victories. While continuing to win all over the globe, he earned his first U.S. PGA Tour title in 1993, and added fourteen more in the U.S. (including two majors) before his stunning 2004 season, during which he won nine times (adding one more major) and unseated Tiger Woods as the number one player in the world.

What was now so strange about Singh was the radical difference between his life, as lived, and his public image. His lack of desire to play the publicity game—refusing requests for sit-downs, even skipping occasional tournament-leaders press conferences—displeased the custodians of his reputation, and they consistently made him pay for it.

At the same time, he had a healthy relationship with the rest of the golf community. Singh was one of the most (if not the most) well-liked players on Tour. He got along famously with most of its bit players (equipment reps, officials and the like: when a photographer who often shot him for sponsor Cleveland Golf was diagnosed with cancer, Vijay offered him whatever help he needed, including the use of a private plane). There were even two or three golf writers with whom he had good rapports. Singh often lunched with *Golf World*'s Bob Verdi. One evening, at dinner at Emeril's in New Orleans, Vijay had a little wine in him, and was spotted ruffling the hair of one of the press corps' junior members.

If the Tour was broken up into Tiger guys, Phil guys, and Vijay guys—as, for the most part, it was—Singh's faction was by far the largest. One reason was his sense of humor—he was quick with a joke, the real payoff being his high-pitched squeal of a laugh. Another was the way he embraced many new arrivals, dispensing swing tips and offering to play paternal practice rounds. Yet another was that many of the foreign players—not just the Europeans, but also the Africans and a few Asians—knew how tough his road had been, because they had, at certain points, traveled it with him. They understood the desperation he faced during his ban-imposed years of exile in Borneo, making $200 a month and playing lumber tycoons and oil company executives in high-stakes games for money he didn't have, just to try to get off the island and resume his career.

Singh's party was undoubtedly the best measure of his popularity. And one of the best reflections of his personality was the way he pulled out all the stops. The first thing guests noticed at the 2006 shindig was a new wrinkle: valet parking. The second, perhaps, was the wine. This year, he had spent over $20,000 on what Mike Weir termed "some pretty impressive vino," a selection that included cases of 2001 Silver Oak, 2001 Opus One, and 2002 Far Niente Reserve.

Upstairs were a couple of poker tables with hired dealers. Dozens of attendees, including Adam Scott and Singh himself, sat and played for a while, trying to beat Hold 'Em cardsharp Tim Clark. Outside on the patio, Charlie Niyomkul—a close friend of Vijay's and the owner of Atlanta restaurants Tamarind and Nan (the latter of which hosted an annual Wednesday night players' dinner during the Tour Championship)—was grilling up 120 pounds of marinated lamb chops. Darren Clarke, Niyomkul reported, was the chop-eating champ "for the second year in a row; Nick Price had a chance, but Darren cleaned up the last batch." As sides, Niyomkul brought along forty pounds each of shrimp curry, lamb curry, and chicken panang.

The main dining area was a big temporary tent, two days in the building, that Scott said looked like something out of *The Great Gatsby*. It was right on the sand, the roaring surf providing the dinner music. The merriment lasted until about 1:30 a.m.

By far the most unusual thing that happened during Players week was Tiger Woods' sudden departure on Tuesday afternoon. His trip back to California, according to confidants, was precipitated by Earl's refusal to eat. When Tiger walked in the door, his father greeted him by saying, "What the hell are you doing here?"

Woods only came back to the Players, he said, to give his father "something to look forward to every day. Hopefully I'll get on TV and hit some good golf shots, and he can watch." When someone asked, "Is this a situation where you might not play The Masters?" Woods replied, "You never know."

It helped that Woods was paired this week (as he was two months earlier in Dubai) with his friend Darren Clarke. Heather, Clarke's wife, had been diagnosed with breast cancer in 2002. Like Earl's cancer, it came, then went, then returned. Few players understood what he was going through the way Clarke did.

Stephen Ames, Tiger's La Costa foil, had been through something of the same struggle with his wife, Jodi, who in mid-2005 underwent surgery for lung cancer. Ames hadn't won since, but by Saturday night was in position to claim his second Tour victory. His lead, however, was only one and barking at his heels were Singh and Sergio Garcia.

But on Sunday both Vijay and Sergio got off to horrid starts. Retief Goosen, coming from four back, tried to challenge, but Ames was playing too steadily to be overtaken. He wound up shooting a stellar final-round 67 and coasting to victory.

Now, as the Tour packed up and headed to Atlanta and Augusta, the season was almost three months old. Yet no dominant storyline had emerged. Tiger had won twice. But because of his father's health, how he would play—indeed, how much he would play—during the coming months was an open question. Good young players had notched a few wins, but the ones everyone expected to break out in 2006—Adam Scott, Sergio Garcia, and Sean O'Hair—had yet to be heard from, except in the case of Garcia, whose final-round meltdowns at Torrey and Sawgrass were bad omens.

Among the top players, Ernie Els, Vijay Singh, and Retief Goosen had yet to win, muffling the Big Five talk that had defined 2005. Phil Mickelson was the biggest mystery. He had four top tens and six top fifteens in his seven starts, but he hadn't yet sniffed the winner's circle. That, however, was about to change.

6

AUGUSTA RE-MASTERED

The Masters

It was 1:50 p.m. on Masters Sunday, exactly one hour before the day's final tee time, and Fred Couples was running late.

Hustling down the central corridor of the clubhouse at Augusta National, he neared the reception desk, made a U-turn, and headed up a flight of narrow, creaky stairs. When he reached the top he turned left and crossed the threshold of the Champions Locker Room, the most exclusive room in all of golf.

As he entered he saw Billy Casper, the 1970 tournament winner, sitting with his son Bob at one of three small card tables. They were watching the closed-circuit telecast on a television in the corner. They appeared to be the only people there.

Couples breezed past them on his left on the way to his locker. He was oblivious to the figure on his right, a man lying on a padded bench with his eyes closed and a rolled-up towel under his head.

Now, less than an hour before his and Couples' tee time, Phil Mickelson was flat on his back, fast asleep.

You couldn't blame him. It had already been a long day. Because of the usual bad weather—there hadn't been a dry Masters since 2001—

the third round had to be completed that morning. Mickelson began his day at 7:45 a.m., on the 6th hole. He finished at about 11:20, signing for a 70, which lifted him into the lead.

Then he had time to kill. He hit some post-round practice putts, came back to the locker room, and had a sandwich with the Caspers. Although they were both San Diegans, Mickelson had only gotten to know Billy in 2005, at the previous year's Masters. But already he trusted him enough to use him as an alarm clock. At about 1:30, right after lunch, Mickelson lay down and told Casper to wake him at 2:00. Then he shut his eyes and was out like a light.

Mickelson was still asleep as Couples slipped on his saddle shoes. What was going through his mind was anyone's guess.

Maybe he was replaying, on the undersides of his eyelids, his break-through 2004 final round. Maybe he was watching a highlight reel of other great Masters moments, like his pal Fred's final round tee shot at the 12th hole in 1992—which, hanging up in the grass near the front of the green, refused to roll down into Rae's Creek, and made his victory seem like the will of the gods.

Later, no one could say what Mickelson was dreaming about, or if he was dreaming at all. Not his wife, nor his caddie, nor Billy Casper, nor Bertis Downs, a friend who seemed to be present at every memorable dinner Mickelson had that month.

Mickelson couldn't remember himself. Who knew? Perhaps he had a premonition about winning the 2006 Masters for his second straight major, and doing the unthinkable: making people believe, just for a moment, that Tiger Woods wasn't the best golfer in the world.

Maybe that was it. Or maybe it wasn't. But whether he dreamed it or not, it was about to come true.

Back in 1975, in *Sports Illustrated*, Dan Jenkins wrote that the Masters doesn't begin until the back nine on Sunday.

But it's not true. At least not for Phil Mickelson. His 2006 Masters began a full ten days before he hit his opening tee shot.

After signing for a final round 74 at the Players Championship (good for a tie for fourteenth), he got onto his plane—a GII with the mono-grammed tail number N800PM—and took off for Augusta. With him were Jim Mackay and Dave Pelz. They landed at the little private airfield on the south side of town, near the Augusta Municipal Golf Course, hopped into the Ford Explorer that reliably awaited him at every Tour stop (compliments of a local dealership) and rode to their hotel.

The next morning Mickelson played a practice round at the National. Such pre-tournament visits were by now a staple of Mickelson's Masters preparation. Every year since 2004 he had spent Monday and Tuesday of the week before the Masters in Augusta, then left to compete in that week's PGA Tour event. The idea behind playing the week before a major was to keep his game "tournament sharp." He kept the same schedule for the other U.S. majors and, beginning in 2005, for the British Open.

His preparation for this Masters, however, had a novel wrinkle. The night before, when they left the Players, Mickelson pulled a second driver from his locker and tucked it in beside his normal driver. His regular stick was forty-five inches long, with the clubhead weighted to produce a controlled cut, for accuracy. The new one was an inch longer, designed to produce a draw: he could fly it about 305 yards, fifteen farther than the other. Mickelson had been testing longer drivers for almost a year, even putting one into play for two rounds at February's AT&T Pebble Beach National Pro-Am. But he hadn't yet thought about using both during the same tournament. Until now.

On Monday morning at Augusta, he hit the draw driver on the first tee. It soared into the distance with a tight, left-to-right ball flight. On the second hole, a downhill par-five, he hit the cut driver, again producing the desired effect. As Mickelson stepped off the tee box with Mackay and Pelz, he said to his coach, "You know, I'm going to keep doing this all day, just to see how it works."

By the time he made the turn during his Tuesday practice round, he had made a decision. He would play the Masters with both drivers in the bag. He would also do it, just to get used to it, over the next few days at the BellSouth Classic in Atlanta, the lead-in to the Masters.

Getting used to it didn't take long. In Atlanta on Thursday afternoon, Mickelson birdied six of his first seven holes and shot 63. On Friday morning he backed that up with a ho-hum 65.

The early end to Mickelson's Friday round gave him liberty to split town. Just before rush hour he and Mackay jumped into the Explorer and headed north to Athens. By 7:30 they were being seated on the veranda at Five & Ten, on South Lumpkin Street, a couple of blocks from the University of Georgia campus.

To say Five & Ten was the best restaurant in Athens didn't quite do it justice. It was often listed among the ten best restaurants in Atlanta, even though it was seventy miles outside the city limits. Its chef and owner, Hugh Acheson, a 35-year-old Canadian who looked like a harder-working version of Josh Hartnett, had in 2002 been named one of *Food & Wine* magazine's ten best new chefs in the U.S.

Dining with Mickelson and Mackay were Mike Mills and Bill Berry. Mills was the lead guitarist for R.E.M., the unassuming little Athens band that, with fellow locals The B-52's, accidentally conquered large chunks of the music world in the early eighties. Berry, the band's former drummer, retired, for the most part, after an suffering a near-fatal brain aneurysm onstage in 1995. (He still appeared with the band on special occasions.)

Also at the table were Bertis Downs and his wife, Katherine. Downs, 50, was R.E.M.'s longtime manager. Raised in Georgia, he was a lawyer by training, and looked like one: his rock 'n' roll hair had left him long ago, and his heavy brow seemed built to think. It wasn't hard to pick him out in photos of him and the band: he was the one wearing a tie. His manner, however, was anything but staid. His enthusiastic, energetic way of talking was just like Mackay's, which helped explain their long friendship.

Mackay—who lived in Athens before moving to Scottsdale—first met Downs, Mills, and Berry in 1994. A longtime R.E.M. fan, he heard that the two musicians would be playing that year in VH1's "Fairway to Heaven" tournament, an annual charity event bringing together rockers and golfers. Mackay wrote a letter to Downs introducing himself and volunteering his services. He got the gig, and brought his brother, Tom, along for the ride. Jim looped for Berry and Tom for Mills.

Before long Mackay was part of Downs', Mills', and Berry's casual games at Athens Country Club. Mickelson too soon began coming by for social rounds. After Berry's aneurysm, Mackay organized a campaign to lift his spirits, convincing every PGA Tour player who had ever heard of the band to fax get-well wishes to the drummer at the hospital.

As Downs became part of Mickelson's and Mackay's social circle he began throwing a regular Masters Friday dinner party in Augusta. The affair—catered, of course, by Five & Ten owner Acheson—always included Mackay, Couples' caddie, Joe LaCava, and Davis Love's man, Cubby Burke. Couples and Love themselves often came by. That's how those two players, along with Mickelson, became part of Downs' personal "Big Three."

Mickelson grew fond enough of Downs to include him in spur-of-the-moment golf outings. In 2002, Bertis had flown to Scotland for the British Open at Muirfield. The Wednesday of that week was supposed to be a day of pre-tournament rest for Phil, so on Tuesday night Mackay and Downs hit the pubs, and Bones wound up crashing at Downs' rented house. Early the next morning Mackay was in the kitchen eating a piece of toast when his phone rang. It was Mickelson.

"What's up?" he asked.

"Not much," Mackay blearily answered.

"What are you doing?"

"Hanging out with Bert."

"Well," said Mickelson, "I'm going to come over and pick you guys up, and we're going to play St. Andrews."

Two hours later, the three men were standing on the first tee at the Home of Golf.

At home in Athens, Downs was a regular at Five & Ten. He liked the New American fare, but he loved the wine list. Although he pshawed such terms as "connoisseur," he vacationed in places like the Napa Valley, and kept a well-stocked cellar whose most valued items were first-growth Bordeaux from great years.

Downs' oenophilia had always influenced his gift-giving habits. When Davis Love won the 1997 PGA Championship, Downs sent him a vintage bottle from his cellar. Unfortunately, Love didn't realize how special it was, and ended up drinking it with some barbecue. After Mickelson won the 2004 Masters Downs repeated the gesture. Again, it wasn't just any bottle. It was a 1982 Château Margaux, one that (a vulgarian might point out) would retail for about $3,000. Mickelson had never opened it. He told Downs he was waiting for him to come out to San Diego and drink it with him.

Now, at dinner at Five & Ten during BellSouth week, the diners tried not to talk too much about golf. Such is the protocol of dining with a tour pro: after a long day on the course, the last thing he wants to talk about is his game. But with Mickelson trampling the field in Atlanta, they couldn't resist. Downs, in fact, couldn't help pointing ahead to Augusta.

"Wait 'til you see the bottle I'm going to send you if you win the Masters this year," Downs said.

Perhaps the best way to appreciate Augusta National is to stand just outside the main gate on Washington Road and breathe deeply of the ugly, soulless, overcommercialized mess.

The street fronting the club brings together the worst of Main Street, America, from the grimy gas stations to the foul-smelling fast-food joints and hulking valu-marts. Even the strip's church—Whole Life Ministries, directly across from Gate 3, the club's main spectator entrance—is an eyesore. It's still the very same building it was back in the eighties, when it housed a Piggly-Wiggly supermarket.

During Masters week Washington Road turns itself up to eleven. The traffic is impenetrable. Peddlers hawk everything from counterfeit badges to wretched landscape paintings of famous golf holes. The deep fryers are on hyperdrive, and the smell of beef tallow is everywhere. The scene's only levity comes from the religious zealots who occasionally stand outside the club waving homemade poster-board signs and barking about repentance. One particularly memorable sign presented a quirky list of sinners, all marked for eternal damnation. Prominently mentioned were "homos," "democrats," "atheists," and "fornicators"—as if they weren't all the same thing.

Then you shut your eyes, click your heels three times, and you're transported to a different world.

Well, not immediately. First you have to walk through the gates, and past the club's capacious parking lots. After encountering the badge checkers, you enter a long, 300-yard pedestrian mall. Bisecting it, at five- or six-step intervals, is a row of flagpoles flying the colors of the Masters' participants. To the left are buildings dedicated to tournament history and memorabilia. To the right is—well, another monument to crass commercialism, the colossal Masters souvenir shop, selling everything from calendars to Augusta-scented candles.

Gradually the walk narrows, and doglegs slightly to the left. Coming under a canopy of small trees, you pass two more buildings—on the left, the small, white clapboard members' golf shop, and on the right, the gargantuan multi-story press center. Waist-high metal cattle fencing funnels you through another slight bend, and towards a clearing.

Then suddenly—voilà!—everything's gone green.

From the moment you leave the concrete and set foot on the huge, immaculately kept lawn that is the golf course, it's hard to find anything that doesn't partake of the club's signature hue. Sure, there are people and scoreboards and flower beds. But they almost get lost in the oppressive uniformity of the color scheme.

The other striking thing about the National is the vastness of the place. Viewed from the clubhouse (about 100 yards uphill and left of the spectator ingress), the property looks like a big, snowless ski resort. It spills downhill in three directions. To the left, cut into the trees like ski runs, are the 10th and 18th holes. To the far right are the 9th and 1st. In between is a bare valley as wide as a football field (or bunny slope) whose only duty is to feed traffic to other holes.

What people tend to remember about visiting Augusta National are the little things, from the throwback food and beverage prices (hot dogs are $2.00 and beers $3.00) to the smartly positioned spectator mounds, which, along with the restricted spectator numbers, make it the best place in the world to watch a golf tournament. But what makes it visually unique—distinguishing it from every other tournament venue in golf—is so obvious that it's easy to miss. At Augusta, grandstands are scarce, and there are no such things as corporate tents or skyboxes. That's the reason the vistas are so uninterruptedly pure. It's the club's way of demonstrating that this week at least is all about golf, for as far as the eye can see.

It's also the one of the National's many ways of saying that no matter what pressures are applied—economic, political, or otherwise—it remains in full control of everything within its gates. Indeed, its restrictions against what normally happens at Tour events make it the golfdom capital of the word *No*.

For spectators, there is no running. Also, no autographs. Also, no lying down flat on your back. Seriously. Fall asleep and a Pinkerton security guard will march over and wake you up.

No caddie ever thinks about working without a white boiler suit.

For print media, there is no inside-the-ropes access. For CBS, for fifty years the tournament's U.S. broadcasters, there are the famous nomenclature "suggestions." At Augusta there are no "fans" or "crowds" or even "rough"; instead, there are "patrons" and "galleries" and the "first cut." There certainly aren't any "bikini-waxed" greens or "body bags" buried on the 17th hole, as Gary McCord found out in 1995, the last year he participated in a Masters broadcast.

The *Nos* affect even the contestants. For this one week many of the usual privileges of Tour life are rescinded. When the players roll their white courtesy Cadillacs onto Magnolia Lane, they aren't simply waved through; each person in the car must have his or her badge scanned. When they get out of their cars, they must leave their cell phones behind. Coaches cannot walk inside the ropes during practice rounds. Only one person (besides a caddie) can accompany a player onto the practice range. And if a man wearing shorts tries it, he's out of luck. In 2006 Bob Duval, David's dad, was denied the privilege of watching his son hit balls until he changed into long pants.

No player ever complained about such rules—at least not publicly—until a few days after the 2006 tournament. David Toms, referring to the badge scannings as "CIA stuff," said that Augusta was "the only place all year where players don't feel like they're the most important things there." Plenty of players agreed. Privately.

Historically, the most important Augusta National restrictions have been its unspoken exclusionary policies on gender and race. In 2003 activist Martha Burk demanded that the club admit women members, threatening a boycott of Masters corporate sponsors. Then-Chairman Hootie Johnson replied that no one would ever tell the National how to run itself, especially "at the point of a bayonet." The question of race is asked less frequently with each passing year, although little time has passed since 1975, when Lee Elder became the first African-American to compete at Augusta—and even less since 1990, when the first black member was admitted. (In 2003, the last time a membership list appeared before the public eye, there were five.)

The one *No* that never prompts any objections has to do with the way the Masters is televised. CBS's broadcasts are limited to no more than four minutes of advertisements per hour. That, more than anything else, is the reason the tournament earns every year's best golf television ratings, and the reason Minnesotans who've never set foot on a course know every square inch of Augusta's back nine. Sure, there's tradition and excitement. But mostly people love the Masters because they hate commercials.

One of Augusta National's most recognizable features is the 150-year-old live oak on the golf-course side of the clubhouse, near the practice putting green and the first tee. Every spring, golf people—equipment company bigwigs, agents, player friends and families, sports psychologists, swing gurus, big hitters from the governing bodies—renew acquaintance under its sprawling branches. They're joined, of course, by the players themselves, who stop after practice rounds, say their hellos, and feed the media their early-week stories.

On Wednesday, prior to the par-three contest, Tom Lehman recounted perhaps the most harrowing Masters story ever. On Tuesday night he was driving to the airport to pick up his family. An SUV roared by him and he heard what he called a "huge, loud explosion." Later, he found a bullet hole in the rear driver's side door. Had he been on his way home instead of on his way to the airport, his 3-year-old son, Sean, would have been in that seat, he said. (By Wednesday night a 26-year-old Augusta man had been arrested in connection with this and another similar shooting. Lehman's wife was told he bore a grudge against Cadillacs, as opposed to Masters participants.)

Annual recipients of plenty of pre-tournament ink were the Masters rookies. This year there were sixteen. Six were amateurs, whose invitations served to honor the memory of Augusta National founder and life-long amateur Bobby Jones. The foreign-born pros were Geoff Ogilvy; Swedish Ryder Cup hopefuls Carl Pettersson and Henrik Stenson; and Thailand's Thongchai Jaidee, a former paratrooper who had turned pro only seven years earlier. In Jaidee's rooting section at Augusta was his uncle, Charlie Niyomkul—the Atlanta-based restaurateur who, in addition to being one of Vijay Singh's closest friends, also caters the yearly party at Singh's Ponte Vedra home during Players Championship week. (A further coincidence: Niyomkul is also uncle to Thai pro Prom Meesawat, another of Asia's finest players.)

Among the Americans were Lucas Glover, Sean O'Hair, and Ben Crane, the latter of whom brought along a big-name caddie for Wednesday's par-three contest—his Westlake, Texas, neighbor Drew Bledsoe, whose day job was quarterbacking the Dallas Cowboys.

Most of the first-timer attention, however, went to Vaughn Taylor, who, like 2002 rookie Charles Howell, grew up in Augusta. His history at the National was spare. He had played there twice, once each as a freshman and senior during his college days at Augusta State. He attended the tournament twice: in 1986 when Jack Nicklaus won—which, for the media, dovetailed nicely with another big early-week topic, the twentieth anniversary of Nicklaus's last major championship victory—and then in 1987, when it was won by another Augusta native, Larry Mize.

As a player, Taylor had many doubters. He had won twice on Tour, but both those victories both came at the Reno-Tahoe Open, a weak-field event played opposite the richer WGC-NEC Invitational. Still, he had recently registered top tens at two of the toughest tournaments of the year, going for a T4 at the Mercedes Championships and a T8 at the Players. Not that it went to his head. He remained unassuming to a fault. After he mentioned he had his picture taken with Billy Casper back in 1986, reporters suggested that he might try to find Casper, now a non-participating attendee, and remind him of the moment. Taylor's reply? "I don't want to bother him." It was a good thing, because Casper was extremely busy not playing.

The headliners, naturally, were the three players who had recently enjoyed the most Masters success: Phil Mickelson, Chris DiMarco, and Tiger Woods.

Mickelson, of course, had won the Masters two years earlier. He also wound up winning the lead-in BellSouth Classic by a whopping thirteen strokes. He was unquestionably the hottest player on the grounds.

DiMarco had come close to winning the previous two Masters, playing in the final groups with Mickelson in 2004 and Woods in 2005. What made him truly conspicuous, though, was his jubilation over the Florida Gators' NCAA basketball championship victory on Monday night. DiMarco's wardrobe for the week, heavy on the orange, invariably made him look like half a pylon.

His current form was questionable at best. He had missed nearly a month (including the Players Championship) after bruising his ribs, during Bay Hill week, while skiing at Beaver Creek. On his last run of the day he was sideswiped by a pair of speed freaks coming out of the trees; he hurt himself falling onto the hard sunglass case in his backpack. DiMarco had missed the cut in Atlanta, in his first start back. It appeared that he was still feeling the effects of the injury.

The state of Woods' game was also a mystery. His preoccupation with his father's health was abundantly evident during his mediocre performance at the Players, and he had spent the week before the Masters at his dad's bedside in California.

Bob Verdi's post-Masters *Golf World* column related that Earl had "lost 50 or 60 pounds, according to friends, and much of his spirit. For Earl to resist even basic nourishment, to have not dreamed about wanting a smoke in such a long while, you know he's in tough shape. Earl had preferred the recliner, but he's been confined to bed lately. No way he could give Tiger a bear hug now, as he did after the landmark Masters victory in 1997."

Woods himself said little about the situation, except that Pops was "fighting." The only loss he seemed ready to concede, in the midst of a year that would be full of transitions, was that of confidants John Cook, 48, and Mark O'Meara, 49, to the Champions Tour.

On Monday Woods played a practice round with O'Meara, whose 1998 green jacket guaranteed him an early-week spot alongside Tiger at the Masters for years to come. All year Mark's game had been in disrepair, not least because of his split, back in March, with longtime coach Hank Haney. (The reason, O'Meara later said, was that Haney, now Woods instructor, "just didn't have enough time" to work with both of them.) Deep down, Woods felt for his friend. But he would never openly admit it. He preferred, in fact, to teasingly suggest that O'Meara was no longer up to Augusta's challenge.

"Hey, Mo," Tiger said as the two stepped off the tee box on the 9th hole. "How much longer are you going to keep playing in this thing? What am I going to do when you're gone? Who am I going to play practice rounds with?"

"I'll keep playing here as long as you give me a ride up on your plane," O'Meara said.

Woods nodded, and readied another needle—this one implying that Mark wouldn't be making many more Masters cuts. "Okay, I'll do that," he said. "But you're going to have to keep going home on your own."

(Knowing his closest friends were about to move on, Woods, in fact, was already recruiting replacements. The following day he and O'Meara played with Sean O'Hair, who was becoming a regular beside Woods at regular Tour stops, during practice rounds, and in the players' dining area.)

Despite all the other plots and subplots, the Masters run-up was dominated by one story, the ongoing changes to the golf course. Since 1997, the year Woods won his first green jacket, it had packed on a whopping 520 yards. Other changes had included the addition of rough in 1999, and the continual reshaping and relocation of bunkers.

Of those 520 yards, 155 debuted in 2006. Five holes were affected. Oddly, the par-four 11th, the hole that added the fewest yards that year (15), received the most attention.

On Wednesday, Johnson used his annual State of the Masters press conference to illustrate why the club insisted on lengthening the course. He said that back in 1998 he had personally watched Phil Mickelson clobber a 300-yard drive at the 11th, leaving himself only ninety-four yards in. "The hole wasn't intended to play like that," Johnson intoned. "I believe Hogan is quoted as saying, 'If you ever see me on that green, you know I've missed my shot.' Well, if Hogan was hitting a damn pitching wedge, he wouldn't have been to the right of the green. He'd have been within three feet of the cup."

Added distance wasn't the only alteration to the hole. The club also planted about five dozen pines on the right side, significantly narrowing the landing area. "If someone wants to swing from the heels and hit it 330 or 340, he'd better be accurate," Johnson declared through clenched teeth.

The backlash against the changes began long before the azaleas began to bloom. Arnold Palmer and Jack Nicklaus both panned them months before the tournament, at a *Golf Digest* function. "I love the place," Palmer said. "But now I'm not so sure. There are some things that are taking the realistic Augusta away."

Nicklaus was less polite. "I still like the course, but I think they've ruined it from a tournament standpoint," he said. "They've totally eliminated what Bobby Jones tried to do in the game of golf."

That last comment spoke volumes. Nothing hurt the Augusta brass more than by saying they had betrayed their inspiration, polestar, and patron saint.

Jones' stated intention in building Augusta National was to create an American St. Andrews. To him and architectural collaborator Alister MacKenzie, that meant a golf course with a premium on strategy and creativity. Ideally, the course would play hard and fast. The greens would be devilish, designed to hold only approaches of the correct trajectory and spin. The fairways would be wide—not to forgive poor driving, but to provide different angles into the green, the preferability of which would depend on a particular day's pin position.

Nicklaus didn't spell out how he thought the changes betrayed Jones' vision, but others did.

"It is less strategic," Bernhard Langer, a two-time Masters winner, told *The Times* of London. "Before they added rough, the strategy off the tees was whether you wanted to be on the left side of the fairway or the right and what angle you wanted to come in from to the green. That has been taken away now because the fairways are narrow. On the 11th, you used to have the option to go way left or way right. I used to argue with Seve [Ballesteros] as to which side was better to come into the green. Now the right side is taken away from us. It seems as though they have taken 40 or 50 yards away from the fairway. The angles are taken out of the tee shot."

A broader concern was how the changes would affect the overall character of the tournament. The longer the course played, the harder it became for shorter hitters to keep up—especially when it rained, which, at this time of year, was often. (Indeed, the Masters' April date militated against Jones' and MacKenzie's vision of a hard and fast golf course.)

Further, a scoring-resistant Augusta limited the back-nine fireworks so beloved by Dan Jenkins and everyone else. Now, on the anniversary of Jack Nicklaus's epic 1986 back-nine charge, it was hard to believe such a rally was still possible.

"It was easier to make a big move in the past," Jim Furyk said. "You could be very aggressive. Guys took more aggressive lines when they had shorter clubs in their hands. That's why you saw more birdies. Now you'll see a more conservative style of play."

Did the short-hitting Furyk still think he could win? "Yeah, I feel like I can win," he said. "But it sure as hell wouldn't be any fun."

All told, the changes brought the Masters closer to the U.S. Open and PGA Championship, whose philosophies favored clearly demarcated shot values over creativity and imagination. In other words, the club had superimposed on Jones and MacKenzie's ideal the dominant ideology of American golf. Never mind Toms' complaints. This was the most pernicious way that Augusta was telling the players how to behave.

Notwithstanding Tom Lehman's early-week shoot-up, the 70th Masters opened not with a bang, but with a series of thuds: hundreds of golf balls falling to earth, hitting rock-hard surfaces, and bouncing off to places they were never intended to go. Only three players broke 70, and twelve failed to break 80. The 11th, unsurprisingly, was the hardest hole of the day, playing to a stroke average of 4.47, bearing out pre-tournament jokes that it was now a nice little par-five.

The leader, after an impressive five-under 67, was Vijay Singh. Rocco Mediate trailed by one. Tiger Woods had a so-so day: despite holing out an 8-iron on the 14th for an eagle, he posted a 72. Apart from the leaders, Mickelson stole most of the attention, mainly because of the way he swashbuckled around the course with his two drivers. He hit a cut where he needed to, but otherwise pulled the longer club, using it to great effect. (He would ultimately lead the field in driving distance for the week.) On the 14th, a 440-yard par-four that doglegs slightly left, he set up on the extreme right of the tee box, with his feet on the long grass, and his rear end brushing the gallery ropes. He had to ask a half-dozen people to relocate themselves and their lawn chairs so he could swing away with Daly-esque abandon.

Singh's low score was the result of a long week of work, during which, in the words of one crony, "the man made the most drastic changes I've ever seen, all in a few days, preparing for the biggest tournament of the year."

After his nightmare final round of 77 at Sawgrass, his caddie, Paul Tesori, suggested that he do something Singh hated: go to the videotape. "Veej, maybe you want to look at your swing on this," he said as his man seethed in the parking lot on Sunday night. The following morning Vijay, Tesori, and Farid Guedra, Singh's longtime friend and part-time tutor, were at the back of the range at the very same course, filming and analyzing his action.

What was wrong was not the "flatness" that people usually perceived (his first move down always involved a flattening of his swing plane). The problem—and the reason it looked flat to everyone—was the height of the backswing. His hands had gotten too low and too close to his body.

Now, during the first round, he looked like a different person. His club was upright and his hands higher at the top. His confidence, moreover, looked unshakeable.

It didn't last. His second-round 74 included three double bogeys. Still, because of difficult conditions—gusty, swirling winds that chilled the air and scattered the course with leaves, making it feel and look like fall—he didn't lose much ground. He finished the day in a tie for second, with

Rocco Mediate and Fred Couples. Passing them all was Chad Campbell, whose low, hard West Texas windcheaters propelled him to a 67.

Before Friday Campbell had been enjoying a quiet week, lazing around a rented house with his brother Mike, the head golf coach at Abilene Christian University, and his caddie and pal, Judd Burkett. Now, back in Campbell's hometown of Andrews, Texas (population 10,000), things were far less subdued. "We've heard from neighbors, friends, people we haven't talked to in years," Campbell's mom, Patsy, told a golf writer from her home state. "We're hopeful to be down there this weekend."

His father, Phillip, an oil field supervisor, listened to the satellite radio broadcast in his Chevy 4x4 while checking on rigs. "I've got XM in my pickup," he told Kansas City reporter Wright Thompson. "I call [Patsy] every time something good happens."

While Phillip, Patsy, and Chad's wife, Amy, were preparing to come out to Augusta, forty-three golfers were getting ready to leave.

The cut-missers included DiMarco and David Duval. The lone bright spot of DiMarco's sojourn was his hole-out eagle on his thirty-sixth and final hole. His finish was ironic, since a mere birdie on that hole on Sunday in 2005, either in regulation or in the playoff, would have won him the Masters. The reporters behind 18 were quick to pick up on it. "What would you give to have done that last year?" one of them asked.

DiMarco's hands were resting on the shoulders of his 10-year-old son, Cristian. He paused for a moment, then pushed him forward. "See ya, boy," he said.

As the reporters laughed, DiMarco pulled Cristian back, leaning over his shoulder and saying, "Just kidding."

"You better be," Cristian frowned.

Merely to say that David Duval missed the cut was to underappreciate the strangest 36 holes Augusta had ever seen. His opening 84 was wild (on the 12th, he made a 9), but his Friday round was positively bipolar.

It started with a double bogey on the 1st. On the 2nd, a long, downhill par-five, his tee shot hooked through the azaleas bordering the fairway, bounded into a small forest, and wound up in a little creek whose existence was previously known only to the club's superintendent. Duval took a penalty drop. (That's two.) Trying to punch out, his ball hit a hazard stake and settled in some nearby pine straw. (Three.) His next hit a tree and ricocheted back into the woods. (Four.) Deeming his lie unplayable, he dropped again. (Five.) He hit another tree (six), then finally reached a greenside bunker (seven), splashed out (eight), and two-putted (ten). No Masters participant had ever made a higher score on the hole. Duval went to the third tee 19-over for his first twenty holes.

Duval's career at the Masters now seemed certain to end in ignominy. This was the last year of his five-year exemption from his win at the 2001 British Open, and the way he was playing strongly hinted that he wouldn't be back. Then, miraculously, he recovered. He played his next seven holes in even par. Making the turn, he morphed into the player he was back in 1999, splitting fairways, hitting it close, and burying putts. He wound up shooting a back-nine 32, the best single side of the tournament.

After signing his card, Duval was immediately surrounded by his family and his coach, Puggy Blackmon. As he neared the clubhouse a clutch of writers was waiting under the oak tree. Thinking twice, he stopped in front of them, only to find that they too were at a loss for words.

Finally someone summoned up a question.

"David, on number 2 . . ."

Duval started to smile.

"To begin with, what did you hit . . ."

"What didn't he hit?" Blackmon interrupted.

"The fairway," cracked Duval, not missing a beat.

Everyone laughed. Then came a long pause. Duval seized the opportunity afforded by the silence.

"Thanks, guys," he said, and turned and walked away.

Friday afternoon also brought the first verdicts on the course changes. Most thought they were a great success. In the *New York Times,* Damon Hack wrote that for the first time in five years, Augusta National played like the "giant pool table" it is supposed to be. The presence in the top ten of relative short-hitters Mediate and Tim Clark (T4) allayed fears—at least temporarily—that only a power player could win on the lengthened layout.

It was clear, however, that the changes had also adversely affected the experience of watching the tournament. The removal of a walkway behind the first tee—necessitated when the tee box was moved back flush against the practice putting green—completely eliminated one of the primary access routes to the golf course. The new trees on the 11th hole led the *Atlanta Journal-Constitution*'s Furman Bisher to complain, "They've planted a black forest between you and the fairway"—one that made it impossible to view approach shots unless you were standing near the green.

"Spectating at the Masters," concluded *Sports Illustrated*'s Gary Van Sickle, "has never been more difficult, or less rewarding."

On Saturday the inevitable happened. It began to rain. Play was called shortly after 1:00 p.m. The last nine pairings had yet to tee off. The stoppage would last four hours and fifteen minutes.

Weather delays at Augusta aren't exciting, but they're not always boring, either. Stories are told, laughs are had, and, once in a great while, a fistfight almost breaks out.

Back in 2005, on Friday, Vijay Singh was playing one group behind Phil Mickelson. During his round, he became convinced the greens were being damaged by Mickelson's eight-millimeter metal spikes, two millimeters longer than conventional models. On the 12th green he complained to two rules officials, who approached Mickelson about it.

Shortly thereafter, play was called because of rain. Singh and Mickelson both went to the Champions Locker Room, where they nearly came to blows. Singh was sitting at one of the card tables when Mickelson entered and took a seat at one of the others. Immediately they exchanged angry glances. Looking on were the likes of Jack Nicklaus, Tom Watson, Billy Casper, Fred Couples, and Tiger Woods.

Mickelson quickly confronted Singh. He used the same language that would appear that evening in a statement to the press: "I was extremely distracted and would have appreciated if it would have been handled differently or after the round." In the locker room, however, his line reading was far more animated.

Singh didn't back down. "All you had to do was take your time and tamp down your spike marks!" he growled. With that, Mickelson got up and moved around the tables to address Singh directly.

After they exchanged a few choice words, Couples intervened. He had been lying on the same bench on which Mickelson would take his 2006 Sunday nap. He bounced up and said, "Hey! I've been in here since 1992, and I have never heard language like that in this locker room!"

Just as he finished, an official came in and said, "Gentlemen, it looks like there's quite a bit of rain coming in. The delay will probably be longer than we initially thought."

From deep left field, Casper cracked, "I guess now you guys are all going to have to play in longer spikes." The interruptions cut the tension and effectively ended the row.

The 2006 rain delay was less eventful. It started, for most players, with lunch. Mickelson ate upstairs with Dave Pelz, Rick Smith, Casper and his son Bob, and 1971 winner Charles Coody and his son, Kyle. Phil's meal included what a nearby diner reported to be a five-scoop sundae. (This, after all, was a man whose 2005 Tuesday night Champions Dinner—lobster ravioli and garlic bread—concluded with pints of vanilla Häagen-Dazs, with spoons stuck in the tops, being placed in front of each diner.)

Afterward, Mickelson returned to the locker room. Vijay Singh was already there. On this day, too, Lefty, along with Darren Clarke, had been playing in the group ahead of Singh. The stage was set for a rematch. But Mickelson short-circuited any possible complaints. "Vijay," he smiled, "just so you know, those weren't my spike marks. I wear only five spikes on my shoes, and the shoes that made those marks had seven. They were Darren's."

Play resumed at about 5:20 p.m., leaving plenty of time for significant movement on the leaderboard. Ben Crenshaw, who had posted surprisingly solid first and second rounds, disappeared from view. More important, Rocco Mediate and Tim Clark both drew within one stroke of Campbell.

Mediate, 43, was a five-time Tour winner whose career was defined by injury. In 1994, his ninth year on Tour, he ruptured a vertebral disc. So uncertain was his future that he took out a sizeable Lloyds of London policy on his back, but it acted up so frequently that Lloyds soon terminated the coverage. There were still days when he played world-class golf, but there were just as many when he could be found at home, crawling upstairs to his bedroom, after an ill-advised attempt to practice.

Lately his primary pastime had been poker. He participated in the 2005 World Series, finishing about 600th in a 5,619-player field. Now, in 2006 in Augusta, he spent his evenings playing online, getting tips from one of his houseguests, 2004 World Series winner Greg "Fossilman" Raymer.

Clark, 30, was an old hand at the Masters. A South African who attended North Carolina State, he first played in 1998, the year after winning the U.S. Public Links. He now lived in Scottsdale with his American girlfriend, Candace, a well-liked young woman with a serious sudoku addiction. Asked by a reporter earlier in the year what he did while Candace worked her puzzles, he answered, "Mostly I sit around in my underwear and watch television." The most distinctive thing about him was his waddly walk. It had earned him the nickname "Penguin," which he'd come to regard fondly. "One day," he once joked, "I'll have to play a tournament in a tuxedo." So far, this one looked ideal.

A big question going into Sunday was how Campbell would hold up. It would be a long day. Plus, ten of the world's best players, including Woods, Mickelson, and Singh, were within three of his lead. When asked about having to cover thirty-two holes on Sunday, he showed a rare glimpse of wit, replying, "It's not like we have to run." But that wasn't the real issue. Chris DiMarco's Sunday morning meltdown just one year earlier served as a reminder that the trick wasn't keeping one's breath. It was keeping one's nerve.

Sunday morning came early, earliest of all for Vijay Singh.

At 4:30 a.m. Big Daddy and his trainer, Joey Diovalsalvi, opened the door of a local gym, using the key the manager had given them on Monday. It was about an hour earlier than they had arrived every other day that week. Their 90-minute workout included 20 minutes on the stationary bike, a full stretch, and some band work, with Singh working against his trainer's resistance on six different swing planes.

Not that everyone else slept in. Tiger Woods was the first player on the National's practice grounds. By 6:30 a.m. he was hitting putts in front of the clubhouse, under the floodlights, with Steve Williams by his side and a lone Augusta National grounds crew member mowing the green around them. Jim Mackay was there, too, waiting for his man, who arrived about fifteen minutes later with coach Rick Smith.

Play restarted at 7:45, with the leaders on the 5th hole, and Mickelson on the 6th.

Woods started on the 10th, which in two ways was the best spot on the golf course. The first was aesthetic. A little secret about Augusta— one that few pros or members are in on—is that the optimal way to play the course is to begin on the 10th tee in early April just prior to 8 a.m. If you do, you wind up walking up the big hill on the 11th fairway just as the sun starts streaming over the trees behind the 12th, bathing Amen Corner in a dewy, diffuse, magical light. The scene only presents itself at a certain time of day, and on certain days of the year. But when it does, it's the prettiest panorama in all of golf.

The other was psychological. Just 364 days earlier Woods began his day in nearly the same place, and blew by leader Chris DiMarco, turning a four-stroke deficit to a three-stroke lead.

Now, in 2006, Woods opened with a birdie on the 10th, and it looked like it might be déjà vu all over again. But on 11 he rinsed his approach and made bogey. He added three more bogeys on the way in, eventually signing for a back-nine 37.

Behind him, Campbell too was faltering, and Mickelson took advantage. His third-round 70 wasn't overwhelming, but it was good enough to get him to –4 for the tournament, one better than Campbell and Fred Couples, who, finishing earlier than Campbell, was awarded a spot in the final group.

Couples in the final pairing was a transgenerational crowd-pleaser. Like peak-period Cary Grant, he was gray enough to please the older crowd, but cool enough to please the kids. One bonus, for their group, was that he and Mickelson were friends. Indeed, the players and their caddies, Mackay and Joe LaCava, were as chummy as any four men on Tour. (As usual, Bones and Joey were rooming together that week.) Another was that a certain 20-year-old record would be at stake. Couples, slightly older than Nicklaus was in 1986, had a chance to become the oldest man ever to win the Masters.

To be sure, it was a quality leaderboard. Right behind Mickelson, Couples, and Campbell were Clark, Singh, Mediate, and Woods. Still, it had been a strange Masters. Birdies, as everyone predicted, were now harder to come by. (In the end, 2006 would see fewer birdies than all but sixteen of the tournament's sixty-one editions.) When players moved up the leaderboard, they most often did so because of other players' bogeys. But that didn't make the golf any less riveting. On the contrary, it seemed like every shot weighed that much more heavily on the outcome.

Just before 11 a.m. Bertis Downs was standing outside the First Presbyterian Church in Athens. A friend, also a golf fan, approached him and said, "Looks like it's going to be Mickelson and Couples in the final group."

Wow, Downs thought. That would be like Christmas morning.

He sat through the services slightly distracted. When he walked back outside at 12:05 p.m., his phone rang. It was Mackay.

"Are you coming?" he asked.

"Are Phil and Fred in the final group?"

"Yeah. Their time is 2:50."

"Well, yeah, I'm coming!" Downs answered.

Still in his church clothes, Downs kissed his wife and kids, got into his car, and headed southeast on State Road 78. His phone rang again.

"Bert, do you have tickets?" Mackay asked.

"No, but I'll figure something out."

"Okay. Let me call you back."

Two minutes later, Mackay phoned again.

"It's all set. There will be a ticket waiting for you at the front gate."

It was about 1:55 p.m. when Couples finished changing his shoes. He slammed his locker shut, and Mickelson's eyes sprang open. Phil got up, wiped his eyes, changed his shirt, and hustled downstairs to warm up.

Fresh legs weren't the only thing Mickelson had going for him. History was also on his side.

Beginning in 1991 every Masters winner had come out of the final pairing. Even better, only four times during that stretch had someone other than the third-round leader gone on to win the golf tournament. These recent precedents suggested that no one had to wait for the back nine for the Masters to begin; in fact, it was more or less over when Mickelson stepped off the green after his third round.

But they played golf anyway. Spain's Miguel Angel Jiménez made some early noise, birdieing three of his first five holes to climb into a tie for the lead. His ascent inspired a pressroom wisecrack contest. One scribbler remarked that Miguel was exacting revenge for U.S. Customs officials having relieved him, seven days earlier, of his stash of beloved Cubanos. Another riffed on his legendary Spafro, saying that if he won, the National would have to order stronger conditioner for the locker room.

As the round progressed, Clark stayed in touch but never threatened the lead. The same was true of Woods, who three-putted three times (six on the week), and missed 12-footers for eagle on both 13 and 15. He came off the 18th saying, rightly, that he had putted "atrociously."

"I felt so in control of my ball from tee to green, and once I got on the green I was a spaz," he added. (Much to Woods' surprise, the remark sparked an international incident: when a British writer pointed out that the term, overseas, insults the handicapped, Woods was forced to issue an apology.)

Mediate remained in the hunt until he reached the 11th. As he hit his approach, his back "went psycho," as he put it, seizing up and making it all but impossible for him to play. He made bogey there, and then made a 10 on the 12th, depositing three balls into Rae's Creek, sending him from three-under to irrelevance.

Singh was on Mickelson's tail until the back nine, where he too suddenly found himself incapable of making a putt. (He had 19 on that side alone.) His three putts on the 16th were the end of his chances.

Couples provided the day's only drama. His birdie on the 1st tied Mickelson for the lead. The two walked in lockstep, at −4, and then −5 through the next six holes (accompanied in the lead at different points by Jiménez, Mediate, and a late-charging José María Olazábal). After matching birdies at the 7th, they bumped fists like teammates. Mickelson pulled ahead with a birdie at the 8th, and Couples handed him another stroke when he bogeyed the 11th.

Couples remained two back until the par-four 14th, where he drilled a short iron to four feet above the hole, giving himself a chance to cut Mickelson's lead to one. But the putt wasn't a gimme. It was a tricky little slider. As he got over the ball, there was dead silence, save for the distant sound of a barking dog.

The putt grazed the lip and rolled five feet past the hole. Too firm. The comebacker, an uphill five-footer, was easier, but Couples hit this one too softly, and it dove off to the right before reaching the hole. Freddie couldn't believe it, and neither could Mickelson. Walking off the green, Phil had taken it for granted that his friend would make par. But now, catching the miss out of the corner of his eye, he stood up straight with surprise.

"I was nervous and I got a little jumpy," Couples later admitted. "That was pretty much the ballgame for me." He was right. Mickelson was now three shots clear of his nearest pursuers.

In the end, Couples, like Woods and Singh, was undone by his putter. On the week, he ranked forty-fourth out of forty-seven players in the putting stats. He too had six three-putts. A sharp contrast were his ballstriking stats: he ranked second in driving distance and led the field in greens in regulation.

As Mickelson hit his tee ball on 18, he still had a three-shot cushion. So he wasn't all that perturbed when he found his ball in the first cut on top of a twig. Calmly he settled over the ball and sent it sailing toward the pin.

At that moment Billy Casper was sitting on the left side of the green, in one of the folding chairs he and his son had planted there, reserving their spots, much earlier in the day. As the ball flew through the air, he thought to himself, Phil's going to walk up here and knock his ball in the hole and I'm not going to have a chance to say a word to him.

Then, just like that, Mickelson's ball was at Casper's feet. It had drifted left, the twig having added some unwanted sidespin. When Mickelson arrived, Casper was standing. He had to be, since the marshals were clearing the area so Phil could play his shot.

"You just had to hit it over here, didn't you?" Casper asked, taking Mickelson's arm with one hand, and patting him on the back with the other.

"That's right, Billy." Phil smiled, grabbing Casper by his arm.

A chip and two putts later. Mickelson had a two-stroke victory, and his second green jacket. The moment, bereft of drama, could not have been more unlike 2004. This time there was no airless, splay-legged leap, no "Oh my God," and no "Can you believe it?" This time, everyone believed it. There was nothing about Mickelson's victory that wasn't utterly convincing.

Instead, he simply removed his visor, said, "Thanks, man," to Couples, hugged Mackay, shook hands with LaCava, and waited for his kids to start climbing all over him.

After signing his card, Mickelson headed to the Butler Cabin for CBS's version of the green jacket ceremony. Mackay was coming off the green when he spotted Bertis Downs, who was all smiles. Bones took his friend inside, where they watched Woods slip the jacket over Mickelson's shoulders.

Next was the more elaborate ceremony on the practice green, where the two found a spot behind the rows of golf dignitaries visiting from around the world. In the fading light, with flashes now attached to the photographers' cameras, Woods put the jacket on Mickelson once again. After he did, Mickelson repaid the favor.

"I'd like to take one moment to ask if we could all say a little prayer tonight," Mickelson said. "Tiger's father is not feeling well. We all know how important parents are in our lives."

Mickelson then went to the press center. For twenty minutes he answered questions, with the television hanging in the corner of the room improbably tuned to a *60 Minutes* profile of Michelle Wie.

Afterward, as the pundits settled in at their desks to coin the term "Mickelslam," the 2006 champion climbed into a golf cart. A tournament official drove him back toward the clubhouse, steering the cart parallel to the first fairway, through the spillway where spectators catch their first big view of the golf course, and then around the white clapboard pro shop.

While Mickelson was with the media, Downs and Mackay had been packing up his gear and pulling his car around. Now they were standing there waiting to hand over the keys, getting ready to say their goodbyes, both to Phil and to each other. Mickelson saw them from the golf cart.

"What are you doing?" he asked, stepping down.

"Waiting to get out of here," Mackay said.

"No you're not," Mickelson said. "You're both coming to the Champion's Dinner."

Just earlier, Amy Mickelson had had a similar exchange with Dave Pelz. Pelz and his son Eddie (who also served as his father's aide-de-camp) were on their way to their plane, waiting for them at the little airfield near the municipal course, when Amy called to issue the same invitation.

None of the three—Downs, Mackay, or Pelz—had attended the Sunday night Champion's Dinner in 2004. Mackay had gone straight home because his wife, Jennifer, was nine months pregnant with their first child. Pelz and Downs had also rushed off. This year, Phil and Amy made sure it didn't happen again.

The Sunday Champion's Dinner took place, as it always did, in the Trophy Room, the club's principal dining room. Inside were ten large tables, each accommodating eight to ten people. Eight of the tables were occupied by Augusta members and tournament officials. At the ninth were Phil and Amy, Mickelson's parents, and, from Augusta National, Hootie Johnson and competitions chairman Will Nicholson, along with their wives.

At the tenth were Downs, Mackay, Rick and Tricia Smith, Dave and Eddie Pelz, Sean Cochran (Mickelson's trainer), and Amy's parents, the McBrides.

Toasts were made and dinner was served. The wine was a California cabernet that Downs later described as "very nice" but whose name did not stick in his mind. Halfway into the meal Downs felt a hand on his left shoulder. It was Mickelson, who all of the sudden was addressing the room. He said, "Two years ago, after I won the Masters, my friend Bertis sent me an incredible bottle of wine. I just want to say that it better be a good one this time, too."

A few days later, lounging at his home in Rancho Santa Fe, Mickelson heard the doorbell ring. He answered it and signed for a package. It was from Downs. He took it into his kitchen, put it on the counter, and opened it. Inside were two bottles. One was a magnum, and a rare one at that: it was 1982 Château La Tour, one of the most prized wines in the world. It was accompanied by a smaller bottle, a 1995 Harlan Estates Bordeaux blend, a personal favorite of Downs'.

The card read: "Looking forward to your next win. I think my cellar can stand to lose a few more bottles."

Mickelson had no idea what to do with a bottle like the La Tour. But eventually he hit on one.

A week and a half after the Masters, he was vacationing in Cabo San Lucas, a resort town in Mexico, at the tip of the Baja Peninsula. With him was his friend Mack Brown, head coach of the University of Texas football team.

Toward the end of 2003, the worst year of Mickelson's life both on and off the golf course, he had dined with Brown in San Diego while Texas was in town to play the Holiday Bowl. They made a pact. They promised each other that the following year Mickelson would win the Masters, Brown's Longhorns would win the BCS title, and they would go down to Cabo together to celebrate.

But it didn't happen. Brown didn't hold up his end of the bargain. But Texas won the National Championship in January of 2006, and Mickelson again won the Masters, so off to Cabo they went. Inside Mickelson's luggage was Bert's bottle of wine.

After dinner one evening, Mickelson told Brown about Downs, handed him the bottle, and said, "Let's make another deal. I've put

Bertis's name in one corner, and I signed it in another corner. You can sign the third. Then, Mack, when you have a friend who does something special—whether it's a coach who's just won a high school championship, or a friend whose kid's just gotten straight A's and gotten into Harvard, or whatever it is—you have him sign the other corner, and we'll all get together and drink this big bottle of wine."

7

THE KATRINA CLASSIC

The Zurich Classic, New Orleans

Late one Sunday evening, four days before the start of the Zurich Classic in New Orleans, Tommy Toefield sat behind the big, wooden counter at Art Accent Tattoo and Piercings, watching *SportsCenter* on the TV hanging over the shop door. He was working late because . . . well, because late is when a lot of people get tattoos. A couple of browsers had been in and out, but right now there were only three people in the shop—Toefield and two artists, who were hanging out in the back. Then, at about 11:30 p.m., the door opened. The man who stepped inside looked like a lot of French Quarter tourists. He was wearing shorts and an untucked golf shirt. But he was bigger than most—six-foot-four, Toefield guessed. He was fit, but with a belly that seemed borrowed from a different, softer body. He was carrying his flip-flops in his hands and he looked scared.

This man didn't browse. He came straight to the counter. He had been out on Bourbon Street, he explained, having a few drinks, trying to have a little fun. He'd gotten into a little trouble and no longer had his wallet or cell phone. Why were his flip-flops in his hands? Because barefoot, it was easier to run. He wanted to call the police, he said, not so much to report a crime, but because he had no other way to get home.

Toefield dialed the local precinct for him and handed him the phone.

While the man talked to the police, Toefield—a trim, good-looking 40-year-old, with short dark hair, a chinstrap beard, and small neo-primitive discs in his earlobes—didn't think all that much about the situation. This, after all, was New Orleans. Besides, the kind of trouble tourists got into seemed mild to him. He grew up in the city—you could tell from his Yat accent, which made him, and fellow natives, sound like Alabamans trying to talk like Brooklynites. He left home early and bounced around the streets until being informally adopted by Jacqueline Toefield, who'd opened Art Accent back in the seventies. He inherited a brother, Gregory (who his mom called Boobie), with whom Tommy now ran the shop. No one ever guessed they were related, since Tommy was white and Gregory black.

The man finished up his conversation with the police while standing near the counter, in front of a showcase full of rings, bars, and other bits of metal designed to decorate every place on a person's body, from ears and nipples to bellybuttons and points south.

Toefield took back the phone and chatted briefly with the man about Art Accent's 40-year history, and Faith Hill's and Tim McGraw's visits to the shop. Then he watched him putter around, waiting for the cops to arrive. It was, if anything, a visually rich environment. The walls were Carnival colors, gold with green and purple trim. Across from his counter were an ATM and big swinging panels—the kind you'd see in poster shops—filled with tattoo designs. On the same wall was a still from the old Clint Eastwood movie *Tightrope,* one of whose scenes had been filmed in the shop. Nearer the door was a white bench and a magazine rack whose contents, depending on the week, ranged from *Family Circle* and *Self* to *Budget Traveler* and *Inked.*

The man flipped through a couple of magazines and dipped into the fishbowl of lollipops on the counter—the kind of candy stash every tattoo parlor keeps to raise a customer's blood sugar if he or she starts to feel faint.

Finally, after about a half hour, the police arrived and escorted the man out. Toefield closed up for the night. Days passed. As the weekend approached the town was revving up for JazzFest. A golf tournament was going on, too. Toefield was mildly aware of it because of ads in the newspaper and on television.

The following Sunday night he was in the same spot, behind the counter, watching *SportsCenter* again. After a while the anchors got to the golf highlights. When the winner's face appeared on the screen, a weird feeling came over him.

Jeez, he said to himself. That guy looks familiar.

The next morning, back behind at the counter with his coffee, he was flipping through the newspaper's sports section. He stopped dead at a picture of Chris Couch with his arms held high in triumph.

Holy shit, Toefield thought. That's the guy who came in here last week to call the cops.

Chris Couch's golf shirt was neatly tucked into his neatly pressed pants as he stood behind the 18th green earlier that Sunday evening, getting ready to go up and accept his surfboard-sized Zurich Classic winner's check. He had just canned a miracle chip shot for his first PGA Tour victory, one he doubted would ever come. The $1.08 million almost tripled what he'd made on the PGA Tour since turning pro in 1995.

Couch walked back onto the green behind the Joe Simon Jazz Band. The horns were blowing and the big bass drum thumping. Raining down from the grandstands were Mardi Gras beads of green, purple, and gold, the same colors Couch had seen on the walls at that tattoo parlor. He might have taken it as a private reminder of how his week had started out.

He stood alongside the tournament officials as they made their short speeches. Then it was his turn. He gathered himself, adopted the Tour-preferred manner of the gentleman golfer, and delivered all the necessary thank-yous, concluding with the head greenskeeper, whose name someone had written down for him on a little cheat sheet. He paused for effect and whispered, "I have just one more thing to say." Then he leaned back and let his inner Bourbon Street reveler reemerge, yowling a wild, five-second "*Whoooo!*" that almost blew out the PA system, and screaming, "*Let's party!*"

In a way, the outburst seemed wildly inappropriate. New Orleans was trying to recover from one of the worst disasters in U.S. history. Large swaths of the city were devastated. The Toefields had all lost their homes. So had over 200,000 others. Art Accent had since reopened, but hundreds, if not thousands, of other businesses were still closed. Since the storm, damage estimates had gone from $25 billion to $125 billion to, well, incalculable. A $250 million aid bill lay dormant on Capitol Hill. Tommy Toefield was only one of many natives so affected by the tragedy that he commemorated it by having tattooed, on his left leg, the now iconic Katrina cross.

On the other hand, Couch's party whoop sounded just the right note. The tournament had been touted as an important step forward in New Orleans' economic recovery. But more than that, it was an excuse for the city to look away, however briefly, from its problems. Couch's unreflective determination to have a good time, looked, at that moment, to be just what Dr. John ordered.

It was something of a miracle that the tournament was played in the first place. Its future was uncertain as late as mid-November, five and a half months before it would be staged. Zurich, the title sponsor, had agreed to return (there was an out-clause in their four-year contract), but venue questions abounded. In 2005 it had been played at the brand-new TPC of Louisiana, in Avondale. But that course, built on low-lying land, now lay in ruins, as did every tournament-worthy course in the area, except for one. English Turn Golf and Country Club, across the Mississippi in a relatively unharmed part of the West Bank, had hosted sixteen prior editions of the tournament. The PGA Tour decided to come back to New Orleans in 2006 only when the club agreed to host it. "It was our only option," said Mike Rodrigue, chairman of the Fore!Kids Foundation, which ran the event.

The Tour's return to New Orleans was indisputably good news. The first major sporting event since Katrina, it was expected to have a $25 million impact on the city's economy. That figure was dwarfed, of course, by the $250 million impact of JazzFest. But four days of national television coverage (with the weekend on CBS) would help send a message that the city was up and running and open for business.

To further that end, the Tour used the event to promote corporate interest in recovery efforts. It moved its annual Commissioner's Cup—a pro-am gathering executives from some of its leading sponsors—to New Orleans, scheduling it for the Monday and Tuesday of tournament week. It also organized a business forum for those two mornings, inviting Rudy Giuliani and Louisiana Governor Kathleen Blanco to address its guests. On Monday, in a suite at the Windsor Court Hotel, Giuliani began his remarks by making an almost obligatory 9/11 comparison, saying that parts of the city reminded him of the World Trade Center site after the attacks. He hastened to add, however, that New Orleans' devastation was on a "much bigger scale."

Three for three for three: Ashley, Ella and Stuart Appleby collect Stuey's third straight Mercedes Championships trophy at Kapalua. (Mia would arrive two months later.)
Reuters/Wire Image

It's always something: Michelle Wie asks playing partners Chris Couch and Camilo Villegas to let her take a scuffed ball out of play during the first round at the Sony Open. They declined. Marco Garcia, Wire Image

A Hono-lulu of a victory: David Toms finishing off his win at the Sony Open.
Robert Laberge, Getty Images

Tiger and Earl: the world's best player and his father in one of their last public appearances together, the trophy presentation at the 2004 Target World Challenge. Scott Clarke, Wire Image

A model family: John Daly, wife Sherrie, and son Little John during less tempestuous times, after John's win at the 2004 Buick Invitational. Scott Halleran, Getty Images

Well worth the trip: J.B. Holmes leaps into his father Maurice's arms on the 18th green in Phoenix. Dave Seibet, Arizona Republic

Saturday smiles, Sunday frowns: Sergio Garcia and Vijay Singh enjoying the tournament lead on Saturday at the Players Championship. The next day wouldn't be nearly as much fun. Scott Halleran, Getty Images

Good playing, partner: Phil Mickelson feeling the love from Freddie Couples on the 18th at Augusta. Harry How, Getty Images

Sin in their hearts?: Richelle and Aaron Baddeley after hubby's win at Hilton Head. Kevin C. Cox, Wire Image

Party at the tattoo parlor!: Chris Couch whoops it up after his victory at New Orleans' Zurich Classic. Gregory Shamus, Wire Image

Soggy celebration: Jim Furyk after holing out to win the
Wachovia Championship, with a pint's worth of rain flying
off his sleeve. Streeter Lecka, Getty Images

Chaotic Canoe Brook: With hundreds stampeding the fairway during the afternoon round of her U.S. Open qualifier, Michelle Wie had no choice but to play to the green.

Nick Laham, Getty Images

"I am such an idiot": Phil Mickelson cursing his fate on the 18th green at Winged Foot. Jamie Squire, Getty Images

Nothing accidental about it: Juli and Geoff Ogilvy, with baby Phoebe on the way, on Sunday afternoon at Winged Foot. Mike Ehrmann, *Wire Image*

Ryder Cup here we come: Gator-lover Chris DiMarco and Ryan "New Guy" Rue during the final round at the British Open at Hoylake. Pete Fontaine, *Wire Image*

One for Pops: Steve Williams points heavenward as Tiger Woods mourns the physical absence of his father. Ross Kinnaird, Getty Images

Major winners on parade: the marquee group at Medinah, with throng. From foreground, Geoff Ogilvy, Jim Mackay, Alistair Matthews, Steve Williams, Tiger Woods, and Phil Mickelson. Donald Miralle, Getty Images

A different kind of house call: Swing doctors Mike Bennett and Andy Plummer honing the action of Tommy Armor III at June's Booz Allen Classic in Potomac, Maryland. Monte Isom

The picture of determination: David Duval during the second round of the PGA Championship, perhaps his last U.S. major. Donald Miralle, Getty Images

Trial separation over: Steve Lucas shows son-in-law Sean O'Hair the way at the Canadian Open. Stan Badz, Wire Image

High on the leaderboard:
Robert Garrigus after his
Saturday birdie at 13 to take
the lead at the 84 Lumber Classic.
Hunter Martin, Wire Image

An inconsolable winner:
Four weeks after the loss of
his wife, Heather, Darren Clarke,
the emotional center of the Ryder
Cup matches, is comforted
by Tom Lehman after his
Sunday singles victory.
David Cannon, Getty Images

The press in pursuit: Tiger Woods and wife Elin leaving the course on Sunday at the Ryder Cup, with *Sports Illustrated*'s Rick Reilly hot on their tails.
Donald Miralle, Getty Images

A green jacket as sweet as Augusta's: Sergio Garcia and gal pal Morgan Norman, Greg's daughter, at the Ryder Cup closing ceremonies, trailed by Padraig Harrington and wife Caroline; David Howell, and Colin Montgomerie. Action Images, Wire Image

Victory sneeze: Ian Woosnam after Europe's victory at the Ryder Cup, demonstrating that there are more ways for champagne to exit the body than to enter it. Jeff Haynes, Agence France Press

At the golf course, the players were trying to have normal week. Practice rounds were played and practice balls were hit. Recent winners and their caddies and wives were accepting congratulations, cracking jokes, and telling tales. The previous week Stuart Appleby had captured his second victory of the year, winning in Houston in a walk. "If it was a boxing match, they would have stopped stop the fight," his caddie, Joe Damiano, said on Tuesday afternoon. The week before, Aaron Baddeley, another Aussie, had won at Hilton Head. David Toms' caddie, Scott Gneiser, caught up with Baddeley's wife, Richelle, and remarked that on TV she seemed to have a good time celebrating Aaron's victory. "What you didn't see on TV," she replied, extending an arm, "was all these bug bites. I was getting eaten alive."

The native Louisianan pros, however, were busy doing press conferences promoting the tournament. Toms presented $100,000 checks to four local charities and detailed his foundation's other relief efforts. He and Hal Sutton—who, like Toms, lives in Shreveport—had started funneling donations through their foundations almost as soon as Katrina made landfall. By tournament time Toms had collected $1.6 million, much of it from fellow Tour players.

But if this was GolfAid, Kelly Gibson was the week's Bob Geldof, the golf community's lead spokesperson and caller-to-arms. The only player on Tour from New Orleans proper, he grew up playing local munis like City Park and Audubon Park, each just minutes away from Bourbon Street. He turned pro in 1986, but only twice finished inside the top 100 and hadn't been fully exempt since 1998. His sole claim to fame, he often said, was "delivering Tiger Woods to the world": at the 1996 Las Vegas Invitational he had held the lead on the back nine, but stumbled on the final holes, facilitating Woods' first pro win.

When Katrina struck, Gibson was in Milwaukee to play in Skip Kendall's charity pro-am. He watched the storm batter his hometown on the television in his hotel room. "I'm sitting there watching this," he remembered, "and I'm like, 'Who's taking care of the people who are helping the people?' Who's going to take care of the police officers, who have lost everything, too? Who's going to take care of the fireman, the guy in the water? Where is the food for them?"

In the space of two days Gibson and wife Elizabeth started Feed the Relief. They soon had trucks rolling in from all over the country with food, water, and other supplies. Yet he had no idea how he was going to pay for it. After receiving an early food delivery bill he called Toms and said, "I'm on the hook pretty good down here. I know I'm the one who ordered the food, but you'll have to pay the caterers." Toms immediately sent him $50,000. A number of other players, and the Tour itself, soon followed with big checks.

But the pre-tournament buzz wasn't all positive. Much of it concerned the number of stars who had failed to show. Only four of the world's top twenty had come to town. Many of the absent players—Tiger Woods, Vijay Singh, and John Daly, for example—were being held up to scorn. Woods, for example, was blasted in the papers and on the web for skipping the event to be with his father, attend Steve Williams' wedding, or both, although neither was the reason he wasn't there: he was obligated to spend the latter part of the week in Las Vegas for TigerJam, his annual Tiger Woods Foundation fundraiser, which was scheduled long before Katrina, and could not be moved. But he was the only one who had a hall pass. (Williams' New Zealand wedding, at which Tiger was best man, was actually a full week before the start of the tournament in New Orleans.)

Toms—who, with Gibson, served as the unofficial tournament host—tried to be diplomatic about the turnout, but his disappointment was hard to miss. "It all goes back to scheduling, I guess," he said. "A lot of those guys are worldwide players, and it's a long way to travel." All true. But Retief Goosen, who flew in from London, provided a counterargument simply by refusing to be thanked for making the trip. "It's not that big a deal," he said between range balls on Tuesday. "I just went to the airport, got on a plane, and came over. I've been doing it for years."

All the talk of donations added another strange element to the week: the feeling that people were keeping score of more than just golf. Phil Mickelson was atop the donor leaderboard, having contributed a total of $250,000 to Sutton's, Toms', and Gibson's funds. That put the onus on other players to follow suit, which was probably the point. But it wasn't universally appreciated. Some players preferred not to do their philanthropy in public. Said Appleby, "I don't tell people what I'm doing, one way or the other. I've just never been one to do that." Tiger, it seemed, felt the same way. His foundation had donated $200,000 to Baton Rouge education charities, but the gift went officially unannounced. To find out about it, you had to call the foundation and ask.

Elsewhere, the early part of the week was one long series of reminders that the city was striving to get back to normal, but not quite succeeding. Harrah's, the big casino at the end of Canal Street, had reopened and, as usual, welcomed many of the players and caddies. Walking past the tables at night, you might see Padraig Harrington, for example, splitting eights at a blackjack table. Yet the casino's main floor was relatively empty, and the annual Tuesday night caddie blackjack tournament had been cancelled.

While rushing to reopen his three New Orleans restaurants, Emeril Lagasse still managed to stage his annual Tuesday morning cooking demonstration for the Tour wives and girlfriends. Later the same day several of those women took part in a cleanup of a damaged home in a flood-ravaged neighborhood. A few were reduced to tears.

Thursday night's yearly player dinner at Acme Oyster House went off without a hitch, but most of the tournament's usual gastronomic fun was missing. In past years there had always been a raw bar on the driving range and, for the Wednesday pro-am, stations set up on every other hole with food from nine of the city's best restaurants. But this year, none of it was there.

What was plentiful on Wednesday was rain. The pro-am was suspended almost as soon as it began, leaving the players to mill around and kill time. Bubba Watson had yet to tee off and was outside on the porch when he spotted Peyton Manning getting into an SUV, intending to head back into town to wait out the delay. (Peyton, Archie, and Eli, the city's favorite sporting sons, were fixtures at the tournament on pro-am days.) Watson ran over for an autograph.

"You didn't have to ask me now," Peyton said. "We're playing together later."

Most of Wednesday's attention was focused on Phil Mickelson, who was making his first appearance since the Masters. That, combined with the star power vacuum, made him the undisputed headliner. The national focus on the event made for a perfect publicity storm.

Early that afternoon he plopped himself in a chair outside an English Turn clubhouse ballroom and offered himself up to a long series of television interviews. He was completely surrounded by batteries of tungsten hot lights, and white and black screen reflectors and dimmers. The session began at about 2:15 p.m., with remotes for CNN, CNN International, and ESPN's *Pardon the Interruption*. He chatted about a potential Mickelslam, the benefits of carrying two drivers, and his intention to take his kids to see the devastation in the Lower Ninth Ward (just as he had taken them, after 9/11, to view the remains of the World Trade Center). He predicted it would take five to ten years for the city to return to normal and pledged his entire paycheck from the Zurich Classic to relief efforts, in addition to the donations he'd already made.

When those three interviews were done, he went into the ballroom and took care of print media, but immediately returned to the camera setup for The Golf Channel, USA Network, and PGA Tour Productions. While awaiting his next interrogator, his press attaché handed him a multipage document. Mickelson looked at the big blocks of text, many of which were followed by question marks. Their purpose was not immediately clear to him.

"These are questions, or my answers?" he cracked. He was being facetious—his answers today, though somewhat repetitive, weren't scripted. But the questions were so elaborate that he couldn't digest them all. Finally, seemingly speaking to someone not in the room, he said, "It doesn't matter. I don't care. Just ask me whatever you want to ask."

The questions must have been from Fox News, because the next voice in his ear was Neil Cavuto. After that flurry, The Golf Channel waded into the circle for a second pound of flesh. But Mickelson begged off. "I've spent an hour and a half answering questions," he sighed. "I'm just burned out. Let's do it tomorrow. Maybe I'll have more energy."

On Friday afternoon, after carding a five-under 67 to move into a tie for second, Michael Allen had the rest of the day free. There were lots of options. He could stick around and practice. He could go back into town and head over to Mother's, on Poydras Street, for a po' boy or some filé gumbo. He could go over to JazzFest—Bob Dylan was playing an afternoon set over at the Fairgrounds. Eventually he decided to take what the locals called a "disaster tour," a drive through one of the New Orleans neighborhoods decimated by post-Katrina floodwaters.

Allen's choice was predictable. His career had given him a lot more perspective than most other pros. At 47, he'd already lived a full golfing life. He had enough gray in his close-cropped hair, enough of a fondness for cigars, and enough Tommy Bahama shirts in his wardrobe to be mistaken for a Champions Tour player. Though he played most of his life after the advent of sunblock, his skin already showed the signs of a lifetime out in the sun.

It was his résumé, though, that really told the story. Allen's career traversed the dark side of professional golf, where glamour is scarce, the travel is steerage, and every nickel counts. After college and eight years in the minors and abroad, he got his first PGA Tour card in 1990. He became one of its perpetual hangers-on, a guy who perennially faces losing his card but somehow manages to keep it, on way or the other. Usually, it was the other. He went to Q-school as often as some people go to the dentist.

By 1996 that life was getting old, so he gave up the Tour for a job at Winged Foot, the storied club outside Manhattan that would in 1997 host the PGA Championship (and in 2006 the U.S. Open). He loved its two courses and the club's old-school personality. But he soon found that he couldn't earn a living as a teaching pro. The Northeast's golf season was short. And even in the summer, the members, mostly Wall Street types, preferred playing to fixing their swings on the range. Allen knew that the following summer would be no better, since the PGA was taking the place over for more than a month. So he went to Scottsdale with his wife, Cynthia, and two-year-old daughter, Christy, and took a job at SunRidge Canyon Golf Club.

That didn't make him rich, either. Soon he was working construction, hoping for a job in medical supply sales to come through. In January 1997 a friend named Ron Burleson dragged him out to the Phoenix Open, and Allen found himself sitting above the 16th hole getting an earful from his buddy about how he should be playing in the tournament rather than watching from a skybox. Part of Allen agreed, but another believed his time had passed. He was shocked a couple of weeks later when Burleson produced $20,000, raised behind Allen's back by passing the hat among his fellow members at Troon North. By late February Allen was standing on the first tee at Monday qualifying at a Nationwide Tour event in California. He earned a spot and wound up tying for fifth, jump-starting his stalled career.

He didn't make all that much money that year—only $27,000—but he never looked back. He and Cynthia had learned that the real world wasn't kind to 40-year-olds whose only real skill was hitting a ball with a stick. In June of that year their second child, Michelle, was born with juvenile diabetes, and the Allens agreed that golf was the best chance of giving her a healthy future.

It was the right decision. Over the next five years Allen won about $500,000, a pauper's sum by Tour standards, but more than enough to keep Michelle healthy and keep up with the average American middle-class Joneses. He had an abysmal 2003, but managed, with the help of a few well-timed under-par rounds at Q-school, to keep his career on the rails.

He hated living most of his life away from his kids. Michelle, the youngest, always cried when he left for tournaments. But Christy kept saying how proud she was when Daddy showed up on TV. In 2004 he made $496,800 for a runner-up finish at Greensboro, and it seemed to justify everything. "A half-million dollars for second place?" Allen rhetorically asked. "For me, that's a career."

In 2006, Allen was in the same place he usually was nearing the mid-point of the year. At 144th on the money list going into the Zurich Classic, he was a long way from locking up his playing privileges for the following year. Maybe a little practice might have been a good idea.

Instead, he got into a posh courtesy SUV and headed across the river. The driver was Robert Marque, a heavyset tournament volunteer who normally worked as a Jefferson Parish fireman. During the drive Allen took a call from a friend ("You play well enough, everybody calls you," he smiled), ruminated on the fitness regimen of playing partner Justin Rose ("It used to be how many Crown Royals you can drink—now it's how many sit-ups you can do"), and listened to the tournament broadcast on the XM satellite radio. As they made their way toward the bridge to the city, he stared at the FEMA trailers on the side of the road and asked Marque what things were like immediately after the storm.

Marque's stories were grisly. He began by telling Allen about the procedure for dealing with dead people. "You couldn't do nothin' for 'em, so you'd just handcuff 'em to something and go on and try to find someone you could help."

"Did you ever have to kill anyone?" Allen asked.

Marque hadn't, but said that it wasn't hard to imagine, in that chaos, a situation in which he might have had to. He recalled the days immediately after the hurricane, when everyone carrying aid feared they would be set upon by people desperate for relief, or trying to profit from the disaster. He said, "If you had a relief trailer hitched on the back of your truck, and they wanted it, then you would do what you had to do."

Eventually they entered the Lower Ninth. The landscape was other-worldly. It was dead quiet and completely unpeopled. The nature of the damage made little sense to eyes that hadn't seen it before and were used to registering only the orderly layouts of ordinary residential neighborhoods. On the right side of the street three houses were smashed together—vertically, one on top of the other, the highest riding about 30 feet up a tree. On the left the prow of a boat peeked out from one house's window.

On the car radio, the announcer excitedly described how Fred Funk had just made a 30-footer for birdie.

The houses that hadn't been razed all bore the standard Day-Glo orange Katrina X. In the left quadrant was the search and rescue team's number, and the time and date they entered the house. At the top was the date they entered the house. On the bottom were the numbers of bodies they found inside. The right was reserved for hazards the team discovered—anything from snakes or rats to gas leaks. Some of the houses also bore graffiti left by former residents. On one house was spray-painted, in black, the word "Baghdad."

The car turned off Forstall Street onto Prieur Street, where, three weeks earlier, a ten-year-old wearing a backpack had been found dead, crushed between two houses. The men got out of the car. On the ground in front of Allen was a videocassette recording of the movie *Twister*. He pawed it with his shoe and uttered the understatement of the year. "You stand around here and 130th on the money list doesn't sound so bad."

Down the street a man was standing in front of what used to be his house, at 5017 Prieur. It was now an eighteen-foot pile of rubble, crowned by orange cushions from what used to be his sofa.

Allen approached him. His name was George Parker. He had built the house, he said, in 1959, with his father and brother. Now 62, he had spent thirty-five years driving a forklift for a local distribution company, until it was bought by Rite-Aid. He'd spent the past six years working for Balmer Foods, makers of marinades like Cajun Impregnator. He had come back today to find out how much might be salvageable from his house, and what had been done so far to clean up his neighborhood. The answer to both his questions was nothing.

Directly down the street, about 1,200 yards away from what was left of his house, was a levee. Parts of it were still standing, but a huge section had collapsed, leaving a gaping hole. "A barge broke it," Parker said. "Just came right through it."

In the hours before the storm Parker took his mother to the Superdome, and then returned to the house to pick up a boarder, Charles Evans, who had refused to leave.

"He said, 'I'm gonna ride it out.' But I don't think he made it.

"I think he's still underneath all that stuff," he added, gesturing toward the debris.

Walking back to the car, Allen found himself doing math, trying to estimate what it would cost to revive the Lower Ninth. It might take tens of thousands of dollars just to clear one block, he figured, and hundreds of thousands just for the materials to rebuild the homes, multiplied by who knows how many square miles. Finally, he gave up. "There is no number," he said, shaking his head. "There is no number."

Chris Couch woke up early on Saturday morning. He had to. His was one of the first tee times of the morning, 7:39 a.m., because he had made the cut on the number, barely making the weekend.

He rolled out of bed in the back of his RV at about 5:30, and went to the front to rouse Ron Benner. Benner, his trainer, was also working as his caddie, after he'd fired Greg Bitterly. Benner's double duty made good economic sense for a player who had only made $22,000 through the first four months of the season.

The bus was parked in a lot adjoining the course, so it was a short drive in the courtesy car over to the clubhouse. After breakfast they met up on the practice tee with Jason Schultz, a 33-year-old rookie who, like Couch, had spent the previous year on the Nationwide Tour. Couch and Schultz had played together the previous two days and would be playing together again in the third round. Couch ended their conversation with a little pep talk.

"You've only made two cuts this year, too, right?" he asked.

"Right," Schultz replied.

"Time for us to start playing some golf," Couch said. "Let's get it done this week."

Schultz didn't, but Couch did, posting a 64, easily his best round of the year. It was spooky: the night before, Couch's longtime friend Paul Tesori, Vijay Singh's caddie, had called him and left a message that said, "Why don't you go out this weekend and shoot a pair of 64s, just to scare everybody?" After Saturday's round he was halfway there.

The Tour likes to say that any of its players is good enough to win on a given week. But for an unpolished player like Couch the stars have to align perfectly. He has to play the golf of his life, and also catch two or three colossal breaks.

The first break of Couch's week was living through the previous Sunday night. The second was Saturday's weather conditions. Couch played most of his round in a steady breeze, but as he finished his round—at about noon, just as the leaders were teeing off—the winds had started to howl, with gusts of well above thirty miles per hour. No one who went out in the last eight groups broke par. Michael Allen, in the next-to-last group, shot a 77, taking a penalty stroke on the 15th green when his ball moved as he struck his putt.

When Couch finished, his −12 was leading the tournament. And with the leaders moving backward, that never changed. Suddenly, for the first time in a long time, there was a reason to be curious about him.

He wasn't a complete unknown. At sixteen he was the top-ranked junior in the country and made it through Monday qualifying at the 1990 Honda Classic. He was a two-time All-America at the University of Florida, playing alongside his pal Tesori and future PGA Tour pro Brian Gay. (Paul earned a Tour card in 1997, but his year—indeed, his career—was cut short when a rotator cuff was ripped up in an auto accident. Soon after he began the first of his two caddying stints with Singh.) In 1993 Couch sank the putt that won the Gators the national championship. It was only a three-footer, but there was plenty of drama to it. Already beset with the yips, Couch had spent the whole day alternating between regular and cross-handed grips, and wore a glove for the clinching putt to prevent the club from slipping out of his sweaty hands.

In his first PGA Tour start as a professional, at the 1999 Sony Open in Hawaii, he finished in a tie for seventh. But in his next sixty-three PGA Tour events he made only twelve cuts. His fallow periods, like Michael Allen's, were murder. Couch almost quit the game twice. After the 2000 season he applied for an assistant pro position at Gainesville Country Club but was turned down by the head pro, who said he was too good for that kind of a job. At one point during 2003, while on the Nationwide Tour, he was playing so poorly that he had to borrow money from fellow pro Brendan Pappas to get to the next tournament.

It was then that he turned to a higher power, issuing God what sounded like an ultimatum. "I prayed hard, and said, if this is what I'm supposed to do, then show me," Couch had said. Lo and behold, He did. The next three weeks Couch finished twenty-fifth, second, and fifth, earning enough money to punch his ticket back to the PGA Tour.

But soon he was struggling again. In 2004 on the big tour (which started with his T-shirt-commemorated loss to Michelle Wie) he made only $28,000 in the first nine months of the year.

The primary culprit, as always, was his short game. His putting had stabilized, thanks to a switch to a long putter in 1999, but he had always been terrible around the greens. No matter which tour he played, he regularly languished near the bottom of the scrambling stats, which measure a player's proficiency at getting up and down after missing a green. In mid-2004, out of desperation, he started chipping and hitting his bunker shots cross-handed at the suggestion of his coach, Mark McCann, a South African who claimed the method was popular in his home country. It was an improvement, but not by much. Couch finished 2004 196th in scrambling, dead last on the PGA Tour.

That winter, he washed out of Q-school early, not even reaching the finals. Afterward, at the end of November, he went down to St. Augustine to meet up with Tesori for an annual multiday skins game at Deerwood Country Club in Jacksonville. He stayed with Tesori—who, between stints with Singh, had just quit working for Jerry Kelly—and was himself plotting a comeback.

Tesori and Couch had known each other for more than a decade. Both Floridians, they first met at a junior tournament in 1987, when Tesori was fifteen and Couch fourteen. They roomed together at Florida for three years, and spent a lot of time together when they were both PGA Tour rookies. In the years that followed they kept in touch, having the occasional beer during the years Couch played the bigs. But otherwise, they led separate lives.

When they got together in November of 2004, they took a close look at Couch's game. Together they watched hours of tape. Some was of other pros, both male and female. (Couch still maintains that Annika Sorenstam has "the best swing in the history of golf—you look at it backwards and forwards, and the club is always on the exact same plane.") But most of it was of Couch himself. It was a series of lessons from Tesori on the practice tee at Deerfield that would eventually turn his game around. "You're hanging back an awful lot on your right side when you're coming through," Tesori told him. To remedy the problem they worked on having Couch drive through the ball with his legs rather than spinning out, a move that kept the clubface square and level for a longer period of time through impact.

Couch began 2005 driving to tournaments in his Dodge Ram 1500 with his wife, Morgan, next to him in the front and their two kids, son Christian and daughter Cayden, in the back of the cab. The swing changes began to bear fruit in May. Couch won twice in four weeks, helping to establish him as the Nationwide Tour's Crash Davis, the developmental circuit's all-time leading money winner, and guaranteeing a return to the PGA Tour in 2006. But the year also brought changes in his personal life. Late that summer he filed for divorce. "It was my decision," he said, adding that his kids were "the reason I hung around for as long as I did. Hopefully one day they'll understand."

With his earnings from his wins—along with the $100,000 he earned for a T14 in a one-off start at July's PGA Tour Western Open—he bought an RV, a thirty-five-foot Holiday Rambler Imperial, and moved out. Where did he get his mail? "I don't have a home address," he shrugged. "People just send stuff through the Tour."

It was a saga, a lifetime's worth of ups-and-downs in a scant sixteen years.

But the weirdest chapter was written five nights earlier. The AP's Doug Ferguson and *Golf World*'s Jim Moriarity drew the fundamentals out of him after his Saturday round.

Coach arrived on Bourbon Street, he said, at about 9:30 p.m. He had a few drinks and got lost trying to find his courtesy car, which was parked six blocks away. A carful of women picked him up, telling him they would help him find his car. "They looked normal," Couch said, "so I thought I could get a ride with them. I jumped in their car, but it got kind of weird," particularly because they started taking him away from where he thought his car was parked. "I didn't really like the situation, so I hopped out of the car, and I was in the middle of nowhere."

As soon as he jumped out of the car, another pulled up, and a man threateningly asked, "What are you doing in this neighborhood?" At that point Couch took off. He ran, he said, in the direction of some streetlights in the distance. Six blocks later he arrived at a big commercial thoroughfare, and ducked into a tattoo parlor. (He didn't remember any of the details, but the street turned out to be North Rampart, and the tattoo shop Art Accent.) Then the police drove him home (to a hotel, assumed the reporters, who didn't know he was living in an RV).

"It was just a bad Bourbon Street experience," he said. "It happens."

When Couch finished recounting his story, he had lunch, and went off to do what any Tour pro would do on a Saturday afternoon. He went out to buy crickets for his two pet lizards.

Even if Couch had shot a 59 it wouldn't have rivaled the splash made by Reggie Bush when he entered Emeril's on Saturday night. The crowd chanted "Reg-gie! Reg-gie!" as the Heisman-winning USC tailback strode through the restaurant on his way to a back room where he would sign with the Saints, hours in advance of his being chosen with the first pick overall in the NFL draft the next morning.

On Sunday Bush came out to English Turn to continue the lovefest. He took a seat behind the 18th, and when CBS put his face on screen, announcing his presence to the television-equipped skyboxes, they erupted. By the end of the day the Saints' season-ticket office had received over 500 phone calls.

Elsewhere, golf-related numbers were being tallied. Michael Allen, having shot 78–68 on the weekend to finish tied for fifty-third, was in line at Mother's, bemoaning the fact that he'd squandered a chance at a top ten and would have to go to Charlotte to try to Monday qualify for the following week's Wachovia Championship. When Phil Mickelson finished his round he promised to bump his Katrina relief contribution from $81,720 (his check for a tie for fifteenth) to another $250,000. In the trailers near the clubhouse, Classic organizers were guessing that 65,000 people had passed through the turnstiles for the event's final two rounds. In another trailer, player services chairperson Anne Barnes estimated that only "twenty or thirty" of the pros had filled out the winnings-donation forms made available earlier in the week.

Couch, one day from his thirty-third birthday, played the final round in a threesome with Joe Durant and Charles Howell III. Howell had a history with Couch, though Charlie was the only one who remembered it. When Couch was at Florida, the Gators played a tournament in Augusta, Georgia, Howell's hometown. The skinny, bespectacled sixteen-year-old was given a choice of caddying for Couch or Justin Leonard. He chose Couch.

On a course sopping wet from overnight thunderstorms, Durant played well but quickly fell behind Howell and Couch, who each birdied four of their first six holes. The old Augusta acquaintances continued to trade birdies around the turn.

At the same time, Paul Tesori was enjoying an afternoon off. He had hit balls with his boss earlier in the day on the range at the TPC at Sawgrass and was now playing a recreational round on its Valley Course with a friend named Scott Brady. He had been keeping abreast of the scores on the internet via his smartphone.

While the players were on the 15th hole, Tesori decided to call Couch again, just to leave a message. "Tell Charlie Howell to slow down," he said. "He's already got his one win. Now it's time for you to get yours."

As they reached the 17th, it looked like he would. At –18, Couch held a two-shot lead over Howell and Fred Funk, who had roared up from the back of the pack with a course-record 62. But standing on the tee, Couch looked like a lock to unravel. Waiting out a backup on the 202-yard par-three, he nervously cleaned the grooves of his six-iron with a golf tee, then took a long, deep breath and rolled his eyes at the sky, as if he'd already made the double bogey he was so afraid of.

When he finally hit, he pulled his shot left into a greenside bunker, finding an uphill lie on sand caked hard by the rain. Unable to get his wedge under the ball, he bladed it over the green and wound up in the rough, forty feet from the pin. His indifferent chip left him a twelve-footer for bogey. Once again his iffy short game was killing him. Indeed, a quick look at the Tour stats revealed that Couch was dead last (184th) in the 2006 scrambling stats. But he gutted it up, drilling the putt into the back of the hole, and walked off the green holding tight to a one-shot lead.

On the 18th, a long par-four, Couch caught a flier with a pitching wedge from the rough. Back in Ponte Vedra, Vijay Singh, an incurable watcher of golf television, was at home on the couch in his living room. He had gotten to know Couch through Tesori, and they had played a number of practice rounds together, both on Tour and in Jacksonville, in early 2006. He picked up his phone, called Tesori, and caught him up.

"He's one shot up on Howell and on Funk, but Freddie's already in the clubhouse," Singh told his caddie. "Chris just bogeyed 17, and he just airmailed the green on 18."

Again Couch was in a bunker—this one long and right of the

green—and once more faced a lie that could make Gary Player cry. His ball lay inches from the back lip on a downhill slope, forcing him into an awkward stance with his back leg outside the bunker, his knee nearly touching the grass. Afraid of repeating his mistake on the previous hole, he nearly whiffed it, barely getting it out of the trap. He now had to get up and down from 55 feet away just to earn a spot in a playoff with Funk and Howell.

Frustrated, he got over it quickly. He lobbed his ball into the air, landing it just on the green. It began rolling toward the cup.

"Bro, this ball could be going in," Singh said to Tesori as it tracked toward the hole. It never even thought about staying out.

"Holy shit!" Lanny Wadkins exclaimed on CBS's air.

"It went in!" Singh yelled into his phone.

Tesori could hear the crowd going crazy in the background. "He made it! He made it!" Tesori shouted at his friend Brady.

After delivering his "Let's party!" victory yowl, Couch came into the press room. Someone asked him if he would be going back to the French Quarter, the scene of his earlier misadventure, to celebrate.

"You never know," he said. "You might see me down there. I like Bourbon Street."

He was also asked whether or not he'd share his winnings with local relief agencies. "I haven't thought about it yet," he replied. "I didn't think I was going to win at the beginning of the week."

Neither did anyone else. And no one was expecting any kind of donation decision by Monday morning. Not from a guy like Chris Couch. Not in New Orleans.

8

PLAYING THROUGH

The Wachovia Championship, Charlotte

Mark O'Meara walked onto the driving range early Wednesday afternoon at Quail Hollow Country Club with his morning pro-am round behind him, and a quick lunch settling in his stomach. Picking a spot next to Tom Lehman, he sent his caddie off to fetch a bag of balls. While he and Lehman chatted he idly reached into his golf bag to grab his phone. He hadn't turned it back on since coming off the golf course.

As he did, the wind freshened, blowing directly into the players from the far end of the range. It caught the backs of a few of the wood-and-canvas director's chairs behind the range line and blew them over. It was a prelude to the thunderstorms the forecasters had been predicting since Monday.

O'Meara's phone lit up, and he saw he had a message. The date and time stamp told him it had arrived shortly after he began his round. It was from Tiger Woods. Tiger said that his father Earl had passed away early that morning. He wanted O'Meara to give him a call.

O'Meara had called Woods the previous day, just to check in, but Tiger hadn't called back. The news, therefore, did not surprise him. He hung up his voicemail, scrolled through his contacts, and selected Tiger's name.

Woods didn't pick up, so O'Meara left a message of his own, and absent-mindedly grabbed a wedge from his bag. He hit one ball, and then another, his mind blank, his body operating by habit. Gradually he began thinking again, remarking to himself that Woods' call, coming from the West Coast, had been placed very early that morning, long before sunrise. After about ten balls his phone began to vibrate in his pocket. It was Tiger, but it didn't sound like him. His voice had none of its usual confidence. He seemed badly shaken up.

Woods was sparing with details, and O'Meara carried most of the brief conversation. "Look," he said. "I want to be there for you. I'm out of here. I'll be there tomorrow."

O'Meara waved to his caddie, who quickly shouldered his bag, and the two walked back through a parking lot toward the clubhouse. He asked for his car at the valet station, walked the twenty or so steps back to the clubhouse, and went into the locker room to gather his gear. Then, still in a kind of fog, he went back outside to get his car and leave.

John Cook wasn't scheduled to play in the pro-am. He was at the club to get in a little practice, and had left the short-game area, far to the right of the range line, at about the same time O'Meara arrived. They had just missed each other going in and out of the clubhouse, entering and exiting through different doors, and then again in the player dining area, with Cook arriving just minutes after O'Meara left. Now Cook, done eating, came out of the locker room and saw O'Meara loading up the trunk.

Cook and O'Meara weren't just friends. They had in many ways lived parallel lives. Both were born in 1957, O'Meara in January, in North Carolina, and Cook in Ohio, in October. Mark's father, who was in the insurance business, moved their family often, and by the time he was a teenager the family had settled in Mission Viejo, California. John's dad was an executive at Firestone, and his responsibilities in auto racing and golf brought him to California so often that he eventually bought a second home in Palm Springs. The two boys got to know each other playing Southern California junior events. Cook went to college in Ohio (at Ohio State) and O'Meara stayed in California (attending Long Beach State). But they stayed in touch, and often reunited during the U.S. Amateur. Cook won the Amateur in 1978; defending his title the following year, he lost to O'Meara in the finals. As the two turned professional, they grew closer. O'Meara, a lifelong teetotaler, said the only real drink he'd ever had was at Cookie's wedding.

In mid-career, they both found themselves living at Isleworth, a posh, gated community near Orlando. In 1996 they welcomed a new neighbor, Tiger Woods. Both assumed a kind of mentor role. O'Meara's was more significant than Cook's, but no one was really keeping score. Together they spent hundreds of hours during the first years of Tiger's pro career on Isleworth's driving range and golf course, in the clubhouse, and then, in the evenings, at dinner at Mark's and John's homes. No two players on Tour were closer to Tiger than they were.

Now, at Quail Hollow, it seemed fated that Cook and O'Meara would run into each other on one of the most important days of their young friend's life. "What's going on?" Cook innocently asked as he approached O'Meara, still standing near the trunk of the courtesy car.

"I think you need to come with me," O'Meara replied, and motioned to Cook to follow him. Leaving the car at the curb, they walked back to the clubhouse and into the locker room, and looked for a deserted corner in the back, attempting to keep the news secret.

"I just got word," O'Meara began. "Tiger just called me. His dad passed away. I'm going back for the service."

"Oh, my God," Cook said flatly. "Do you think he would mind if I went out with you?"

"He already mentioned it. He told me to tell you. He wants you there, too." In his ten minutes of sleepwalking, O'Meara had forgotten that request.

"I've got to withdraw," Cook said. Only then did it occur to O'Meara that he had to do so too.

O'Meara approached a clubhouse attendant, who radioed tournament director Kym Hougham. Hougham, a tall, lean, bespectacled gray-haired man who was universally liked and respected by the players, was out on the golf course, near the seventh hole, checking some gallery roping. Putting his radio down, he got in his cart, drove back to the clubhouse, and went inside to find the two players.

Together Cook and O'Meara made their apologies. Hougham understood completely. "That's far more important than this," he said. "Of course you have to go." Cook and O'Meara then headed for the airport and went back to their homes at Isleworth. The following morning they would fly out to California together.

•　•　•

Earl Woods' death only made stranger the year's most unusual week. None of its most interesting happenings—and there were plenty—seemed to have anything to do with the golf being played at Quail Hollow. John Daly's book *My Life In and Out of the Rough* was released, every sentence a tabloid headline. Tom Lehman convened his first meeting of potential U.S. Ryder Cup players. Hootie Johnson resigned his post at Augusta National, bringing to an end to one of the most tumultuous chairmanships in the club's history. Half a world away, in Korea, Michelle Wie made her first cut playing against male golfers. To top it all off, Joe Ogilvie, the young Dukie who was one of the Tour's model citizens (even serving on the PGA Tour Policy Board), got arrested for drunk driving.

All those things conspired to deflect attention from what had quickly become one of the premier events on Tour. Just four years after its debut, the Wachovia Championship was already the players' favorite regular-season event. Its charms began with its perks, which—along with the 84 Lumber Classic, the Western Pennsylvania event that ran from 2003 through 2006—raised the bar for every other stop on Tour.

The swag started four months before the tournament itself, with Hougham traveling to Kapalua and placing a bottle of Dom Pérignon in each player's locker. Once in Charlotte, contestants all received Mercedes courtesy cars—except for the defending champion, who got a chauffeured $400,000 Maybach, about which 2003 winner David Toms had said, "It's a little embarrassing when you take it through the drive-thru at Burger King." The defending champ's caddie (in 2006, Vijay Singh's man Paul Tesori) drove the leftover Mercedes. The caddies also got to use valet parking and received playing privileges at nearby Ballantine Country Club, a considerable switch from their bench-and-a-sandwich treatment at most Tour events. The players' wives were hardly left out. One year they were taken by private jet to Asheville to visit the Vanderbilt Estate and do a little wine-tasting; in 2006 they were shipped off to Charleston, South Carolina, for a luncheon at an historic plantation and a horse-drawn carriage tour of the old city. In the players' eyes, however, the hands-down best perk was the shrunkenness of the pro-am groups. During Wachovia week each pro played with two amateurs, rather than the usual four.

The royal treatment was only part of the story. What the players truly loved was the golf course, a fifty-year-old, old-school track whose beauty and shot-values made it a pleasure and a challenge to play. The standard compliment was that it was worthy of a U.S. Open. After one typically trying but no less enjoyable round, Jay Haas said, "I must have shot a hundred today. But with another inch of rough and another foot or two of speed on the greens, you could play whatever you wanted to play on it."

As often as the national championship was mentioned, the major to which the Wachovia was most closely related was the Masters. There were material links: Quail Hollow's architect, George Cobb, built the par-three course at Augusta National and retouched the main course in 1967 and 1977. The most impressive commonality, however, had to do not with a man but with nature. The club's rolling land featured just as many elevation changes as Augusta, and the holes, similarly shapely, were lined with the same loblolly pines.

But in 2006, what happened on that course seemed relatively unimportant. At least not until Sunday, when the Wachovia staged another terrific finish, and toasted a winner who by summer's end would be the second-ranked golfer in the world.

Nowhere was there a man more different from Earl and Tiger Woods than John Daly. It therefore made a ridiculous kind of sense that on the afternoon before Earl's death, Long John and his tell-all autobiography were the center of attention.

Thanks to review copies and magazine-published excerpts, most of the reporters on hand in Charlotte had already read at least part of Daly's book. It stated, almost boastfully, that his gambling, over the years, had cost him $60 million. Other lowlights included Daly's father pulling a gun on him, stretches of weeks during which John consumed a fifth of Jack Daniel's a day, and a girlfriend not only visiting a strip club with him, but suddenly deciding to disrobe and do a little pole-dancing.

The most outrageous episode involved a trip to Las Vegas immediately after Daly lost to Woods in a playoff at the 2005 AmEx Championship in San Francisco. Emboldened by his $750,000 payday, Daly went right from the plane to the new Wynn Casino, stood in front of a $5,000-a-pull slot machine for an hour and a half, and lost $600,000. Discouraged, he went to another casino, Bally's, and won $175,000 on the slots. What next? A return trip to the Wynn and another $600,000 marker. He proceeded to lose that, too. All told he lost $1.65 million in less than five hours.

When Daly appeared on the range on Tuesday, a few days before the book's release, the scribblers made a beeline for him. When he finished hitting balls, they pounced.

Puffing on a Marlboro Light, Daly said the book had already resulted in a fifteen-minute face-to-face with Tour commissioner Tim Finchem in Charlotte, just a day earlier.

Conduct unbecoming a professional?

"My life is unbecoming a professional, basically," Daly shrugged.

"He's just concerned," he continued. "He thinks gambling is an issue. Our conversation is sort of confidential, but he said he's concerned."

Asked if Finchem told him not to gamble, Daly shook his head. "No," he said. "He said he thinks I should have counseling. But he said, 'I won't make you.'"

Will you be seeking counseling voluntarily?

"I'm not really into that," he said.

Daly was candid about the financial motivations behind the book, confessing that he perhaps should have made it clear that his gambling losses were offset by $20 or $25 million in winnings. What was clear was that he was keen on the idea of other, similarly profitable projects.

"Hopefully, there'll be a sequel or a movie," he said. One could only imagine what a sequel would be like.

That night Daly appeared onstage at a local bar as the featured attraction at an annual party thrown by Quail Hollow founder John Harris. With his guitar resting on his belly, he belted out a version of Dylan's "Knockin' on Heaven's Door." Peyton Manning, a club member, was in attendance, as were NASCAR drivers Jeff Gordon and Jimmie Johnson. The year before, at the same party, Sergio Garcia had offered up the weirdest-ever version of "Mustang Sally."

Daly's beers were on the house, but that didn't mean he wasn't tipping. According to the *Charlotte Observer*'s account of the evening, one female bartender said that after she handed him a bottle, "he kissed me on the cheek, patted me on the butt and gave me a $100 bill."

Earlier that evening, a slightly different kind of affair was taking place back at Quail Hollow. At the pool adjacent to the clubhouse, Tom Lehman and a group of would-be Ryder Cuppers had gathered for a barbeque, the first of a few such events that year. It drew a crowd: the list of invitees included everyone who had a decent shot at making the team.

At subsequent team meetings, that would change. The next one, four weeks later at the Memorial Tournament, welcomed only the top 25 on the points list. The new exclusivity rule was Lehman's little way of sounding a wake-up call. At the Memorial, when Stewart Cink saw an envelope with a Ryder Cup logo taped to Ben Crane's locker—but none to his—he thought to himself, *Tom's sending me a message by not sending a message.*

Here in Charlotte, however, pressure played no part. This get-together was more like a family picnic. Laid out on a table were chicken, hamburgers, coleslaw, and potato salad. An official from the PGA of America—the governing body that runs the Ryder Cup, along with the European Tour—handed out logo'd baseball caps, urging each player to take a few for friends and family. A rep from Polo was there, showing the players what the team uniforms would look like.

There was no prearranged seating, but the veterans took care to pair up with the younger players. Jim Furyk, for example, sat with first-time Cup hopeful Zach Johnson. Over a couple of beers, they talked about kids, baseball, and what a great job they thought Lehman would do.

Tapping Lehman as Ryder Cup captain wasn't odd or objectionable. Yet his playing record (five Tour wins, with one major, the 1996 British Open) wasn't nearly as strong as some past captains, or other men who had also been up for the 2006 captaincy, like O'Meara (sixteen wins and two majors) and Larry Nelson (ten wins and three majors).

Lehman knew his paper-based qualifications were thin and even brought it up as he began speaking, trying to inspire some of the less decorated attendees. Ryder Cups, he said, weren't about résumés. That's why the Europeans always out-performed expectations. The matches were about guts, determination, passion. That feeling, he said, was what made his three Ryder Cups the highlights of his career.

He wasn't making it up. His emotional investment in the event was abundantly clear to anyone who'd ever seen him stand next to a *USA*-embroidered golf bag. His 3–0 singles career included rousing wins against Seve Ballesteros in 1995 at Oak Hill, and against Lee West-wood in the all-important leadoff Sunday match at Brookline in 1999.

But Lehman's most telling Ryder Cup experience may have come in 2001, a year he didn't make the team. That summer (which, because of the matches' sudden 9/11-related postponement, wound up as the qualifying period for the 2002 event) was the worst of Lehman's life. On July 23, the day before the sixth birthday of his son Thomas, Lehman drove his wife, Melissa, to the hospital. She was five months pregnant. Two days after she was admitted, she delivered a stillborn son. They gave him a name—Samuel Edward Lehman—but couldn't give him anything more. "Tom sat in a rocking chair and held Samuel as though he were alive," *Sports Illustrated*'s Rick Reilly wrote a month later. "He held the 10-inch-long baby in his big hands for two hours, rocking and touching and weeping worse than any infant in that maternity wing."

Two weeks after the funeral Lehman returned to the Tour. He was heartbroken, but he was still in the top ten in the points standings, and more determined than ever to make the team. Playing the last two qualifying events despite the circumstances was his way of demonstrating his commitment, although most people felt certain that if he hadn't, and fell out of the top ten, that captain Curtis Strange would have made him a captain's pick.

Predictably, Lehman missed both cuts and dropped from tenth to eleventh. Forty-five minutes after the end of the PGA Championship, the final qualifying event, his phone rang. It was Strange.

"Seems like you've been struggling," Strange said, as Lehman remembered it. "I'm not picking you."

If his three Ryder Cups had been the best experiences of his golfing life, that was the worst.

Lehman didn't tell that story in Charlotte. Instead, he dwelt on the immediate future. He said, "All the guys who have the potential to make the team should get together, try to play some practice rounds, get to know each other well, and have some fun. Get used to stuff like this. We're going to be getting together a lot more. I want this team to have a lot of camaraderie." They were already off to a running start.

That evening notwithstanding, the beginning of Jim Furyk's sojourn in Charlotte unfolded the same way as almost every other week of the year—with daddy running the Clark Griswold playbook, preschool edition. He and his wife, Tabitha, arrived on Monday evening, and headed straight to the nearest all-suites hotel. No room service for this family—they wanted a kitchen. Neither daughter Caleigh nor son Tanner had reached four years of age, so macaroni and cheese and spaghetti were still king.

Furyk savored the hardships of traveling this way, because he knew this period in his life was drawing to a close. Caleigh would start school the following year, and except in summertime, she and the rest of his family would be staying at home. Jim and Tabitha rejected out of hand the idea of keeping the kids on the road and home-schooling them, as some other Tour parents did. They wanted them to grow up the normal way, going to a normal school, just like they had.

Their one travel-week concession to their tax bracket was that one of their two nannies always went with them. Having nannies around, Furyk confessed, had always felt "a little strange." He comes from Western Pennsylvania immigrant stock, and not until his parents' generation had his forebears sniffed the middle class. His mother, Linda, worked with the handicapped and developmentally disabled until she had Jim. His father, Mike, was a slim-walleted club pro while Jim was in his teens.

Meeting Mike—a burly, good-natured man in the mold of Roseanne's TV husband, John Goodman—had always been the best way to understand Jim's average-guy code of conduct. Try to address his father as "Mr. Furyk," and he would say, "It's Mike," even before you reached the *k* in his last name. Mike was also the authority on the evolution of his son's idiosyncratic game. He loved to tell stories about rebuffing instructors who wanted to fix his son's naturally loopy swing, and about the conversations with Gary Player and Arnold Palmer ("If you could start over again, what would you do differently?") that resulted in Jim's putting cross-handed decades before it was fashionable.

Conventional wisdom was that Furyk's background also informed his style of play. The epithet "gritty" was so often used to describe him that "Jim" had started to look like his middle name. Few gave him credit for any innate talent. And—heaven knows!—his success couldn't be due to his technique. It was presumed to originate with blue-collar practice habits and a have-not's resolve.

There was no doubt Furyk had more try in him than most other golfers. It helped account for his stellar Ryder and Presidents Cup singles record (which, in early 2006, stood at 5–0–1). When he ran into fellow University of Arizona alumni at Tour events, the greeting exchanged was always the school slogan, "Bear down." But Furyk didn't need any reminders. For him, it was second nature. Often he seemed like one of those very few players—like Nicklaus and Woods—who actually played better when the pressure was on.

Two such instances were head-to-head battles with Woods. The most memorable was their playoff at the 2001 Bridgestone Invitational, where Furyk stirringly holed a bunker shot on the first extra hole to stay alive, and hung tough for the next two hours, extending the playoff to seven holes. But just as telling was their Sunday final group face-off at the 2003 Buick Open in Flint, Michigan, two months after Furyk's triumph at the U.S. Open at Olympia Fields. Furyk led by four at the start of the round, and went on to win by two. But what was impressive about his performance was that he never flinched. His one bogey of the day came at the 11th hole—the same hole Tiger birdied to pull within two. Just about anyone else on Tour would have buckled. But Furyk birdied three of his next four holes, and Tiger never got any closer. On the round, Woods shot a 66, and Furyk a nerveless 68. Performances like these earned Woods' unreserved respect, and eventually led to Furyk's assuming his job as Tiger's Presidents and Ryder Cup wingman.

When Furyk heard about Earl Woods' death, he too was on the range, working his way through a post-pro-am practice session. It was about 2:00 p.m. He and his caddie, Mike Cowan, just looked at each other. Neither thought about phoning Tiger, knowing that today that line, on this day, was reserved for those closest to him. They packed up and left almost as soon as they heard the news. If the practice session was a little short, it may have been because they knew the media would soon be looking for sound bites.

Although few people knew how tight Furyk and Tiger had become (they'd fallen into the habit of calling each other, for example, whenever one of them won), he was likely to get a grilling anyway. But it was Cowan who would have taken the brunt of it. Fluff, of course, worked for Tiger during the young star's first three years on Tour, and knew Earl well. Despite his sudden excommunication from the Woods camp in 1999, for being a little too comfortable in the spotlight, he had a lingering respect for both Tiger and Earl. That everybody knew. Had he stayed on the range he would have spent all afternoon answering questions.

Furyk talked about Earl's death that night with his father. Race aside, Mike and Earl had a lot in common. Each was a generous, unpretentious man who loved watching his son compete. Mike also shared Earl's body type (if not his bad habits). That commonality introduced a reflective note into the conversation that night. "I'm fifty-nine," Mike said to his son on the phone, "and it seems like every year one or two people my age are passing away."

The following afternoon, during the first round, Furyk and Cowan's conversation was, as Furyk put it, "a little subdued." Usually, they were chatty, dissecting the previous day's football or basketball games. Given the time of year, they would ordinarily have been talking about the NBA playoffs. Cowan was fonder than most of pro hoops; he even watched broadcasts in which Bill Walton was involved. (He once explained, "I just love it when the acid kicks in.") It was surprising that neither of them had tuned in to the previous evening's Miami Heat play-off game, after which Shaquille O'Neal, in a post-game interview, publically expressed his condolences for his Isleworth neighbor.

But that night, neither had been in the mood. And the following day they carried their downbeat demeanors out onto the golf course. The 68 Furyk shot seemed incidental, even if it did grab him a share of the lead. Their thoughts were elsewhere.

Because of the time change, Cook, his wife, Jan, and O'Meara woke up early on Friday. They were staying at the Cooks' place in Corona del Mar. They puttered around the house and eventually went out for breakfast. On the way Cook took a little detour to show O'Meara the house Tiger had just bought. It was barely a mile from his home, just like back at Isleworth.

John and Mark had been in touch with Tiger the day before, and discussed the possibility of having breakfast together down at the Coco's on Pacific Coast Highway. But the timing was wrong—Tiger had to be at the funeral home well before they did. As things turned out, O'Meara and the Cooks decided to go to Coco's anyway. When they entered, Woods—in a black suit with a black shirt and black necktie—was at the cash register paying for his meal with Elin and friends Jerry Chang and Brian Bell standing alongside him.

The service—in the chapel of a funeral home nearby Tiger's boyhood home, where Earl had passed away—was relatively small, attended by about fifty people. They included Tiger's inner circle—his wife, his mother, agent Mark Steinberg, caddie Steve Williams, and his closest friends, Chang, Bell, Greg Nared, and Vencie Glenn. Also there were a few of Earl's old service buddies, some of the men he had played golf with in Orange County, and Earl's children from his first marriage, as well as some of Tida's relatives, Darius Rucker from Hootie and the Blowfish, another friend of Tiger's, would sing two songs during the service—"Amazing Grace," and an old Southern gospel hymn called "Will the Circle Be Unbroken."

Four people got up to say a few words. First was Pete McDaniel, a *Golf Digest* writer and longtime family friend. Next was Bill Stark, a buddy of Earl's from his days as a Green Beret. Then came Earl's eldest son, Kevin. Tiger was last. He was "a rock," his friends later said. He reminded Cook of Tracy Stewart when she spoke at her husband Payne's funeral. Tiger told a few anecdotes—most harkening back to his boyhood—and drew a few laughs. Then he grew more serious, trying to put into words how much his father meant to him. He finished by saying that now it was time to take everything he had learned from him and move forward.

The group then moved to a second, larger service, at the Tiger Woods Learning Center, in Anaheim. Woods was exceptionally proud of the place—it had opened in February, and he, by all accounts, was involved in every facet of the design. The building itself was a memorial to Earl. It was meant to be a place where children could grow in the most supportive environment possible. As Earl himself might have said, it would help provide some of the educational opportunities usually denied to underprivileged kids.

Arriving early, Tiger took a few minutes to give the Cooks and O'Meara a tour. Upstairs, he astonished them by detailing the purposes of every room, from the computer workshops to the science labs. Eventually they returned downstairs to the ground floor, where the service was being held. Thirty or so tables had been set up, along with a small dais and a microphone. The room was just beginning to fill with people. In the end there were about 250 attendees, ranging from local golf people who had known Tiger early in his life, to businessmen like former Nike CEO Phil Knight, to celebrity friends like Charles Barkeley, Gabrielle Reece, and Laird Hamilton. (Woods had met Reece while the former volleyball player, trying to transition to pro golf, was working with Woods' then-coach Butch Harmon; pro surfer Hamilton was her husband.)

Here, because of the open mic, the speakers were more numerous. There were more than a dozen, some of them recognizable names. A few were talkier than necessary—they were the kind of people who, in the words of one of Earl's old friends, "liked to let the coffee get cold." Most of the testimonials, however, were heartfelt. It was clear that Earl had touched many people. They showed their appreciation not so much by mourning his passing as by celebrating what his friendship meant to them.

Elsewhere on Friday—long before those services and miles away, both physically and emotionally—Michelle Wie made her first cut in eight tries against a field of male players, at the Asian Tour's SK Telecom Open in South Korea. Locally, it caused a huge swell of national pride. The child of two Korean-born parents was embraced as one of their own, lovingly referred to as *on-ni*, big sister, by young girls in the gallery.

Yet in the States, it hardly made a ripple. For one thing, it happened on the other side of the globe. For another, the tournament was as minor as major leagues gets: the entire purse ($600,000) was less than the second-place check at the Wachovia, and the field was accordingly weak. (Wie received a reported $700,000 for making the trip.) The kicker was that the feat wasn't unique. Se Ri Pak had finished tenth at the Korean Tour's SBS Super Tournament in 2003. All these factors—combined with the media's preoccupation with Earl Woods—had turned it into a non-event.

Back in Charlotte, the Wachovia Championship was becoming a big, wet mess. Thunderstorms halted Friday play at 4:00 p.m., well before the second round ended. But with rain expected all weekend, Tour officials rushed the players back out after two hours indoors. It was a mistake. Another cell was on its way in. The players had been out on the course only thirty-five minutes when a terrific boom came from the skies, sending some terrified players sprinting off the course. The horn sounded about half than a minute afterward.

"What the fuck!" John Daly roared as he came into the locker room.

Olin Browne was right behind him. "Are you going to leave us out there 'til you kill us?" he growled at a Tour official. Later, a different official explained the logic. "It was huge to get those extra holes in, because it got TV back on schedule." The Saturday broadcast, he noted, was slated to end just prior to the start of the Kentucky Derby.

The third round did indeed finish on time, safely before the Derby. But on Sunday morning the weather was lousy, and looked like it would only get worse. As the final threesome stood on the first tee—with Furyk leading the tournament at eleven-under and Retief Goosen and Trevor Immelman one stroke back—it felt like London in November.

There was a heavy mist in the air. The players could see their breath. A few yards away a concession-stand barbecue was belching complementary smoke, but it seemed like rain might douse the coals at any moment. All three players were already wearing the bottom halves of their rainsuits.

As play began most eyes were on Goosen. He had been hunting a win for several weeks: in the three-event stretch from the Players to the Masters he hadn't finished worse than fourth. But around him hovered suspicions about his ability to close. Although he had won the previous August in Denver, he still seemed haunted by the shadow of his meltdown at the 2005 U.S. Open at Pinehurst, where, going into the final round up by three, he shot an 81. Before that day he seemed to rival Tiger as the best tough-course player in the world. Now no one knew what to expect from him.

Not that anyone had him figured out before then. Indeed, the only things people knew for sure about the number five player in the world was that he was exceptionally quiet, and had once been hit by lightning. Goosen hated it when people claimed the two were related, once saying, in his distinctively clipped South African accent, that the notion was "a load of crap."

His mother, Annetjie Goosen, thought otherwise. She said as much in a profile ABC aired on the 2005 *Battle of The Bridges* (which teamed Goosen and Phil Mickelson against Daly and Woods). Part of the profile was filmed at Annetjie's home in South Africa. It opened with Goosen recounting the day on which it happened. He was fifteen, he said, playing at his home course with a cousin when a storm rolled in. They were headed back to the clubhouse when they passed a stand of three pine trees. A huge thunderbolt hit one of them. "I was standing next to it, and it blew me apart," Retief said.

Annetjie said that when her son arrived at the hospital, "he was black from head to toe, smelling of sulfur. He said, 'Tell them to put some ointment on me. I'm burning. I'm burning.'"

Under her voice, the cameras showed her taking the clothes Retief wore that day from a small, child's suitcase that usually resides in a closet. She held up the most telling item, his brown pants. The waist, the right-side back pocket, and the front, down to the bottom of the zipper, were intact. But most of the seat, and the entire left leg were completely gone. The lateral half of the right leg hung down in one long, disheveled thread.

Goosen celebrated his 16th birthday in intensive care, where he would spend five days. Miraculously, he was back on the golf course two weeks later.

At the end of the piece Goosen repeated his usual stance. "If it did change me, it's nothing I know about," he smiled. Annetjie had a different view. "I think he became quieter," she said, measuring her words. "It was as if he was more"—here she paused, motioning her hands toward her chest—"more into himself."

Every player on Tour got along with the Quiet Man, but only one, countryman and contemporary Ernie Els, seemed truly to know him. Saying they were like brothers was an understatement. They played junior golf together, served in the South African Air Force together, and started their careers together on the European Tour. Ten miles separated their houses in South Africa. Even closer were their residences in London (same neighborhood) and Orlando (same block). Amusing stories circulated about their antics together. They usually involved beer or wine, and wound up with Els as the butt of the joke. Goosen once described an evening that ended with his friend "making handbrake turns" in his Lake Nona driveway at two in the morning. Els protested, with a telltale smile, that he was "never anywhere near his house that night."

Most of what Els had to say about Goosen's personal history only reinforced Goosen's image as an introvert. He was always shy, Els said, hiding behind "these huge glasses that he used to wear. He was quite a sight." As children, their socio-cultural background made both of them reserved. "We come from Afrikaans backgrounds, and in those days the whole golfing community was English. Afrikaner kids don't quite socialize with English kids. We tended to stick to ourselves."

On Tour, Goosen's entourage consisted of one person, his caddie, Irishman Colin Byrne. (Goosen has never minded that Byrne wrote a weekly newspaper column for the *Irish Times*, a clear sign that he was perturbed by nothing.) He tended to pshaw coaching. Yet by most accounts it took an intervention by one kind of coach, a sports psychologist, to get Goosen playing his best golf. At the 2000 U.S. Open at Southern Hills, Jos Vanstiphout, working with Goosen at Els' suggestion, read him a very loud and very public riot act that stopped just short of a bitch-slap. That week Goosen won his first major.

His second came at the 2004 U.S. Open at Shinnecock, where, in the final round, Goosen put on the most flawless display of championship golf this side of Tiger Woods' 2000 U.S. Open victory at Pebble Beach. On a day that lives in golf infamy, the USGA allowed the greens to dry up and die. Addressing a putt—even a putt with little or no slope—was to know what it felt like to have your finger on a hair-trigger. "We were all busy complaining about the golf course," said Els, "and Retief just kept quiet and did his thing." Afterward, Dave Pelz said he'd never seen anyone—anyone—putt that well.

That win, more than anything else, was why Goosen looked like such a lock to finish off his third U.S. Open victory at Pinehurst. Victory seemed so certain that every weekly golf writer in the world had finished his Sunday story by Saturday night. But by 4:00 p.m. on Sunday they were all pushing delete. Goosen's explanation was typically succinct and straightforward. "What can I say? I messed up badly," he said.

Through the first five holes at Quail Hollow, Goosen hit the ball so poorly that a repeat of his North Carolina nightmare didn't seem out of the question. He was spraying his tee shots everywhere, yet somehow managed two birdies, and led by one as the trio walked off the 6th green. Eventually, though, his errant driver caught up with him, and it was Immelman who took advantage. He made his second straight birdie on the 8th, a short par-four so thick with pines that it smelled like Christmas, and now led Goosen by two strokes, and Furyk by three.

Of the three players, Immelman seemed the least likely winner. He was young—just 26—and was ranked eightieth in the world, with most of his points having been earned in Europe and South Africa. He had never played a full year on the PGA Tour (this was his first; he had bought a house at Lake Nona, on Els' and Goosen's advice, earlier in the year) and had only three top-tens to show for his forty-two career PGA Tour appearances.

Indeed, his American rep was tainted by the appearance of nepotism. Immelman was a captain's pick at the 2005 Presidents Cup, even though he was at the time ranked fifty-sixth in the world. (Ten other eligible players were ranked higher.) The man who picked him for the team was captain Gary Player. Player wasn't a blood relative, but he might has well have been. During that Presidents Cup Player privately said that he had "known Trevor since before he was born." Actually, they had first met when Trevor was six. His father, Johan, was a leading figure in South African golf and had long been a friend of Player's. (He had been commissioner of the country's Sunshine Tour since 1990.) "I have photos of myself with him when he was this big," Player added, holding his hand about waist-high.

The controversy surrounding that selection didn't die easily. It was present, in fact, at Trevor's every 2006 PGA Tour start: his exemption was the product of a rule that automatically granted status to any member of a Presidents or Ryder Cup team, whether qualifier or captain's pick.

But that didn't mean Immelman wasn't a better player than half the guys holding Tour cards. His four international victories proved it. If testimony was needed, his circle of friends—which included Tim Clark, Adam Scott, and Geoff Ogilvy, the man who perhaps most deserved that Presidents Cup spot, but never complained about not getting it—were happy to provide it.

The friends had known each other since they were teenagers, meeting often as the top players at international junior tournaments. They later cut their teeth together on the European Tour. From the beginning Immelman was a little different, his golf pedigree having imbued an early seriousness about the game. "He always carried himself like a professional, even in those days," Ogilvy said. Adding to his resolve was the fact that he was slightly undersized. But he always had a sense of humor about himself. It, like Clark's, was reflected in his choice of headcovers. On Immelman's driver was Grumpy, one of the seven dwarfs.

As the final group went to the 9th, it finally started to rain. Up went the players' umbrellas. The caddies hustled dry towels out of their bags and hung them from the metal girdings. Goosen and Immelman slipped on the other halves of their rainsuits. But Furyk did not. He made do with his V-neck sweater. Rain jackets, he said, always make him feel "all bound up." Being soaked to the skin posed no problem at all.

Despite all the talk of coolness under pressure, Furyk was in fact chock-full of nervous tics. His inveterate greenside nail-biting was only the beginning. Before every shot, he rubbed his elbows against his sides as if to hitch up his pants, although his pants never moved an inch. Strolling around the greens, he tweezed the fronts of his pants legs with his fingers. (What he was doing was making compulsive adjustments to his boxer briefs.) Every so often he released some saliva from his mouth, not so much spitting as drooling. His elaborate putting routine was maddeningly wacky. As *Golf Magazine's* Cameron Morfit once put it, it featured more changes of address than Larry Brown. But all this served a purpose: keeping him calm and focused. And in these conditions, that was paramount.

By the time they reached the 16th, the rain had stopped. Immelman was still leading, at −13, one ahead of Furyk. Goosen, for his part, had fallen off the pace. At −10, he was more or less done.

The final three holes at Quail Hollow make up the toughest home stretch on Tour. The gauntlet begins with a long par-four, then moves to a 217-yard par-three whose left side is bordered by a lake. The 18th, another par-four, is pucker material all the way, with a creek running all the way down its left side, and a green whose traditional Sunday front-left pin placement, just a few yards from the hazard, is impossible to get close to. Forget birdies. These holes are about survivalist pars.

Furyk and Immelman safely negotiated the 16th and 17th. On the 18th they got their balls in play—and then paused to watch a horror movie. Goosen found the creek off the tee. He took a penalty drop, and had 208 yards left. Then he fatted his three-iron, sending his ball back into the hazard. He had to drop again, but this time needed a ruling to determine the proper place.

Immelman started to look antsy, but Furyk didn't mind it a bit. He said to Fluff, "He's putting the old four corners on him." Basketball again. Translation: Goosen's troubles were frustrating Immelman, applying the golf equivalent of Dean Smith's old North Carolina stall. About the delay Furyk later said, "I knew it wasn't hurting me, if you want to put it that way." (Goosen eventually made a nine, moving him from solo third to a tie for tenth, and costing himself $264,600. What could one say? He messed up badly.)

When Immelman finally hit his approach, it finished long and well right of the front-left flag. With Furyk in position to make par, he would have to get down in two to win. But his first putt wouldn't be easy. He was facing a treacherous 35-footer, downhill all the way, and virtually impossible to stop near the hole.

As Immelman sized up the putt, Furyk noticed something odd. Half of the Jumbotron to the right of the green displayed Immelman's picture. The other half detailed a statistic: on the year, the South African was 154th—almost dead last on Tour—in three-putt avoidance when putting from beyond 25 feet.

A little weird for that to be posted up there, Furyk thought to himself.

Right on cue, Immelman rolled his first putt twelve feet past the hole, almost onto the fringe. His missed the comebacker, making bogey. Play-off.

Furyk had mixed feelings about play-offs. He was, at the time, 1–6 in extra innings on the PGA Tour. One of the losses had come exactly fifty-two weeks earlier, at the hands of Singh. But Furyk wasn't thinking of that. Instead, he dwelt on his international streak of one straight play-off win, which began over the winter at the Nedbank Challenge in South Africa, where he chipped in on the second extra hole to defeat Goosen, Adam Scott, and Darren Clarke.

This time the play-off was mercifully short, and the result again to Furyk's liking. Immelman made another bogey, and Furyk's paint-by-numbers par earned him the eleventh Tour victory.

After an indoor trophy ceremony—it had started to rain again—Furyk got into his courtesy Mercedes with his family. Tabitha had already packed up the car, so they headed straight to the airport. Jim was, in his words, "a vegetable" when he got on the plane, and he quickly dozed off. When he woke up, he and his family were in Dallas, having arrived a day early (according to their usual schedule) for that week's Byron Nelson Championship. Furyk turned on his cell phone and zipped through his messages. One of them was from Tiger Woods.

9

THE DOG DAYS
OF NOT-QUITE-SUMMER

The Colonial

The weeks between the Masters and the U.S. Open were traditionally the snooziest on the PGA Tour schedule. Occupied mostly by lesser events such as Harbour Town, New Orleans, and the Colonial, they were like baseball's midsummer dog days, only with slightly cooler weather.

Two tournaments were exceptions. The Wachovia Championship, since its inception in 2003, had become the new belle of the post-Masters ball. And the Memorial, positioned two weeks before the Open, had a kind of glamour because of its host, Jack Nicklaus. Still, they weren't majors. During this stretch, following the Tour was like being on a long plane ride with multiple refueling stops. No matter where the landings were, it was hard not to think of them merely as inconvenient delays on the way to one's final destination.

The movement of the Players Championship into May, beginning in 2007, figured to change that. But it couldn't change the mood of most of the surrounding tournaments. These were low-key weeks. And yet, there was a certain edginess about them, with many of the rank-and-filers—especially those whose seasons had started poorly—trying to right their games in time for the three summertime majors.

Their anxiety had a trickle-down effect on the Tour's supporting cast—the caddies, trainers, sports psychologists, and swing gurus who made up the players' retinues. They were easy scapegoats for substandard early season play. The period between April and June always saw plenty of pink slips. But that wasn't necessarily a bad thing, since every job that went vacant was another job that had to be filled.

As far as caddie changes went, the 2006 mid season was typically busy. At Hilton Head, Sean O'Hair, the 2005 Rookie of the Year, decided to try his young wings without father-in-law Steve Lucas, who had caddied for him ever since he graduated from Q-school. Lucas's replacement was Bobby Verwey, a nephew of Gary Player's whose biggest prior gig was looping for Michelle Wie in her first PGA Tour appearance, at the 2004 Sony Open. John Daly let go his longtime bagman, Peter Van Der Reit, in Houston. Bubba Watson unceremoniously canned John Hillerbeck after he failed to show up for his man's Thursday tee time at the Nelson. At the Colonial, Tim Herron rehired his caddie of seven years, the compulsively affable Scotty Steele, after a brief separation.

Transitions among trainers, sports psychologists, and swing teachers happened less frequently. But when they did, they were often more interesting. Splits involving top players were noisy affairs: think, for example, of Tiger Woods' split with Butch Harmon in 2003. They could also be comical, as when dedicated junk-food addict Chris DiMarco signed on with Vijay Singh's disciplinarian trainer, Joey Diovisalvi, in early 2006.

Every once in a while the Tour welcomed a brand-new face, who, after a quick success or two, becomes the most talked-about person on the range. It's almost like what happens when a cute new girl or boy arrives at the local high school, except for the money involved.

In 2004, it happened twice. Gio Valiante, a young, charismatic sports psychologist from Florida's Rollins College, started out working with two players who at that point were relative newcomers, Chad Campbell and Heath Slocum. Their success became his success. By the middle of that year his client list had doubled in size, as he took on Charles Howell, Justin Leonard, and Chris DiMarco. When Leonard and DiMarco both wound up in the three-man playoff at that summer's PGA Championship at Whistling Straits, Valiante's name was writ large in every substantial tournament recap. Before long he was a regular on The Golf Channel, a bona fide TV star.

Toward the end of that same year, a man named Jim Weathers suddenly became ubiquitous at Tour venues. He was hard to miss—a six-foot-four, fu-manchu'd bruiser whose deeply tanned biceps strained his short-sleeved shirts, like Bill Bixby caught in mid-Hulk transformation. By trade Weathers was a trainer—kind of. His business card said "chronic pain specialist," "motivational speaker," "shiatsu master," and "reflexologist." But to his clients he was a healer, whose very touch seemed to relieve all kinds of aches and pains.

Weathers' left bicep, emblazoned with a highly visible Marine Corps Green Beret tattoo, told only part of his story. While in Asia, he was injured during a parachuting drill and wound up seeking help from a renowned female spiritualist in Tokyo. The woman, said Weathers, immediately recognized him as a shaman. "You have so much energy running through you that I can't sleep at night," she told him. "I've been looking for you for thirty years."

Weathers wound up on Tour by accident, running into perpetually ailing pro Ted Purdy in the weight room at the Westin La Cantera resort on the Wednesday of September 2004's Texas Open in San Antonio. Weathers gave Purdy a 10:00 p.m. massage, and the next day Purdy shot a course record 61. Eight weeks later, Weathers treated Jerry Kelly at the Tour Championship. Kelly's left shoulder was in such bad shape that he had been planning on hitting one shot, withdrawing, collecting $90,000 last-place prize money, and flying home to have surgery. In the end, Kelly wound up playing all four rounds, canceling the surgery, and finishing third.

In 2006, most of the mid-season non-caddie movement involved swing gurus. O'Hair also parted ways with David Leadbetter, who, preoccupied with Michelle Wie, had also been let go two months earlier by Charles Howell. (Howell and Leadbetter would reunite by September.) O'Hair took up with Gary Gilchrist, O'Hair's original instructor at Leadbetter's Bradenton Academy.

Another instructor, Matt Killen, was also moving up in the world, even though he was only 21. At first, Killen's only client was Kenny Perry; he had gotten to know the nine-time Tour winner through Perry's son, Justin. In May 2006, Killen took on his second student, former PGA Champion Sean Micheel. By the end of the summer he would also start working with J. B. Holmes, who, after winning in Phoenix, had been struggling to make cuts.

But the hottest names on the range were Mike Bennett and Andy Plummer.

The two initially hung their dual-practitioner shingle out on Tour in 2004. They had their first success in late 2005, spurring Steve Elkington to a second-place finish at the PGA Championship at Baltusrol. Now, in 2006, their stock was going through the locker room roof. The primary reason was a first victory, with Aaron Baddeley at Hilton Head. For new Tour-based instructors, heading out to the range with a first win—especially with a player like Baddeley, who had seemingly lost his way—was the equivalent of wearing a steak suit to a dog pound. Suddenly Bennett and Plummer were besieged by pros looking for help.

Tim Herron was asking questions. John Cook was taking notes during his practice rounds with Tommy Armour III, who regularly worked with the pair. Scott McCarron wanted to have lunch. Ben Crane and Bernhard Langer started sniffing around. So too did Colombian Camilo Villegas, Trinidadian Stephen Ames, and Canadian Mike Weir. "If things keep up like this," Plummer joked, "we're going to wind up with half of next year's Presidents Cup team."

"It's funny how the dominoes fall," Bennett said. "If you have success with one guy, everyone wants your phone number."

They hardly seemed suited to all the attention. Minus their video-cams, they both looked like misplaced high school English teachers. Plummer, a 39-year-old native Kentuckian, invariably wore white polos and khakis. (Players joked that he was his profession's answer to Chad Campbell.) Bennett, 38, from tiny Jordan, New York, near Syracuse, was similarly unshocking. Although he owned one or two striped golf shirts, they were usually covered up with beige pullovers. His little square eye-glasses only emphasized his bookish, unathletic look.

Both began teaching by accident. In the early nineties, when they were both mini-tour grunts looking to improve their games, they went out to Palm Springs to work with legendary eccentric Mac O'Grady. O'Grady had just more or less retired from a twenty-year pro career that included sixteen flunked Q-schools, two Tour wins, and a famous weeping fit on the 15th green while in contention during the final round at the 1987 U.S. Open at San Francisco's Olympic Club.

O'Grady's bible was a curious little yellow tome called *The Golfing*

Machine, a dense, physics- and mathematics-laced manual penned by a golf nut named Homer Kelley, who worked in the jewelry business but moonlighted as a consultant for Boeing. The book had been all the rage in the early 'eighties, chiefly because it underlay the youthful success of current CBS broadcaster Bobby Clampett. Clampett, "Mr. Golfing Machine," lived by the book and had become the youngest player in PGA Tour history to amass $500,000 in career earnings.

In 1984, however, Clampett's game went south, and the book's reputation went right along with it. Indeed, it was blamed for destroying his career. That, along with its forbidding terminology, sent it into an instructional exile that would last twenty years. As far as PGA Tour pros were concerned, Kelley's swing elixir may as well have been Jonestown Kool-Aid.

Yet O'Grady never lost the faith. He had grown up with the *Machine,* reading and rereading it (along with Kahlil Gibran's *The Prophet*) with a battery-powered lamp as a homeless teenager living in a storage bin in Los Angeles. It now became the cornerstone of his single-minded search for the ideal swing.

When Bennett and Plummer arrived in Palm Springs to work with O'Grady they too embraced its principles. They soon became "Macolytes," giving up playing for teaching and working alongside their mentor in his invitation-only swing symposia. Eventually, however, they were excommunicated from the flock. Bennett's transgression, he said, was a week of poor caddying for O'Grady at one of his boss's rare Tour appearances, at the 1997 CVS Charity Classic. In Plummer's case it was disobeying O'Grady's edict not to work with pros like Elkington. One after the other, the two moved back east and took club pro jobs.

Over the years, they kept in touch with each other, and with Elkington. When the 1998 PGA Championship winner invited Plummer out to work with him, they realized they had a foothold on Tour. By the end of 2005 they had also hooked up with Armour; Dean Wilson, the Hawaiian-born grinder who was Weir's college teammate at BYU; and New Zealander Grant Waite, whose claim to fame was his second-place finish at the 2000 Canadian Open, where he was beaten by Tiger Woods' famous 6-iron out of thick rough over a lake to a tucked pin on the par-five 18th hole, perhaps the best shot Woods has ever hit.

Bennett and Plummer's teaching drew heavily, but not exclusively, on *The Golfing Machine.* "For us, the basic principles are absolute," Bennett explained. "But when it comes to actually playing the game, some of it is just brutally poor."

They also adopted some of O'Grady's teachings. Their humility, relaxed demeanors, and teaching styles, however, were worlds away from O'Grady's. "Mac demanded a lot—he had you standing out on that range ten hours a day," said Elkington, whose history with O'Grady dated back to the eighties. "But Mike and Andy can fix most guys in two swings."

Baddeley's win wasn't the only thing working to their advantage. It also helped that Armour and Wilson were hyperactive evangelists, singing Bennett and Plummer's praises like doorstep Jehovah's Witnesses. Armour also brought them attention from outside the Tour. His Hollywood connections included actor Mark Wahlberg and his entourage. By the week of the U.S. Open, the real-life Johnny Drama (Wahlberg's cousin) was ringing Bennett's BlackBerry for swing tips. Also enhancing their visibility were their practice rounds with Armour, a frequent Tuesday partner of Tiger Woods.

During the summer of 2006, their appointment books swelled. The demand forced one or both of them to attend every Tour event from Monday to Wednesday, Invariably they worked 12-hour days. (From Thursday through Sunday they held down their club jobs. Bennett was at Metedeconk in Jackson, New Jersey, and Plummer at Aronimink in Newton Square, Pennsylvania, near Philadelphia.)

Not that they minded being busy. Both were self-professed golf junkies. Bennett, who was married in July, videoed himself hitting balls off a pier into Lake Winnipesaukee, in New Hampshire, while on his honeymoon, with his new wife, Heather, sunbathing in the foreground.

Despite their new popularity, some players still saw their teaching as anathema. Their association with O'Grady was a lingering stigma, as was their fondness for *The Golfing Machine,* whose angles and tilts and multiple planes reminded some of a class they almost failed in high school. It didn't help that Bennett and Plummer insisted that students grasp its basic principles. "Some guys just want you to fix the computer," said Elkington. "Mike and Andy want to open up the computer and show you how it works."

One night at dinner during the week of the U.S. Open, Dean Wilson aped the response he sometimes witnessed while practicing with his teachers. Turning his head as if to cough, he muttered, "Fucking cult."

Besides, the swing Bennett and Plummer were teaching was just plain funny-looking.

Most brand-name, Golf Channel–trumpeted teachers—from Leadbetter to Harmon to Haney—advocated a big move off the ball, loading into the right side to produce power, with the shoulders remaining level. Bennett and Plummer, on the other hand, stress staying stacked over the ball, with much less weight shift, and a steep shoulder turn. Their signature move resembled one that teaching pros reflexively drilled out of beginners' swings. "At first it looks and feels like a reverse pivot," Baddeley said. "But now I absolutely love the feeling of being right on top of the ball."

Wilson was easily the most outspoken proponent of their methods. Early in his career, he said, he "bounced from one top teacher to another, but things kept getting worse. There was a time, in the middle of 2004, when I didn't want to hit balls in front of people anymore."

His game came together only when he ditched the distance-oriented swing models in favor of Bennett and Plummer's emphasis on consistent ball striking. The power game, he said, "is fine for guys who hit it as far as Tiger, Phil, and Vijay. But what about the rest of us? We're not going to beat anybody trying to play that way."

To underline the ills of those dominant swing models, Wilson liked to tell the story of his clubhouse lunch with Jack Nicklaus at the 2006 Memorial. Wilson had recently purchased (on eBay) a copy of Nicklaus's hard-to-find 1980 book *The Full Swing*. He took it with him to that lunch and went over some swing sequences with his host.

"These pictures," Wilson said, "make me think that all these new teachers are wrong. They all say you have to get your weight behind the ball, and onto the right side, to get any power. But you didn't do that, and you were known for your driving."

Nicklaus shook his head and said, "I've never believed all that modern stuff."

Of the dog days' weaker events, the ones with most personality were Dallas's Byron Nelson Classic and Fort Worth's Colonial.

The Nelson's public image was defined by the man for whom it was named. Late in his life—in his eighties and early nineties—Lord Byron would sit in a chair above the 18th green, near the scoring trailer, not only shaking the hand of each finisher, but asking about their rounds and pointedly thanking them for participating.

All of them knew of his greatness as a player, though most knew that it came with an asterisk. About twenty of the fifty-two wins and two of the five majors in his eleven-year career (he more or less retired in 1946) were earned against fields weakened by peers' World War II military obligations. (Sam Snead and Ben Hogan, who were born in the same year as Nelson, both served; a blood-clotting deficiency kept Nelson home.) The players' respect, however, was only partly based on his record. Early each year they received personal handwritten invitations from the last of the gentleman golfers. You couldn't drink them, like the Wachovia's bottles of Dom, but they were far more cherished. When Nelson passed away on September 26, 2006, every one of those old letters became cherished keepsakes.

But the Nelson had another side that was as dark as a private booth at a strip club. Its secret preoccupation, in a word, was sex. There was, of course, the infamous 2005 pre-tournament party at Armour's house, steps from the far end of the Las Colinas driving range: that year sushi was served atop the prone, naked bodies of two young women.

There was also the Pavilion, the Nelson's answer to Phoenix's Bird's Nest. It was first and foremost a tented Oktoberfest. But it was also a notorious meat market. In the early nineties, a familiar sight was a group of men sitting in folding chairs and holding up scoring placards, Olympics-style, to grade the looks of female passers-by. There was talk that some of the men were members of the Salesmanship Club, the organization that ran the tournament.

Tour Rats—equipment reps, writers, caddies, and their ilk—ranked the local talent as the best all year, though they often made connoisseurs' complaints about surgical torso enhancement and bigness of hair. Their walks past the pool at the Four Seasons, where Tour wives and nannies liked to lie out, featured more covert glances than a year's worth of detective films.

In 2006 Brett Wetterich won the Nelson. To most he was a relative unknown. Coming out of the tournament most reporters worked the family angle, emphasizing the recent death of Wetterich's brother. The story was touching enough. But that didn't mean his win wasn't deeply disappointing to the event organizers. Yes, they smiled when the photographers snapped the group pictures at the trophy presentation. But inwardly they knew it would be hard to sell tickets to the following year's event with Wetterich's picture in all the pre-tournament advertising.

(At that point in time, the possibility that he might quickly become a star—maybe even a Ryder Cupper—never crossed their minds.) It was what tournament directors called the Curse of the No-Name Winner.

Any of the other players in contention on Sunday would have been a preferable winner. Adam Scott had played in the final group—he would have been a big hit. Same for South African Trevor Immelman, who, improbably, had a history in Dallas. He lived there for a year as a pre-teen while his father, who was in the spirits business, had come to the States to develop a new brand. Local boy Chad Campbell, playing a group behind them, would also have been a popular winner. Even UNLV alum Charlie Hoffman, who played in the next-to-last group with Campbell, would have been better, simply because he was so weird-looking. With his slouch, baggy clothes, and impossibly long blond hair, he looked like the secret love child of Craig Stadler and Cousin It.

Two secondary aspects of Wetterich's victory, at any rate, did merit some interest.

One was the way he won. Those close to the game had long known that Wetterich was one of its most powerful players. Some swore that before Watson and Holmes came along, he was the longest guy on Tour—longer even than Woods, Daly, or Hank Kuehne. Despite that advantage, Wetterich went around Las Colinas hitting 5- and 3-woods. It was a refreshing change to the way Bubba and J.B. slashed their way around, and showed that sometimes there's a better way to exploit one's power than hitting driver everywhere. Two months later, a slightly better-known player would employ a similar strategy to win the British Open.

The other was its Ryder Cup implications. Indeed, Wetterich's win made Captain Tom Lehman break out in a cold sweat. Coming into the week, Wetterich was forty-first in the U.S. team rankings. But the new Cup points system—which Lehman helped devise—so heavily weighted 2006 Tour wins that the Nelson winner suddenly climbed to number ten. A week later, Lehman could only feel worse. Paired with Wetterich on Thursday and Friday at the following week's Colonial, Lehman watched him shoot 73–74 and miss the cut by six shots.

When the Nelson was over, the Tour caravan packed up and drove to its next stop, the Colonial Invitational in Fort Worth.

No two Tour stops were closer together on the map. They also shared a few traits. One was an association with a legend. For years, Colonial Country Club was Ben Hogan's home course. He also dominated the tournament, winning it five times in the forties and fifties. The Club's Hogan Room, packed with memorabilia, was as impressive as any exhibit at any golf hall of fame.

Another, less seemly commonality was determined drinking. On Thursday morning of the 2006 edition, the first margarita of the day was sold at 8:30 a.m., which prompted *Dallas Morning News* golf writer Bill Nichols to quip, "It was surprising that anybody who drinks tequila that early was up that early."

On the whole, however, the Colonial was markedly more subdued. The heat had a lot to do with it. Despite the geographical and seasonal proximity, the Colonial always seemed twenty degrees hotter than the Nelson. In recent years it wasn't unusual to see players, between shots, ducking under the trees that lined the fairways. In the afternoons the practice range was often empty. Those who weren't obliged to be on the golf course fled to their hotel rooms and hugged their air conditioners.

The other reason was the weakness of its field. After his 1997 appearance Tiger Woods never again played the tournament. In 2004, asked about his annual snub, he said the tight little track "didn't suit my game." (He was right, but the Colonial's MasterCard sponsorship might have had something to do with it, given his deal with American Express.) Apart from sporadic visits from Phil Mickelson, the only recent buzz had been generated by Annika Sorenstam's 2003 visit. (After 2003 Vijay Singh stayed away, so as not to have to relive his "hope she misses the cut" incident.)

Everyone who did play claimed to do so because they loved the course. It was a ballstriker's paradise, they said, a place where accuracy and shot-shaping (as opposed to raw power) were paramount. Kenny Perry meant it when he said it. He had won the event twice between 2003 and 2005, and was more or less the place's sheriff. David Toms did, too. He certainly didn't come to town to visit his friends at Links Sports, who were headquartered in the area; during his 2005 Wednesday press conference, where he first publicly mentioned his lawsuit, one of Links' agents came in, sat down in the back, and taped the proceedings in case he said something actionable.

Most of the other players came for the same reasons they went to any other tournament: to find some magic and make some money. In 2006, those tasks, for two players in particular, had developed a certain urgency.

• • •

One of the consequences of the riches of the Tiger Era is the temptation, for many pros, to slack off.

Each player arrives on Tour working hard, looking to build a reputation, and trying to find out how good he can get. One win comes, and maybe another, establishing him as a recognizable name. Then something happens. Family becomes a distraction—a happy distraction, but a distraction nonetheless. Age creeps up, his body fills out, and late in his rounds tucked pins get harder to find.

He finds it hard to admit he's slipping or that he should work any harder because the money's so good. Just a couple of top-fives per year—not a tall order, given the abundance of weak-field events on the inflated Tour schedule—keeps his salary north of $1 million. His endorsements are another quarter-mil. Throw in the odd, accidental win every couple of years, and the endorsement bonuses alone are enough to buy the house out from underneath his next-door neighbor, no matter how fancy your neighborhood.

Staying hungry only gets harder, since he's so well fed. He may even find that he doesn't really like golf—as everyone knows, it's ultimately a pretty stupid game. And playing all the time can't help but become a grind. Gradually it becomes harder to leave the house for tournaments. Who wants to be out in the hot summer sun all day, every day? Or worse, finishing up a rain-delayed round at 8:45 p.m., when he could be at home, driving his kids home from the ice cream parlor?

In one way he's drawn the long straw. He gets to enjoy the spoils of the Tiger Era, but doesn't have to put up with the hassles of stardom. In another way, though, he's let himself down. Golf has become just another way to earn a living. He's become a clock-puncher.

This kind of mid-career malaise isn't exclusive to golf. Every year the corporate community spends millions of dollars combating it, in the form of executive seminars and retreats. Golf's motivational speakers, of course, go by a different name. They're called sports psychologists. But the lessons are the same: try to stay fresh, do what you can to have fun with your work, and try to find the right balance between career, family, and outside interests.

It doesn't always work. It's especially difficult for athletes—for whom anything less than total commitment can't help but result in an attenuation of skills. It's hard to stay happy when the very concept of a balanced lifestyle means accepting a performance downturn. With age working against him, spending more time with his family can be the royal road to losing his job.

When the Tour reached the dog days of 2006, Chris Riley was starting to stare that possibility square in the face. For Tim Herron, things weren't quite that bad, but there were some foreboding signs.

By the numbers, Herron's career was healthy. Lumpy was just coming off three of his best seasons on Tour—his money list finishes in 2003 through 2005 were three of the four highest in his ten-year career. The theory was that his recent play had everything to do with his starting a family. His wife, Ann, gave birth to their first child midway through 2002. Playing well right after starting a family was a common phenomenon. It even had a name, the "first-baby bounce." There were golf bettors, notably in England, who invested large sums of money in it.

Still, not all was right in his world. He hadn't won since 1999, when he was 29, and he wasn't getting any younger. Those three solid years from 2003 to 2005 featured only eight top-threes. Closer inspection of his earnings showed that he made a lot of his money through the back door, shooting some of his best rounds on Sundays, the day that less seasoned pros normally head south. He'd earned his only big check of 2006—a T7 at New Orleans—that way, with a Sunday 67. Going into the Colonial, he'd earned $389,706 on the year, the kind of figure that could easily convince you that you were playing great. On the money list, however, he was ninety-third.

Perhaps more telling was a decision he made in late 2005. With twins on the way (two more boys, who would be born in November), he and Ann decided to sell their house in Scottsdale and live full time in their native Minnesota. The reason was child care—the kids would be easier to raise with grandparents around to help out. Of Scottsdale he said, "We knew it was going to be difficult raising the children there." It was "just as important to be around family" as it was to be able to practice year-round.

Herron's next sentence, however, sounded a different note. "I felt like I could still have a career up there," he said. It showed that he knew the move would adversely affect his game. Some might have argued—indeed, Herron himself may have argued—that the move only reflected a confidence in his skills. But there was another way to look at it. Saying he could "still have a career" after the move was tantamount to saying, "Yeah, my game might slip a little bit, but I'll manage to keep afloat."

Had there been a list of clock-puncher warning signs, the sentiment he was expressing would have ranked at about number six.

Chris Riley's straits were more dire.

The red-haired native San Diegan had always been a happy-go-lucky sort. Guileless and lighthearted, he was the kind of guy Tiger Woods, a friend since junior golf, referred to as "a beaut." A few years earlier, in sunnier times, a reporter, reading through a list of softball profile questions, asked him if he had any pets.

"I have a pet rat," he replied.

C'mon, Chris. Really?

He never flinched. "I have a pet rat named Felix."

Felix the rat?

"That's right!" he said, his poker face finally cracking. "Felix the rat!"

Never much of a ballstriker, Riley lived on his putting, still taking some money from Woods during occasional practice-day putting contests. (Once in a while, when putting badly, Woods hit putts during tournament rounds with his head stock-still, his eyes never looking up to following the ball, just listening for the sound of it hitting the bottom of the cup. He got the idea from Riley.)

In December 2002 Riley married Michelle Louviere, an LSU alum who had played two years on the LPGA Tour and the Futures Tour (the LPGA's feeder circuit). Theirs was a New Orleans jazz wedding, complete with a march down Bourbon Street. (In attendance were pros Craig Barlow and Chad Campbell. Both were Riley's UNLV teammates; Campbell was his roommate.) Michelle was from Lafayette, Louisiana, a brunette whose easy smile seemed custom-built to enjoy Riley's goofy humor. Her mother, Barbara, smiled the same way when Riley, during their courtship, would call the house and ask, "So, is the moss still hanging from the trees down there?"

Chris and Michelle settled in Las Vegas, built a new house, and made plans to start a family. Their future looked bright. Between 2001 through 2004, Riley's second through sixth years on tour, he placed in the top sixty on the money list four times, and just inside the top twenty-five twice. He had won once, at the 2002 Reno-Tahoe Open.

Still, most golf fans only knew Riley for his disastrous appearance at the 2004 Ryder Cup. After winning a Saturday morning four-ball match alongside Woods, he was benched for the afternoon session. Word leaked out that he had begged out of playing, saying he was "tired." He was pilloried for it and never bothered to defend himself, even though his fatigue would have been perfectly understandable: his first child, daughter Taylor Lynn, had been born only sixteen days earlier.

Early 2005, however, saw the start of a pronounced downslide. That year he made just eleven of twenty-five cuts and had only one top twenty, a T18 at the Hope, in January. He finished 184th on the money list. His start in 2006 was no better. In eleven starts, he had missed four cuts and withdrawn twice; in the other five never finished higher than thirty-first. Coming to Colonial, he was 181st on the money list. It was still early in the year, but the writing was on the wall. His prospects for retaining his card were not good.

Many blamed his slide on that miserable Ryder Cup experience. But that wasn't it. It was another first-baby bounce, only this time in the wrong direction. "I don't know what to say," he shrugged on Friday afternoon at Colonial, after a one-over 71 that left him at -1, in a tie for twenty-fifth place. "I haven't been the same for about a year and a half now. I had put so much work and energy into it. That was my whole focus—golf. And now it's just that I really love being with my daughter. I'm happy for the opportunity to play on Tour. But still." He already seemed resigned that the following year, he would be playing somewhere else.

The following day, he shot a 66, his best round since January 2005. In his first decent post-round mood in some time, he sat down on a bench in Colonial's low-ceilinged locker room and unburdened himself about Tour pressures, shifting priorities, and what really happened at that Ryder Cup.

"When I made that Ryder Cup," he started out, "it was almost like, okay, I've reached my goal. And that same week"—actually, two weeks earlier—"we started our family. So all of the sudden I'm really not as focused on golf. I'm probably, like, seventy-five percent focused on [my family]. I still try hard but I'm not—I mean, it's not the same."

Leaving home to hit balls, he said, "it's almost like I try to hurry up and practice and get back home to see my kid. I don't know. It's just weird. And then, when I'm on the road, I miss being at home. Some guys can go three or four weeks without seeing their kids. But I can't.

"And then when you take them on the road, you wind up wanting to kill somebody!" he laughed. It wasn't just her crying at night that drove him crazy. It gave him the creeps to have his daughter in any hotel room at all. When Taylor Lynn was with him, he said, he traveled "with a can of Lysol—you know, everywhere we go, spraying everything down."

It didn't figure to get any easier. He and Michelle were expecting another child the following month. At a point that demanded he get in as many starts as possible, he was about to take four weeks off.

"I'm not throwing it in or anything," he continued. "I may have to go back down to the Nationwide Tour. But I'm not afraid to do that. I love the game of golf. But right now I'm getting my ass kicked."

The conversation eventually turned, as it had to, to the 2004 Ryder Cup, and that fateful conversation with Hal Sutton.

Riley's version was this. "We were walking down the 13th hole, a par-three. I had hit it in there like this close." He held up his hands, with his index fingers extended in front of his chest. "Hal goes, 'You going to be ready to go again this afternoon with Tiger?' And I go—I think these were my exact words— 'Man, I'm tired, but this is awesome!' You know, you're a rookie at the Ryder Cup, and you're tired just during practice rounds." On top of that, the new arrival in his house meant that he "hadn't been getting much sleep. Like, four hours a night.

"It's funny," he continued. "That was the best time of my life, the Ryder Cup. And it might have been my downfall.

"If you had told me I'd have just eight, ten years, out here, I would have taken it. I don't need to play at the highest level. I don't need to be on the grand stage all the time. Do you know how well I played golf in '02, '03 and '04? I was getting *everything* out of my game. *Everything.* I was chipping in from everywhere. I didn't miss any of these putts." He stretched his arms out wide. "Now I'll miss two or three in a row. I'm a good player. But dude, it's tough out there. These are the best players in the world. I mean, if you don't play good, you're going to get run over. I don't care if you play halfway decent. Some of these guys, like Davis Love or Tiger, can just play decent and still be up at the top. But if a guy like Chris Riley doesn't play good, I'm missing the cut. That's all there is to it.

"It's tough out here. You have to be so focused on just this. I know I'm not good enough to just come out here and play like I've been play-ing—half-assed—and keep my card. These other guys work way too hard for me to do that. But whatever happens happens. I'm not living or dying with it, like I used to. Who knows what's going to happen? How I'm going to feel, in three or four years from now? Maybe I'll find a way to get hungry again."

One reflection of Riley's vacillating feelings about the game was what happened when he reached out for help.

Just prior to the 2006 season, Riley had spent several days hitting balls on the driving range at the TPC at Summerlin with Andy Plummer.

Not surprisingly, their connection was Wilson, who also lives in Las Vegas. Plummer had been flying out to see him throughout 2005. Riley noticed, and by December he too was taking private lessons.

In January Riley thought about formalizing a relationship with Bennett and Plummer. He even sought Wilson's advice about which of the two to work with.

"Who do you like better?" he asked. "Mike or Andy?"

"Chris, it doesn't matter," Wilson deadpanned. "They're the same guy."

Yet when the time came to make a commitment, Riley demurred. When they saw each other in January in Hawaii Riley told Plummer, "I don't know if this is going to happen."

"Is it the money?" Plummer asked. His and Bennett's yearly fee was $30,000.

"That's not it," Riley replied. "I've got plenty of money. It's just that I see you with your guys out here, and you're all together, hitting balls and playing practice rounds and everything. Frankly, I don't know if I want to practice that hard."

Tim Herron's acquaintance with Bennett and Plummer started in May 2006, during New Orleans week. Once again, Wilson was the broker. Herron had admired the way Dean was hitting the ball and scheduled a Tuesday practice round with him. Rain foiled those plans, but he wound up sitting down that morning with Bennett, Tommy Armour, and Tommy's brother Sandy.

The group was encamped at a grated metal table on the covered patio at English Turn. Wilson had with him his copy of Nicklaus's *The Full Swing*, and Bennett explained some of his and Plummer's ideas by way of the book's pictures. What astounded Herron, however, was that Bennett was already thoroughly familiar with his swing. The team's footage of Steve Elkington from the 2005 PGA Championship inadvertently featured Herron: in some of it he was simply standing behind Elkington, staring and smoking the occasional inquisitive cigarette; in other frames he was hitting his own practice balls.

When Wilson told Bennett that Herron was interested in them, Bennett returned to that old footage, this time studying not Elkington, but the guy hitting balls in the background. He had printed some stills from that footage and now had them laid out in front of Herron, dissecting his swing picture by picture.

At one point Mark Calcavecchia stopped by, and Bennett gave him the treatment too. Patiently he explained how Herron's swing resembled Calc's, drawing diagrams and explaining spine angles and swing paths. Calcavecchia, who had never taken a lesson in his life, was quickly lost.

He waited for a lull. Then, with his characteristic glibness, he muttered, "I gotta go," and walked away.

Fucking cult.

Three weeks later, at the Colonial, Herron was ready to give that practice round another try. He walked onto the first tee on Tuesday morning at about 8:45 a.m. Standing alongside Wilson was Chris Riley.

This time, the tutor would be Plummer. He was running a little late; he was about fifty yards up the fairway from the 2nd tee when he spotted them. He positioned himself under a tree, opened up his Sony TRV38, and began filming the threesome's drives.

After his tee shot, Herron made a beeline for Plummer. He peppered him with questions, trying to figure out why he was consistently blocking the ball right. Plummer spent six holes explaining how the excessive rightward tilt of his spine was making it impossible to square his clubface. Riley couldn't get a word in edgewise.

Finally, on the ninth tee, Herron made a swing that pleased both him and Plummer.

"Alright," Herron said. "I've got it. I see what I've got to do. I'm out of here. I've got to go practice." From there he walked directly to the range.

On Thursday, Herron shot a 67, good for a tie for fifteenth. He improved his position with a Friday 65, landing him in a tie for fifth. He shot a pair of 68s on the weekend and ended up winning the tournament.

He nearly won again the following week in Memphis, where he held the lead until late on the back nine on Sunday.

During those two weeks Herron did a lot of interviews. He talked about how good it was to have Scotty Steele back on the bag, how well he was putting, and how the win made him feel a lot better about his decision to move back to Minnesota. Not once did Bennett's or Plummer's name pass his lips.

Weeks later he would privately explain his silence to a reporter, saying that he didn't want to appear disloyal to his longtime coach, Mark Nelson.

Those close to him, however, knew the story. On Monday in Memphis Herron and his wife, Ann, had run into Bennett and Plummer in the player's dining room. "These are the guys who've been helping me with my swing," he said to Ann, by way of introducing them.

For some people that wasn't enough. Dean Wilson, for example, believed that public props were in order.

"You guys really helped him a lot," he remarked to Plummer that same week. "But he hasn't said a thing about it in all those interviews."

"I guess you're right," Plummer said. "But you know what? He's going to need that help again."

10

OF FATHERS, SONS,
AND A DAUGHTER

The Memorial

On Monday, June 6, while hundreds of adult male golfers and one teenage girl were trying to qualify for the U.S. Open, an odd-looking quartet was walking the fairways at the ACE Club in Lancaster, Pennsylvania, just outside Philadelphia. Adam Scott and Sean O'Hair—standard-issue, fit and trim tour pros—were ordinary enough. But with them were John Daly—whose paunch and chain-smoking, as usual, made him look like a bowling alley attendant—and a clubless man who walked along stiffly, as if his back and head had been strapped together on a plank. His name was Jim Furyk.

The occasion was Furyk's charity event, the Exelon Invitational, which annually raised about $200,000 for local Boys & Girls Clubs. Over the years, every pro you'd ever heard of had participated, except for one. But Furyk understood. When Phil Mickelson showed up it was bedlam; a Tiger Woods appearance would have required so much security that that the charity would have had to write Furyk a check, rather than the other way around.

To commit to the date, the four participants' U.S. Open eligibility had to be a settled issue. Furyk was exempt from qualifying because he had won the U.S. Open three years earlier. Scott and O'Hair were in off their top-thirty finishes on the 2005 PGA Tour money list. John Daly wasn't in the Open, but he didn't care. He had withdrawn his entry the previous week, citing a back injury, just as he had withdrawn from his three previous PGA Tour events. But he looked plenty limber today, perhaps because he had hoisted some of the beer sponsor's product even before teeing off, proclaiming, in true Ricky Bobby fashion, "That new Heineken Light—it's pretty good!"

Furyk's injury was very real, even if its genesis was bizarre. That morning, in his hotel bathroom, he had just finished brushing his teeth and was hunched over the sink. From that position, he put a couple of Aleve in his mouth and threw them back. Suddenly pain shot through his upper spine, and the muscles in his upper back seized up. It was the Tour's first-ever case of self-inflicted, anti-inflammatory-related whiplash. Jim Furyk was gonna need some more Aleve.

All afternoon the four men played to the crowd. Daly was head ham, and Furyk, as host, spent most of his time along the ropes, shaking hands, signing autographs, and thanking people for coming. Scott and O'Hair weren't wallflowers, but interacted with the layfolk less than the others. Instead, they spent most of their time between shots continuing to get to know each other.

After Sergio Garcia, Scott and O'Hair were probably the two best young players in the world. Yet they were only starting to get acquainted. They first played together in Los Angeles, at February's Nissan Open. Then, in Dallas at May's Byron Nelson, they were paired for the first two rounds. Sean was struggling; at one point he turned to Adam and said, "What do you do when nothing's going right?" It was the kind of exchange that, between any two people, cultivates trust and confidence. Next was their third round together at the Memorial, a stop-and-go, rain-delayed affair during which they both played poorly—mostly they shook their heads at each other about the weather and their games.

Now, in Pennsylvania, they were building on that foundation, checking each other's technique and trading the occasional word about Winged Foot, the host venue of the following week's U.S. Open. Scott had gone and played an early practice round. O'Hair had never seen the place.

The national championship always concluded on Father's Day, and was therefore a kind of celebration of the way dads passed the game along to their sons. The four players in Philadelphia had been all been introduced to the game that way. Furyk's father, Mike, raised his kid in sports; for a time, he was a club pro. Scott's father, Phil, was a lifelong teaching pro, and Adam literally learned golf at his feet, at Adelaide Golf Club. There was a moment during his adolescence when Adam drifted away from the game, preferring to go surfing. But by the time he was thirteen, he had almost wholly given himself over to the sport that would become his livelihood. After school he went straight to the club, and hit balls endlessly while his dad worked in the shop. When Phil managed to sneak away, they played holes together. It was hard to imagine a stronger bond being formed around the game by a father and a son.

Daly's father too had led his son to golf, but also to the habit that almost destroyed John's life. Jim was a drinker, and his behavior was erratic. When John was growing up, he has said, his father beat both his wife and his son. In 2002 Jim held a loaded shotgun to John's head. John was 36 at the time, but the episode provided some indication of the nature of their relationship.

Sean O'Hair's experience with his father, however, was perhaps more disturbing. His father, Marc, was the kind of nightmare sports dad who served as a stern warning to any parent who harbors dreams for a child of professional success. For Sean, golf was always less a sport than a job. It was entirely predictable that the way Marc forced the game on his son would end in their mutal alienation.

O'Hair's status as one of the game's best young players was still based largely on promise. The 23-year-old, who lived in nearby West Chester, Pennsylvania, had won the 2005 PGA Tour Rookie of the Year award, largely on the strength of his victory at that year's John Deere Classic. He began 2006 as the 37th ranked player in the world. He still had a lot to prove, but his potential seemed limitless.

Scott's résumé, on the other hand, already qualified him as a world-class player. On the advice of Greg Norman (who had watched Scott's development from an early age) he started his career in Europe; Norman paved his way by helping to secure exemptions for him. Scott's success on that tour was immediate. In 2000 it took only eight starts to lock up his playing privileges for that year and the next. In 2001, his first full season, he finished thirteenth on the money list.

In Europe Scotty found not only success but also friends, quickly falling in with countryman Geoff Ogilvy and South Africans Trevor Immelman and Tim Clark. He also found love. He first met Marie Kojzar, a young Swede, while she was working as a nanny for Ryder Cupper Thomas Bjorn. They hit it off quickly, and by Christmas 2001 Marie was headed to Oz to meet the parents.

The trip, however, ended badly, with Scott witnessing an incident in which his father, Phil, almost lost his life—and might have if his son hadn't saved it.

In January, Adam and Phil were jet-skiing near South Stradbroke Island, off the Queensland coast, when Phil was thrown by a rogue wave. It broke his back, smashing a number of vertebrae. Adam watched it happen and had to pick his father's limp body out of the waves, slide it onto his own jet-ski, and take him back to shore. The island, relatively undeveloped, had no medical facilities. It was only because a surfer had his cell phone with him that they were able to call the Coast Guard. A water ambulance back to the mainland was out of the question, because the water was rough, and because Phil's injuries were so severe. He lay on the beach for four hours, sheltered from the sun by standing surfboards, before a rescue helicopter arrived. For months he was in a back brace. He almost had to miss Adam's debut at Augusta that April.

On the golf course, however, Adam never broke stride. He notched his first European Tour victory in March of that year in Qatar and went on to finish seventh on the money list. With his reputation growing, he and Kojzar (who by now was attending university in England, studying architecture and design) became a London glamor couple. Occasionally he ran with new friend Sergio Garcia's posse of European sporting elite. After Sergio dragged Scott to his first football match, to watch Garcia's beloved Real Madrid, they spent a night on the town with Ronaldo and David Beckham.

At the time Scott came to America only sporadically, for majors and World Golf Championship events. His most frequent practice round player was Harmon stablemate Tiger Woods. Adam and Tiger—whose swings at that point were hard to tell apart—wound up facing each other in the semifinals of the 2003 Match Play in Carlsbad. (Scott lost on the 19th hole.) He truly arrived as a star in 2004, when he won the Players

Championship at 23 years of age. It was then that he decided to play full time in America. He ceased playing in continental Europe (except for the Scandinavian Masters, his participation there being mostly Marie's decision). Yet unlike his contemporaries, he never relocated to the States. It lead to some ribbing from Ogilvy and Clark, now based in Scottsdale, about their friend's constant preoccupation with U.S. tax statutes, which forbade him from spending more than 120 tariff-free days on American soil. (Charity outings like Furyk's don't count.)

In the wake of his Players win, Scott became golf's reigning Mr. Sexy, appearing in the popular press in features like *Esquire's* "Best Dressed Men in the World," where he rubbed padded shoulders with George Clooney, Bill Clinton, and Donald Trump. His peers teased him about it mercilessly. Even caddies said things like, "Hello, gorgeous," when he passed by. Scott just rolled his eyes, knowing that protests would make matters worse.

Less unpleasant were the overtures from women. LPGA cheesecake queen Natalie Gulbis once left a signed pinup for him at Harmon's place in Las Vegas. Marie, who was with him when he was presented with it, "wouldn't let me hang it in our home," Scott said, so it stayed at Harmon's. At tournaments he unfailingly drew a coterie of gallery swooners, some of the teenybopper variety, but others who seemed of age and quite willing. Once a reporter approached a Kojzar look-alike and asked if she was indeed Adam's girlfriend. "No," the young woman smiled. "But I'd like to be."

Scott wasn't a perfect player. His short game was an ongoing concern: on the PGA Tour he had never ranked better than 135th in scrambling. His win at the Players, he conceded, was largely the product of a Band-Aid lesson from Norman. "I probably would have lost the tournament, to be honest with you, if I was chipping the same way as I did earlier in the week," he said after the victory. His ballstriking, though his strong suit, had both champions and doubters. Early that same week Johnny Miller proclaimed Scott's "the best swing in golf right now"—just before the young Aussie yanked his last approach shot of the tournament in the lake. "Let me tell you something," Mark O'Meara said privately a few weeks later. "If he's got the best swing in golf, there's no way he rinses that ball on 18. He hits it right, long, short—anywhere but in the water."

Scott started 2006 as the ninth-ranked player in the world. But he wasn't happy. Still a committed surfer (even despite his father's accident), he loved going to Hawaii, but was denied entry to the winners-only Mercedes Championships, despite his apparent qualification. He had won the 2005 Nissan Open at Riviera. That rain-soaked event was called after two rounds, and the Tour deemed it an unofficial victory. Scott felt that he was being punished for something that wasn't his fault. When his petition for entry was refused he was really miffed, "especially when all those other guys didn't show up."

He nearly won Riviera again in 2006, and finished third at the Wachovia and Nelson, the two events directly preceding the Memorial. During a Tuesday practice round at Muirfield Village he and Trevor Immelman had a skull session about their failure to beat Wetterich down the stretch in Dallas, despite their both being in the final group with him. It was a unique opportunity for the two friends to help each other out: instead of trying to describe rounds the other hadn't seen, they could now dissect some of the strengths and weaknesses in performances they had eye-witnessed. Scott later said that the conclusion they reached about him was that he "was a little too blasé out there." Trevor, they thought, "was too much the other way. We both thought it was a missed opportunity." They looked forward to another, and a better result, at Jack's place.

Had Norman Rockwell been a golf fan, the Memorial would have been his favorite event. Mr. Nicklaus's tournament, as it's known, is held on and around a national holiday, in a small town, Dublin, Ohio, where big commercial boulevards haven't yet entirely replaced quaint little store-fronted streets. Fresh chlorophyll fills the air, overlain with the smell of a thousand busy barbeque grills. There's always—infamously—a little rain, but otherwise the weather is perfect for lying on the ground, putting a blade of bentgrass in your mouth, and spotting shapes in the clouds. The galleries are among the politest in the country, and the most drably dressed. The untanned legs, along with the ambient aromas and frequent breeze-borne dandelion snowstorms, create the very picture of early summer in the American Midwest.

Dublin is just outside Nicklaus's hometown of Columbus, Ohio. In the late sixties, when the area was nothing but farmland, Nicklaus came out and bought a parcel of 1,300 acres. Whispers were that he meant to build a golf course. An old friend of Nicklaus' is fond of saying that every time Jack came out to visit the property, it resulted in the sale of 100 more acres in the surrounding community.

Helping to define the Memorial was an entirely intentional resemblance to the Masters. Muirfield Village members wore green jackets. The caddies wore the same cursed white boilersuits. The sandwiches were wrapped in the same green cellophane. But mostly it was defined by Nicklaus himself. He was always the headliner, despite Tiger Woods' annual presence. In recent years those headlines often had to do with Nicklaus's hints of retirement. Every year Nicklaus suggested it would be his last Memorial appearance; the following year, he invariably showed up again to play. It drove the golf writers crazy. One year, two scribblers were sitting in the press room when one suggested that a member of their fraternity should tell Nicklaus to make up his darned mind. "You think the food in the press room is bad now?" the other replied.

The 2006 Memorial turned out to be the first one Tiger Woods missed since he turned professional. As the tournament approached, whether or not he would participate was the cause of much speculation. Most thought that it would be an index of how hard he was taking his father's death—the Memorial's Wednesday pro-am would mark four weeks since his father's passing. If he returned, the occasion would be loaded with symbolism: over the years Nicklaus had become a kind of spiritual father to Woods.

Yet up until May 26, the Friday preceding the Memorial (and the deadline to commit to the tournament) Tiger and his camp were completely silent about his plans. Until that day, not even Nicklaus knew whether or not he would show. He had called Woods several days earlier. They had what Nicklaus, according to friends, described as a "heartfelt" conversation. But they didn't discuss Tiger's participation in the tournament.

(Once it was established Tiger was skipping the Memorial, speculation turned to the U.S. Open. But most Woods watchers solved the riddle pretty quickly. On the Friday the Memorial's commitment window closed, Tiger appeared in the Bronx to watch a Yankees-Royals game, and the following day played a practice round at Winged Foot.)

The 2006 Memorial was also the first ever without Nicklaus himself in the field. As much as he loved Muirfield Village, he had wanted his last playing appearance to be at St. Andrews, the stage for the 2005 British Open. And it was.

Still, the host made his presence felt. At the eleventh hour he made a dramatic rules change, decreeing that every other tooth on the bunker rakes would be removed. That created furrowed lies in the bunkers, stiffly penalizing errant shots. As the tournament began, the players' lack of control over their balls, particularly in greenside bunkers, provoked some hissy fits. "It's a joke, really," Paul Azinger said. "It neutralizes everybody who is a good bunker player." True enough. But a moment later he unwittingly supplied the counterargument. When a reporter mentioned that Nicklaus himself was never a great bunker player, Azinger shot back, "But he was never in them." Exactly.

The move produced the desired effect. By the end of the week the field's sand save percentage was 43.8, down significantly from the 2006 Tour average, 49.1. The scoring average for the week was 73.003, radically higher than 2005's 71.932.

Adam Scott didn't mind. The changes played to his strengths. Over his first thirty-six holes he missed only six fairways and seven greens, taking the bunkers all but out of play. After the second round he found himself in second place, behind leader Carl Pettersson.

Tied with Scott was none other than Sean O'Hair. Struggling so far in 2006, his first-round 67 was his second-best of the year, and he backed it up with a two-under 70. The sudden return to form seemed to validate all of his recent decisions—firing David Leadbetter to work with Gary Gilchrist, and replacing Steve Lucas, his caddying father-in-law, with Bobby Verwey.

As important as the instructor change was, replacing his caddie had more bracing effects. It meant that for the first time in his life, O'Hair, 23, was traveling alone. Since he arrived on Tour, Lucas had been with him every step of the way. His wife, Jackie, had also been by his side, except for the beginning of his 2005 rookie year, toward the end of her pregnancy with their first child, daughter Molly. Almost immediately afterward, Jackie and Molly rejoined them on the road.

Before that O'Hair's life on the road had been harrowing, because of the treatment to which he was subjected by his father, Marc O'Hair.

In 2002, when Sean was 19, he and Marc appeared on CBS's *60 Minutes II,* as part of a segment entitled "The Tiger Formula." It focused on the pursuit by some families of the riches Woods brought to the game. It opened with father and son on a hotel room sofa. Marc, once co-owner of a family shutter and blind business, cast his son as an equally saleable commodity, and talked about him in terms that would drop the jaw of any parent. "I was in business twenty-plus years, and I know how to make a profit," he said. "You've got the same old thing—it's material, labor, and overhead." Then, nodding toward Sean, he added, "He's pretty good labor."

The six-foot-three, 260-pound Marc O'Hair—whose large brow, small eyes, and tiny mouth conspired to fix his face in a stern expression—spoke with chilling detachment. Sean seemed to have no more importance to him than a pile of lumber or a band saw.

At the time, Sean's cheeks still carried some baby fat. The rest of him looked to be assembled from chopsticks. Always thin, Sean, during the summer of his sixteenth year, underwent a terrific, six-inch growth spurt. (He still bears stretch marks from that period on his back.) As he sat before the camera he was the same height as his father, but half his age and weight.

Yet he was already a third-year pro. He had made the jump in the summer of 1999, after his junior year in high school. It happened suddenly, without any formal announcement, and attracted little attention, even in golf circles. Yet it was the first time in decades that a highly touted male teenage golfer had turned pro.

It was nothing like the ascension, for example, of a promising young basketball player. There was no draft to usher Sean into the bigs, no guaranteed salary or place to play, and no coaching staff to help polish his skills. There was certainly no sneaker company to sign him to an endorsement deal. He did draw one sponsor, TaylorMade, but his status as a former top-ranked junior player was good only for a one-year, four-figure deal.

The circumstances under which he turned pro were not pleasant. Earlier that summer, during the second of a three-round American Junior Golf Association event, Sean, playing unremarkably, faced a four-foot putt on his final hole to shoot even par. Looking on, Marc growled, loudly enough to be heard by both his son and other spectators, "If you shoot over par, we're going home." Sean missed the putt. His father was true to his word, and more. The O'Hairs withdrew, and Sean never played another junior tournament. In retrospect, it seemed fitting that professional golf was introduced into his life as a form of punishment.

The decision bound the two together as if with handcuffs. Marc repudiated the last semblance of his and Sean's homelife. Leaving Sean's mother and little sister behind in their home in Lakeland, Florida, they hit the road together, with Marc serving as Sean's caddie, swing coach, nutritionist, fitness guru, cook, and chauffeur. During the next two years they put 90,000 miles on Marc's Ford Taurus, driving from one tournament to the next, with Sean doing schoolwork in the passenger seat, earning his high school diploma via correspondence courses.

The O'Hairs drove from city to city, paying entry fees at some tournaments and attempting to qualify at others. A typical noncompetitive day began at 5:00 a.m., with breakfast and a mile run. When their hotel had a weight room, Sean used that, too. Marc prepared their meals on an electric hot plate to ensure that Sean "didn't wind up eating crap."

It was no accident that the routine seemed borrowed from Fort Bragg, because boot camp, in a way, was Marc's model. "The military, they know how to build a champion," he told CBS. "Somebody who slacks off, that's a loser. The typical high-school kid is hanging out at the mall. That's a loser. You have to have a goal or you are just wasting time."

This was what the world knew of Sean O'Hair when he arrived in Palm Springs for the 2005 Q-school finals. What had happened in the intervening years was a mystery. The question that presented itself with the most immediacy was the identity of the middle-aged man serving as Sean's caddie. The few golf writers who recalled the *60 Minutes* segment remembered Marc O'Hair's size, but that was about it. The man now carrying Sean's bag was also big, but no one was sure it was him.

All week long that small clutch of reporters eyeballed the pair with a combination of intrigue and apprehension. Was this still his father? Was this horror show still in progress? The temptation to find out was countered by a respect for what Sean was trying to do—no one wanted to approach him, bring up his past, derail his concentration, and ruin his chances to earn a Tour card.

Basic information was gleaned—well, ostensibly—on the sly. During Wednesday's second round one clever reporter, noticing that Sean's caddie constantly had his lips around a cigar, approached him between holes, cigarette in hand, and asked for a light.

The second question had to be carefully crafted. "You've been doing this"—that is, caddying—"for a while now, haven't you?" he asked, believing "yes" would betray him as Marc O'Hair, and "no" meant the caddie was a hired hand, no relation.

"Yeah, a little while, I guess," the man replied.

Plan B was to sit and wait for O'Hair to play well enough to warrant conventional news-gathering attention. But all week he remained at a comfortable distance from the leaders. Eventually he finished in a tie for fourth, winning a double victory: he earned his card but avoided the media spotlight.

It didn't last. As soon as the new PGA Tour season started, his past was scrutinized anew. *Golf World* ran a feature on O'Hair out of his first tournament, the Sony Open in Hawaii. *Sports Illustrated*'s star columnist Rick Reilly weighed in after his second, the Buick Invitational in San Diego.

The two pieces showed that *Sixty Minutes* only scratched the surface. In truth, Sean's mistreatment at his father's hands had been worse than anyone had thought.

If Sean's schedule was reminiscent of the military, so too was father Marc's idea of discipline. For years Sean was forced to run a mile for each bogey he had made in the course of a day's competition. In 1998, for example, at a summer junior tournament in California, Sean shot a score of 80, and spent the afternoon running eight miles in 93-degree heat. Worse was Marc's way of responding to challenges to parental authority. He smacked his son's nose bloody, Sean told *SI*, "20 times—at least." Somehow, he also convinced Sean that he deserved it. "It's weird, but when I got hit, I thought I was the problem."

The *SI* and *Golf World* pieces also delivered some good news. Most of it involved Sean's new family, in particular his new wife, Jackie, and father-in-law, Steve Lucas.

Steve Lucas, it turned out, was the man on O'Hair's bag at Q-school. The easy-going, amiable Philadelphian was now the person showing Sean, on a daily basis, what male parenting was supposed to look like. Helping to make him Sean's ideal cohort was his background in sports. His six years of service as an NCAA college basketball referee in the northeast's Division I Metro Atlantic Conference did nothing if not teach him how to deal with young athletes.

Sean met Jackie Lucas while the two were practicing on the putting green at the Tournament Players Club at Heron Bay, in Coral Springs, Florida, a former site of the PGA Tour's Honda Classic. It was early in the summer of 2002, not long after the airing of the *60 Minutes* segment (which she had not seen). She was a member of the golf team at Florida Atlantic University. Sean, though 19, had never been on a date and never kissed a girl. So narrow was his upbringing that he'd never been allowed to buy a pair of jeans. This was not a young man apt to strike up a conversation with a young woman. So Jackie, admiring his form, did it for him. "So what tour do you play on?" she asked, and their romance had begun.

It wasn't long before she noticed that Sean's father was dominating his life, and she spoke up about it. Sean later said of Jackie, "She was the one who kind of opened my eyes a little bit, let me know that, 'Hey, your dad is overstepping his boundaries.' She just said, 'Look, this isn't right, and you don't deserve this.' So I realized that I needed to do something about it. I didn't go up to my dad and say, 'Up yours, I'm leaving.' I didn't say that, but I started to take a little firmer action. Whenever he did something I thought was wrong, I'd say, 'No, this isn't right.' And I think I just started to become my own man because Jackie was allowing me to."

A few months after Sean and Jackie met, Marc said "something ugly about her," as Sean recalled, while the two were riding between tournaments. This time, for the first time, the threat of physical violence did not back Sean down. One ultimatum lead to the next, and when Sean got out of the car, their relationship was over. He moved in with the Lucases and went out and bought his first pair of jeans. Six months later he and Jackie were married.

The last time Sean talked with Marc O'Hair was on his wedding day, in September 2003. There the two exchanged only the most cursory greetings, not even shaking hands. By 2005 there were other, happier things to think about. Sean and Jackie's first child, daughter Molly, was born on February 17. On the golf course, his talents were coming into full bloom. His second at the Nelson, his win at the Deere, and then his tie for fifteenth at the British Open, his first major, brought his season earnings to over $1.8 million. He spoke of his father only when the press asked him to.

Still, it took a long time for Marc O'Hair to let go. In 2005—three years after they had parted, with Sean now a rookie on Tour—he was still holding over his son's head a pair of contracts (one signed at age 17, the other at 19) obliging not only repayment of monies spent on Sean's golf (with interest, at the rate of prime plus two percent), but also 10 percent of any and all future professional earnings.

In *Golf World*, Marc O'Hair repeated what he had said to his son at the time the contracts were signed. "I told him, 'I can't blow this kind of money without a return. When you make it, there has to be payback someday.'" The rationales from the past were accompanied by up-to-the-minute threats. "As soon as he gets famous, I am going to lower the boom," he said. "I am going to show everybody what he did to me. I intend to crucify him in the media, because what he did to me is not right."

Then, in August of 2005, two weeks after the British Open, an unexpected fax arrived at PGA Tour headquarters, select newsrooms, and the pressroom at the Buick Open in Flint, Michigan, where Sean was playing that week. It read, in part:

> Because I love Sean, I put a long-term plan together and financed it producing one of the best young players in the world. I demanded long hours and a commitment to excellence that I do not regret. You are just now seeing what I knew all along. . . . [H]e's a player. In those stale years from the fall of '99 thru the fall of '02, Sean's game went into seclusion as a result of being bitterly frustrated because he was stuck between adolescence and young adulthood. I didn't recognize the problem and we had a very painful split. It wasn't until after Sean's marriage that I realized that he simply needed his independence from me and wanted his own space with his woman to spread his eagle wings and fly. But Sean and his wife, in almost a vindictive tantrum, began a media assault a couple of years ago that has branded me forever. I wish Sean had just given me a call to tell me how bitter he was and why he was so bitter instead of unfairly bashing me in the press. It makes my life miserable. Even though Sean must sooner or later assume responsibilities for his own actions, I will bail him out of another one of his problems by releasing him from liability concerning the contracts. And in closing, I would like to tell all my dear friends in the media to kiss my ass.

Sean first found out about the statement the previous evening. A copy had also been sent to the offices of his lawyer, Lucas family friend Michael Troiani, who happened to be with him in Grand Blanc. "We were sitting at dinner and he kind of told me about it," O'Hair told reporters after his Wednesday pro-am round. "And I said, 'Well, is there anything I need to know?' And he said, 'Not really,' and kind of summarized it, and I just shrugged my shoulders, and then we had a nice meal."

O'Hair's dismissiveness about the statement and the contracts he had signed in the first place was anything but offhand. Rather, it was rooted in talks he had been having with Troiani for years. The contracts had indeed been a concern, Troiani admitted Wednesday afternoon, standing under a shade tree while Sean hit chip shots on a nearby practice green. But not because he thought they were enforceable. What Troiani was afraid of was that legal action, however unfruitful, would probably have resulted in months of emotional chaos.

"That was the big fear," Troiani said. "We were never worried about the contracts. We were worried about the commotion Marc would try to make with them. To that extent, yes, this statement is a welcome thing."

The release would not be the end of the story. It would, in fact, turn out to be a prelude to Marc's new campaign to insinuate himself back into his son's life. Two weeks later, the *New York Times* sent a reporter to Marc O'Hair's house in Lakeland, Florida (which he still shared with Sean's mother, Brenda). "I love Sean," he told her. "I love Sean, damn it. And somehow we've got to put this thing back together. That's the bottom line. I don't give a rat's ass about anything else other than I want my son to be my son again. And I want to be his father. And that's the only thing that counts. Putting the family back together."

His pleas didn't take. Over the next few months, Marc, whenever contacted by the press, used the opportunity to reach out to his son, but never received a response. Toward the end of the season Sean was asked if he ever thought about renewing his relationship with his father. "Sometimes I think I do," he said. "But he's not going to change. He is what he is. It would be stupid for me to bring that back into my life."

Still, Marc never drifted far from Sean's thoughts. How could he? Golf only sustained the memory of their time together. Whenever Sean set foot on a course, he was walking the path his father chose for him. The miseries he endured at Marc's hands—the forced roadwork after bad rounds, the bloodied noses that followed challenges to parental authority—were inviolably a part of his journey. Most difficult to countenance was that Marc's training methods, however severe, were now contributing to Sean's success. How else could one explain his rare mental toughness, his ability to handle pressure down the stretch at big tournaments? Indeed, it was impossible to say whether Sean was flourishing despite his father or because of him. Either way, there was no erasing Marc's role in sculpting his dreams and his skills. Sean's success only protracted his residence in the gilded cage his father had built for him.

The 2006 season, at any rate, was about breaking with the past. The presence on the road of Steve, Jackie, and then Molly kept him swaddled in stability and security. His parting with coach David Leadbetter became a necessity when he found himself struggling early in the season. At the end of February he was sitting at home stewing after missing four of six cuts on the West Coast; he had just exited the Match Play in the second round. "I didn't even feel close," he said. "I mean, the stuff I was working on technically, I was confused, I had no confidence in it. It just didn't feel right. I really had no idea where the ball was going. I just didn't feel good about my game."

He and Gilchrist, his original instructor at the Leadbetter Academy in Bradenton, got together at Doral. They didn't try to rebuild his swing. Mostly they left well enough alone and focused on the part of his game he thought was really slipping, getting the ball in the hole. Steve's eventual departure was always part of the plan. During Masters week Sean found himself thinking the time might be right. He brought it up with Lucas one evening while they were having dinner at the house his management group, IMG, rents for its clients every year.

"Steve," he said, "I've been thinking about making a change, you know, like we've always talked about."

"You know that any time you want to do it is fine with me," Lucas said. "Just say the word. And if you want me to help you find someone else, let me know, and I will."

At that point, they dropped the topic. But it came up again the following week, as they were driving up to Hilton Head, in Sean's new extended-cab Denali. (He had gotten a sweetheart deal on the vehicle from a golf-crazy car dealer in Jacksonville, and it was now being used for an extended road trip.)

When Sean brought it up this time, the question wasn't if, but when. He and Steve agreed on the following month's Wachovia Championship, the first event Sean would play after Hilton Head and two weeks at home.

It was, as O'Hair said, "a big step. But it was the right step." He wouldn't say much more than that, except to talk about how it affected Steve. "I think he's happier. When he was caddying he didn't get to play golf at all. He didn't get to see his friends much. Imagine a successful businessman who makes great money, doesn't have to travel, plays golf as much as he wants with his buddies—and then he gives that all up." In the end, Sean felt that he owed Lucas back his freedom.

About what it meant for O'Hair himself, Gary Gilchrist said, "When Sean told me Steve wouldn't be on the bag, I said to myself, this is important. This is a big change. Steve has meant so much to him."

Steve was at Jackie and Sean's house, set to look after the baby while Jackie took Sean to the airport for his flight to Charlotte. As he walked out the door, Steve pulled him aside and said, "If you ever need me again, I'll be there for you."

When Sean boarded his flight, he realized it was the first time he had ever been on a plane alone.

That week in Charlotte, it took Sean a while to adjust to all the time he had on his hands. At night he predictably spent a lot of time on the phone with Steve and Jackie. Otherwise he did the same things he would have done had they been around. He puttered around on his computer, spending long stretches on the Dupont Registry website (a popular site among car nuts), and watched a pay-per-view movie starring Jennifer Aniston. In the mornings, he wasted a little more time than usual watching *SportsCenter*. The biggest change was the way he ended his days at the golf course. There were no discussions with Steve about how many balls he should hit or where to have dinner. He simply did what he wanted. And he didn't mind that at all. By the time he went to Columbus for the Memorial, he had settled into his own habits and routines.

Still, "it felt strange. It still feels strange," he said at the end of his week in Ohio, just before heading home to Pennsylvania for Furyk's charity event. He loved that he could "just go out and do my business." On the other hand he missed them, and was glad we would soon rejoin them. "It has been a little loney," he confessed, "especially at night, whenever you've got to go to dinner and eat by yourself. It's going to be cool at the end of the round not to sit at dinner by myself."

The Memorial turned out to be a weird week for everyone. A Saturday rain delay threatened to push the finish back to Monday, a potential disaster since so many players had U.S. Open qualifiers that day. That wouldn't have affected O'Hair or Scott, but the stop-start aggravation may have had something to do with their weekend setbacks. Finishing the third round (during which they played together) on Sunday morning, they signed, respectively, for a 73 and a 74, effectively shooting themselves out of the tournament. Scott bounced back on Sunday for a back-door top-four: O'Hair played a so-so fourth round, but his T12 was still his best finish of the year.

Sweden's Carl Pettersson wound up winning the tournament, but its most memorable moments were produced by Phil Mickelson, who put on a dazzling short game display. On Saturday, from just off the 10th green with the pin just fifteen feet away, he took a huge swing with his lob wedge and grinned as the ball went straight up in the air, landed three feet from its original position, and trundled down the steep downhill slope directly into the cup. On Sunday, his tee shot on the par-three 16th plugged in a front bunker; another huge swing sent up a cloud of sand and another miraculous birdie. He wasn't hitting the ball particularly well from tee to green, but if his short game was this sharp at Winged Foot, he would be hard to beat.

The following day, while Scott, O'Hair, Furyk, and Daly were in Pennsylvania, 152 other players were at Canoe Brook Country Club in Summit, New Jersey. One of them was Michael Allen. His quest to make it back to Winged Foot, his old place of employ, would have been the best story on the grounds had it not been for the presence of Michelle Wie.

By Michelle's side, as usual, were her mother, Bo, and her father, B. J. Wie. As a golf parent, B.J. was more hands-on than Phil Scott but thankfully less so than Marc O'Hair. True, he had his critics, principally because of his role in fast-tracking his daughter's career. But those close to the family—indeed, anyone who had ever talked to his strong-willed daughter—knew that B.J.'s place in such decisions had more to do with "letting" than "forcing." His sin, if there was one, was an unwillingness to say no.

Michelle's dream of becoming the first female to participate in a men's major might have been fulfilled if she had not had to qualify in the midst of a Fellini movie. On hand at Canoe Brook were 300 accredited members of the media, half of them armed with cameras. Published spectator estimates ran from 2,000 to 4,000 to 6,000, although the 1,200 guessed at by Mark O'Meara, among those competing for eighteen spots in the U.S. Open, was probably correct. Whatever the number actually was, it was too many, considering that most were making liberal use of their cellphones and otherwise disregarding the usual Silence Is Golden code of golf spectator conduct. In at least one respect it was like an early Tiger crowd: they came out not to watch golf but to see a celebrity.

After the first seventeen of her thirty-six holes, Wie was two under par, but her score could have been better: she had missed six birdie putts from inside 12 feet. On the 18th, she hit what might have been her worst shot of the round, a push that only the rough prevented from finishing in a pond. She also got lucky with her lie, and was able to reach the green in two. Her ball was in the tall grass to its left, nestled among some low lying mushrooms, but was almost pin-high, about 60 feet from the back-right flag.

Elsewhere on the grounds, the other players went about their business in complete anonymity. Michael Allen, already finished with his first round, was chomping on a cigar on the driving range, trying to convince himself that his opening 74 hadn't scuttled his chances. Mark O'Meara was nearer the hub of the action. He was in a golf cart, driving alongside the hole Wie was playing. He too had shot a 74, and was on his way to begin his afternoon eighteen. Worse than his score was the warning ringing in his ears. Earlier, Tiger Woods had called, imparting a simple message. "You'd better not let a girl beat you," he said.

Just after O'Meara rolled by, Wie holed her chip for an eagle. Her 68 put her in a tie for thirteenth; she was leading all but about 135 of the men, including O'Meara and Allen. It was true that she had played the easier South Course and would face a more difficult test in the afternoon. But that hardly stemmed the enthusiasm as she sat down to sign her scorecard, under a temporary, open-sided canopy tent beside the green. Checking her math, rubbing the cap of her Sharpie over each number, she was flanked by her playing partners, Rick Hartmann, the head pro at the Hamptons' tony Atlantic Golf Club, and former U.S. Amateur champ and PGA Tour winner David Gossett. Surrounding the trio was so much TV and radio equipment they looked like jurors right after the O.J. verdict. A microphone from local news radio station WINS was an inch from Hartmann's temple; an unlabeled television camera was brushing the bill of Gossett's Titleist cap. The strange thing was that none of the newspeople were saying a word. All were completely silent, straining to catch stray syllables.

As Wie and her partners returned from lunch and started their second round, things only got worse. After their opening tee shots several members of the ever-growing crowd took advantage of the absence of gallery ropes and blithely walked out onto the first fairway to inspect the players' balls. Wie's was in a kidney-shaped left-side fairway bunker. By the time she arrived, spectators and TV crews had completely surrounded it.

Three cameramen pushed through the throng and planted tripods on the fairway side of the bunker. Michelle took a while to examine her lie and test her stance. She would have to hit the shot with her right foot in the bunker, and her left outside it, her knee resting on the grass. When she looked up, she saw that the crowd had only thickened. The lower lip of her tiny mouth dropped in amazement, and she turned up her palms, wordlessly pleading for people to back off. Her round was only two minutes old, and it was officially out of control.

Eventually, everyone figured out that they had to give the players some space. Wie managed to play the front nine in two over par and still had a reasonable chance to post the even-par round (for a total of -4) that she would need to qualify. She parred the first three holes of her back nine, with B.J. watching every step of the way, in his usual visor and glasses, and an off-red Nike-logoed shirt that seemed stolen from Tiger Woods' closet. "Are you incredibly nervous, or are you used to this by now?" a reporter asked him. He laughed. "By now, I'm used to it." Fortunately, he was out of earshot a moment later when an especially genteel fan of his daughter's, watching her settle over a testy par putt, muttered, "C'mon, G-string, make it."

That par putt dropped, but it was the last she would make for a while. She bogeyed the next three holes, two of them via three-putts. She finished with a 75, missing the playoff for the last qualifying spots by five strokes.

"I'm very proud of her," B.J. said after her round. "A little disappointed, but very proud. I think Michelle demonstrated that it's possible for a woman to play in a men's major."

About that opinion there was little dissent. Her reviews, almost universally, were glowing.

"There are more believers now than there were before." wrote *Sports Illustrated's* Michael Bamberger.

Dave Anderson's lead in the *New York Times* was, "Michelle Wie didn't make the United States Open, but someday she will."

She was only 16. There was plenty of time.

11

LEFTY AGONISTES

The U.S. Open

It was only minutes between the act and its consequence, but it felt like forever. Walking up the fairway with his head bowed, he looked disoriented, like a boxer who had taken a knockout punch but somehow remained upright, his body refusing to register what his head already knew. He managed, somehow, to continue to hit golf shots—a third, then a fourth, and now the fatal fifth. Still the ball wasn't in the hole. The stunned silence of the witnesses, all 35,000 of them, made the scene all the more unreal.

It wasn't just a tournament that had slipped away. It was a singular opportunity. So much had been at stake. A championship that, three times before, had been taken from him, or given away, at the very last moment. His third straight major, a feat previously accomplished by only four men, all giants: Jones, Hogan, Nicklaus, and Woods. The chance to prove that a new work ethic and a revamped approach to the game had transformed him, finally, into the player he always should have been. And the final exhibit in an unassailable case that right now, Phil Mickelson, not Tiger Woods, was the best golfer in the world.

But there he was, squatting on the green, with his head pressed between his hands, coming to terms with his fate, rehearsing the words to which he would give voice a few minutes later, and which, the following day, would be splattered like a stain across newspapers all over the country. *I am such an idiot.*

Considering the occasion, Mickelson's disaster made a certain kind of sense. This, after all, was the U.S. Open. And this was Winged Foot, the most demanding and unforgiving of all Open venues.

The national championship was supposed to be this way—a theater of pain, a symphony of despair. Just look at what the past ten years of Open Sundays had wrought. Colin Montgomerie weeping in his wife's arms behind the 18th on Sunday at Congressional in 1997. Tom Lehman, on the same day, standing in the 17th fairway in a pose eerily similar to Mickelson's, after drowning his approach in a lake. Retief Goosen's dejection after his final round 80 at Pinehurst in 2005.

In between, no one endured more U.S. Open anguish than Phil Mickelson. There he was in 1999 at Pinehurst, looking on helplessly as Payne Stewart drained a forty-footer on the 72nd hole to beat him. And again in 2002, at Bethpage Black, looking heavenward after missing a two-foot par putt on the next-to-last hole. And then at Shinnecock in 2004, shutting his eyes tight as his final-round par putt on the burnt-out 17th green sped wildly by the hole, costing him a bogey and the championship.

Other majors, too, had their heartbreaks. But at the U.S. Open, they seemed to happen by design. Every fairway was as thin as a supermodel. The rough on either side and around the greens was infamously high and thick, wrapping itself around ankles like second pairs of socks. Off-the-charts green speeds made putting as exacting as brain surgery.

It was no coincidence that the USGA, the governing body that ran the event, had a reputation for sadism. Nerves were always a problem at majors, but here, course setups gave human nature a helping hand, fraying them from the very first tee shot. The idea, it seemed, was to make the contestants play at the edge of frustration. That's why the U.S. Open so reliably produced catastrophes. That's why the great Bobby Jones, over half a century ago, said, "Nobody ever wins the National Open. Somebody else just loses it."

Winged Foot's West Course, built in 1922 by A.W. Tillinghast (who also designed Bethpage Black, Shinnecock, and Baltusrol), had hosted four previous U.S. Opens. Jones won the 1929 edition, just a year before his half-am Grand Slam. Billy Casper won in 1959, and Fuzzy Zoeller in 1984. But easily the most memorable was 1974's "Massacre at

Winged Foot." That was the one cementing the championship's reputation for brutality. A year earlier, Johnny Miller had shot a final round 63 at Oakmont to win the championship; the USGA replied by putting the screws to the West Course, turning each hole into a bowling alley surrounded by a jungle. Asked what he thought of the setup that year, Jack Nicklaus said, "The last eighteen holes are very difficult." In the end, Hale Irwin won it at seven over par. But that's not what most people remembered. What they remembered was then-USGA president Frank "Sandy" Tatum responding to critics by saying, "We're not trying to humiliate the best golfers in the world. We're simply trying to identify them." What made the line famous was that no one ever quite believed him.

In 2006, the Tour's lead-in to the Open was the Barclays Classic, at Westchester Country Club, just five and a half miles from Winged Foot. With the events so close, many players spent the entire fortnight in the same hotel room or rented house.

Vijay Singh encamped in a big suite on the ninth floor of the Crowne Plaza in White Plains. During the Barclays, the hotel, he said, was "full of businessmen." They wore suits, carried briefcases, and strode in and out of conferences in the ballrooms. But when Vijay returned to the hotel on Sunday night, after the first win of a trying season ("Finally," he had sighed immediately afterward), he couldn't help but notice a change. The entrance and the lobby were now crawling with golf people. Newly arrived players were hauling their gear out of courtesy cars. Agents and equipment industry execs were checking in at the reception desk. Caddies and media guys were perched atop stools at the hotel bar.

Same thing, different year. The U.S. Open always overran the host community like an occupying army. Most of the fans shuttled in from nearby Manhattan by train, but those closer to the game sold out every local hotel, and made local homeowners rich. The approximately 5,000 bivouackers broke down this way:

- Players, friends, caddies, and relatives (including children): 1,200
- Golf business people (agents, equipment manufacturers, instructors, etc.): 600
- Volunteers (nonlocal): 2,500
- Media (including TV): 1,000
- USGA staff and contract vendors: 500

Many of them lodged in the Crowne Plaza's 402 guest rooms. The hotel's unfamiliarity was something golf people rarely experienced. One of the comforts of Tour life was that one could, in every city, bunk at the same hotel, or rent the same house, year after year. But at the majors, all bets were off, because the year's four biggest tournaments, with the exception of the Masters, rotated venues. That meant spending a week in a place you'd probably never seen before. Even the few who had stayed at the Crowne Plaza before—during the 1997 PGA Championship, the last time there was a major in town—barely remembered it.

Geoff Ogilvy's philosophy about new hotels owed something to Forrest Gump. As with boxes of chocolate, he said, "you never know what you're going to get." After checking into the Crowne Plaza on Sunday evening, he opened the door of his room with some apprehension—he had asked for a suite, but feared, considering the unexpectedly low room rate, that he had been given a standard room. He was relieved when he saw the sitting room, with a roomy couch, set off from the bedroom. His wife, Juli, was five months pregnant, and the couple needed space to spread out. Walking over to the window, he saw signs for a Morton's Steakhouse, a Cheesecake Factory, and a Neiman Marcus. At least there's something to do around here, he thought.

By Monday, the hotel had taken on a dormitory feel. You couldn't walk down a hallway or board an elevator without running into someone you knew. This was not entirely welcome, especially for the players, who during the week of a major generally want to be left alone. Running into media members could, for obvious reasons, be awkward. Since most everyone knew where you were staying, you were also subject to unwanted social calls from other players. Your corporate sponsors knew where to find you, introducing the prospect of dinner offers that you wanted to refuse, but couldn't. Strangely, though, everyone in the hotel did their best to ignore the contestants. "It's a funny thing," Ogilvy said. "Everybody in the world is there, but most everyone knows better than to ask you to do anything."

All the shops and eateries—a switch from the previous year's Open, in rural Pinehurst—were a big bonus. There were in fact over a dozen restaurants within walking distance, making room service happily unnecessary. For fussy-eating Tour wives, there was a Whole Foods around the corner. The Neiman Marcus across the street made them happy in other ways.

If the hotel was like a dormitory, the restaurants were like college dining halls, with familiar faces at every table. On Tuesday night at Morton's, Joe Damiano, Stuart Appleby's caddie, and Tony Navarro, Adam Scott's, were chatting at the bar. Colin Montgomerie was in a booth with his agent, Guy Kinnings. Dean Wilson and his swing coaches, Mike Bennett and Andy Plummer, were at one table. David Toms and his wife, Sonya, were at another, getting reacquainted with two old friends who lived in New York City. (The female half of the couple had had been one of Sonya's bridesmaids.) In a large private dining room sat Chris DiMarco and about a dozen relatives.

Not everyone was staying at the Crowne Plaza. USGA officials were at a Marriott closer to the course, and with good reason: some were on site for as many as sixteen hours per day. Perhaps the busiest of the group was Mike Davis. He was the organization's new director of competitions, taking over course setup duties from his oft-criticized predecessor Tom Meeks. Meeks, of course, was the man responsible for 2004's greens-baking disaster at Shinnecock Hills. For his finale, at Pinehurst in 2005, Meeks offered a tamer, uncontroversial setup. Now, with Davis at the helm, no one quite knew what to expect.

Davis, an even-keeled 41-year-old employed by the USGA for nearly twenty years, knew the West Course didn't need much toughening up. Its small, severely sloped greens were guarded by deep, forbidding bunkers. It was so testing off the tee that as far back as 1937 one member had become known for replaying tee shots after all-too-frequent unplayable drives. That member's name was David Mulligan, and the custom still bears his name.

Davis's most noticeable innovation was his introduction of graduated rough. For the first time, the USGA would vary its length, cutting the first twenty feet from the fairway to three and a half inches and the rest to five and a half. The idea was to penalize slight misplays less severely than drives that were way off line.

But Davis also came up with a few new punitive wrinkles. He ordered fresh sand for the bunkers, increasing chances of buried and fried-egg lies, and at the very least diminishing the players' ability to spin and control shots from the traps. He pushed back gallery ropes so that fewer wild drives would draw clean lies on spectator-trampled grass. Acting on the recommendation of Executive Director David Fay, he also introduced circular drop zones, typically placing them in the gnarliest patches of rough, so that players entitled to free drops didn't benefit, for example, from hitting it into a grandstand.

(Before play began, the USGA unveiled one more surprise, announcing that it would be taking the Open back to Merion in 2013, flying in the face of prevailing sentiment that the course was too short to host the championship. It had been emboldened by the course's sturdy showing during the previous weeks' U.S. Amateur.)

Among nonparticipants, Davis was the runner-up as the week's man to watch, trailing only Johnny Miller. Once one of the finest players in the game, the NBC color man was simultaneously the fans' favorite broadcaster and the most hated among the players—the latter of which only went to prove that where tour pros were concerned, there was often nothing more controversial than the truth. His outspokenness took many forms. He was unusually insightful: he understood, before almost any other member of the media, that the PGA Tour was now "a three-club game: driver, wedge, and putter," making that pronouncement at Doral in early 2005. He could also be brilliantly contrary: at the 1999 Ryder Cup, two months after Jean Van de Velde's catastrophe at the British Open, he remarked that the Frenchman was "the first guy in history to have a grandstand cost him a major championship." (He was right: if Van de Velde's first shot to the green hadn't hit a greenside stanchion and bounced 180 degrees backward, it never it wouldn't have wound up in that awful burn.) Sometimes he was gratuitously insulting, as when he said that 2004 Doral winner Craig Parry had a swing that "would make Ben Hogan puke."

Even before he arrived in Westchester, Miller set the stage for the championship more succinctly than anyone else. Talking to Mark Cannizzaro of the *New York Post* prior to leaving his home in the mountains near Salt Lake City, Utah (hard by Alta and Park City), he said, "Phil is the best player in the world right now. If it comes down to the last nine holes on Sunday, though, I'll take Tiger. Phil hasn't shown the golf world yet that, with nine holes to go, he can beat Tiger. Tiger is the ultimate guy to make people shrink. If Phil can win the U.S. Open playing with Tiger and they're even with nine holes to go and wins, he's going to probably be the dominant player for the next five years."

Tiger Woods and Phil Mickelson were made to be rivals. The differences between them were impossible to miss, even when they were inside the ropes. Woods, ever the "hard kid" his father once described, was stone-faced, imperturbable, grim. Mickelson, on the other hand, always sported that goofy smile. True, it was partly public relations. But it was also partly sports psychology, a way to remind himself to stay upbeat. More generally, though, it was a reflection of his everyday demeanor, a tendency to engage and enjoy the attention showered on him rather than pretending it wasn't there.

Those differences came into bold relief when the two were paired together. Standing on the first tee at the 2002 Tour Championship, Tiger was typically indifferent as the announcer listed his victories for that year—Bay Hill Invitational, Masters, U.S. Open, and so forth. Mickelson jokingly interrupted, crying, "Alright, already," to indicate he'd heard enough.

The words they exchanged with each other often reflected those same differences. Before they teed off at the final round of the 2001 Buick Invitational, Mickelson walked over to Woods and said, "Good luck today, Tiger. I've got a red Titleist 7."

Woods' over-the-shoulder reply was characteristically terse. "Nike 1," he said.

Over the years, the press played little bouts of needling as though they were knife fights. The most famous was Mickelson's 2003 *Golf Magazine* comments about Woods' "inferior equipment," augmented by the remark that "Tiger hates it that I can hit it by him now." In substance, Lefty meant to send up Woods' obstinacy in clinging to his short, small-headed, steel-shafted driver. That he didn't explain that afterwards was his only real gaffe.

Mark Calcavecchia liked to tell a story about an early Tiger-Phil encounter at the Masters. In the version he related to *Golf Digest,* he said, "Phil and I were supposed to be first off for a practice round at Augusta, and Phil was getting on Tiger for cutting in front of us. Phil was like, 'You better get your ass out of the way, or I'm hitting.' And I was like, Wow! Tiger was looking at me like, Is he serious? Then Phil comes back with that grin he has, like he was partially messing with him."

Woods wasn't above a little smart-assing of his own. Just before Winged Foot, on his website, Woods wrote, "I won't carry two drivers. I can shape my driver both ways, so I don't need to carry two, although I can understand where Phil Mickelson is coming from." Reading it, you could almost hear Tiger cackle.

Generally, though, there was never any real quarrel between them. One insider called their alleged antipathy "the most overblown story in golf." When circumstances dictated, they never resisted playing a few practice holes together, as they did at Baltusrol, the week before the 2005 PGA, or on Wednesday at the 2004 Players Championship. On the latter occasion they played the entire back nine together. When they arrived at the famed 17th hole, they swapped clubs, Phil hitting Tiger's righty 9-iron, and vice versa. Competitive? Yes. Archenemies? Not quite.

Whatever the interpersonal dynamics, their pending Winged Foot showdown set off feverish anticipation. Mickelson, of course, was playing the best golf of his life. After his dominating display at Augusta, he posted a couple of lackluster results (T15 in New Orleans and T35 in Charlotte, to go with his T4 at the Memorial), but that may have been because he was spending so much time in Mamaroneck. In the weeks prior to the Open, he played a dozen practice rounds at Winged Foot. (His stunning short game display in Columbus was doubtless the product of hours of practice around its tricky greens. Much of it was accomplished with the 64-degree wedge he put in his bag expressly for the Open.)

Mickelson's recent dedication to preparation and his new, less sanguine course-management philosophy made him a much different player than the one who had come up short at so many previous Opens. Mickelson himself resisted the commonly used Old Phil–New Phil distinction, but everyone else embraced it, including one woman who lived in his house. "I think the old Phil would rely on those amazing moments to kind of vault him along in the tournament, eagles and chip-ins, skip the ball across the water, whatever, bend it around the tree," wife Amy said at a Monday morning post-Masters victory press conference at La Jolla Country Club. "That's the way he used to play majors. It's good enough to get you in contention, but the way he manages his game now, he puts so much into preparing. It's very different. He's finally found what works for him."

Mickelson was now 35, but it looked like he was just coming into his prime. (He and Ben Hogan had both won their first majors at 33.) He was starting to look like the biggest obstacle between Woods and his eighteen major championship wins. In one commentator's words, Woods needed, at very least, "to re-establish the long-accepted fact that he's the man to beat in the big ones."

At Winged Foot, Mickelson would also have something of a home-court advantage. His last three major appearances in the New York area—at Bethpage, Shinnecock, and Baltusrol—had seen the development of a love affair with local sports fans. After his victory at the 2005 PGA, someone in the stands had shouted, "You're one of us now, Phil! Let's go get a beer!"

It hadn't quite come to that. But in New York, Mickelson enjoyed getting out and taking in the town. During Baltusrol week, he and his family saw a Broadway show, *Chitty Chitty Bang Bang!* One year during the Barclays, he rode the commuter train down to Yankee Stadium for a ballgame. Shortly after 9/11, he had taken his children to the former site of the World Trade Center and tried to explain what had happened there. Now, at Winged Foot, he said, "They still talk about it today. In fact, Amanda just did a project in her class and she brought in a picture of her at Ground Zero."

Mickelson rented a house near Winged Foot for the Open, and shared it, during the first part of the week, with Jim Mackay and Rick Smith. His family hadn't yet arrived because daughter Amanda was graduating from kindergarten on Friday morning. (When they flew in, they were able to watch the end of the second round on the TV in the plane.)

Woods, for his part, was bunking with wife Elin and their border collie, Taz, on the good ship *Privacy,* easily the week's most enviable digs. The $20 million, 155-foot yacht had a master suite and six staterooms, and slept twenty-one. Its walls were covered in white silk, with appointments of beige marble and cherrywood. It was equipped with a gym, home theater, and an eight-person whirlpool.

It was docked in an inlet on Mamaroneck Bay, at Derecktor Shipyards, which once built the *Stars & Stripes,* the boat with which Dennis Conner won the 1987 America's Cup. It was there because no conventional marina could hold it—it dwarfed the thirty- and forty-footers more typically found in the bay. It also outsized the ferry parked next to it, which shuttled people to and from Manhattan. In fact, getting *Privacy* in and out of the harbor was a problem. Because of the water's shallowness, movement was only possible at high tide.

The yacht was impossible to see from the street, but was plainly visible from next-door Harbor Island Park. All week, gawkers came by for a glimpse. The local papers sent out reporters nearly every day. On Tuesday, one of them breathlessly wrote that two mysterious women had been seen "pushing a baby stroller on the sidewalk outside the boatyard. They were wearing khaki slacks and white shirts with the boat's name so lightly emblazoned that it was almost invisible." Not golf reporters, they didn't deduce that one of the women was Elin's twin sister, Josefin, the other Steve Williams' wife, Kirsty, and the baby Steve and Kirsty's son, Jet, all of whom were staying on the boat.

Woods' Monday practice round was a big event. It was his first public appearance since his father's death (not counting a youth clinic in Arkansas, and a Yankee game, where Woods dropped by on his way for a practice round at the club to see his pal Derek Jeter).

Thanks to a board outside the clubhouse displaying scheduled practice round times, dozens of reporters congregated around the 10th hole at 1:00 p.m., waiting for Woods. Fans were lined up along the ropes on each of the back nine's first two fairways.

But Woods didn't show. Perhaps the posted time was a diversionary tactic. But a half-hour later he appeared on the practice green. Soon after, Tiger and Jeff Sluman approached Charles Howell and Bo Van Pelt, a big, long-hitting Oklahoman, on the first tee. Tiger asked, "Can we make it four?"

His first tee shot traveled 340 yards, straight down the middle. Later Van Pelt said, "He gets up there, and hits it thirty yards by us, as if to say, yeah, I'm back." At first Woods looked happy to be back inside the ropes. But it didn't take long for his mood too change. He soon began complaining about the green speeds. "Man, I can't believe how slow these greens are," he told Van Pelt. "When I was here a couple of weeks ago they were a lot faster."

When Woods finished his nine holes, more than a dozen reporters were standing behind the green, pens at the ready. He breezed right by them, just as he had on Tuesday in San Diego. The implicit message, once again, was that they would have to wait to talk to him, and everyone quickly understood it: after all these years, Woods had them remarkably well-trained. He would not do his talking until his formal press conference the following day.

It fell to Sluman to recap their half-round. When the newsmen asked how his playing partner had fared, the dry-witted veteran decided to have a little fun with them.

"Charles? Charles played really well," he said.

No, the other guy.

"Bo Van Pelt was tearing it up," he responded.

Finally the object of curiosity was mentioned by name.

"He's always good," Sluman smiled. "There's no rust on his game. If he drives it straight, he's going to win the golf tournament. And if he doesn't, he'll have a hell of a chance."

At Tuesday's presser, Woods was predictably laconic about his father's death. But really, what could he say? It takes an artist, after all, to illustrate how hard it is to lose a loved one. Providing more depth wasn't just against his inclination; it was beyond his vocabulary and, to be honest, those of everyone else in the room.

There was, however, an odd tone to some of his answers. Normally, Woods was polite, if not especially forthcoming. Today, however, he was occasionally snippy. At one point he said, "I'm really looking forward to competing because that's when all of you guys go away." The remark was out of character, but there was an explanation. That morning, when he walked off his yacht, he had been greeted by a photographer from the *New York Post*. When he heard the camera click, he cracked, "It's a little early to be taking pictures out here, isn't it?" He then added, "Have a nice fucking day."

Woods played another nine on Wednesday, for a total of fifty-four holes of preparation on the year's most demanding track. Mickelson, for his part, spent Wednesday at Baltusrol, the site of the previous year's PGA Championship triumph. He had set up the round with the head pro, Doug Steffan, on the Sunday of that tournament, well before winning it, promising, "I'll be down the Wednesday before the Open," and now he kept his word.

Jason Dufner was a 29-year-old from Cleveland, Ohio, but he looked fifteen years younger. After checking into his hotel late on Sunday night—just hours after winning the Nationwide Tour's La Salle Bank Open, near Chicago—he was recognizable to precisely no one. He got into the elevator with a bushel of dry cleaning thrown over his shoulder, apparently the last thing he unloaded from his courtesy car. He could easily have been mistaken for an extraordinarily late delivery boy.

Four days, five holes, and two birdies later, he was leading the U.S. Open.

Every major—except for the Masters, with its limited field—has its Cinderella, an unknown who appears at center stage with the suddenness of a rabbit pulled out of a magician's hat. Often, they dematerialize just as quickly. In Dufner's case, a double bogey on his seventh hole did the trick.

Before the tournament started, the leading candidates for that role had been two players who surprised even themselves by qualifying for the Open in the first place. One was Madalitso Muthiya, a 23-year-old from Zambia. The first black African ever to play in the Open, he was a 2005 graduate of the University of New Mexico, and was now beginning his life as a professional on the Canadian Tour. Never for a moment did he try to conceal his joy in participating. Each time he hit a ball, regardless of the result, a big smile appeared on his face, as though it was a natural part of his follow-through.

The other was Tadd Fujikawa, who at 15 was the second youngest man (better, boy) to earn a berth at the Open. He had done so in a sectional qualifier in his native Hawaii, but probably only because Michelle Wie decided to play hers in New Jersey. In local qualifying, Wie had beaten him by two strokes. But that hardly mattered, because his story was so, well, uplifting. Fujikawa stood just over five feet tall. Born three and a half months premature, he spent the first three months of his life in the hospital. During that time, he related, he was small enough to fit in the palm of his grandfather's hand.

By early Thursday afternoon, however, their tournaments, like Dufner's, were more or less over. Tiger Woods', on the other hand, had yet to begin. His Thursday tee time was 1:25 p.m. He started his practice session hitting practice putts from sixty and seventy feet, still trying to get a feel for the speed of Winged Foot's greens. Conventional wisdom said that after a layoff, the last thing to come around was one's putting; his preoccupation was a sign that he wasn't confident in his form.

Tiger's Thursday was a long day, in more ways than one. His group started behind that of Niclas Fasth, Europe's answer to Ben Crane. It took them twenty minutes to complete their first hole. As the round wore on, Woods had lots of time to dwell on how poorly he was playing. He wound up hitting only three of fourteen fairways, taking thirty-three putts, and shooting a six-over 76.

Two days earlier, practice round partner Bo Van Pelt had said Tiger was having trouble picking lines off the tee. For the long-hitting Woods, the turns in Winged Foot's fairways, at between 260 and 280 yards, were in all the wrong places. If he hit driver, he had to shape his ball as expertly as Trevino to keep it in the short grass; even the straightest ball with his 3-wood was bound to run through the fairway. His 2-iron would have offered a solution, but it was at home in his garage.

After his round, Woods explained (or explained away) his score by criticizing the putting surfaces. He wasn't alone. "The greens are getting a little . . . *irregular,*" was how Geoff Ogilvy put it. What he meant was that they were quick, but also soft, which meant footprints. The combination drove everyone nuts. Because of their speed, players couldn't putt aggressively. But being cautious meant bumpy rolls, and watching your putts wander toward the hole as haphazardly as drunks.

(After Darren Clarke's Friday round a reporter asked him, "Are these the worst greens you've ever seen?"

"Yes. Comfortably," he replied.)

It was easy to blame Mike Davis, the USGA setup man, but doing so was to oversimplify the problem. The USGA wanted fast greens. Yet the greens had to be regularly watered, so they wouldn't dry out. (Remember Shinnecock?) That's why they were soft. Even the best chef could make mistakes with such a delicate recipe.

Apart from the greens, most players spent Thursday chanting the same mantra: tough but fair. The day's scoring average was about 76. Only one man broke par. That was Colin Montgomerie.

The majors, of course, had been Monty's own personal trail of tears. There were near misses at the 1992 U.S. Open at Pebble Beach (after his round, he was congratulated on winning by Jack Nicklaus, but was then overtaken by Tom Kite); at the 1994 U.S. Open at Oakmont (where he lost in a playoff to Ernie Els); at the 1995 PGA Championship at Riviera (another playoff loss, this one to Steve Elkington); and in 1997, in the U.S. Open at Congressional (he was again nipped by Els). He also had a chance to win—kind of—at the 1997 Masters, where he was in second place after second-round play, trailing Tiger Woods by three. That evening, he memorably said of Woods, "There's more to it than hitting the ball a long way. The pressure's mounting now, and I've got a lot more experience in the majors than he does." The following day, they were paired together. Woods beat him by seven strokes.

The most disappointing, perhaps, came on the Scot's home soil, at the 2005 British Open at St. Andrews. During the third round he had tidily outplayed Tiger Woods; all day flags were flying behind him, turning the event into a weird golf version of *Braveheart*. Woods, he later said, "was playing with the wrong guy in the wrong country that day." On Sunday he hung with Woods through the turn but scuttled his chances with bogeys on the 11th and 13th holes.

In earlier years, the man who owned the European Order of Merit (at one point winning it seven consecutive times) was also the man everyone loved to hate. It was hard to miss his haughtiness and his rabbit ears—his habit of noticing sometimes phantasmal distractions in the galleries and singling out offenders with contemptuous stares, if not a few choice words. Along the way he was pinned with nicknames like the Goon from Troon, Scotland Lard, and Mrs. Doubtfire.

Now, years later, he seemed to be at the end of a transformation from detestable lout to sentimental favorite. One reason was his play at the Ryder Cup, which made it impossible to disrespect his game, no matter what he did at the majors. Another was the personal turmoil that began in 2001.

He and his wife, Eimear, had been married for seven years. Once an attorney, she had given up her career to travel with her husband, and care for their three children. They parted company though in 2001, and Montgomerie left their Surrey estate to live in a flat in Chelsea. During long, drawn-out divorce proceedings that were finally settled in January of 2006, he dropped out of the world top fifty, even failing to qualify, in 2005, for the Masters and Players Championship. What he went through couldn't help but elicit pity. His wife was spotted out at night with actor Hugh Grant, much to the enjoyment of the tabloids. (Both insisted they were just friends.) During a 2004 British Open qualifier, Alasdair Hadden-Paton, a man Montgomerie believed was Eimear's new beau, came out to watch him play, throwing him off his game. "I can't believe he's here watching!" he howled, according to multiple British tabloids. "That's unbelievable!" (Hadden-Paton too denied any romantic involvement with Eimear.) In his autobiography, Monty spoke of aimless, sob-ridden bachelor walks through the streets of London.

He was believed to have amassed a personal fortune of about £30 million, but the divorce reportedly cost him about £12 million. By mid 2006 he had at least discovered a sense of humor about it, saying at one point, "I was financially secure for life, and now someone else is."

In 2005, toward the end of the proceedings, he rededicated himself to the game, and ended the year with an eighth Order of Merit title.

But not everything was right in his golfing life, especially not in the locker room. In March of 2005, at the Indonesian Open in Jakarta, there was an incident that impugned his integrity and, according to some observers, turned much of his home tour against him.

One afternoon, preparing to play a shot near a greenside bunker, Montgomerie saw a flash of lightning and sprinted from the course, a few moments ahead of the horn that officially stopped play. He neglected to mark his ball, and overnight it disappeared. When he returned the following morning he replaced it in a spot that conspicuously improved his stance: the previous day it seemed necessary for him to place his feet in the bunker, and now it did not. He had in accordance with the Rules of Golf asked for help from his playing partners, India's Arjun Atwal and Thailand's Thongchai Jaidee, but they deferred to his judgment. "We never saw his lie because we were on the green," Atwal said. "He said, 'Is this where you think the ball was?' We were like, 'Yeah, you should know.'"

Another European Tour player, Denmark's Soren Kjeldsen, was watching on television and reported the apparent infringement to the tournament referee. For some reason, officials could not or would not review the video until after the tournament ended. Eventually, the video showed that he had replaced his ball a foot and a half away from its original location.

In the wake of the scandal—and Montgomerie's donation of his prize money to charity—John Huggan, one of Europe's most respected golf writers, wrote, "it remains true that the rank-and-file on the European Tour retain a lingering antipathy for [Montgomerie] in the wake of what they typically see as an outrageous—and largely unpunished—breach of the rules." Months later, at the PGA Championship at Baltusrol, a European player was quoted as saying, "there's still a lot of anger about what happened."

Tiger Woods' second round was no better than his first. He needed only a single word to describe how he felt after his second straight 76, and that word was "pissed." The other operative word was "rust," but that one he didn't like. "No, it's not rust," he said. When he said, "I was not ready to play golf," it pointed to two things: his father and inadequate preparation for this particular course. His missed cut was his first ever at a major as a professional.

Phil Mickelson, for his part, had a steady start: his rounds of 70 and 73 had him tied for seventh. He had decided (contrary to expectations) to play with only one driver, a model designed to hit a cut. It worked out well on day one, when he hit nine fairways, but not so well on day two, when he only hit six. His key, more than anything else, was the short game that bailed him out of trouble time and time again.

Whatever else it was, his Friday round was entertaining. For his birthday, New York produced a Lefty love-in. One quartet of fans wore bow ties and tuxedo shirts, the letters of his first name inked on each one's chest. On the 7th tee, the crowds sang a rousing rendition of "Happy Birthday," caring little that the threesome ahead of his was putting out 160 yards away. That night, back at the house, his personal chef prepared his favorite dish, lobster ravioli. His kids delivered the cake and presents.

The halfway leader was Steve Stricker, a fourteenth-year player with three Tour wins and a silky putting stroke who had nevertheless fallen prey to apathy and lost his card after the 2004 season. He started 2006 playing on sponsor's exemptions. He showed signs of life with a third-place finish in Houston, but no one expected this.

It was, in fact, far less surprising to see David Duval having a good week. His round of 68, backing up a 77, was Friday's best, and enabled him to play on the weekend at a major for the first time since 2002.

On the year Duval had made six of fourteen cuts, a number that looked spectacular in contrast to the previous three years. Each time he made one, the local writers greeted the occasion as if it were the reappearance of the dodo. Each time, Duval responded in the same way, saying that he had been playing quality golf all along, even if it hadn't been showing up on his scorecards.

Now that such conversations were taking place regularly, they were becoming a little tiresome. National writers, concerned less with tournament particulars than a developing story, looked in on them casually and started to see a pattern develop. The questioning would start innocently enough. Then, pressed for particulars, Duval would understandably get a little bored, and his answers a bit shorter. To bring the conversation to an end, he would usually say something like, "Well, what do *you* think? Did you see me hit any shots out there today?" The answer, of course, was invariably no—only friends and family hoofed it around with players who weren't in the lead. With the reporters flabbergasted, the interview was over.

The exchange on Friday wasn't very different. When Duval was asked about the state of his game, he said, "I guess you haven't been listening.

I've been saying that I've been playing well for I don't know how long, and nobody seems to listen. I'll say it again: I'm playing well." After that, he didn't need the bit about reporters walking the course.

On Saturday, the 2006 U.S. Open's true Cinderella finally arrived. Only she looked like a dockworker.

Kenneth Ferrie, 27, was a veteran of five European Tour seasons, his best coming in 2005, when he took the prestigious Smurfit European Open at Ireland's K Club, and finished eleventh on the Order of Merit. He was also a sight. He stood 6-foot-4. Despite having recently dropped about fifty-five pounds—from 280 down to about 235—he still looked to be wearing about sixty jiggly pints of lager around his waist. Just below it was a belt buckle bearing the Superman logo. Farther south, things got really troubling. His Depeche Mode gray-plaid pants were so tight they looked like they had been purchased in the Stylish Teens department. It was the first time most Open-watchers had seen a male camel toe since the heyday of The Bee Gees.

Apparently, he looked just as strange undressed. His shoulders and upper arms were rumored to be tattooed with Maori tribal symbols.

After his Saturday round of 71, which pushed him into a tie for the lead, he stopped by the press tent to give the American media a crash course on who the heck he was. The European media, of course, already knew, and seized the opportunity to grill him about a scandal of his own. A month earlier, at the Irish Open, he was playing with Paul McGinley, the Irishman who holed the winning putt at the 2004 Ryder Cup. At one point, Ferrie's ball, resting on a green, was moved by high winds. He was stumped about whether or not he could move it back. McGinley told him, incorrectly, that he could, and it wound up costing Ferrie two strokes. Afterward, he threw a tantrum, and accused McGinley of misleading him on purpose.

He later apologized, but now, at Winged Foot, that didn't stop the European press from trying to grill him about it. "Can't we talk about something else?" he growled. "After all, it's Saturday night, and I'm leading the US Open!" That rerouted the discussion to more basic topics, like his background and his round. He said was from Ashington, a small mining town in the North of England. He also said he was from a working class family, and it was true—you could tell by his grammar. Asked to describe his putts on 18, he said, "Well, there was three of 'em."

Nobody gave him a canary's chance against Mickelson, who was tied with him for the lead at two-over. Clearly, Mickelson himself wasn't too worried. It showed in the way he light-heartedly engaged in a little matchmaking outside the clubhouse on Saturday evening after his round.

As Mickelson signed autographs, a stunning blonde was leaning against the waist-high cattle fencing, waiting her turn. It was apparent she wanted more from him than just an autograph. When he arrived in front of her, he signed, but ignored her attempts to talk with him, and moved down the line.

Sports Illustrated's Rick Reilly, standing nearby, saw an opportunity. Reilly was something of a friend; he had covered Mickelson's earliest triumphs back when he was a lowly golf writer, before both he and Phil became pop culture icons. He was also recently divorced. As Mickelson moved away from the blonde, Reilly moved toward him and whispered in his ear, "Don't forget your divorced pal, Rick. Your pal Rick, who hasn't had a date in a month."

Mickelson looked up and smiled at Reilly, and stepped back toward the woman. "Have you met my friend Rick Reilly?" he asked her. "He writes the back page column for *Sports Illustrated*. He's really famous. You should go out with him! Why don't you two go to dinner together? I'll make a reservation for you at my favorite Italian restaurant in the city!" With that, he took down her number, and handed it to Reilly.

A half hour or so later, Mickelson, now in his car, and already having made the reservation, rang Reilly's phone. "Rick, it's your Pimp Daddy," he said. "You owe me big time! Just remember—I want details!"

Mickelson's hottest pursuer on the leaderboard was Geoff Ogilvy, who was just one stroke behind him and Ferrie.

A lot had happened to Ogilvy since the young Aussie's victory at the Match Play. His Masters debut had gone reasonably well. Although the architecture critic in him disapproved of Augusta's changes, he still posted a top twenty, and had the time of his life.

That is, until May, when, while playing the Byron Nelson in Dallas, he received an unexpected invitation. The President wanted him to come to dinner.

"That was quite surreal really," Ogilvy told the *Sydney Morning Herald*. "Apparently, they couldn't find our address. Quite weird. They're the White House. They should know everything."

The occasion was a black-tie state dinner honoring Australian prime minister John Howard. Shocker: Geoff and Juli got there early. They were bug-eyed as they watched the other guests arrive. "Cheney, Rumsfeld, Rice, Murdoch—Juli and I looked at each other and said, 'Wow, why are we here?'

"I thought, before we went to the dining room, maybe we'd be in a queue to shake Johnny and Bush's hand. We were, but the President caught Juli's accent. 'Are you from Texas?' In thirty seconds they'd established that she had a friend who had babysat the Bush children."

The biggest surprise was the location of Ogilvy's placecard. "I said to Jules before we were ushered into the dining room, 'I'll see you later.' Then I found my table. 'Table 11. Where the hell is it? Right up the front. Not bad. Wonder who's on the table?' I looked at the place names. Condoleezza Rice. Wow. Rupert Murdoch. The President. John Howard and Mrs. Howard, Julie Eisenhower. What the hell am I doing here?"

A nonsurprise, perhaps, was that no one expected him to talk politics. The war in Iraq came up only when Bush told him he'd stopped playing golf when it began. "All he wanted to do was talk sport," Ogilvy said. "No politics. Maybe that was the reason I was there. I'm an Australian and we love our sport."

In one way, Ogilvy didn't figure to play well at Winged Foot. For a player apt to slide quickly toward frustration, it would surely pose problems: if ever there was a course to try one's patience, this was it. Also, he would likely be unsettlingly critical of the setup. "What I typically do," he said of his experience at past U.S. Opens, "is stand on the tee and bitch and moan about how high the rough is, and that sort of thing."

On the other hand, he was in the middle of great run at the majors. In 2005, he had finished T5 and T6 at the British and PGA; in the two majors before those, he had posted top-thirties.

Maybe his head, at least at the majors, wasn't that much of a problem. "It's funny the way you get at a major," he said. "My brain just sort of switches on. You know you've only got four chances a year at this kind of thing. With regular tournaments, it's just like, oh, well, there's another one of these next week. At a major, it's not like that at all. There's not another one of these for a year.

"At the others, you don't fly the white flag, but you just don't dig quite as deep, and do everything possible. You think, ah, I'll get 'em next week. In a regular week, I have to remind myself to be patient. In a majors week

I don't. It just happens." In other words, Ogilvy didn't have to focus for the majors. They focused him.

At one point on Saturday afternoon, however, Ogilvy looked ready to let old tendencies derail his chances. Playing the superlong 640-yard par-five 12th, he hit a colossal drive. Walking toward his ball, he thought to himself that if there was ever a time he could reach this green in two, this was it. He remembered: "After I walked about three hundred yards, I said, I'm going to be able to go for this. This is awesome. So I'm winding myself up, getting ready to go for this green."

Alistair "Squirrel" Matheson, Ogilvy's caddie, wasn't having it. The quiet young Englishman patiently told his boss that on this day—with the pin front left, just over a bunker, and next to a precipitous fall-off on the left—hitting a 3-wood would more likely result in a six than an easy four.

"I tried for three minutes to talk him into letting me go for the green," Ogilvy said weeks later. "He just waited me out. He was brilliant." But those words came out of a calmer head than the one on his shoulders that day.

The wait—and the irritation evident in Ogilvy's body language as he and Matheson talked—caught everyone's notice. His playing partner, Kenneth Ferrie, the championship leader, had already laid up, and stood idly 150 yards ahead, tapping his wedge against his shoe. When Ogilvy finally hit his seven-iron, Ferrie gave him a mock happy-face, and a thumbs-up.

Ogilvy had accepted Squirrel's counsel, but he wasn't happy about it. His next shot showed it. The worst wedge he'd hit since he was 12 finished a good forty feet right of the pin.

"I was never annoyed with [Matheson]," he later said. "I was annoyed with the situation. I was annoyed that I tried to talk him into going for the green. I knew it was the wrong play. And I had tried to make Squirrel feel bad for not letting me, by walking in front of him twenty yards, which is a petty little thing. Two holes later, we were back to reality."

Unfortunately, on both those two holes, he made bogey.

On TV, Johnny Miller and Dottie Pepper psychoanalyzed Ogilvy the whole way. After the second bogey, Miller remarked, "Something happened. His demeanor—well, it's not dark, but it's not happy."

"You're right," said Pepper. "His attitude has completely changed since that exchange at the twelfth."

"Isn't that part of winning the U.S. Open, handling that stuff?" Miller asked.

Juli Ogilvy was watching in the clubhouse. Early along in Miller and Pepper's dialogue, she had to leave the building. She just couldn't bear to listen. "Of course they're going to have disagreements," she said of her husband and his caddie. "It's like a marriage. They've been together seven years."

Later that night, Ogilvy got a phone call from Judy Rankin, the LPGA great and former ABC commentator, and one of the best people in golf. She was at home, battling breast cancer. She and Geoff had become friendly because Rankin's son, Tuey, was married to Juli's sister.

A veteran of twenty U.S. Women's Opens—which could be just as brutal as the men's—she wanted to offer a few words of encouragement. As Ogilvy remembered it, she told him, "You're always going to be surprised at what score wins the U.S. Open. So never let yourself think you're in bad shape." It would turn out to be perfect advice.

On Sunday Mickelson arrived at the course at 10:30 a.m.—four and a half hours before his 3:00 p.m. tee time—and hit about 300 putts to prepare for the long afternoon. His mother, Mary, met him on his way to the clubhouse. The two walked in arm-in-arm. While he sat down for lunch, Geoff Ogilvy was settling in front of a locker room television to watch Australia play Brazil in the World Cup.

Mickelson and Ferrie were in the final pairing. Just ahead would be Ogilvy and Ian Poulter, an old European Tour comrade of Ogilvy's, who today was dressed in pink from head to toe. ("He looked like the Easter Bunny," Ogilvy later said.) The second-to-last pairing was Colin Montgomerie and Vijay Singh.

By the time the leaders teed off, it was already plain that the day would be tough on them all. The 90-plus degree heat would have been unbearable if not for the slight breeze. The greens were a crusty championship-brown. The rough was just as ugly as it had been earlier in the week. On the 5th hole, Mickelson was in Davis's kinder but nonetheless evil three-and-a-half-inch cut, with 141 yards left into the green. The grass was so thick that he believed he needed a 4-wood to advance his ball to the green. He managed to advance it about three feet.

Up ahead, Ogilvy's second straight birdie, on the 6th, moved him into the lead. On NBC's broadcast, Johnny Miller said, "Well, he can tell his family some day, if he never gets a major, hey, I was leading the Open." The implication that Ogilvy didn't have a chance to win at Winged Foot was enough to send Juli running from the TV once again.

As the leaders limped around the turn, all of them over par, Ogilvy led by one. Right behind him were Mickelson, Ferrie, Montgomerie, and Jim Furyk, who, at two under, was playing the round of the day. Vijay Singh and Padraig Harrington were two back.

Mickelson, however, soon regained the lead, holing a tricky 12-footer for birdie at 11. He extended it to two with another birdie on the 14th. With five holes left, all the week's promise was coming to fruition. Three straight majors. The brink of the Mickelslam. And maybe, just maybe, the best golfer in the world.

Walking along with Mickelson, ducking in and out of the trees, Rick Smith was already receiving congratulations. But he wasn't accepting them. At least not yet. "I'm still nervous as hell," he said, behind the 15th green, watching his man tap in for par.

He had reason to be. Mickelson may have been leading, but he had only hit two fairways all day. Yes, he had made three birdies. But as Smith knew, even Harry Houdini never did acts of longer than three hours.

Play-by-plays of a tournament's final holes are usually pretty tedious. But what happened over the last hour at Winged Foot featured more mood-swings than three Mahler symphonies. It would be the strangest major championship denouement in decades.

Off the 16th tee Mickelson hit another foul ball, this one a pull left. He managed to advance it to the green, but wound up with a horrid fried-egg lie in the front bunker. It doomed him to bogey.

At the same time, Colin Montgomerie was playing the 17th. That hole began with a classic Monty moment, with crowd interaction that, among the watching European pressmen, produced several different but equally damning stories. As Monty readied himself to hit his tee shot, he was disturbed by a young boy in the gallery, who was in the act of kneeling down. He treated the child, according to one account, "to one of his patented, prolonged stares." After driving way right, almost into the other fairway, he picked up his tee and threw it at the boy. Depending on who you believed, it either sailed by his head or hit him in the chest.

In any case, he hit a splendid recovery into the middle of the green, and rolled in a miracle fifty-footer for birdie that gained him a share of the lead at four over par.

At that point, both Geoff Ogilvy and Jim Furyk were one shot behind Lefty and Monty. Over the next half hour, all four would have a golden opportunity to win the championship. All but one of them would refuse it.

Jim Furyk was first. Playing 18, he drove it into the fringe, and then played into the front left bunker. He hit a terrific sand shot that left him five feet below the hole. The nerve endings were virtually popping out of his forearms. He backed off the putt once, then twice, then a third and fourth time. In the end, he left his putter blade open, shoving the ball right.

Ogilvy, meanwhile, was having trouble at the 17th. After a terrible drive, he had to punch his ball back into the fairway, and try to get up and down for par. His sand wedge took a strange bounce, and rolled onto the left fringe, thirty feet from the cup. He looked done for. But at least two people thought otherwise.

Due to her pregnancy and her distaste for television, Juli had been watching the round from a golf cart, with one of the tournament officials driving her around. As her husband approached his ball, the cart was parked on a hill overlooking the green. Any sudden movement might spill it over. "You'd better put the parking brake on," she told her chauffeur. "Who knows what could happen?"

Squirrel, Ogilvy's caddie, had a funny feeling, too. For some reason, he decided to pretend he was Bruce Edwards standing next to Tom Watson at the 1982 U.S. Open at Pebble Beach. "Why don't you just chip it in?" he suggested. Sure enough, his boss's ball landed soft, released, broke at the right time, and tumbled into the cup. Ogilvy was still in the hunt.

Now came Colin Montgomerie's tournament-defining—and perhaps career-defining—moment. Standing on the 18th tee, he needed a birdie to overtake Mickelson (who, at the time, was busy parring 17, after hitting his drive, of all places, into a garbage can). A par figured to ensure a spot in a Monday play-off.

His drive was perfect, a signature fade that landed on the right side of the fairway. Another of his cuts would get him close to the middle-right pin. Monty likes to play fast, but that was not an option. Yes, another distraction. A few days later, the 42-year-old, now 0–58 in the majors, would say, "I was nervous and all that, but it didn't help that Vijay," his playing partner, "had driven into the tents and was about five minutes getting a ruling. I honestly believe that if I was able to walk up to that shot and hit it immediately I would probably have won."

And he probably would have won if he had picked the right club, and hit a decent shot. But neither happened. At the last moment he shoved his 6-iron back in the bag and pulled a 7, then hit it heavy. "What kind of shot was that?" he asked himself as the ball flew through the air. It finished in what he called "position Z," right of the green, the short side, in the heavy rough. A mighty rip was required to get it out, but the ball flew far past the flag. Three more putts, and he had a double bogey.

(Naturally, there was more controversy as Monty left the green. Walking past the Mickelson family, he—again depending on who you believed—either bumped into or shoved a state policeman.)

Ogilvy was right behind him, in the fairway, looking at the unluckiest break of the week: his center-cut drive had finished in a sand-filled divot. Yet Ogilvy refused to become unnerved. If he had, it would have been the first time all day. No matter what happened—bad shots, funny bounces, all the little horrors that were part of Winged Foot's nature— he never lost his composure. Saturday's frustrations seemed like ancient history. His patience had been sublime.

His 6-iron came off the ground in a cloud of sandy smoke. It looked brilliant, but when it hit the green, it didn't release as it should have. Instead it spun back and rolled off the front of the green, winding up twenty yards short, back in the fairway. No matter. He settled over it and hit a spinny little wedge that landed five feet left of the pin, checked up, released and rolled right, finishing five feet above the hole. Now it was his turn to wait. As fate would have it, Ian Poulter, playing with him, had the same exact putt, from the fringe, that Greg Norman had holed to force a playoff with Fuzzy Zoeller at the 1984 Open. Watching his idol drain it was one of Ogilvy's earliest golf memories. Poulter missed his putt— just barely—but Ogilvy did Norman's legacy credit, rolling in his curling little putt to finish at five-over. A stumble from Mickelson, still leading by one, and Ogilvy might have a chance.

The rest was ugly to watch. Mickelson's tee shot on 18 was punctuated by a cry of "Oh, no." It bounced off the railing outside a corporate tent, well left of the fairway. His second shot, an attempted cut around a tree from 210 yards, caught a branch and went forward only about 45 yards. Rick Smith was standing right behind him. "It was like a nightmare," he said. On TV, Johnny Miller, complaining about Mickelson's "crazy shot selection," said he would have punched back into the fairway. He also said that "Phil the Thrill" had returned. One more thing: "Right now, Ben Hogan has officially turned over in his grave."

Mickelson's next shot, his third, found another fried-egg lie in the front left bunker. From there, Mickelson had to get up and down for bogey to force a play-off.

Because of the dogleg shape of Winged Foot's 18th it was impossible for those standing around the green to see what was happening. One of them, Amy Mickelson, was smiling when she saw her husband start to walk toward the green. When she heard what had happened, she put her hand over her mouth in shock.

Geoff Ogilvy had a better view. He and Poulter were in the scoring area as Mickelson hit his second shot. Ogilvy was still checking his card when Poulter, who was already looking at the nearby television, stuck an elbow in his ribs and said, "You might want to watch this." Together they saw Mickelson play his third. "You're looking pretty good here," Poulter said to Ogilvy.

Open officials, preparing for Mickelson's entrance, soon ushered Ogilvy, now joined by Juli, into the locker room. There they watched the rest of Mickelson's tragedy unfold.

Mickelson's fourth shot came out of the bunker with absolutely no spin. It sped across the green and entered the right rough, pin high. He had one more chance. Holing out would mean a play-off. But he missed. Behind the green, Amy turned to her nanny and told her to take the kids home.

Winged Foot's two-story locker room is perhaps the most unusual in golf. Its first floor is broken up into halves; to get from one side to the other, you have open a door, go outside, take five or six steps across a walkway, and re-enter through another door. The second floor, however, crosses the walkway uninterrupted, hanging above the path like Venice's famous Bridge of Sighs. Inside are the same metal lockers that were installed in 1921. On the walls, and at the end of each aisle of lockers, are framed newspaper clippings that go back as far as Bobby Jones' U.S. Open victory in 1929. There's no air conditioning, only ceiling fans.

One of the locker room's few concessions to modernity is its handful of television sets. Geoff and Juli Ogilvy watched Mickelson's last three strokes on one of the sets upstairs. Grouped around them were other players and their wives, and some agents and officials. Also in the locker room, and hovering just outside it, were two dozen eager reporters, committing to their notebooks every little scene.

When Mickelson's bogey chip went past the hole, there was a vacant, incredulous look on Geoff Ogilvy's face. Then Juli threw her arms around him. He buried his face in her shoulder. When it re-emerged, he was wearing an ear-to-ear grin.

"This is a big deal!" she said, with her eyes open wide, but her voice, though excited, in an embarrassed hush.

The first player to congratulate Ogilvy was Jim Furyk. He was at the bottom of the stairs as the couple came down, holding his shoes in his left hand and shaking Geoff's hand with his right. "I just said, 'Hey, great playing,' or something simple like that," he remembered. "At a time like that, it really doesn't matter what you say to the guy, because he's not really hearing it."

Colin Montgomerie was next. "Well done," he said, on the same principle. More interesting was what he said to Padraig Harrington when they ran into each other later. "Why on earth do we put ourselves through this?" Montgomerie wondered. Monty's formal press conference produced a classic moment of black humor. "I look forward to coming back here again next year for another U.S. Open." Pause. "Disaster."

After receiving his locker room congratulations, Ogilvy called his father, Mike, back in Melbourne, and wished him an Americanized Happy Father's Day.

Mickelson, for his part, remained in the scoring area after his round for what seemed like a half hour. He and Amy sat there at the table, hunched over, as if in mourning.

His words to the press were unforgettable. "I still am in shock that I did that. I just can't believe that I did that. I am such an idiot."

At about the same time, Adam Scott, Geoff Ogilvy's best friend on Tour, was sitting on a couch in Ernie Els' nearby rented house, watching NBC's post-round highlight package. Outside, Els, Darren Clarke, Thomas Bjorn, and their wives and caddies were loading up the cars, getting ready to go over to the Mamaroneck airport to fly home in Els' G5.

As Scott watched, he was trying to piece together what was going on at the course. Foremost in his mind was the scene when he had won the Players Championship two years earlier: Bjorn had hung around after his round, knowing that Adam's girlfriend, Marie, was going to have to stand around for three hours, virtually clueless, while he took care of media obligations. Now Scott was thinking that Juli, Geoff's wife, would be going through much the same thing. "I was wondering if I should go back," he later remembered, "because I wanted to shake his hand and have a drink with him, but also because I could sit with Juli, because she was going to be out on a limb for a while."

Trying to make a decision, he eventually found himself standing outside with Bjorn.

"Do you think I should go back?" he asked.

"He's your mate. What do you want to do?"

Bjorn's voice is distinctive. He is a native of Denmark and has long had a house near London, but through it all, he has somehow emerged as a dead vocal ringer for a Scot, Sean Connery. Maybe it was the way he inflected his words, or simply the Bondish tone in his voice. At any rate, Scott turned around, got in his courtesy car, and made the short drive back to Winged Foot.

As he neared the course, the awards ceremony was getting started on the 18th green. Mickelson gamely went out to receive yet another silver medal, but Montgomerie and Furyk, also runners-up, chose not to attend. Scott arrived just in time to see Ogilvy raise the trophy and say, "Thanks to all the Australians in the crowd, and all the others pretending to be Australian."

Moments later, The Golf Channel approached Scott for a comment. "Geoff was this much better than everyone else when he was twenty," he said. "He just didn't know it. It just took him a few years to figure it out."

When the presentations were done, Mickelson dutifully signed some autographs, cleaned out his locker, and made the long walk to the parking lot, his arm around Amy's waist. When he drove off he was wearing sunglasses, even though it was dusk.

He wouldn't begin to recover, he said a couple of weeks later, until he was reunited with his kids.

"Did you win, Daddy?" asked his daughter Amanda, who was born the day after Mickelson lost the 1999 U.S. Open to Payne Stewart.

"No," her father said.

"I'm sorry. Do you want pizza?"

She also added, "Daddy, second is just so good. That is so great, Daddy."

Ogilvy's encounters that night with the press were odd affairs. At times, they verged on being overtaken by gleeful Aussie writers punctuating each of their questions with a hearty "mate." The American writers, in contrast, asked Geoff Ogilvy as many questions about Phil Mickelson as Geoff Ogilvy. But he was a realist. He understood. "I think I was the beneficiary of a little bit of charity," he candidly said. "I think I got a bit lucky."

He was also asked to speculate on the reasons Tiger Woods was not, for a change, in the hunt on a major championship Sunday. "It had to be the two months off," he said. "He's never missed the cut before, but he's never taken two months off before, either. There's got to be a connection. The trouble is, it will annoy him that much that he'll hit a ton of balls and win next time by fifteen."

Smart guy.

Regardless of who blew a golden opportunity, and who wasn't around to challenge him, Ogilvy was the most deserving player at the most demanding championship since—well, since the last time they held a U.S. Open at Winged Foot. And now it was time to enjoy the spoils.

That evening, at about 10:00 p.m., he returned to the Crowne Plaza, carrying the trophy. He got into the elevator with a businessman who had just checked in; the hotel was already beginning its transition to a normal work week. He and the trophy drew what he remembered as "a pretty weird look."

He changed into his preferred downtime outfit, jeans and a T-shirt, and spent the next several hours in the hotel bar, exchanging grins with Juli, Adam Scott, and a dozen other friends, and drinking champagne from the trophy. The party went until about 2:30 a.m. The following morning he had the luxury of rising late, but it was still a work day. He checked out of the hotel at about 10:00 a.m.—characteristically pausing to hold the door open for a luggage-laden sportswriter—then got into a limousine and went into Manhattan to make his Monday media rounds.

There were stops with CNN, ESPN, and Fox News, but the highlight of the day was his appearance on David Letterman. In his dressing room, he met Adam Sandler, who offered his congratulations. "That was big!" Sandler, a golf nut, enthused. "That was insanity!" Sandler then looked over the Top Ten list Ogilvy was about to read. "Pretty strong," was his assessment.

The list—*The Top Ten Things That Went Through Geoff Ogilvy's Mind After Winning the U.S. Open*—went like this.

10. This is one of those things you never forget—like seeing John Daly in the locker room naked.
9. I wish I hadn't put all my money on Phil Mickelson.
8. Even I've never heard of me.
7. Now I can take a vacation from the grind of playing golf all day.
6. Crap—I'm gonna have to go on Letterman.
5. After all these years, I can finally use my "World's Greatest Golfer" mug.
4. I can quit my day job at Outback Steakhouse.
3. What would Retief Goosen do?
2. I hope this victory isn't overshadowed by America's World Cup excitement.
1. Thank you, Balco!

By Wednesday, he was back in Australia. The hero's welcome included another political function, this one hosted by the premier of Victoria, his home state. Part of the affair was the screening of a video. Ogilvy was seated at the dais while highlights of his victory, accompanied by the audio from the American television broadcast, ran behind him. At a certain point Ogilvy, twisted around in his chair, heard for the first time what Johnny Miller said about being able to tell his family that once upon a time, he held the lead at the U.S. Open. Everybody laughed, but no one enjoyed it more than Ogilvy did.

12

"THIS ONE'S FOR POPS"

The British Open

Much is made every year of the romance and charm of the British Open. But it's never enough.

It's impossible to do justice to the uniqueness of the event, how it manages to reflect both golf's humble origins and its global reach. It's played in out-of-the-way, unassuming little coastal towns in Scotland and England, populated, for the most part, by people who love and care about the game, and who are rewarded with the chance to host each season's most international field. Every Open Championship therefore produces an unmatched combination of worldliness and hominess. It's like moving the U.N. General Assembly into a old friend's drawing room.

That's not to say it's an entirely comfortable affair. The towns—most of which host the event only once every ten or so years—can't help but be overwhelmed by it. Transportation is never better than frustrating. Most housing options are often of the far-flung, last-resort variety, and they're rarely cheap, thanks to profiteers who like to make sure things don't get too hospitable. Going to the Open year after year means getting used to Cheshire-grinned bed-and-breakfast owners charging you £2,000 per week for stuffy rooms with rickety beds, moldy old electric teakettles, and broom closet-sized showers.

For the players—especially the Americans—the golf too can be maddening. The nine courses that make up the Open rota are advertised as masterpieces of strategic golf, living testaments to the way the game was meant to be played. But once you push a tee in the sandy seaside soil, your score often seems governed by the will of the gods. A bad bounce can leave you in an angry-looking gorse bush or a pot bunker you never knew was there. Even legendary St. Andrews drew complaints: Scott Hoch famously called it "the worst piece of mess I've ever played." Then there's the weather, whose changeability, even in mid-summer, perennially explains why Francis Galton, Britain's first official meteorologist, ended his life by slitting his own throat.

There was a time when all the good and bad fortune evened out over the course of four rounds, and the Open could be counted on to produce the best possible champion. It's hard to remember a year between 1960 and 1995 when the claret jug wasn't raised by a legend like Palmer, Player, Nicklaus, Ballesteros, Norman, or Faldo. Recent years, however, have seen a spate of perceivedly undeserving winners (Paul Lawrie, Ben Curtis, and Todd Hamilton). Their victories were hard to explain, but probably had a lot to do with technology. It was rapidly making some of the venues obsolete, and the rough that was grown to combat it only enhanced the role of luck. Even when the best player won—like Tiger Woods, at the 6,600-yard St. Andrews in 2000 and 2005—it seemed to have less to do with strategy and finesse than his ability to overpower the course. Before the 2005 Open, veteran English caddie Grant Berry said of Woods, "Of course he'll win. There's absolutely no flair required around there anymore. He can hit it his 350 yards and it won't matter where it goes."

Royal Liverpool—which because of infrastructure shortcomings hadn't hosted an Open in thirty-nine years—wasn't anything like St. Andrews. Renovations to its teeing areas extended it to 7,258 yards, making it the second-longest course in Open history. Its fairway bunkers were still in play, unlike those at most courses in the rota. When they weren't, the shapes of the holes, combined with the firmness of the fairways, made it impossible to predict where even the straightest drives would finish.

Tiger Woods, Hank Haney, Steve Williams, and Woods' trainer, Keith Kleven, flew to Liverpool on the Saturday before the Open, arriving at about 2:00 p.m. Their traveling party was smaller than usual. Tiger's wife, Elin, was already in Europe, after watching the World Cup with her family. Tida, a usual visitor to Britain, had passed on the trip. Woods' camp offered two explanations. One was that she needed a little more time to get over Earl's death. The other was that a particularly scary moment during 2005 Open week was still fresh in her memory. That Thursday she was in London, and was just across the street from one of the four terrorist bombs that exploded that day on the city's bus and rail lines.

After the four men landed, they found their lodgings and dropped their bags. Haney was staying at the house rented by the staff of *Golf Digest,* about two and a half miles down the road from Royal Liverpool, in West Kirby. Woods, Williams, and Kleven were a little further down the street. Their place wasn't auto racer Nigel Mansell's mansion, nor footballer Michael Owen's spread, nor the posh, nineteen-room, 250-acre Hillbark Hotel—all of which had been named in the local press as Woods' accommodations for the week. Where he actually stayed was a relatively humble three-bedroom house ordinarily peopled by a local middle-class family.

By 4:00 p.m. they were on the golf course. Only one, Williams, had ever been there before, but that was back in the eighties. His recollections were dim at best.

That day Woods played eleven holes at Royal Liverpool (or "Hoylake," as it was also called, after the small town in which it was actually located). He immediately recognized the course would be a challenge off the tee. Hazards were everywhere. There were ninety-two bunkers and the usual thickets of gorse, broom, and thistle. Out-of-bounds loomed on ten holes, most conspicuously on the dogleg-right 18th, where many players would have to start their second shots on the wrong side of the white stakes. (In a preview article, an American golf writer had nicknamed the course "Royal O.B.") The sun-baked fairways added an element of unpredictability, especially when Woods took his driver out of the bag. Soon after they began on Saturday he said to Haney, "If I hit this thing, even if I land it in the middle of the fairway, what's going to make it stop?"

The sun was setting as they walked in. The orange clay brickwork of the clubhouse glowed like a hearth; the windows in its turrets and dormers were lit up in reds and yellows. No one yet had given voice to it, but they were already halfway to a decision that would all but determine the outcome of the 135th Open Championship.

The following day they came out for a full practice round. As they made the turn, Steve Williams finally said what everyone had been thinking. "Let's just forget about the driver, eliminate all the fairway bunkers on this course, and take double bogey out of play," he proposed. "It'll make the course longer, but it will still be playable."

Woods and Haney immediately agreed. What sealed the deal was the recognition that there was little advantage, on the par-fours, to being a little farther down the fairway. Whether one had 120 or 190 yards in, the firmness of the course dictated playing to the middle of the greens. Even with a wedge, it was going to be impossible to stop the ball close to the hole.

While Woods and his team were working out their strategy, everyone else had old British pop songs running through their heads. Number One on the retro hit parade was the Gerry and the Pacemakers' tune "Ferry 'Cross the Mersey," a nod to the river running through the host city. It was closely followed by every song the Beatles ever recorded. Liverpool, of course, was the hometown of the Fab Four. They honed their musical chops at the Cavern Club, once a dank little hole-in-the-wall public house and now a shrine to the band that made it famous. The papers let no one forget that 1967, the year Hoylake last staged the Open, was also the year the Beatles released *Sgt. Pepper's Lonely Hearts Club Band.*

The other popular preoccupation among Open visitors was fear. The city's rough-and-tumble natives—"scousers," as other Englanders called them—were known to delight in meancing out-of-towners.

Golf Digest's Tom Callahan brought back from a pre-tournament trip an anecdote that perfectly described the breed.

A man parked his car near Anfield Stadium before a Liverpool Reds football game. He was approached by a young entrepreneur who asked, "Mind your car for a quid?"

"I left my Rottweiler in the back seat," the man defiantly replied.

"Can he put out fires?"

The scouser flag-bearer, if there was one, was a Liverpudlian foot-baller named Wayne Rooney. In that summer's World Cup, playing for his national team, he brutally stomped the leg of a Portuguese player in the quarter-finals. The red card he received for the deed led to England's elimination.

The city's symbolic Open-week greeter was a kid who was riding the local rail lines on Tuesday. His shaved head bore the scars of a dozen pub brawls. Alongside him was his off-the-leash pit bull.

Thankfully, Hoylake and Royal Liverpool were fifteen minutes outside the city, on the coast. Most of the locals were law-abiding types who worked in the nearby Cadbury and Squibb factories or on the dairy farms just inland.

But thuggery sometimes travels. On Wednesday night, Jim Weathers, the thick-armed ex–Green Beret who served as a trainer to Jerry Kelly, Ted Purdy, and a handful of other pros, was out for a drink with Eric Meller and Brett Waldman, Kelly's and Ben Crane's caddies. It was late, and the pub was dark. After a while a skinny but evil-looking lad inched up behind them. He was holding in his hand a long iron that, until that moment, had served as a wall decoration. His appetite for violence was rivaled only by his lack of common sense. "Are you with those faggot American golfers?" he growled. Weathers promptly picked him up by the throat, lifted him in the air comic-book style, and gave him a good shake. That was the end of that.

Play began on one of the hottest days ever at a British Open, with temperatures well into the nineties. The links hadn't seen substantial rain in months. Most of the grass was the color of oatmeal, and was so brittle that two fire engines were stationed beside the third hole from the first shot of the championship to the last. Royal Liverpool's official club history was called *Mighty Winds, Mighty Champions*. But this week, the title's first half seemed nonsensical. The only breeze on the premises issued from the air conditioners over at the compound of the Royal and Ancient Golf Club of St. Andrews, the body that ran the Open Championship, and made the rules for most of the golfing world.

In one respect, at least, this Open was like every other since the late nineties. The crowd's nearly singular concern was Tiger Woods. Unlike American fans, the British only saw him one or two weeks per year. Every time he appeared on the course, it was like Oscar night. One afternoon a little girl appeared on the beach a few hundred yards off the 11th hole with orange stripes painted onto her brown Great Dane, so that it looked like a Tiger.

This year Woods' visit came with a bonus, his hotly anticipated pairing with Nick Faldo. From the moment the Thursday-Friday tee times were announced, the press sold it as a grudge match, recalling critical remarks Faldo made about Woods on television at the end of ABC's broadcast of the February 2005 Buick Invitational at Torrey Pines. On the final hole Woods had hit a weak push short and right of the green. Afterward he said it was "a good miss," claiming the ball wound up right where it should have after a slight mis-hit. Faldo insisted he just plain fanned the shot, and that Woods was too haughty to own up to it.

Asked about his relationship with Faldo on Tuesday, Woods said that they "didn't talk much." The follow-up was whether or not he expected any conversation during their rounds. "I've only played with him two times since I've been a pro," Woods said, "and there wasn't a lot of talking there, either."

The papers played it like Tiger intended to give Faldo the cold shoulder, but that was hardly what he meant. He was simply acknowledging Faldo's stoic, tight-lipped on-course reputation. Of Faldo in his heyday, Jim Furyk once said, "He rarely spoke. It was tough to get a 'good shot' out of him. And if you said 'good shot' to him, the joke was that you were never really sure what came back. It was more of a grunt than a 'thanks.' That was just his style."

It was natural for members of the media to try to set Faldo up. Throughout his playing career the six-time major winner had always been hostile toward them, memorably thanking them, after his 1992 British win, "from the heart of my bottom." Nowadays they returned the favor by mocking his transformation into Hollywood Nick, the television alter ego he trotted out, they said, to gain the money and the attention he could no longer earn with his golf.

At Hoylake, he did all he could to legitimize the derision. He showed up on the first tee on Thursday afternoon in smoky, mirrored amber sunglasses (not sports-specific shades, but the kind Tour wives buy in upscale shopping malls). Later that day he donned a Superman baseball cap, insisting it was the idea of his son, who was caddying for him. Knowing he would be humbled alongside Woods, he was playing it for laughs. Some considered him a golfing lounge act, and compared him to an aging English pop star trying to smile through the knowledge that he hadn't charted in years.

When Woods arrived on the tee, he hugged Ivor Robson, the genial, white-haired, longtime Open starter whose ten-hour days on the job never include a potty break. (Tiger was careful not to squeeze too hard.)

He didn't have much to say to Faldo, but that didn't necessarily mean anything. For one thing, Woods is never chatty on the first tee, especially not at a major. For another, he had already said his hello-how-are-you's to Faldo on the practice range on Wednesday. It was tempting to say that they had hugged it out, but the truth—as their laughing and joking showed—was that there was never any true animosity between them in the first place.

By the time they teed off, plenty of good scores had already been posted. If much thought was being given to strategy, none of it resembled what Woods was planning.

"I was playing a practice round with Seve [Ballesteros]," said Argentina's Angel Cabrera, who by Saturday would be among the tournament leaders. "And I said to Seve, 'How do you play this golf course?'

"Seve said, 'The closer you get to the green the better your chances.' So that's the way I've played it. I hit driver wherever I can. I've played an iron off the tee on the 2nd, 4th, and 8th holes, and everywhere else I hit driver, except on the par-threes. The last nine holes, all driver."

That's not how Woods went around. Starting out, he mostly hit 2-irons on the par-fours and 3-woods on the par-fives. The lasting image of Tiger on that first day had him standing in the middle of the fairway fifty yards behind playing partners Faldo and Shingo Katayama. Not that Woods was short; his low-trajectory 2-irons were rolling out to 275 yards, and his 3-woods were finishing at about 300. He hit one driver all day, on the 16th hole. It sailed way right, into the adjacent 18th fairway. He wouldn't touch the club for the rest of the tournament. But the quality of his play was already arguing that he didn't need to. He shot an opening round five-under 67, finishing one stroke off the lead.

On day two, most of the men who had shot low first-round scores—hitting their drivers but somehow avoiding Hoylake's perils—began to move backward. Woods gained a share of the lead for the first time with a tap-in birdie at the par-five 10th, joining Chris DiMarco, who had gone out in 31, and then birdied 10 and 11. Tiger eventually overtook him with a spectacular 4-iron hole-out on the par-four 14th hole.

DiMarco's appearance on the leaderboard was a surprise. He had won early in the season, in Abu Dhabi, but hadn't been heard from since his ski injury in March. On the year, his PGA Tour results showed eight missed cuts in seventeen events. The slump made it seem as though Tom Lehman's Ryder Cup team would be without its most fiery player.

He was also fighting through a family tragedy. His mother, Norma, had passed away on July 4 during a Colorado vacation with Chris's father, Rich, with whom she had just celebrated their forty-sixth wedding anniversary. She had gone up a flight of stairs at their condo; Rich, following her at a distance, heard her groan and then fall. When he reached her he tried CPR, breathing into her mouth and compressing her chest. The EMTs then tried to revive her for what Rich remembered to be ninety minutes. The cause of death was a pulmonary embolism.

Indeed, one of the strangest things about this Open was the surfeit of heavy hearts. There were Woods and DiMarco. The news about Darren Clarke's wife, Heather, was increasingly dire. Mark Calcavecchia's mother, Marjorie—a "little woman," in Calc's words, who filled scrapbooks with her son's newspaper clippings and taped every golf broadcast she thought might feature him—had also passed away just before the Open.

DiMarco came to Hoylake with a small entourage that included his father and father-in-law, his son, Cristian, and Ryan Rue, his new caddie. Rue and DiMarco had been friends for over twenty years. They grew up playing the same course, Sweetwater, in Orlando. Rue was now a relative: his brother had married DiMarco's sister. The other players and caddies nicknamed him "New Guy," because no one had ever seen him before. But he was an essential part of the week's support system. Having another friend close at hand—especially one who had known Norma—helped Chris work through his mourning.

DiMarco's play during the first two rounds was inspired. After Friday's play he was at nine-under, three behind Woods. He was characteristically blunt about how Norma might have felt about his decision to compete so soon after her death.

"My mom has always been a huge supporter," he said. "She followed me around so many times, drove me around everywhere as a junior player. She would be absolutely pissed off if I didn't play."

Between Woods and DiMarco in second place was another unexpected name, Ernie Els. Since his 2005 knee surgery, the big South African had never quite regained his form. He had won late in the year against a weak field in his home country. But other than that, his best finish had been in Dubai, in February, where for the seventh time in his career he finished second to Woods. His duck hook on their first playoff hole, which cost him the tournament, suggested that Tiger would always have him hexed, whatever the state of his health. In the wake of that loss *Sports Illustrated*'s Alan Shipnuck wrote that Woods had once again "taken occupancy in the time share he owns inside Els' head."

It was a shame, because "Big Boy," as Tiger Woods called him, was perhaps the best-liked player on Tour. Indeed, no one was fonder of him than Woods. Together their foundations sponsored junior tournaments between Southern California and South African junior golfers; late in 2006 they would announce a partnership in a resort development in the Bahamas.

Heading into the weekend, it was hard to take seriously either Els' or DiMarco's challenge, simply because Woods was playing so well. Indeed, an eleventh major championship win seemed almost inevitable. It wasn't just Woods' strategy; it was his control of his golf swing. Laying back off the tee, he was playing a much longer course than everyone else, but it didn't matter. On Friday he missed only two greens, fewer than anyone else in the field.

Intimates like Haney and Williams were begin to whisper that it was the best they'd ever seen him hit the ball. They'd said it before, but this time their claim was credible. They and a few other observers knew that just two weeks earlier, at the Western Open, Woods had made a swing adjustment that had set him up for one of the finest stretches of golf in his career, and may eventually be judged as one of its major turning points.

Woods was always measured against his incredible run between the summers of 2000 and 2001—probably the best in the game's history—when he won nine PGA Tour titles, including four majors in a row.

When his game slipped in the years that followed, there was plenty of second-guessing about Woods' decision to split with teacher Butch Harmon and take up with Haney, dedicating himself to a swing change that no one thought he needed. "It was like Michelangelo going back to chisel a more impressive six-pack on the David," Jaime Diaz wrote in *Golf Digest,* summarizing the reaction of Woods' critics.

Tiger insisted he knew what he was doing. And it was hard not to believe him, because he had done it before. It was a major renovation in the wake of the 1997 Masters that produced his dominant stretch in 2000 and 2001.

The young Woods always had plenty of power. What concerned him was a lack of control. In an early-round interview during the 1997

Masters, David Feherty complimented him on a few spectacular recoveries that followed wild drives. "I've had a lot of practice," Woods said. "I've spent my whole damn life in these trees."

In the two years that followed, he and Harmon worked diligently to improve his accuracy. It culminated in May 1999's famous eureka moment, when Woods, on the range at the Byron Nelson, finally felt everything click, telephoned Harmon, and simply said, "I got it."

If Woods missed a shot between June 2000 and April 2001, no one remembered it. It therefore seemed crazy when he started to contemplate another overhaul toward the end of 2002. But to Tiger it was a necessity, for three reasons.

One was a perceived technical problem. From his junior days to the height of his powers, Woods fought a tendency to "get stuck," to let his arms drop too far behind him, making it impossible to return to club squarely at impact. The swing he developed with Harmon—with a vertical takeaway and a slight reroute back to the inside, a so-called two-plane swing—held little promise of curing the fault.

The second was the way the game was changing around him. Club for club, he had always been the longest player on Tour. But new technology (along with a new, Woods-instigated emphasis on fitness) was closing the gap. Other players were now wielding longer, graphite-shafted drivers with heads the size of toasters, while Woods stubbornly clung to his small-headed, 53-and-three-quarter-inch steel-shafted driver (part of what Phil Mickelson once infamously called his "inferior equipment"). In 2002 he fell to sixth in the Tour's driving distance stats. He still lead the Tour in par-five birdie average (perhaps the most important of all Tour statistics), but his margin was shrinking.

The third reason was a chronic injury. Throughout his career, Woods "regularly snapped his left knee into hyperextension," as Diaz wrote in *Golf Digest* in 2004, in the best piece ever published on the evolution of Woods' swing. "Woods considered the move a key source of distance; he would exaggerate it when he needed an extra 20 yards."

Said Woods, "The more the knee hurt, the more I'd have to make alterations in the swing to try to make solid contact. The more alterations I made, the more distance I lost, because I was actually moving away from the ball a lot, slowing down, trying not to make it hurt."

In December 2002 he had surgery to drain the knee, and remove cysts that had formed around the anterior cruciate ligament. He won five times in 2003, but was still dissatisfied, and severed ties with Harmon that summer.

Gradually he began spending time with Haney. At first the relationship was informal. As instructor to Woods' pal Mark O'Meara, Haney already traveled in his orbit. Then he began visiting Haney in Dallas. Woods tried to keep it secret, in his inimitable Mata Hari way. But word leaked out. By 2004 beat writers were making jokes about Woods rappelling down from a helicopter, ninja-style, into his new teacher's backyard.

Woods liked what he saw in Haney's flatter one-plane swing. The absence of a reroute seemed to discourage getting stuck; it also encouraged more clubhead speed, and therefore more distance. Additionally, its roundedness allowed him to swing around his left leg, rather than into it, helping to preserve the health of his knee.

Results, however, were anything but immediate. His 2004 PGA Tour season was a career worst. He won only once (at the Accenture Match Play at La Costa), flopped at the majors (his best finish was a T9 at the British), and in September was supplanted by Vijay Singh as world number one. He picked up a couple of yards off the tee, but was wilder than ever, hitting only 56.1 percent of his fairways (182nd on Tour).

All year the press asked him what was wrong.

"I'm close," he'd always answer.

Things finally started to come together in December of 2004, when he won the Dunlop Phoenix in Japan, his first stroke-play victory in twelve months. In 2005 he went on to win six PGA Tour events, including two majors.

Still, he wasn't quite firing on all cylinders. His driving distance was suddenly way up (reaching 316.1, from 301.9 the previous year), due at least in part to the addition of a longer, graphite-shafted, large-headed driver. But his driving accuracy was again abysmal (54.6; 188th). His two major victories came at what were then the two least demanding driving courses of all the major venues, Augusta National and St. Andrews. At Augusta he won despite back-to-back bogeys on the 71st and 72nd holes, both the product of wayward drives, and at St. Andrews—well, Grant Berry was right. He hit it all over the place, but it didn't matter.

To most, the new swing was the problem. Butch Harmon would later say that Tiger's plane, now twenty degrees more horizontal than it used to be, encouraged the clubface to come from too far inside, rather than "out toward the target. When this happens, his head dips, the clubface never squares up, and the ball goes a zillion miles right of the target." Woods and Haney believed that the solution lay in perfecting his takeaway and swing plane. It would come; it was just a matter of time.

After missing the cut at the U.S. Open, Woods did what Superman always does after coming out on the wrong end of a fight: he repaired to his Fortress of Solitude. True, it wasn't as solitary as it used to be, before the additions of a wife and a dog. But little had changed about the way Tiger pursued excellence while encamped at Isleworth.

Isleworth was a flashy address, home to not only a half dozen or so Tour players, but also the likes of Shaquille O'Neal, Vince Carter, and Ken Griffey Jr. Yet Tiger's townhouse (like that of next-door neighbor Wesley Snipes) was a humble dwelling, indistinguishable from the others surrounding it. One evening in 2001, veteran pro Jeff Sluman went over to Tiger's for dinner. Unsure exactly where Woods lived, Sluman finally identified his place by peeping in all the front windows on the street, until he found the one with all four major championship trophies lined up on the living room coffee table.

The house was ideally suited to its one true purpose, preparing Woods to play his best golf. He loved his weight room, the furnishings of which lent a clue to his competitive psyche: the only picture on the walls was the famous photo of Muhammad Ali scowling over a fallen Sonny Liston in Miami in 1965. He also loved the difficulty of the community's golf course—so much so that after buying his new $38 million spread near Palm Beach, he insisted he would keep the place at Isleworth, because of the way the course got him ready for the majors. And the driving range was perfectly situated—it was directly across the street, just steps from his front door.

After Winged Foot, Hank Haney, Woods' coach, spoke frankly with Tiger about "stepping it up in terms of practice time, and getting refocused," as he later put it. It wasn't exactly a riot act, but Tiger needed something to reawaken him, as anyone would after losing a parent. They wasted little time getting back to work. The following week they spent long hours on Isleworth's course, and hit plenty of range balls. In the weight room, Woods rechisled the muscles that on sticky summer days, with his hairless arms sweaty and his shirt clinging to his torso, made him look like something produced by Mattel—a Tiger Woods action figure.

He was also spotted that week running windsprints on the driving range while wearing a sixty-pound weighted vest.

The week after, Woods went to Chicago to play the Western Open, and shot an opening round 72. By the numbers, he drove the ball well, hitting nine of fourteen fairways. But he was dissatisfied. He was particularly troubled by a foul ball off the 15th tee. His right hand came off the club halfway through his follow-through, and, all in one motion, he immediately extended it to Williams for a reload.

That evening, he made a few loose swings on the range, and began to voice his frustration. He couldn't give Haney an explanation for what was going wrong, except to say that he had experienced the same discomfort on the golf course.

Haney turned to Williams. "What did you see out there?" he asked.

"The same thing as always—his head moving around and winding up back here," Williams said, as he pantomimed the fault, with his head winding up near his right shoulder.

"You know what?" Tiger interjected. "I want to fix this. I've *got* to fix this. Now, what do we do about it?"

"It wasn't a new thing," Haney would later say about the problem. But that exchange, he said, "renewed our commitment to fixing it."

The focus of their attention, in their terminology, was Tiger's fluctuating "eye tilt"—a left-and-right rocking of his head ended in that telltale rightward dip. They had always treated it as the product of poor positions throughout the swing—when the takeaway and plane were solid, the problem would disappear.

Now they went straight to the head, in essence trying to fix the cause by fixing the effect. That evening—as well as the following afternoon, in a three-hour range session—Haney spent most of his time with his hand on the Woods' right cheek, keeping the head stabilized. When he backed off, Woods conspicuously craned his neck and shrugged his right shoulder, trying to ingrain the proper spacing between them.

In the weeks that followed, Woods consistently referred back to those two visits to the range at the Western, saying that they "turned it around" for him—not just with the driver, but throughout the bag— and got him "hitting the ball more crisply, more solid" than he had in a long time. At Royal Liverpool, he wasn't hitting any drivers, but otherwise his ballstriking was pure. By Saturday, keener eyes were starting to look past Hoylake, and wonder what Woods might accomplish during the second half of the season.

Apart from making Woods the prohibitive weekend favorite, his Friday round at Hoylake also helped settle a few other storylines. By then it was clear that neither Phil Mickelson nor Geoff Ogilvy would be contending. One hadn't quite recovered from his Winged Foot disaster, and the other hadn't recovered from his celebration.

Darren Clarke shot a Friday round of 82, and abjured future tournament plans to be with his wife, Heather. "I won't play again for the foreseeable future," he said. "I've got other more pressing things to think about."

Then there was sideshow Daly. John made news all week, first for his Tuesday gig at the Cavern Club ("Knockin' on Heaven's Door" again), then for his annual snub of Wednesday's Champions Dinner ("They can't get this fat boy into a shirt and tie," he said). Yet the family highlight of the week, however, was his wife Sherrie's return to the public eye. England's *Guardian* reported that on Friday, as her husband was finishing up his cut-missing 72–73, she was in the R&A pavilion making bets on how John would make out on the 18th hole. When he hit his drive out of bounds, the paper said, it cost her thirty-two pints. A double or nothing bet on his next tee ball—also O.B.—made it sixty-four. (Daly's camp denied Sherry even went to Hoylake.)

During Saturday's play the biggest change on the leaderboard was the appearance of Sergio Garcia's name. His 65 was the round of the day and earned him a spot in the final pairing alongside Woods, who had unexpectedly stalled: his third-round 71 featured three three-putts. With Garcia, DiMarco and Els just one shot behind Woods, and Jim Furyk one behind them, the stage seemed set for one of the best Open finishes in history.

Still, overtaking Woods seemed like an uphill task. He was nearly invincible—thirty-four for thirty-seven—going into a final round with a lead. At the majors, his record was a perfect ten for ten. Garcia, like Els, had plenty of mental baggage when it came to playing head to head against Woods, and some of it was freshly packed: in the same situation in January's Buick Invitational, he had shot a 75 to Tiger's 72. As for DiMarco, Woods had stared him down as recently as the 2005 Masters.

Woods woke up early, as he always does, and began the arduous process of killing time before playing a late round of golf on a Sunday afternoon. He went for a six-mile, forty-minute run with Elin, Steve Williams, and trainer Keith Kleven—they had discovered a bike path that ran right along the coast, and afforded a scenic look at Wales across the Irish Sea. On their return, Elin made breakfast. Then Tiger settled onto the couch with his housemates to watch some television. As usual, Tiger had the remote, and quickly landed at CNN. They took in some Tour de France highlights, and saw aftermath footage of the previous day's bombings in Lebanon that included jarring pictures of injured children. "Compared to that," Woods remarked to Williams, "the golf seems pretty unimportant." Nevertheless, he soon clicked over to the BBC's early coverage of the Open, to perform—again, as usual—their Sunday morning scouting of the day's pin positions. They knew the practice might not be condoned by the men who originally wrote the Rules of Golf. But after so many mornings just like this one—whiling away the hours before a late major championship final round tee-time—their thinking was simple. You'd be a fool not to do it.

When they got to the range, they were quick to spot Garcia. It wasn't had to pick him out: he was sporting yellow pants and a clingy, high-tech yellow shirt with a stiff, mock-turtle collar and a zippered neck. He would later take a fair amount of abuse for it, even from the European pundits, who should have realized it was a cool, fashion-forward nod to the Tour de France, which was also winding up that day.

When play began, Tiger continued treating Hoylake like a chess-board and parred his opening four holes. Garcia, in contrast, was struggling. His putting stroke in particular looked ill-equipped to handle the pressures of the final round at a major. He three-putted twice in his first three holes to dig himself an early hole.

Woods' eagle on the par-five 5th distanced him from the peleton. From then on, no one could touch him. He allowed DiMarco to pull within one when he bogeyed the 12th, but three straight birdies on 14, 15, and 16 settled the issue.

When Woods hit his tee shot on 18—the last of a few dozen 2-irons striped right down the middle—his twirl of his golf club indicated that he knew it was over. Still, he was all business, riffling through his yardage book as he approached his ball in the fairway. Just before he and Garcia hit their second shots, a chorus of boos came from ahead of them, up near the green. A man had thrown onto the green a half-dozen powder bombs, which left purple splatters when they hit the ground. Woods hardly noticed. He drilled a 3-iron over the green and began the last portion of his long march.

He had made this walk before, and this one showed little deviation from those that preceded it. He smiled, and tipped his hat to the cheering crowd, knowing that once he reached the green, he would switch right back into grinding mode. He still had to finish the race, as his father used to say.

Halfway to the green, Steve Williams tried to remind him of the gravity of the moment.

"This one's for Pops," he said, throwing his arm around Woods' shoulder.

Tiger looked at him for a moment. "Yeah, you're right," he said. But that was all. Reminiscence was not part of the on-course job description. Even if part of him wanted to give in, he fought off the urge.

Woods settled over his ball, lying just behind the green, and putted it back toward the hole, threading it through a pair of purple splotches. Two putts later he was in with a par, finishing off his two-stroke victory. He pumped both fists over his head, reflecting his pride in the way he'd manhandled the golf course.

He was still smiling when he buried his face in Williams' chest. He held on tight for what seemed like a full minute. But as he hugged him, his upper body started to heave. When his face became visible again he was sobbing uncontrollably. He was still overcome as he embraced Elin, Kleven, and Haney behind the 18th green.

The hard little kid from Cypress hadn't cried like this since he was a child. In all of his life as a public figure—indeed, even at his father's funeral—he had never shown this kind of emotion. It was easy, until now, to think it was no longer in his nature.

Woods gathered himself as he made his way to the scoring trailer. Just before he entered, he passed Chris DiMarco, who called out, "Hey Tiger, why don't you give me a little bit of a chance for once?" No way. That certainly wasn't in his nature, then or now. That wasn't ever going to change.

13

TIGER MACH THREE

The PGA Championship

It was a scene right out of a movie. Two young, fashionably unshaven men wearing oversized sunglasses were walking across the tarmac at a small airfield, heading for a private jet. Hustling behind them was a scruffy reporter, dragging his luggage, looking hopelessly out of place. At the rear of the group were two impossibly good-looking women. It was pretty clear which of the three men they weren't with.

"So, Geoff," the reporter said. "Ever see that Cameron Crowe picture, *Almost Famous*?"

"I have," said the U.S. Open champion.

"This remind you of anything?"

"It does," he said, getting the joke.

"How about that other scene, where they're in the air, and that storm hits. . . ."

"Yeah," he said, interrupting. "I remember that one, too."

Golfers, as a rule, don't like wisecracks about plane crashes. Payne Stewart's memory ruled them out. But Geoff Ogilvy's fears, in this particular case, didn't have anything to do with that. He had cut the reporter off in deference to Richelle Baddeley. Aaron's wife was trying hard not to show it, but she was an uneasy flier. If Chicago was anywhere near Scottsdale, she would have driven.

The other members of the group were Tim Clark, the young South African who was runner-up at the Masters, and his girlfriend, Candace. Richelle's husband, Aaron, wasn't there because he was, at that very moment, finishing off his final round at The International, in Denver. He and his wife would meet up later, at the DuPage County airport near Chicago, a couple of miles from Medinah Country Club, site of the upcoming week's PGA Championship.

For now, Ogilvy was Richelle's chaperone. The math worked out because Juli, Geoff's wife, couldn't make the trip. Now seven months pregnant, her travel was restricted. She was also dealing with gestational diabetes, which deprived her of the opportunity for nonstop noshing. "What can you eat?" Candace had asked Juli at the airport, where she was seeing her man off. They were standing next to a late-model, limited-edition Porsche that was parked on the lobby floor, with a $200,000 for-sale sign on it. (It was used; the odometer said 201 miles.)

"Very low carbs," Juli sighed. "Basically, nothing."

For Ogilvy and Clark, flying private wasn't a way of life. Yes, they were rich. Clark's career earnings, on the PGA Tour alone, now hovered at about $7 million. Ogilvy's were $10.5 million, but his actual income was nearly impossible to calculate. His triumph at Winged Foot would lead to a considerable boost in endorsement money, appearance fees, and the like.

Still, neither was profligate. As they got settled on the plane, the first topic of conversation was the surf bum clothing they were wearing. Clark's baggy shorts, he said, had cost him $20 at an outlet mall. Ogilvy's entire ensemble—T-shirt, shorts, and flip-flops—looked like it might have been purchased at Wal-Mart for half that price. Around his wrist was perhaps the only leather-banded watch on Tour. The women were wearing what, in the summer of 2006, was the standard outfit of every attractive young woman in America—tight jeans and equally tight, low-plunging T-shirts. The only blingy piece of jewelry between them was Richelle's diamond-encrusted crucifix.

All five passengers spent the first twenty minutes of the flight ferreting out the goodies on the plane. The drinks were in a closet up near the cockpit; candy bars were hidden underneath the armrests. After a while, Clark discovered a stash of macadamia nuts in a nearly invisible drawer underneath his seat. Jackpot.

During the rest of the two-hour flight, the conversation pinballed everywhere. Clark talked about his recipe for beer-can chicken, the condo in the Bahamas he was thinking—*thinking*—of buying, and how, a couple of days earlier, after days away from the range, he had bruised up his hands by hitting balls for two and a half hours.

Ogilvy shook his head. "You can't do that. You've got to do a little something every day, no matter what it is—short game, putting, whatever."

Clark and Ogilvy remembered how, when they first moved to Scottsdale, they lived in the same apartment complex. "It was like Melrose Place," Clark said, chomping on the banana pepper that had been packaged with his sandwich.

They talked about movies (taking care to sidestep one). Geoff was well versed in indie and foreign films. He admitted that he had only seen Wim Wenders' classic *Paris, Texas* because it was named for his wife's hometown, but when he mentioned that it had won the grand prize at Cannes (pronouncing it *Kahn,* like a Frenchman) it seemed like he had this kind of conversation fairly often.

Eventually, the talk came back around to golf, particularly the coming week's PGA Championship. "I'm playing with Tiger and Phil," Ogilvy said, arching his bushy eyebrows and smiling his Stan Laurel smile. "Should be interesting."

As they touched down, the reporter turned to Ogilvy. "Can I say it now?"

"Say what?"

"The line from *Almost Famous.* I've been dying to say it."

"Okay," Ogilvy said. "But not too loud."

"'I'm flying high above Wichita, Kansas,'" he quoted, "'with America's hottest band, and we're all about to die.'"

Richelle, quiet the entire flight, suddenly leaned forward in her seat, her head peaking into the aisle. "I heard that!" she barked.

The plane taxied forward, rolling around Phil Mickelson's parked GII. You could tell it was his by the tail numbers, N800PM. (Tiger Woods, too, had just arrived, but it was difficult to tell which plane was his, particularly since he owned shares of three: a 1997 Citation X; a 2005 Gulfstream G-200; and a 2000 Gulfstream G-IVSP. Each was suited to a trip of a different length.)

When the door to Ogilvy and Clark's plane opened, Aaron was already waiting for Richelle on the tarmac, standing next to his courtesy car. Geoff's and Tim's cars were pulling up to meet them. For them, at least, the year's fourth major had begun.

Ogilvy was right. His pairing with Woods and Mickelson would be interesting. So interesting, in fact, that it was the near-exclusive focus of the first part of the week.

The PGA's pairing Woods and Mickelson together wasn't a plot. It was the championship's long-standing policy to put the winners of the three previous majors together. But because of a recent spate of lesser-known major champions, this was the first time in a long time they wound up with a group featuring the game's two most popular players. Previously, Woods and Mickelson had only faced off a total of four times. Now they would do it for two straight days.

And they would do it at what had recently been the best of the year's four majors. True, the club pros added some clutter, but if one looked past them, the PGA presented the season's strongest field. Teeing it up at Medinah would be ninety-eight of the world's best 100 players.

As far as excitement went, no other major could rival its recent run of fantastic finishes. Over the past seven years, there hadn't been a lemon in the bunch. Working backward, there was Mickelson beating Thomas Bjorn and Steve Elkington down the stretch at Baltusrol; Vijay Singh taking a play-off from Chris DiMarco and Justin Leonard at Whistling Straits; Shaun Micheel edging Chad Campbell at Oak Hill; Rich Beem's triumph over Woods at Hazeltine; David Toms squeaking past Mickelson at Atlanta Athletic Club; and Woods' epic battle with Bob May at Valhalla.

The one that started the streak had been right here at Medinah, with Woods outlasting a post-pubescent, scissor-kicking Sergio Garcia. That little bit of history also weighed heavily at this year's event because it was one of the turning points of Woods' career.

If Tiger's first great run was the one with which he started his career— five victories in twelve tour events, highlighted by the 1997 Masters— then Medinah was the launching point for the second. Ending a ten-major winless streak, his 1999 PGA victory was his first after refashioning his swing, along with Butch Harmon, for accuracy and control. What followed was history's best-ever run of golf, featuring eighteen Tour wins and five majors in a period of twenty months, capped off by the TigerSlam.

Hoylake, it seemed, had seen the birth of Tiger Mach Three. His lone start since then was a dominating performance at the Buick Open in Flint. Hitting twenty drivers all week (in comparison to the one he hit at Hoylake), he hit two-thirds of his fairways, bogeyed just four holes, and made a career-best twenty-eight birdies to win by three. Clearly, he had found his form. Indications were that his work with Hank Haney, from the Western Open forward, had refined all the iffiness from his swing. It helped that his club selections off the tee had become more conservative, but Flint's revelation was that when he did pull the driver, he could now hit it straight. He was starting to look a little scary.

The anticipation the Woods-Mickelson matchup resembled that at Winged Foot, except that the tables were turned. Now Tiger was playing the best golf in the world, and the question marks surrounded Mickelson. Phil's tie for twenty-second at the British was his best result in three starts since his meltdown in Mamaroneck; the week before the PGA, in Denver, he had missed the cut. It was hard not to think he was dealing with some psychological scarring. On the other hand, expectations surrounding Mickelson had been similarly low the previous year at Baltusrol, and he surprised everyone by winning delivering his gutsiest-ever performance at a major and taking the championship.

The previous week in Denver, Dean Wilson had finally broken through, claiming his first victory on Tour. (Sadly, the Flyin' Hawaiian didn't do his long-promised backflip. "At this point," he said, "I'd wind up killing myself.") The win was also the third of the year for his coaches, Mike Bennett and Andy Plummer, if you counted Tim Herron's at Colonial.

The man Wilson beat, in a play-off, was Tom Lehman. Had Lehman won, he would have earned a spot on his own Ryder Cup team. He was loathe to admit it, but he was sorely disappointed.

Slumping Chris Riley, in the wake of the June birth of his second child, daughter Amanda, was enjoying a second-baby bounce, making his fourth straight cut. "I don't know how to explain it," he said. "I guess I'm getting hungry again."

The tournament's most intriguing presence, however, had been David Duval. For him, Denver was a home game; he had moved to the mountains in 2004, marrying a native, Susie Persichitte.

His new family came ready-made. Susie had three kids from a previous marriage—two boys, aged twelve and ten, and a seven-year-old daughter, Shalene. Dating a single mom had been tricky business. Naturally, she was protective of her kids, not wanting them to meet her new beau until she was sure about him. But her sons, Deano and Nick, were golfers. They knew the voice on the answering machine belonged to David Duval well before she wanted them to. The couple married in March 2004, after a five-month engagement. Together they had a third son, Brayden, who was born on April 21, 2005.

For Duval, Susie and the kids filled a long-standing gap. When he was nine, he lost his twelve-year-old brother, Brent, to aplastic anemia; weeks earlier, David had endured a bone marrow transplant to try to save Brent's life. Soon after, his parents divorced. The experience encouraged a certain introversion. He found solace in golf, and the game rewarded the time he spent with it by turning him into a great player.

His new family also answered a question he had been asking since winning the British Open in 2001. After that victory, he went through a kind of malaise, all but losing interest in the game. Duval referred to that period as his "existential moment," but the problem was better stated by Peggy Lee than Jean-Paul Sartre. He wondered, *Is that all there is?*

"David always assumed that because golf was his life, when he reached his goals in golf, he'd find fulfillment," Gio Valiante, his friend and former sports psychologist, told *Golf World* in 2004. "When he reached his goal, and saw that he still wasn't fulfilled, he truly realized for the first time that golf isn't life."

Now, Duval had changed. But he was also the same. He was still on the shy side. He could still grow impatient with some of the banalities of Tour life (for example, post-round interviews). He was still a Democrat, one of the only two or three on Tour—in an early summer *Golf Digest* piece, he admitted to voting for John Kerry, a hideous breach of Tour etiquette. He was still bookish, although his tastes had migrated from Ayn Rand to, say, Bill Bryson, perhaps reflecting a shift from an inward gaze to an eager curiosity about the outside world. Yet he still grew self-conscious when people tried to paint him as an intellectual. *Digest,* for example, had asked him to pose in a chair, reading a book. He obliged but considered it "weird."

Through his struggles, Duval liked to say that his new family was the reason he kept playing golf: he wanted to show them that he was still capable of being a great player. Of the relationships that once defined his Tour life, he would say, "I'm out of that loop." But neither was entirely true. He still loved the game. And he was still close with a few of his Tour cronies.

Justin Leonard, for example, bunked in at Duval's new house near Cherry Hills during the week of the International. Placed, however, in opposite ends of the draw, they didn't spend much time together. While Leonard slept in (relatively speaking) on Thursday morning, Duval woke up at five and headed to Castle Pines. Although on the early side, he was a lot like a typical Denver commuter. Driving onto the property, he breezed his Range Rover past the physical therapy fitness trailer—a happy new circumstance, considering his six-year string of health problems (shoulder, back, and wrist, and even a bout of vertigo). Once inside, he headed "right for the coffee machine," he said. "They've got the good stuff there, Lavazza."

He knew the place well. Castle Pines was a regular hangout. He played there as often as he did at Cherry Hills and sometimes came in just for lunch. He usually went the healthy route, going for the half-Cobb salad, rather than the specialty of the house, tacos made with filet mignon. The clubhouse was filled with friendly, familiar faces.

By the time he finished hitting balls, Susie, Deano, and Nick had arrived to watch him play. Initially small, his gallery steadily grew as the day progressed. Most onlookers knew him personally; every member of Susie's wide, hometown-girl circle of acquaintance had embraced him. For his most recent birthday party, she said, "we invited about two hundred people, and about three hundred showed up."

On the golf course, Duval looked almost exactly like he did back in 1999, when he was the number one player in the world. The sunglasses were on, the chew tucked under his lower lip. After a few lean-waisted years, he was back in what somebody called his "buffet zone." (The half-Cobb salads only did so much good.) There were only two discernable differences. One was that the top half of his fu manchu was gone. The other was the yellow LIVESTRONG bracelet on his left wrist.

Actually, there was one other difference. Rarely did ten minutes pass without Duval looking out into gallery, finding Susie, and flashing her a smile. It was a departure from the old, stone-cold David, and indeed a rarity on Tour. Most players wanted to stay focused on the business at hand. While they liked having family supporting them out on the course, interaction was out of the question. It was inconceivable for Tiger Woods, for example, to do such a thing. When he played, Elin, who often walked his rounds, might as well not have been there.

Watching Duval play confirmed what he had been saying all year. He wasn't far away from his former level of excellence. But it also confirmed an age-old pro golf truism: there was a very fine line between great golf and poor golf. He missed only three shots all morning. Unfortunately, they were all drivers, and led to three double bogeys. A streak of cold putting kept him from righting his score. During one stretch, he singed five straight lips.

Afterward, a reporter remarked, "You must have missed those five putts by a total of twelve centimeters."

"Do you think it was that much?" he replied.

That week, his evenings were relatively quiet. He worked the grill when he had time, and the family ordered Chinese food on the one day he finished late. He wound up missing the cut, and on Sunday night started packing for Chicago. He had planned to fly out on Monday, but decided, at the last minute, that he "wasn't ready to leave." Because of their guest, and all the activity surrounding the tournament (which, for Duval, didn't end until Saturday, because of a rain delay), he felt like he hadn't spent enough private time lately with Susie and Brayden.

On Monday they went to "the baby store" to get diapers and formula, then went to the bookstore. There, Duval said, Brayden was "a brute." He wouldn't stop whining. He shifted gears at the mall, where David needed to get a couple of pairs of pants. "We set him down, and he started walking around," something he'd only started doing four weeks earlier. "Before we knew it, he had walked right out the door."

Early Wednesday morning, at Medinah, Duval hit two buckets of balls with Puggy Blackmon, his old coach at Georgia Tech, to whom he had returned in 2004 to help him make his way back. Then he played a practice round. Afterward, changing shoes in the locker room, he talked about his hopes for the week and for the upcoming Ryder Cup. He said, "I still think I can make the team, frankly. I'm playing great, and I feel pretty confident that if I won this week, I'd be picked."

It wasn't as crazy as it sounded. He had had a good week at Winged Foot, tying for sixteenth, and again at the British, where one bad round, a Saturday 78, kept him from a top ten.

Medinah offered plenty of good memories. Back in 1990, when the only people who had heard of Tiger Woods were college golf coaches, Duval, then a college freshman (with coach Blackmon toting his bag) was leading the U.S. Open after five holes. He hung around on the leaderboard until late Friday afternoon. On the weekend he almost wrested low-amateur honors from two-time NCAA champ Phil Mickelson.

From the locker room, he walked over to player dining and sat down for a late lunch with Blackmon and Dr. Mike Lardon, a San Diego-based physician and sports psychiatrist. Duval leaned into his cheeseburger, his blond hair standing straight up, his white cap and sunglasses resting near his right arm, clamped together in one piece, looking a little like a football helmet without the chin guard.

Soon Nick Price stopped by. The three-time major winner had just returned from a vacation on the Baja Peninsula, in Mexico. He spent much of his time, he said, surfcasting for roosterfish, easily the ugliest fish on the planet. With coal-black eyes and a weirdly stepped snout, it looked like a horizontal version of the Creature from the Black Lagoon.

The two made some small talk and eventually wound up telling Simon Hobday stories. Hobday, a South African–born contemporary of Price's, had a reputation as a world class drinker and carouser. Both were exaggerated. He was, however, one of golf's zaniest characters. Players of Price's generation told Hobday tales the way baseball fans quoted Yogi-isms. There was the time, for example, that the grizzled old pro asked a clothing manufacturer for $500,000 *not* to wear its line of golf shirts. One evening, he arrived at a reception, noticed a sign that said "Ties Only," and entered wearing only a tie.

Price's favorite Hobday story, he said, dated back to the early eighties. One day Simon's bank manager phoned him, and told him his account was overdrawn by $2,500.

"So?" Hobday asked.

"What are you going to do about it?" the banker inquired.

"How much did I have in the bank at this time last month?"

"About $4,500."

"Well, I didn't phone you to ask about it, did I?"

Duval didn't know Hobday. But his father, Bob, had played the Senior Tour alongside Simon for a few years, and passed on to his son a couple of tales that Price had never heard. The one David now related had Hobday late for his tee time at a tournament in Arizona, racing to the course at roadrunner speed. When he was pulled over, the state trooper, relishing the chance to dish out a steep fine, said, "You know, I've been waiting for somebody like you all day."

"Well, I got here as quick as I could," Hobday replied.

After Price left, Duval had one more joke to tell. Leaning back in his chair, he said, "Okay, Puggy. Let's go hit a couple more buckets of balls."

His coach laughed. "Once David's fanny hits the chair, we're done for the day," he explained, "especially if Susie is in town."

On the surface, it was another reminder that golf was no longer the most important thing in Duval's life. Yet something about it rang false. Why make a point of it? If the feeling was that deeply ingrained, he wouldn't have bothered saying it at all; he simply would have gotten up and left. Somewhere, it seemed, there still resided a piece of him that really did want to go out and practice some more.

David Duval would play more majors. His status as a past British Open champ guaranteed him a spot until he reached 65 years of age. But this was the last year of his five-year exemption into the other three. It might well be the last major he would play in America.

Nothing about his behavior said he was okay with that. If he was, he wouldn't have been on the range at seven that morning. If he was, he wouldn't have slogged through three long years of wretched playing. This company, these clubhouse chats, the challenge of the game, was part of him. However much he claimed that competitive golf had faded in importance, much of what he did argued otherwise. He wasn't going to give it up without a fight.

Thursday was the kind of morning so often poeticized in golf's commemorative, Chris Schenkel–voiced highlight films. As the sun peeked over the horizon, it poked through the trees and dappled the fairways. The mist was still heavy on the course's ponds and lakes.

The tee time for the Woods-Mickelson-Ogilvy group was 8:30 a.m. They were to start on the 10th tee, which was so distant from the clubhouse that the players were chauffeured there, via surface streets surrounding the course, in SUVs. Each emerged from his vehicle like a heavyweight prizefighter with his cut- and cornermen. Mickelson was accompanied by Jim Mackay and Dave Pelz, and Woods by Steve Williams and Hank Haney. Ogilvy trumped them both. By his side were Alistair Matheson and Richelle Baddeley. She wasn't there to carry cards around the ring between rounds. She simply needed a lift—again—to join her husband, who was teeing off just ahead of the marquee three-some.

All three players had their game faces on. Preparing to tee off, they staged an elaborate dance that seemed designed to prevent them from talking to each other. Each put his bag down at a different corner of the tee box, and wandered into the tent to pick up their scorecards at different times. Not a word was spoken between them, save for Ogilvy saying "good luck" to each of his partners.

Tiger was the first to tee off. This being a par-five, he pulled driver, and hit it off the world. He had to punch out from behind a tree, found the back fringe with his third, and, because of the green's steep back-to-front, wound up making bogey. It was only 8:45 a.m., but Woods was already throwing clubs at his bag.

Meanwhile, Ogilvy and Mickelson both made birdie. Phil's was an easy tap-in set up by a sweet 3-wood approach from the first cut. Geoff's came on a wedge and a beautifully holed, curling fifteen-footer.

Because of the 10th tee's far-flung location, few fans had seen them tee off. But by the time they were in the 11th fairway, their gallery numbered about 1,000. It only got bigger.

Their rounds progressed in dramatically different ways. Tiger's bogey on his first hole was his last of the day. He had to hole a 35-footer for par on his second, but otherwise the sailing was smooth. He found his worst trouble on his fifth hole, the par-five 14th, missing his driver again and finding an icky lie from which he could only advance his ball about 80 yards. Yet he managed to grind out another birdie, canning a 25-footer. From that point on he played tidy golf.

Mickelson hit a fair number of loose shots but always managed to recover, and never lost control of his round. Ogilvy, on the other hand, had a five-hour roller-coaster ride, making seven birdies, two bogeys, and a double.

They finished with identical, highly respectable scores of 69.

Of the three, Ogilvy was easily the best interview.

The round, he said, was "lots of fun, one of the biggest, best atmospheres I've ever played in—at least on a Thursday morning." The reporters laughed. "Everyone was looking forward to watching those two play together, and I had the best seat in the house."

He was entertained by the "controlled craziness" inside the ropes, with nearly a hundred writers and photographers stalking the group. He said, "The first few holes I wondered who was guarding the media center. Someone could have picked it up and taken it away, and no one would have noticed."

What most pressmen wanted to know about—flogging a horse that was never really alive—was the supposed hostility between Tiger and Phil. Allowing that the two "probably weren't on each other's Christmas lists," it was "exactly the same as in any group during the first round of a major, unless it was best friends. It was exactly like a normal group. You talk in between holes, and when you both hit a good shot you have a bit of a talk. But when one of you hits a bad shot you're not the first to say something. It was just perfectly normal. First rounds at majors are a bit serious. And everyone was just being serious."

His most insightful comments related to Woods' play. "He's back to playing conservative," he said. "He's back to playing the way he did in 1999. Tiger's playing textbook golf now. For a while there he was hitting a lot of drivers, but now he makes conservative decisions." Having watched Mickelson hit recovery shots all morning, Ogilvy also had choice comments about Phil's short game. "It's pretty special, isn't it? He very rarely has a chip shot or a bunker shot that he doesn't look like he's going to make. It's always going at the hole. I wouldn't want to say who's got the better short game out of Tiger and Phil. They're both very special. But Phil's is extra special. He hits the hard shots really well."

Both of the players tied for the lead at day's end, with 66's, were interesting stories. One was Lucas Glover, the likeable young Clemson grad who all year had his heart set on making the Ryder Cup team. He had been grinding perhaps too hard, throwing away several point-earning opportunities with poor rounds. (Most recently, he had played in the final group with Woods at the Buick Open, and shot an even-par 72, falling all the way back into a tie for 15th.) He wasn't helped by the early-season death of Dick Harmon, a member of one of golf's great teaching families. Harmon had been not only Glover's teacher but something of a father figure, mentoring the young man from his early teens.

The co-leader was the newly hungry Chris Riley, the slumping former Ryder Cupper who was having such difficulty, after starting a family, maintaining his enthusiasm for the game. Even with a win, he probably had no mathematical chance of making Tom Lehman's team for the upcoming trip to Ireland. But if he somehow won the PGA, it would certainly put pressure on Lehman to make him a captain's pick.

David Duval was paired with Chad Campbell and Retief Goosen, and went out on Thursday morning four groups ahead of Woods, Mickelson and Ogilvy. He opened his round, as he did so many others in 2006, with a wild drive. He bogeyed his first two holes, but bounced back with two straight birdies.

His driving further deteriorated on the back, where he missed every fairway but one. But hole after hole, it seemed, he wound up rapping in a seven-footer for par. In a way, it was encouraging. His knack for scoring—getting the ball in the hole despite whatever kind of trouble, the mark of all truly great players—hadn't left him. He finished with a 73.

He came out on Friday afternoon with an excellent chance to make the cut. Son Nick reported that during lunch, at family dining, Justin Leonard had predicted it would fall at one-over.

The day's biggest surprise, perhaps, was the size of Duval's galleries. Though in the same half of the draw as the glamour group, there were people watching him along most every inch of the gallery ropes. It was proof that Chicago loves its golf, takes Fridays off, and has a long memory. Susie, so easy to locate in Denver and during Thursday's round, was now hard to find. David spent much of his first few holes trying to pick her out among the other spectators.

He was having an equally hard time, once again, finding fairways. From the day's first hole—where Duval hit a big block—Blackmon's face couldn't cloak his concern. Ordinarily, Puggy was great company, an outgoing Southerner with an easy smile and an antic sense of humor. During one of Duval's first appearances at the Masters, he was caddying for him, as usual, and staying with him in the same rented house. When Duval went out to their courtesy car on the morning of their first round, he found that Puggy had tied steer horns to the hood ornament. "I wanted him to arrive like Boss Hogg," he said.

Now, however, Blackmon was deadly serious. Walking a few steps behind the family, he tried to explain what was wrong with David's game.

"We're just working on the last piece," he said. "We spent another two and a half hours on the range this morning. He's bringing the club back a little outside and then flattening the club, laying it off. That's why he's hitting it right. He can't hit his cut right now," the shot he relied on during his heyday. "He has to bring his hands up a little more on the inside, so it's more on the outside on the way down."

Three holes later, Duval yanked one left.

Trying to save it with his hands?

"Yep," Blackmon said.

On the third, in between poor drives, Duval hit the fairway, found Susie, and came over to visit while waiting for the green to clear. He gave her a little peck and said, "Are you staying ahead of me? I can't find you."

On the ninth green, while Duval was sizing up a 40-foot birdie putt, he noticed that Woods, Mickelson and Ogilvy were coming off the neighboring seventh tee. He looked over at the walking scoreboard. In red block letters and numbers, it said: MICKELSON 3, OGILVY 6, WOODS 4. He settled over his putt and rolled it in for his first birdie of the day.

Duval turned at even par. By that point, a light rain had come in. The forecast had called for thunderstorms. When an official in a golf cart inadvertently leaned on the horn, everyone mistook it, for a moment, for a suspension of play.

Soon after, his old friend Gio Valiante, who had introduced him to Susie, appeared along the ropes. He had come out to watch his client Campbell. Susie asked how Gio was doing. He told her about having to fly back and forth to Reno to tape episodes of The Golf Channel's *The Big Break* that involved young women from the Futures Tour, the LPGA's developmental circuit.

He hated the travel, he said, but when they tried to sign him on for more episodes, he thought about how cute the players were and accepted.

Susie laughed. "I know how you are. I've seen you in action."

She was referring to the night she first met David, back in 2003. Valiante had taken him out for a beer in Denver, during tournament week. Duval was in a rut, Gio insisted, spending too little time outside his hotel room. At the restaurant, Valiante dragged him over to a table of young women. David immediately fixed his eyes on Susie. The attraction was mutual. It was Valiante who was talking to her, but as he remembered it, "you were looking way past me, right over my shoulder. And David was looking at you like he was a hunting dog."

Approaching the clubhouse, Duval was hanging tough at one-over. He drove his last tee shot into the trees, punched out to about 100 yards, wedged it to eight feet, and rolled the putt in for par. But it wasn't enough. By now it was clear that Leonard was wrong, and the cut would be even par.

Every Friday afternoon on Tour, you could usually spot the players who had missed the cut just by looking at their faces. Invariably, they wore tight-lipped frowns all the way from the scoring trailer to the car. As Duval walked into the clubhouse, with Blackmon on one side and Susie on the other, he wasn't frowning. But he wasn't smiling, either.

Mickelson's Friday 71 dropped him well back in the pack. Woods and Ogilvy, however, held steady, shooting matching 68's. The leaders after two rounds were Billy Andrade, one of the other admitted Democrats on Tour, and Henrik Stenson. The 30-year-old Swede had long been tagged as one of Europe's next great players, but in 2001 he suddenly saw his game desert him. It took him three years to recover fully. His coach, English sage Peter Cowen, said, "It's the biggest overhaul I've ever done, including Lee Westwood," referring to the Ryder Cup stalwart he'd brought back from the abyss in 2002.

Saturday's sentimental-favorite pairing was Billy Mayfair and Shaun Micheel, who were two and three strokes back. Mayfair, the tow-headed 1987 U.S. Amateur champ and five-time Tour winner, had five weeks earlier discovered he had stage-one testicular cancer. Within three days he was on the table. The surgery was a success, and the scene in the recovery room testified to how popular he was among Tour folk. When he woke up Phil Mickelson and Jim Mackay were at his bedside.

In the wake of his 2003 dream win at Oak Hill, Micheel hadn't had much success. He never followed up with a second Tour win, and never finished better than eighty-second on the money list. He sometimes complained of feeling lethargic, but most figured it was a by-product of racing around the country to see his favorite band, Kiss. (He had developed a friendship with their golf-junkie lead guitarist, Tommy Thayer, and had an unlimited supply of backstage passes.) More seriously, he was often depressed. The prospect of seeking out medical help scared him, especially since his mother had long battled bipolar disease.

His problem, as he found out in April 2005, was low testosterone. It was easily remedied by the application of a cream ointment, and by late summer, he was starting to feel like his old self.

Also helping was his liaison with Matt Killen, the 18-year-old boy genius swing coach who began his career on Tour with Kenny Perry. When Micheel arrived at Medinah he was feeling good, playing well (three top-fifteens in his last three months), and talking up his new fondness for a slightly heavier shade of metal. He had recently discovered the ear-splitting, guttural sounds of Motörhead.

On Saturday, Woods played with SoCal junior golf buddy Chris Riley, but they were moving in opposite directions. Riley shot a 73, while Woods shot a 65. Tiger, on the brink of his second straight major, would play in the final group on Sunday alongside Englishman Luke Donald, a local favorite who went to college at Northwestern, and still kept a condo in Chicago.

It was intimidating enough that Woods was 11–0 in the majors when beginning Sunday with at least a part of the lead. But he was also playing near-perfect golf. He had made precisely zero bogeys between his first hole on Thursday and his sixteenth on Saturday. Finding a groove on Saturday with his driver, he hit eighty percent of his fairways, and only missed one green. Even his 2006 bugbear, the tendency to three-putt (seven at the Masters; four at the British) was starting to disappear. So far at Medinah, he'd only had one.

Hank Haney was unusually upbeat. "All year long he's been around the top of the Tour stats in proximity to the hole," the measure of how close to the pin players hit their approaches. "But he's been near the bottom of the rankings in three-putt-avoidance. Two weeks ago he was 171st, and there are only 179 guys on tour. What does that tell you? The putting has been the last thing to fall into place."

On Sunday Donald showed up in a red shirt, copying Tiger's traditional final round wardrobe choice. But it didn't help. Neither he nor anyone else in the field had a chance. Woods went out in four-under and never looked back. Micheel, the eventual runner-up, finished five behind him.

The day's only real drama involved the several Americans making a last-minute run at a berth on the Ryder Cup team. The prospect seemed especially interesting because the bottom two players in the Cup point standings, Zach Johnson and Brett Wetterich, had both missed the

PGA cut. A top ten from any of several players would probably be enough to secure a spot.

Stewart Cink, in twelfth place in the rankings, shot a solid 69, but started too far back in the pack to place among the top finishers. Give or take a few strokes, the same was true of Jerry Kelly and Lucas Glover.

Davis Love and Tim Herron were better positioned, but shot over-par final rounds. Steve Stricker and Ryan Moore shot 69s to earn top-tens, but neither had enough points to build on.

Although Sean O'Hair's ranking and his starting position precluded his chances of making the team, he shot a tidy 68. His principal motivation was fear. His new regular practice round and dining partner, Tiger Woods, had scolded him in Flint, telling him, "You'd better make this team. And if you don't, it'd better be the last one you miss."

If you've ever wondered what the wife is saying to the agent as the husband is finishing up a tournament, here's the answer. She's asking how fast they'll be able to get out of town.

On this particular Sunday, Mark Steinberg was saying to Elin, "it won't be for a while, because Tiger's got a lot of things to do." He was right. There was the trophy presentation, and a champagne toast with PGA officials and Medinah members, and a formal press conference. Also, an interview for the Tour's cable radio station, and a Tour-favored website called insidetheropes.com. And then five separate sit-down one-on-ones with various television outlets. The routine was exhausting, especially if you weren't actually part of it and had to kill time waiting for it to end. Steinberg knew it. Stevie Williams knew it. Even Elin knew it. This wasn't her first rodeo. Still, she frowned. She and Tiger had an appointment to keep, and this peripheral stuff wasn't going to make that easy.

When Woods arrived in the press center, he was asked many questions. Almost all of them were pointless. This was the kind of occasion, as they say, on which you could just print the stat sheet.

Driving average: 318.0 (field rank: 2nd)
Fairways hit: 64% (T36—not great, but better than his PGA Tour, nonmajor average of 57%)
Greens in regulation: 78% (T1st)
3-putt greens: 1
Birdies: 21 (T3rd)

Bogeys: 3
Scrambling: 87.5% (1st)
Consecutive wins: 3
Consecutive majors: 2
Total major victories: 12 (surpassing Walter Hagen)
Majors needed to surpass Jack Nicklaus: 7
Age at time of twelfth major victory: 30 years, 8 months
Nicklaus's age at time of twelfth major victory: 33 years, 7 months

The only truly relevant question was whether or not this Tiger Woods compared with the one who so completely dominated the game between 1999 and 2001. He said yes, but it really wasn't up to him to say.

But the week did provide a simple lesson to the sport's other players. In a nutshell, it was that there were only two kinds of professional golf: Tiger in the middle of a swing change and Tiger on fire. Better catch him while he's not hot.

As Woods fielded more questions, Mark Steinberg stood against a wall on the left side of the room, growing bored. A scribe asked Tiger, "What did you think when you saw Luke come out wearing a red shirt today?"

"Jeez," Steinberg sighed. "This is stupid." His cell vibrated, and he took the call. He said into the phone, "Have you heard anything from Lehman yet?" Presumably the Ryder Cup captain had already made up his mind about captain's picks, and IMG was supposed to be among the first to know.

Just as he hung up, the PGA's head press official, Julius Mason, approached him. "A reporter just called to ask what kind of dog Tiger has." Yes, it had come to that. These were the kinds of questions that came up when the popular, nonsporting media got interested in Tiger. It was a sure indicator that Tigermania was ramping up again.

"I don't know," said Steinberg, apparently not a dog person. (For the record: border collie. Name: Taz. Tiger's second career dog. First one, a boxer, lived in California with mom Tida.)

The one-on-ones were the most tedious portion of the post-victory media gauntlet. They took place back in Medinah's clubhouse. It had been built by the Shriners, a splinter group of the Masons with a pronounced fetish for things Middle Eastern. (Medina, in Saudi Arabia, was

276

the resting place of the prophet Mohammed. The sign on the gate as one left the club read, "Allah Be With You.")

Two DuPage County sheriffs led Woods into the building, through the lobby, and past its immense fireplace, whose tilework was emblazoned with images of fezzes, camels, and Muslim crescents. They took him up the stairs, which ran up the side of a big, domed area that that resembled the transept of a cathedral. The markings on the gold-leaf ceiling were decidedly non-Christian. There were more Muslim crescents, stars of David, and some decorative, Middle Eastern paisley-like squiggles that looked like a Western child's notion of Arabic script. Conspicuously absent, however, was explicit Mason iconography like pyramids and compasses.

Woods entered a hallway on the second floor. It was lined with doors that led to meeting rooms named after past Medinah major champions—Cary Middlecoff, David Graham, Hale Irwin. The Golf Channel was set up in one room, ESPN in another, and so on. Over the next forty-five minutes, Woods would bounce from one room to another, like the Beatles or the Monkees in one of their cheesy old sixties films.

Inside each, he would be asked more or less the same questions he had already answered four times that afternoon. This was one of the principal job requirements of a major champion—the ability to repeat yourself indefinitely without falling asleep.

When it was over, the sheriffs took Woods down the stairs, through the locker room, and out the back door, which opened out onto the practice putting green. On the far side were ESPN's and The Golf Channel's big temporary stages. Their klieg lights flooded the green, attracting gnats in the fading early evening light. Two full hours had passed since Woods holed the winning putt. But he hadn't yet reached the parking lot.

Tiger stopped to sign autographs on the way to his courtesy car. Waiting in the driver's seat was Steve Williams. The satellite radio was on and foreign newspapers were scattered around him. He had been using both to do some catching up on his hometown sports. "It's a big rugby weekend," he explained. "The All-Blacks are playing Australia."

Finally, Steinberg ushered Woods into the car, using the door to squeeze him, like so much toothpaste, through the last dozen signature-seekers. Now he could go meet Elin. Where were they off to? Not home, but to Houston to see a breeder, and pick up a second dog for their household. For the record, the breed was labradoodle. Name: Yogi.

The popular press would love the new pooch. They loved everything about Woods when he was playing like this, dominating the game. For others, however, such performances provoked a certain sinking feeling. It was hard not to wish that somebody—Mickelson, Ogilvy, even Duval—would step up and challenge Tiger when he was playing his very best.

14

EIRE'S MUD IN YOUR EYE

The Ryder Cup

It was Monday morning in Dublin, Ireland, and Padraig Harrington was everywhere. He was on the sides of buses. He was on the brick walls outside the pubs. At Shannon Airport, he was endlessly replicated in those long, interterminal corridors with the moving walkways: he waved to you once as you got on, again twelve seconds later, and a third and a fourth time before you stepped off. He was in restaurants both splendid and mean, even in the bathrooms. A few evenings earlier, his wife, Caroline, dining out, had walked into a ladies' room, entered a stall, and sat down. She looked up to see her husband staring down at her from the inside of the door. "My God," she said to herself. "I can't get away from him."

That, at least, was how the locals were telling the story during the run-up to the 2006 Ryder Cup. It helped illustrate how big an event it was to the Emerald Isle—by all accounts it would be the largest sporting event in its history. But mostly the point was that things had gone just a little over the top.

The American team came into Shannon early on Monday, on an overnight flight from Washington, D.C. They were supposed to arrive like the Beatles, greeted on the tarmac by popping flashbulbs and hordes of screaming fans.

Inside the plane they were more like the Charlestown Chiefs at the end of a two-day bus ride. Clothes were flying everywhere as the players scrambled through their first of the week's approximately twenty uniform changes. Today's costumes were elaborate: shirts and ties, plus wool sweaters, topped off by mustard wool jackets in a pattern close to houndstooth (some players were calling them their Sherlock Holmes coats). The players were all putting them on at the same time. A crush had formed in the galley behind the cockpit. Some wound up changing in their aisles or in their seats.

"I know we've just met," Stewart Cink said to Brett Wetterich's girl-friend, Erin Noel, as he slipped out of one pair of pants and into another in front of her. "But I don't have much of a choice."

Since no mirrors were available, no one was quite sure how he looked. That was where David Toms came in. Ready ahead of everyone else, he roamed around playing fashion consultant, even helping Wetterich tie his tie.

Most of the players were still groggy. Sleeping had been difficult, owing to the party going on behind them. The forward half of the plane was occupied by players, coaches, caddies, and wives, but the rear held about 50 hangers-on—sponsors and their guests, who had purchased their seats. Their presence, according to one passenger, got things off the wrong foot; from the start the trip had the feel of "a glorified corporate outing." The picture and autograph requests early in the flight had turned six hours of potential rest into four.

Not everyone had to endure the hassle. Phil Mickelson's schedule kept him home until later that day; Tiger Woods and Jim Furyk were already across the ocean, having played the previous week in the World Match Play at Wentworth, near London. (Woods fell 4 and 3 to Shaun Micheel in the first round, ending a five-tournament winning streak that included post-PGA victories in Akron and Boston.)

When the rest of the team finally touched down, they had to figure out an exit order. "Hey, New Guy," captain Tom Lehman shouted to Ryan Rue, Chris DiMarco's caddie. "Why don't you lead us off the plane?"

Ultimately, of course, it was Lehman who assumed the responsibility. As they descended the stairs they were met by a handful of pressmen and officials, a few fans, and European captain Ian Woosnam, who held the Cup in one hand and extended the other to Lehman.

In the end, the most memorable thing about their arrival was the miserable cold, drizzly weather, which over the course of the week rarely got any better. It answered any lingering questions about why the country was so green. But it also provoked another: how did Harrington, or any other Irishman, every get good at golf in a country where it never seemed to stop raining?

Certainly the Ryder Cup deserved a smoother, grander kickoff. It was now a global mega-event, broadcast to 140 countries around the world. Over 40,000 spectators attended each day. In 2004 the host organization, the PGA of America, had grossed a reported $80 million. The formal early-week banquets had the feel of state dinners. The flashiness of the opening ceremonies was rivaled only by the Olympics.

On the other hand, the confusion of the Americans' arrival was a perfect metaphor for the week. For seven days, a bunch of mostly low-key athletes would be required to behave like dignitaries, diplomats, defenders of the flag. The pomp and circumstance felt strange to them, even disorienting.

How they were going to get comfortable and play their best golf was a question no one was prepared to answer.

"The Ryder Cup," Jack Nicklaus once said, "is not a war. It's a friendly competition."

In his heyday, those words rang true. Before 1981, his last appearance as a player, the biennial matches, which then pitted the Americans against teams from Great Britain and Ireland, were quiet, invariably lopsided affairs. The handshakes and bonhomie were their only reasons to exist.

That all changed in the eighties, when the newly added Europeans, led by Seve Ballesteros, transformed the event. In 1985 his side won its first cup in twenty-eight years. They won again in 1987 and in 1989, the year a new contentiousness entered the matches. Its figureheads were Ballesteros and Paul Azinger. They spent their Sunday singles match squabbling over scuffed balls and penalty drops, and after it was over, the Spaniard griped that the American team was made up of "eleven nice guys, and Paul Azinger."

The following edition—"The War on the Shore," in Kiawah Island, South Carolina—was contested a half year after Operation Desert Storm. God and Country types like Azinger, Corey Pavin, and Payne Stewart used the occasion to ratchet up the patriotic rhetoric; Pavin even wore a camouflage cap. Along the ropes the fans indulged in a kind of raucous flag-waving previously reserved for soccer's World Cup.

The acrimony and jingoism reached their high points—or low points—in 1999 in Brookline, where the premature celebration following Justin Leonard's presumed clinching putt stirred bitter controversy, and nearly overshadowed the Americans' spectacular Sunday comeback. It was Lehman, of course, who was singled out for most of the scorn, accused by captain Sam Torrance of provoking the chaos. "And he calls himself a man of God," Torrance famously grumbled.

During play, things had been no better. There were accusations, for example, that a marshal had stepped on Scotsman Andrew Coltart's ball, lying just off the fairway in the rough, while directing him to look for it thirty yards away in the woods. The night the matches ended, American Jerry Higginbotham, who had caddied for Spain's Sergio Garcia, was beaten up in a Boston bar.

By 2006, however, things had changed. Brookline had embarrassed everyone. The growing internationalism of the U.S. PGA Tour made it harder for the Americans to summon up animosity for opponents who played alongside them all year. The terrorist attacks of 9/11 made partisanship unseemly. So did the war in Iraq.

Just the same, the Americans, once in Ireland, unflinchingly proclaimed their loyalty to the stars and stripes. Rookie Zach Johnson talked about getting "pretty juiced" when hearing the national anthem; Phil Mickelson spoke of an "obligation" toward "the citizens of the United States." Yet their words had a forced feeling about them. It was hard not to think they were only uttered because the hype machine demanded it, and that the players' true feelings had actually drifted back toward the Nicklaus ideal. Admitting as much, of course, was impossible: anyone who declined to salute would have been labeled unpatriotic and pilloried in the press. It was awkward to have to pay lip service to the nationalistic atmosphere of Ryder Cups past while being uninvested in it.

The Europeans' feelings about the event were different. The American players were their friends too. More deeply, however, they had a huge reservoir of anti-American feeling to tap into, simply because of the cultures in which they were raised. To them, Old Glory couldn't help but mean cultural imperialism, unpopular military installations, and McDonald's franchises despoiling centuries-old streets. It wasn't hard to imagine that a youthful Luke Donald or Sergio Garcia might once have encountered an American tourist in a Hawaiian shirt, asking directions to the Tate or the Prado while standing directly in front of the building.

Only rarely did that kind of ideological baggage get unpacked. In 2005 Paul Casey caused a furor when, reflecting on the 2004 matches at Oakland Hills with the *Times* of London, he said that he and his teammates "properly hated" the Americans, and thought their fans were "bloody annoying." In the aftermath the young Englishman—an affable, good-natured 29-year-old who attended Arizona State, had long dated a pretty young American named Jocelyn Hefner, and lived part time in Scottsdale—was quick to say that he only made the remarks in the context of Ryder Cup competition. But that didn't explain where the sentiment came from. The U.S. players knew it was nothing personal; they understood, as did most people, that the Ryder Cup has sociocultural underpinnings for the Europeans that it will never have for the Americans.

Ryder Cup week began with both sides claiming to be underdogs. For the Americans this was novel. So was the fact that they were clearly correct.

They were coming off a lopsided 18½-9½ defeat at Oakland Hills, the worst in Ryder Cup history. They had lost four of the previous five competitions. More importantly, they looked seriously undermanned. Notably absent were old warhorses like Fred Couples, Davis Love, and Kenny Perry. Replacing them was a bumper crop of four rookies, Vaughn Taylor, Zach Johnson, J. J. Henry, and Brett Wetterich. The youth movement was overdue. After all, Love, Couples, and Perry bore a good deal of responsibility for the Americans' recent poor record. Still, none of the rookies had the kind of résumé that suggested they belonged on such a stage: between them they had only five PGA Tour wins. Not that there were other young American who were more deserving. The only real solution would have been finding citizenship loopholes for Adam Scott, Trevor Immelman, and Geoff Ogilvy.

Four weeks before the trip, in Akron, Tiger Woods had taken the rookies to dinner, aiming to give them the benefit of his Ryder Cup experience.

Each of the four said he enjoyed himself. Yet it was hard not to suppose that the occasion felt a little strange. Socializing with Woods was an odd proposition to begin with: his reality was so different from theirs that they may as well have been breaking bread with a Martian. That they were Woods' contemporaries (Henry and Wetterich were slightly older, and Johnson and Taylor both about two months younger) would only have contributed to the awkwardness, since this, their first Ryder Cup, would be Woods' fifth. A small solace may have been that they all had better Ryder Cup records than he did.

The K Club received some criticism as a host venue, mostly because its Palmer Course parkland layout was more characteristically American than Irish. (Its selection, it was openly acknowledged, was financially motivated; owner Michael Smurfit, like Valderrama's Jaime Ortiz-Patiño before him, had essentially purchased the privilege of hosting the Cup.) But the on-site hotel drew nothing but kudos. The five-star monument to luxury looked like it once belonged to Napoleon, and no expense was spared to keep the players happy.

Especially impressive were the team rooms. They were located on the ground floor, on opposite wings. The U.S. team's, which looked to be a converted portion of one of the hotel's restaurants, was spacious but homey. It had a big-screen TV, computer terminals, a karaoke machine, and pool and Ping-Pong tables. On the left were big windowed doors that opened onto a patio, overlooking the 17th hole and the Liffey, the river that came all the way from Dublin to run through the golf course. At the far right was a separate barroom, which would prove to be a popular postmatch hangout.

In a way, the team room came with its own staff. The barkeep, of course, was a local. But Lehman had also conscripted Dennis Trixler, an old mini-tour crony, as team chef: his big gas grill was set up out on the patio. Four-time Tour winner Duffy Waldorf, another old friend, served as the wine steward. In all, the setup's only downer was a big table covered with materials—flags, pictures, and the like—that the players were expected to sign.

For the players and their wives, the first part of the week was like summer camp, at least after practice rounds. Tiger Woods owned the Ping-Pong table, except when he had to face Chris DiMarco. ("In that game, at least, I have his number," DiMarco said.) Woods took advantage of a rare rainless evening to walk down to the Liffey and go fishing with wife, Elin. The karaoke machine got a workout, with Chad Campbell's wife, Amy, making the strongest impression. In the bar, the players, wives, and coaches were developing a taste for Guinness. Back in their rooms, they played with the new toys that filled their gift bags—Rolex watches and Cup-logo'd cell phones, for example—as well as ones that didn't fit into them, like new freebie mountain bikes.

It was hard for anyone not to applaud the hospitality. The scribes certainly did: the free Guinness in the pressroom, along with the chortle-inducing Caroline Harrington stories, helped them forget their crappy off-site accommodations. The most spoiled of the nonplaying attendees, however, were clearly the corporate guests. They spent most of their time in a colossal three-story chalet that had been built alongside the 18th green, in the spot where the grandstands should have been. Its size and comforts (wood paneling, carpet, furniture better than the local Marriott) made some Americans wonder why they never saw such structures back home. Three or four would have gone a long way toward solving post-Katrina housing problems in New Orleans.

The only thing to complain about was the seemingly interminable wait for the golf. Most everyone had arrived on Monday, if only to justify the length of the trip, but play wouldn't begin until Friday. There was only so much YouTube a man could watch. Golf writers who had previously covered football compared it to Super Bowl week. Even the Guinness couldn't quell the boredom.

The press conferences didn't help much. For the most part they were tepid affairs. Captains Tom Lehman and Ian Woosnam, who held two each, had spent their best material long ago, in promotional talk-ins that had been taking place since February. The choicest nugget from those affairs was a story Lehman told in Los Angeles about his first impressions of Woosnam. Oddly, they didn't involve an actual meeting, but a look over the backyard fence of Woosie's fairway home in Barbados. Lehman was in the middle of playing a *Shell's Wonderful World of Golf* match when, walking by Woosnam's house, he spotted a keg sitting next to the pool. "I figured, that's my kind of guy, right there," Lehman said.

Darren Clarke's visit to the media center was anticlimactic. His wife, Heather, had lost her long battle with breast cancer on August 13, a month before Ryder Cup week, and he had done all the talking he wanted to do about it when he returned to the game at the previous week's Madrid Open. "I didn't want to come in here and answer the questions that I was asked last week," he said. The scribblers complied.

The only conference with real news value was that of Tiger Woods. When he sat before the microphones on Wednesday, he looked like a man whose wife had just been publicly insulted—which, in fact, he was. The September issue of *Dubliner* magazine had run a story called "Ryder Cup Filth for Ireland," complaining that "Most American golfers are married to women who cannot keep their clothes on in public. Is it too much to ask that they leave them at home for the Ryder Cup?" Accompanying the article was a photo of a naked woman purported to be Elin Woods.

"I'm very disappointed in the article," Woods grimly said. "My wife, yes, she has been a model, and she did do some bikini photos. But to link her to porn websites and such is unacceptable." He also made vague promises about a legal action. (He would make good on them in November.)

(Internet surfers were eventually able to place the woman as one Kimberly Hiott. The means of identification was the distinctive tattoo on her lower back. It affirmed the old Biblical prophesy that ye shall know the true porn models by their tramp stamps.)

With so little to write about, the scribblers held their usual derby to try to determine the cause of the U.S. Ryder Cup ills. The most popular hypotheses were these.

- The Spoiled Millionaires Theory. The Americans were motivated only by money. They cared little about competitions without purses.
- The Camaraderie Theory. On the European Tour, the players travel together, stay in the same hotels, and rub elbows at nightly meals. The Americans travel in cocoons. An early 2006 piece in *The Sporting News* read, "Putting a U.S. team together is not unlike forging a complicated merger. That's the task captain Tom Lehman will face before the 12 corporations playing for the United States meet the 12 drinking buddies playing for Europe."'
- The "Constipation" Theory. Jim Furyk, in an interview with *Golf World's* Bob Verdi, put it better than any writer could. "Every two years, when the time comes, it's like we're all constipated. We just get too tight. Any other week, including the Presidents Cup, we have

more fun. Guys are on the range, talking, joking, loose. But when it's the Ryder Cup, everybody's mood seems to change. It's like we're going to work instead of going to the golf course."

- The Stroke Play Stigmata Theory. Whether recreationally or competitively, young Europeans play match play all the time. When they become pros, they're used to it. The Americans, on the other hand, always play stroke play, and are especially befuddled by the team-play foursomes and four-balls formats. (The evidence for the latter claim was strong: in the last four Cups the Europeans had outpointed the Americans 39½ to 24½ in team play.)

- The Tuxedo Theory. Just before the 2006 Cup, 2004 assistant captain Jackie Burke sounded off in *Golf Digest* about the "opulence" surrounding the cup, making a special target of the formal dinners. How could the U.S. team concentrate on golf, he reasoned, when they were being treated like movie stars?

- The Cups-Runneth-Over Theory. This held that the Americans were ruined by having to play such events every year, alternating Ryder Cup competitions with the Presidents Cup.

- The Europeans-Are-Simply-Better Theory. Naturally, a British paper, the *Daily Telegraph,* said it best, opining that "any confidence in the U.S. team is misplaced, because they have so little to offer outside their top trio." Beyond Woods, Mickelson, and Furyk, the Americans had only two players ranked in the world's top twenty, for a total of five. The Europeans had eight.

All the arguments had merit. Worse, they all pointed to factors that were impossible to change. Tom Lehman did all he could to reverse the losing trend. He had rejiggered the qualifications criteria. He picked the brains of legendary coaches like John Wooden and Mike Krzyzewski. He tried to instill camaraderie by bringing the team to Ireland three weeks before the event for practice rounds. He imported the comforts of home, packing the team plane's cargo bays with tortilla chips and salsa.

But he couldn't change the one decisive difference-maker. The Ryder Cup simply meant more to the Europeans. And they were about to demonstrate it for the fourth straight time.

With just twenty-four players on the grounds and eight playing in the first set of matches, the practice range should have been a lonely place on

Friday morning. But it wasn't. When Tiger Woods appeared at 7:00 a.m., an hour before his tee time, already milling about were a hundred fans, six team captains or assistants, and two dozen members of the media. Woods wasn't even the first player there. Swedish rookie Henrik Stenson was already hitting balls. He wasn't scheduled to play that morning, but had to do something to calm his nerves. (Stenson's history at the K Club could only have made his anxiety worse. This was the place where he walked off the course after nine holes of the first round of the 2001 Smurfit European Open, his swing so lost that he believed he'd never find it again.)

Woods' opening-match partner was Jim Furyk. Furyk arrived at about the same time as Dublin-born Padraig Harrington, one half of the European opening pair. The other, Colin Montgomerie, was nowhere to be found. He finally showed up at about 7:45, wearing a broad smile that said: You others may have gotten here first, but this range—indeed, any Ryder Cup range, in any city, in any year—is my range.

Over at the first tee 1,600 fans were already packed into the horseshoe of grandstands. And there were almost as many people inside the ropes. A few were necessary presences—the marshals, for example, and the first tee announcer, Ivor Robson, moonlighting from his regular job as the starter at the Open Championship. Then there were the television crews, print reporters, and photographers. The others, who were granted no such access at ordinary events, included nonparticipating players and caddies, player's wives, and officials from various European and American governing bodies. The female American officials were easy to spot: they were the ones wearing matching red leather jackets. Their outfits helped explain the cost of the duck confit over in the corporate tents.

The atmosphere was raucous, with the fans' lungs already in Sunday form. It affected everyone, even Robson, who announced, "This is the first match of the Friday morning foursomes." The crowd laughed. Their programs said "four-balls."

After a deafening ovation for Harrington, the opening shot of the competition, a Jim Furyk 3-wood, split the fairway. Tiger Woods was next. He pulled his ball so far left, into a lake, that he would have needed his scuba gear to retrieve it. No wonder he liked having the steady Furyk as a partner.

Furyk's approach was even better than his tee shot: he stuck a 9-iron to eight feet. Soon it became clear why he and Woods needed four days' worth of practice rounds together. Their putt-reading choreography was more complex than Swan Lake. After sizing up his putt, Furyk assumed his stance over his ball, then backed off, went behind it, crouched down, and gave it another look. Tiger, clubless, moved in over the ball, making right-handed, open-palmed practice strokes. When he finished, he walked to the other side of the hole, across from Furyk, looking at the putt from above the hole. Then he went and joined his partner, still buried in his crouch, and reread the putt over his shoulder. Monty, who liked to play fast, looked on with unmistakable chagrin.

Ultimately, Furyk holed his putt, and the Americans were in the lead. As the inside-the-ropes armada moved to the second tee, Elin gripped Tabitha Furyk's forearm and yelped, "This is so exciting!" It was the most she'd ever said within earshot of a member of the press.

The U.S. team's lead didn't last long. Behind the first match, all three European pairs got off to good starts, and the scoreboard was soon familiarly blue. Woods and Furyk wound up with a win, and Stewart Cink and J.J. Henry salvaged a halve from Casey and another Swedish rookie, Robert Karlsson. But Europe took the remaining points, and ended the morning session with a 2½-1½ advantage.

The afternoon foursomes produced an identical result. That was particularly frustrating for the Americans. The last two matches seemed destined to produce two points and earn the team the lead. Instead, things went horribly wrong.

The first setback came at the hands of Montgomerie. He and Lee Westwood were trailing Chris DiMarco and Phil Mickelson, 1-down, as they came to the tee at the 18th, a long par-five. Eventually, Monty wound up standing over an eight-footer to steal a halve. The putt was heavy with meaning: holing crucial putts was what made him a Ryder Cup legend, and this one, if he made it, would only add to his air of invincibility. True to form, he buried it. For the Europeans it was a good sign: Monty was still Monty.

The last match of the day was a bitter affair. At its center was Sergio Garcia. Paired with Luke Donald against Furyk and Woods, the young Spaniard found plenty of inspiration amongst the inside-the-ropes onlookers. One source was his new girlfriend, Morgan Norman, Greg's daughter. (His date, though a member of polite golf society, only enhanced Sergio's reputation as a lady-killer. "He's got the gift of gab, that guy," his pal Adam Scott had remarked. "He's smooth. I don't know what they see in him, but he's smooth.") The other was Tiger's pal Michael Jordan. When Donald made a 35-foot bomb on the 5th hole to send the team 2 up, Sergio met his partner at the hole and tauntingly wagged his tongue.

The match was all square when it came to the par-four 17th. Garcia then stiffed an approach to five feet, and the Europeans went one up. Woods hit a perfect drive on 18, but Furyk, from 228 yards, yanked his approach left, into the lake. The hole was conceded for a 2-up European win.

Rather than taking the lead, the Americans had squandered two points and ended Friday's play on the wrong end of a 5–3 deficit.

Things were different on Saturday, but not in ways that counted. Ivor Robson finally got the "four-balls" thing right and was rewarded with hearty, sarcastic applause. Off-and-on rains had players changing clothes more often than runway models during Fashion Week. As for the golf, the Americans did little more than continue to dig themselves a hole.

In the morning session the key American teams—Woods and Furyk, and Mickelson and DiMarco—lost both their matches. The only thing saving the side from complete embarrassment was the unexpectedly solid play of rookies Zach Johnson and J. J. Henry, who produced a point and a half alongside partners Scott Verplank and Stewart Cink.

Johnson and Verplank's victory was clouded by some unwelcome remarks from Johnny Miller. While NBC was on a commercial break, Miller opined that if Johnson "had a partner, they'd have won 6 and 5. Verplunk." He didn't know that the network feed, complete with off-air chatter, was being piped into the U.S. locker room. Verplank missed it, but a few other players heard Miller's remarks loud and clear.

Verplank was benched for the afternoon foursomes, but no one took up his cause. The Americans coughed up two and a half more points, and finished the day down 10–6, the same margin by which they trailed at Brookline in 1999.

The Europeans couldn't have looked more confident. Putting like he was 18 again, Sergio Garcia had gone 4–0–0 in team play. Seven other players had yet to take part in a loss. The only disappointment was Harrington, who was 0–3–1. When reporters tried to summon the ghosts of Brookline, Montgomerie insisted that the situations didn't brook comparison.

"That wasn't 10–6," he said, preparing to explain that the score, in effect, was far closer than that. "That was 10–9 overnight. We had three rookies that had not played before"—Andrew Coltart, Jarmo Sandelin, and Jean Van de Velde had sat out Friday and Saturday—"and they happened to draw the three top Americans at the time, in Tiger, Davis Love, and Phil Mickelson."

Here, he continued, "we have a team with two rookies that have played, and played well. Everybody has played twice, and everyone's gotten at least half a point. It's also being played in Ireland, not in Boston. So I don't want any comparisons with the score line of 10–6. This is a very, very different situation."

What really dampened American hopes was the play of their two top pairs. Mickelson and DiMarco—who had looked so strong at the previous year's Presidents Cup, going undefeated as a team—were both dreadful, managing only a half point over the first three sessions.

Woods and Furyk had won two matches, but they'd played four. They had never played well at the same time. On Friday morning, Woods played some of his worst golf since the U.S. Open, and Furyk carried the team; on Saturday afternoon, Woods finally came to life, but Furyk played his worst golf of the year.

Despite his turnaround, it was hard not to put Woods under the microscope. At turns he looked unenthused, distracted, or just plain tired. His participation in the previous week's World Match Play was easy to second-guess: he never played the week before a major, indicating that the Ryder Cup, in his mind, lacked a certain gravity. When not playing, he seemed to spend most of his time bearhugging his friend Darren Clarke. Jack Nicklaus would have been proud, but no one had ever seen Woods treat any of his teammates so warmly. Somewhere in the back of his mind he was probably thinking of his friend Mark O'Meara, who had been up for Lehman's candidacy but had been passed over, even though he was Irish by heritage and had spent easily more time at the K Club than any American alive. (His pals J. P. McManus and Dermot Desmond made sure of it.) One potential reason for the snub was that O'Meara always considered golf a supremely individual game. Team play had never held much allure for Woods' friend. Now it seemed like Woods was more or less of the same mind.

After Saturday's play the U.S. team took care of their media obligations, hit practice balls, and met briefly in the locker room in the clubhouse, behind the 18th green. Lehman, frustrated and flabbergasted, simply told his players to go back to the hotel and try to relax a little. They would talk later, in the team room.

They reconvened a couple of hours later and had dinner. On previous Ryder Cup Saturday nights, a rah-rah atmosphere had prevailed. Visitors made inspirational speeches, as when then-governor George W. Bush addressed the team in Brookline, reading William Barret Travis's famous speech about defending the Alamo. Team members and their wives were always asked to say a few words about his week's experiences, and their invariably determined feelings about the Sunday singles.

This year, there was none of that. George H. W. Bush was on the grounds, as were former President Clinton and Michael Jordan, but none were invited in. Lehman's policy was No Outsiders Allowed. Even the caddies, usually part of the Saturday night pep talks, were asked to leave directly after the meal. Lehman read the next day's playing order and handed out pieces of commemorative art. The players were given the opportunity to speak. Four of them did (Cink, DiMarco, Furyk, and Verplank), but that was as far as it went. Lehman almost discouraged it from going any farther. "We could sit here and spill our guts," he said, "but everybody knows what we have to do. We were in exactly the same position at Brookline. It's imperative that we get off to a good start."

If Friday's first-tee scene was raucous, then Sunday's bordered on delirium. The fans, some of whom had planted themselves in the grandstands three hours before the 11:15 a.m. start, were already well into their signature chant, *Olé! Olé, olé, olé!* David Toms' caddie Scott Gneiser said, "It was the loudest thing I've ever heard, because the people were right on top of us. I couldn't imagine hitting a shot, because I don't think I could have balanced a ball on top of a tee."

Starting off the first match of the day, his boss somehow managed the feat, but that was as good as it got. There was no beating Europe's lead-off man, Colin Montgomerie, who ran his Ryder Cup singles record to an unbeaten 6–0–2.

Stewart Cink's match, the second off, gave the U.S. a glimmer of hope. Enjoying the best putting day of his life, he throttled Sergio Garcia 4 and 3. Woods won too, beating Robert Karlsson 3 and 2, despite losing his 9-iron on the 7th hole, when Steve Williams accidentally dropped it into a greenside pond.

Those were two of only three full points the U.S. would win all day. Furyk played well, shooting 66 on his own ball, but Casey—who was unstoppable in winning the World Match Play at Wentworth two weeks earlier—was still on fire. He made eight birdies, and won 2 and 1.

Englishman David Howell manhandled Wetterich, and Luke Donald outlasted Chad Campbell. The winning putt was sunk by Henrik Stenson, who defeated Vaughn Taylor 4 and 3.

The spotlight was now on Darren Clarke, the emotional center of the matches. When Zach Johnson conceded the final putt on the 16th hole, the Ulsterman's face crumpled in tears. He spent the next ten minutes being embraced by his friends—caddie Billy Foster, Ian Woosnam, then Sergio Garcia, Paul Casey, and the rest of the European party. Tom Lehman, who had presided over Heather's memorial service at the PGA, held him tight and told him she would have been proud. The last hug Clarke got before he left the green was from Tiger Woods.

What happened thereafter was mostly mopping up. Paul McGinley conceded a long birdie putt on 18 to J. J. Henry, because of the ruckus caused by a streaker. Had he not gifted him that half point, the European margin of victory would have been the largest ever.

Mickelson's ended his Ryder Cup 0–4–1, losing to José María Olazábal. Scott Verplank, steaming about being benched by Lehman for most of the matches, beat Padraig Harrington 4 and 3. Poster boy Harrington finished the Cup with a record of 0–4–1, but he couldn't stop smiling.

The last match on the course was between Lee Westwood and Chris DiMarco. Westwood had birdied five of his first seven holes, but DiMarco fought back. He had a chance to halve the match on the 18th, but wound up hitting his approach in the lake, and finished the competition with a record of 0–3–1. Westwood, unbeaten in this Ryder Cup, was now 10–0–3 in his last thirteen matches.

The victorious team went into the clubhouse and next appeared on the balcony on its second floor. The spraying champagne could have refilled the water hazards twice over. Flags were draped over everyone's shoulders. Henrik Stenson wore a bright green wig.

Darren Clarke was the first to go to an alternative beverage, downing a pint of Guinness in one swallow, then beaming under his foam mustache. Woosnam repeated the feat, then chased it with a long swig from a magnum of bubbly. But he overdid it. His head pitched forward, and when he raised it back up, twin foot-long stalactites of champagne and mucus drooled out of his nose. On the nearby greenside Jumbotron, Sky Sports was kind enough to replay it twice.

The next stop was the closing ceremonies, where Woosnam pronounced the event "the greatest week in history," proving that the Guinness and champagne were working. He reconfirmed it by saying he looked forward to meeting again "at Valhalla in 2006."

The ritual imbibing continued at the press center, where the Europeans sat down with glasses and microphones in front of them, to talk about—what else?—drinking.

Clarke teased Woosnam, "It took ten seconds too long for you to down that pint of Guinness."

"A tenth quicker than you did," the captain replied. "And I'll prove it now if you want to get them out on the table."

"I'm a little bit younger than you are," said Clarke. "Just mind your age."

"There's no substitute for experience," Woosnam shot back.

Padraig Harrington was the last player to whom a question was formally addressed. But as soon as the reporter spoke Padraig's name, he interrupted him. "So," he began, leaning in. "Do you want to know how I won the Ryder Cup for Ireland?"

The rare serious note was sounded by Garcia. Asked about the team's pride in its victory, he channeled Paul Casey and said, "It's always nice to beat the Americans at anything."

That night the K Club saw two parties of very different kinds. One was private, bringing together both the European and the U.S. sides in the American team room. The other was public. It took place in the tented village behind the clubhouse.

The Americans were subdued when they returned to their quarters at about 9:00 p.m. They had dinner, and then sat around commiserating. At about 11:00, Sam Torrance, this year one of the European vice-captains, walked into the room. His long-ago insult of Lehman had apparently been forgotten, and he mingled freely among the Americans. He eventually wound up alongside Scott Verplank, and invited him to the winning side's team room.

"Why don't you come over and say hello?" Torrance asked.

"Will you let me in?" Verplank replied, smiling.

Verplank walked across the hotel with Torrance. He watched the Europeans drink from the Cup and chatted with Westwood, Clarke, and Harrington. After fifteen minutes or so, he said, "Why don't you guys come back over to our room?" They were glad to oblige, and brought along Montgomerie, David Howell, and Luke Donald.

Howell went right for the karaoke machine and launched into a version of "Copacabana" that would have made Barry Manilow weep. It must have been audible in the other team room, because before long eighty percent of the Europeans had made their way over. Verplank and Lisa Cink belted out "Stairway to Heaven"; Furyk and Vaughn Taylor teamed up for a highly ironic duet of 50 Cent's "In the Club." A few players retired early; for others the drinking and singing went on until two.

But as fatigue set in, so did the reality of the loss. When Verplank went upstairs to his room, he found Furyk sitting on the floor in the hallway, mulling over the events of the week.

They sat together for an hour, assessing their team's intensity level, degree of comfort with team play, and the other riddles of its underperformance.

"The new guys just didn't know what to expect," one of them said.

"The grinding isn't working," said the other. "Going out and trying to have a good time gives you the best chance."

"Why is it so hard for us to get relaxed and have fun with this?" they both wondered. In the end, they weren't any better at reaching conclusions than anyone else.

The public party had taken place much earlier, right after the sun had set and the European team had exited the press center. In its way it was a far more interesting affair. Certainly it better reflected the spirit of the week, if only because it included the gleeful people of Ireland.

Its setting was an outdoor, open-sided tent whose atmosphere was dreamlike, almost surreal. The floodlights in the distance barely reached it; the tent itself was equipped only with eerie little yellow, blue, and purple spotlights. There were perhaps 200 people inside, and 500 more clustered around the perimeter. A small pub-rock band was running through a rowdy rendition of "Is This the Way to Amarillo"—a song that, oddly, is virtually unknown in America but is wildly popular in Ireland and the UK, especially on the football terraces. The singing was louder than anything on the golf course all week. On the shoulders of those in the middle of the floor, bouncing up and down in time with the music, were Padraig Harrington and David Howell.

Howell soon departed, but Harrington was held captive. The crowd never let his feet touch the ground. The band went into the chorus from the Beatles' "Yellow Submarine," playing it over and over. After two passes, everyone had caught on to the improvised lyrics:

> *We all live in a dream of Harrington,*
> *A dream of Harrington,*
> *A dream of Harrington!*

On the path nearby, Ian Woosnam rolled by in a golf cart, smoking a cigarette, with a broad smile on his face. The people on the outer fringes turned around and roared. He lifted an imaginary glass in their direction.

Eventually, the man who won the Ryder Cup for Europe managed to scramble out the farside of the tent and disappear. The band played on. Several yards away, a group of about ten young women came bounding around the corner of the tent next door. One of them was tugging down the left halves of her blouse and brassiere, proudly displaying the upper portion of a breast to one of her friends. Now the women broke into their own improvised song.

> *Padraig Harrington signed our tits!*
> *Doo-dah! Doo-dah!*
> *Padraig Harrington signed our tits,*
> *All the doo-dah day!*

It was okay. Catherine would have understood.

THE FALL THAT WOULDN'T FINISH

I t was hard to say how the 2006 season ended, because it seemed like it never would.

Following August's PGA Championship, there were twelve official PGA Tour events, including the Tour Championship—none of which, in the pre-2007 schedule configuration, really mattered. On top of that, there were silly-season skins games and shootouts, plus an assortment of substantial-purse foreign events in Asia, Australia, and South Africa. These pocket-lining opportunities kept most players from putting down their clubs until the week before Christmas.

Apart from the Ryder Cup and Tiger Woods' seeming inability to finish anything worse than second, those four months produced little competitive news. There were, however, some peripheral attention-worthy moments. They ranged from the sentimental (Arnold Palmer putting his clubs down for good, in October) to the controversial (the first truly pointed exchanges about drug testing on Tour, just before Labor Day). And at year's end, there was plenty of analysis to be done, on everything from television ratings to the players' 2006 campaigns.

Concern about performance-enhancing drugs had long been part of pro golf's background music. Yet neither the Tour nor any other organization governing men's professional events had ever taken steps to implement testing. (In late 2006 the LPGA announced plans to begin testing in 2008.) The PGA Tour's inaction in particular drew steady criticism. During the summer of 2006, for example, Greg Norman had accused it of being "asleep at the wheel" on the problem.

The Tour, however, believed that testing was not needed. When Tim Finchem spoke to the press on the Tuesday prior to the WGC-Bridgestone Invitational in Akron, he insisted that "the culture of the sport" was enough of a safeguard against drugs that would enable players to combat nerves, for example, or drive the ball farther. Telling the players that they weren't in the spirit of fair play, he said, was "pretty much all you have to do in our sport at this point."

Then, on Wednesday, immediately following the commissioner's press conference, Tiger Woods issued a response that was just as harsh as Norman's, in tone if not in language. From his point of view, he said, the Tour should "have a program in place before guys are actually doing it."

How soon should it be implemented?

"Tomorrow."

Finchem must have felt shanghaied. Woods had in fact met with Finchem the previous day, just a few hours after the commissioner spoke. Whether or not they addressed the issue during that meeting remained a mystery. But Tiger's "tomorrow" was a slap at the Tour's idleness.

Woods and the other critics were right to say the Tour was dragging its feet. One Tour player, on the condition of anonymity, said that performance-enhancers were indeed available in the locker room, even if they were not widely used. "There are three guys out here every week who can get you that stuff," he claimed.

But even if the commissioner wanted to begin testing, it would be virtually impossible to do so considering the nature and structure of the Tour. Rounding up blood or urine samples from the more than 200 official PGA Tour members would be difficult enough. But if the Tour did that, it would also be formally obliged to test members of its affiliate circuits, the Champions and Nationwide Tours. (Indeed, that same Tour player said, "The real problem is on the Nationwide Tour, and that's the Tour's big headache, trying to police that tour.") Further, any testing effort could turn into a huge legal mess. The players were independent contractors, not employees. And, since there was no such thing as a players' union, there could be no blanket consent from the players' side. Then there was the question of how to handle nonmembers—international players, Monday qualifiers, or those competing on sponsor's exemptions. Imposing conditions on their participation in Tour events could expose it to antitrust actions.

Easier to grapple with were the black-and-white numbers resulting from the television ratings. Once again, they were down almost across the board. The most disappointing ratings came from the Tour Championship, whose Sunday finale barely reached one million households, and the U.S. Open, whose Tiger-less final round drew the championship's second-smallest audience since 1994.

The lone bright spot was the PGA Championship, where Saturday and Sunday numbers were up almost twenty percent over the previous year. This was widely understood as proof of Woods' ability to drive ratings—confirmation that the masses only cared about golf when Tiger won—although probably underestimated was the way early-week interest in the Woods-Mickelson matchup carried over into the weekend.

As far as player performance went, what stood out most was the number of under-30 Tour winners. Young players won thirteen of the Tour's forty-eight events—or, to put it another way, about a third of the events that Tiger Woods didn't win. Only once in the past eight seasons had the under-30's enjoyed such a boom year. It was probably no surprise, however, that fewer than half were Americans. (What was surprising was that Ben Curtis, the accidental 2002 British Open champion, accounted for two of them.)

It was tempting to understand the trend as something of a changing of the guard. Furthering that impression was that Ernie Els and Retief Goosen were both winless on the PGA Tour, and that Vijay Singh, now 45, won only once.

How, then, did the year work out for this book's featured players?

Michael Allen. Made over $470,000, but still finished 153rd on the money list, and had to go back to Q-school. He made it through again—running his record to nine successful finishes in thirteen tries—but had to buckle down to do so. After opening rounds of 76, 72, and 74, he played his last sixty holes bogey-free, closing with 66–69–66 to finish tied for twenty-third.

Mike Bennett and Andy Plummer. Toward the end of the year, the two swing gurus' students seemed to win almost every other week. After

Dean Wilson's victory in Denver (the pair's third of the year), Will Mackenzie won in Reno, and Eric Axley won in San Antonio. Bennett and Plummer's relationships with Mark Wahlberg and Johnny Drama, they said, earned them an unlikely November Las Vegas meeting with Ari Emanuel, the Hollywood superagent who served as the model for *Entourage*'s Ari Gold, and ultimately landed them a television appearance deal on The Golf Channel. Boom!

John Daly. To hear Daly tell it, his abysmal 2005—eight made cuts, eight missed cuts, and five withdrawals in twenty-one events—was the result of injuries to his left hand and his back. (Of the latter, Tiger Woods quipped, "his back is bothering him because he's got his front to deal with.") But it was hard not to suspect that his off-course life had something to do with it. There were no shotgun-wielding fathers or drunken rampages or cavorting with strippers (at least not that anyone knew of) but the health of his marriage was clearly a concern. Sherrie, his wife, filed for divorce on October 17; Daly filed divorce papers on the following day. Nevertheless, the couple was seen together again during Tiger Woods' Target World Challenge in mid-December. In 2007, Daly would have to rely on sponsors' exemptions to play the Tour.

David Duval. Duval had his best season since 2002, making eleven of twenty-four cuts (including two at the majors) and showing consistent signs that he was indeed on the way back. Yet he still lost his card, finishing 172nd on the 2006 money list. His position on the career money list, however, guaranteed him not just a free pass for the 2007 regular season, but also, effectively, for 2008; ending the year twenty-fourth on the all-time money list eked him under the cut-off number for the first, and, if he needed it, he could use a further exemption for the all-time top-fifty in 2008.

Jim Furyk. Furyk's two 2006 wins propelled him to the number two spot in the world rankings. With Singh having an off year, he was the new deputy sheriff in town. He might have even made a run at Woods' number one ranking had it not been for all his runner-ups—his three second-place finishes (at Hilton Head, the U.S. Open, Flint, and the Tour Championship, in Atlanta) ran his total to eight for the 2005 and 2006 seasons.

Robert Garrigus. On the balance, the rookie's 2006 was a huge success. He squandered his one great chance at a big paycheck—shooting 73 in the final round of September's 84 Lumber Classic, and finishing tied for fourth, despite starting Sunday in the final group. Still, he stayed drug-free, and made fifteen of twenty-eight cuts, enough to earn over half a million dollars. A bonus: he played well enough to attract the notice of Ernie Banks, Mr. Cub, a boyhood idol, who called Garrigus on the range at Disney and asked to tee it up with him in Scottsdale. (Garrigus, though raised in Portland, grew up watching Chicago sports on WGN.) He had to return to Q-school, but finished second to regain his card. Year's end, however, also brought bad news: he lost his father to cancer on December 29.

J.B. Holmes. After his win in Phoenix, the big-hitting rookie experienced a sharp drop off—between April and mid August, he couldn't find a fairway and couldn't make a putt, and missed eight of twelve cuts. It might have been the fault of those man-hungry young women back in Campbellsville. But the likelier causes were his needs to recover from his early-season win and, more generally, to feel truly at ease with Tour life. (Remember, his win in Phoenix was only his fourth event as a pro.) He turned to prodigy instructor Matt Killen at the end of the summer (at about the same time Killen starting working with Shaun Micheel), and that seemed to right his game: from that point he made six straight cuts, including good showings in Denver and at the PGA (where he was in the hunt until a Sunday blow-up).

Phil Mickelson. If one needed support for the idea that the 2006 season ended in August, no one was happier to furnish it than Mickelson. He teed it up only twice after the PGA—once in the WGC-Bridgestone Invitational in Akron and the other at the Ryder Cup. (He appeared at both, it was safe to say, because of the way he'd be criticized if he didn't.)

Geoff Ogilvy. The icing on Ogilvy's breakout season was the arrival of his and wife Juli's first child, daughter Phoebe, in October. His newly heightened profile, however, forbade him from taking much time off. He played well at all of his post-baby events, finishing T19 at the Tour Championship, third at November's four-man Grand Slam of Golf, and second at both the Australian Open and Tiger's Williams World Challenge.

Sean O'Hair. O'Hair's solo road days didn't last long. After nine weeks and two caddie-firings, father-in-law Steve Lucas was back traveling with him and carrying his bag. The reunion was probably a good idea. Their first week back together, at August's Buick Open in Flint, O'Hair placed fourth; five weeks later, at the Canadian Open, he finished third. He didn't play particularly well toward the very end of the season, perhaps due to the fact that he and his wife, Jackie, were expecting their second child in January.

Adam Scott. Late in the season, Scott had a star-crossed feeling. Through eighteen PGA Tour events, he had a fourth, three thirds, and three runner-up finishes, but felt like he would never earn another win. The good news was after years of faltering at the majors, he was showing real improvement. His tie for eighth at the British was his best-ever showing, and he followed that with a tie for third at the PGA. He finally broke into the winner's circle in November, winning the Tour Championship. The victory would have looked stronger had Tiger and Lefty shown up, but it still helped redeem all the year's near-misses.

Michelle Wie. By the end of 2006, any support Wie had for her quest to make a cut against the men had more or less evaporated, at least among the Tour's players. True, she had a fair degree of success on the LPGA Tour (six top-fives in eight events, three of them at majors), and almost qualified for the men's U.S. Open. But her four appearances on men's tours during the year's second half were nothing short of disastrous.

In July she withdrew from the PGA Tour John Deere Classic, citing heat exhaustion. (She was eleven-over-par after twenty-seven holes when she pulled out.) In early September, she took two weeks off from school to compete, in consecutive weeks, in the European Tour's Omega Masters, in Crans-sur-Sierre, Switzerland; and the PGA Tour's 84 Lumber Classic, in Pennsylvania. In both events she finished last. Then, in November, she played in the Casio World Open in Japan, and she finished next to last.

Central to Wie's participation in such events was the notion she would improve with each passing year. Yet her results told the opposite story. Her best showing remained her first, three years ago at the Sony Open, when she was fourteen. She seemed to be living proof of the old adage that girls physically mature faster than boys—in the intervening years her progress had not been impressive. (Her short game was getting better, but still wasn't up to PGA Tour standards.) Most importantly, she seemed more susceptible than ever to nerves. It was perhaps no coincidence that her best finish came at an early age. Her inability, at that point, to appreciate what was at stake and be affected by pressure had been her secret weapon, and was now long gone.

The pivot in opinion among her would-be peers was easy to locate. It came during the second round at the Deere. As late as Thursday afternoon, Tour policy board member Joe Ogilvie (not to be confused with Geoff), at that point leading the tournament, could pronounce, somewhat condescendingly, that those who criticized Wie's Tour appearances "just didn't get it"—that is, didn't understand that the attention she brought to the men's game was all for the good. What Ogilvie "didn't get" was that the more often Wie failed, the more often the Tour could be accused of false advertising. When she played badly, as was now so often the case, the Tour looked bad for inviting her. Other players were now questioning what would it prove if she finally survived to play a weekend. "If you give somebody enough chances, they're bound to make a cut," Sean O'Hair said on Sunday at the Deere, just five days after playing a practice round with her. "I just don't know what the big deal is if she makes the cut. I'm not bashing Michelle. I think she's good for the game. But if we're giving her an exemption just to see if she can make the cut, I mean, c'mon. Making a cut in a PGA Tour event and contending in a PGA Tour event are universes away from one another." If one boiled down his sentiments, they were fairly close to those Vijay Singh expressed when he asked, "But can she win?" back in Hawaii.

The second half of her year also saw wholesale changes in Team Wie. A week after the Women's British Open she fired her caddie, Greg Johnston, who said he was "extremely disappointed that no one named Wie gave me the news." Presumably it had been delivered by her agent, Ross Berlin, who one hoped got the courtesy of a personal call when he was fired in November.

Late in the year came the news that Wie had been accepted at Stanford. On the surface, her desire to continue her education was laudable. Still, it underscored a difficulty that was already hindering her development as a player. As a pro, she couldn't play amateur or collegiate events. And because of LPGA age restrictions, she could only play eight events per year on that Tour. If she was going to attend college, it would, on the one hand, only diminish her playing opportunities, especially after she passed the LPGA's minimum age of eighteen. On the other, playing the same number of winter, spring, and fall events as she did during her junior and senior high school years would cut six full weeks out of her academic year. She would, in other words, still be living half-lives as both a golfer and a student. During her hapless outing at the 84 Lumber, one member of her inner circle head-shakingly said, "She's got to pick one or the other—school or golf. She can't do both." Enrolling at Stanford would only perpetuate the problem.

Tiger Woods. One day before the end of the year, on his thirty-first birthday, Woods announced that his wife, Elin, was expecting their first child. It was a fitting, circle-of-life ending to his year. But the four months leading up to it were business as usual, with the emphasis on business.

During that period, he launched a course-design firm (his first would be in Dubai) and a resort venture in the Bahamas (where he partnered with Ernie Els, who was handing the architecture duties, and Joe Lewis, the tycoon who built Isleworth, who obviously was handling most of the money). It also came to light that Woods had signed a new endorsement deal with Nike, although both the timing and the terms of the story were curious. Usually, Woods and his people leaked word to the press about his deals, so as to illustrate his popularity and the signing company's faith in his marketability. But here that didn't happen, and one could only wonder why. The *Chicago Tribune* broke the news in December, although Nike officials had confirmed the deal was done as far back as August's PGA Championship. The length of the deal wasn't mentioned and neither were dollar amounts. The likeliest explanation for the silence was that the terms didn't significantly surpass those of his previous, 2001 deal (five years, at $20 million per). Another reason to keep things quiet, many suspected, was that part of the package was equity, which is far less sexy than cash.

More interesting, perhaps, was Woods' now-annual trip to Asia. In November, in the two weeks following the Tour Championship (which he had skipped), he played the HSBC Champions Tournament in Shanghai, China, and then the Dunlop Phoenix in Japan. The former was the more important of the two, considering Tiger's relationship with Buick. China is the largest car market in the world, and has become increasingly important to General Motors; according to industry projections, more Buicks would be sold there in 2007 than in the U.S. (where the brand's sales continued to decline, despite Woods' efforts as spokesperson).

The golf tournaments might have seemed incidental to Tiger's Asia trip had it not been for the reported $3 million appearance fees he received to play in each of them. They topped off the whopping $98 million in off-course income that Woods collected in 2006 (as reported in *Golf Digest*'s annual survey of player endorsement earnings).

Of course, the golf Woods played toward the end of the year was just short of magnificent. In and around wins at three straight post-Medinah Tour events (running his Tour streak to six in a row) he worked in two second-place finishes in Asia, plus a win at the Williams World Challenge. (The only real blip was getting knocked out in the quarterfinals of the World Match Play in Wentworth, England, the week before the Ryder Cup.)

Only a few months had passed since the world wondered if he was still the best player in golf. But now there was little doubt. It seemed like the only question now surrounding Woods was whether or not he could rival or better his monster run of 2000 and 2001. But there were two others. Would such a run, if it happened, provoke a similar spike in spectator interest? And if it did, would the general public's interest in golf again fall through the floor when it was over?

Allaying that last fear was a marked change in the competitive landscape. Phil Mickelson, for one, was a much better player than he was in 2000. Although some doubted his inability to recover from his disaster at Winged Foot, his history showed that he was nothing if not resilient.

More to the point, golf was probably only beginning to see the most remarkable ramifications of Tiger's presence on Tour. Some of the young fans he initially brought to the game were now nearing the age at which they might begin to compete against him. It was correct to call Sean O'Hair and Michelle Wie the first (nonbiological) children of the Tiger Era: they were the first players to come into—or be rushed into—the game in his wake. But the generation behind them, far greater in number, held more promise. Just after Woods won the 2001 Masters, at a youth clinic in Long Beach, California, a reporter asked him who he thought would be his next great challenger. "It might be one of these kids right here," he replied. At the time, most of those kids were pre-teens. But now their arrival was right around the corner.

ACKNOWLEDGMENTS

A lot of legwork went into this book—thirty weeks in 2006 alone. But it also represents the time and effort of dozens of people—friends, relatives, colleagues, players, caddies, coaches, and even an agent or two—without whose help it never would have been completed.

It would take hundreds of pages to do justice to their time and effort. While I don't have room for that, I can tell one illuminating tale.

In Chapter Eight, one of the Tour's finest makes an unplanned visit to a New Orleans tattoo parlor. Yep, a tattoo parlor. (No spoilers here. You'll have to read the chapter to find out who, and why.) In writing about it, I needed to describe the shop, but didn't have time to stop by myself, since I had to get on a plane the morning after the tournament ended to fly to the next Tour stop.

My friend Tom Albrecht lives in the Big Easy, so I asked him to do some reporting for me. Now, Tom's not a reporter. And he's the last guy you'd ever find in a tattoo parlor. He's an English professor at Tulane (we went to grad school together in California) and although he has the shabby-chic, Lower East Side look of an extra in a Sonic Youth video, his cultural tastes are more high art than body art.

That wasn't the only thing making this an uninviting errand to run. The tattoo parlor in question resides in one of the dicier areas of post-Katrina New Orleans. It's in the kind of neighborhood where it's not uncommon to "get bumped," as the locals say—meaning, to have someone rear-end you on purpose, so as to steal your car or worse. But Tom went ahead and did it anyway.

No one else, I suppose, endangered life and limb for this project. But many others gave me chunks of time that reflected a similar commitment. The primary and heartiest thanks go to the Tour folk who allowed me to chew on their ears—in some cases for hours at a time—on the range, in the locker room, on the telephone, in hotel rooms, in their homes, and even, in one case, on a private plane. Their cooperation was this book's very condition of possibility. I'm still shaking my head about just how many people immediately saw the value in what I was trying to do: show a side of Tour life that conventional media, for the most part, no longer has much time for. Had they not understood and shared that desire, this book couldn't have happened.

I also got invaluable assistance from my fellow golf writers. I always profited from the questions they asked in group interviews (press conferences, post-round scrums, and the like), but more important from their copy, which enabled me, a guy on a longer deadline, to follow up with the players and ferret out more detail. I never, for example, would have known about that tattoo parlor if *Golf World*'s Jim Moriarity and the Associated Press's Doug Ferguson hadn't coaxed out the beginnings of the tale in the first place. I would never have known about Phil Mickelson's nap before the final round of the Masters if Tod Leonard of the *San Diego Union-Tribune* hadn't first mentioned it in one of his post-Augusta stories.

But my press room neighbors offered a lot more than leads. I don't have much experience covering other sports, but it's hard for me to imagine a group of people who, within the confines of their responsibilities to their individual outlets, are so generous in sharing information. Beyond that, their assistance in shaping ideas and opinions—and their expertly pointing out fertile lines of pursuit—greatly improved this book. Those who helped were legion in number, but I'd like to single out Damon Hack of the *New York Times,* Steve Elling of the *Orlando Sentinel,* Sam Weinman of the Westchester *Journal News,* Ron Kroichick of the *San Francisco Chronicle,* Mark Cannizzaro of the *New York Post,* and Jaime Diaz and Tom Callahan of *Golf Digest.*

Biggest thanks, however, go to my *Sports Illustrated* colleagues Gary Van Sickle, Alan Shipnuck, Rick Reilly, and John Garrity, not only for their encouragement and long golf memories, but for setting writerly standards that I'll be trying to reach for a long, long time.

On the edit side, I also owe enormous thanks to *SI* golf editors Jim Herre and Jim Gorant for keeping me on the road and working—a prerequisite to the project, since the cost of doing it out of my own pocket would have been prohibitive. Back at the office, Rick Lipsey unfailingly helped erase my mistakes. Farrell Evans did that, too, but also served as an expert (though not officially licensed) psychotherapist. Librarian Helen Stauder worked magic for me on several occasions, laying the foundation for some of my most crucial reporting.

In terms of helping to edit this book, I also owe a huge debt to everyone who read chapters in their initial stages, particularly Jason Sobel of ESPN.com, whose meticulous, on-the-money comments were invaluable.

Mike Gorman of WireImage and Christian Iooss of Getty Images were clutch performers, helping me gather some terrific photos for the book. I would not have had a clue about what to do with those pictures were it not for Rick Becker-Leckrone, who schooled me in the ways of photo-editing. Darren Carroll took on the impossible task of attempting to make me look good for the author photo. And if that wasn't enough, he also made me to try the green mole sauce at Tucson's Café Poca Cosa. ("Too pedestrian!" I scoffed. I was wrong.) For both things I will be eternally grateful.

It says a lot about the culture of golf that numerous people—from officials at the Tour and other governing bodies, to p.r. folks at the networks—unblinkingly answered every one of my thousands of requests, for everything from stats to memory-refreshing game tapes. My sincerest gratitude goes to Una Jones and Julius Mason at the PGA of America; Jill Maxwell and Glenn Greenspan at Augusta National; Angela Howe and Angus Farquhar at the R&A; Betsy Swain at the USGA; and, at the PGA Tour, Joel Schuchman, Todd Budnick, Nelson Silverio, Mike Veneto, Maureen Callaghan, Denise Taylor, and James Cramer—but especially Colin Murray, who served as much of this book's de facto fact-checker.

Among television people, thanks to Robin Brendel and Kevin Tedesco at CBS Sports, Stacy Adduci at USA, Keenon Perry at HBO, Lindy Barnes and Brian Walker at NBC Sports, Jonathan Bramley at the BBC, and Sean Wheeler at Turner Sports. I must make special mention of ace DVD-burners Seth Fader, at PGA Tour Productions, and The Golf Channel's Jeremy Friedman, who allowed me to ruin (well, almost ruin) his Christmas.

Expert number-crunching came from Brandi Preston at Nielsen Media Research and Judy Thompson at the National Golf Foundation.

I'd also like to express my gratitude to Carol de Onís, copyediting supervisor at Simon & Schuster, and staff—their efforts in getting this book to market quickly were superhuman, and greatly improved my prose.

While those folks ensured accuracy, my friends helped me stay sane. Doing weeks' worth of telephonic babysitting was Gary Touma (the Jason Mewes to my Kevin Smith, but without the heroin—nooch!). Megan Becker-Leckrone performed similar duties and more, editing an entire weekend away during one of my Las Vegas stopovers, while I sat around eating chicken panang and pilfering her and husband Rick's CD collection. Friend and former golfaholic Brigitte Sandquist also pitched in with some last-minute editing. While traveling, I also benefited from the company—and sometimes spare beds—of the best group of friends a road warrior could ever have. In Miami, Harry Sherman introduced me to the wonders of bottle service; in New York, Rebecca Fine reminded me of what a bad influence Harry can be. Kit Millan showed me around Honolulu, and made it crystal clear that Iolani was a much better high school than arch-rival Punahou. During a late-project stop in Tucson, Richard Grant and Shipherd, Julie, and Lincoln Reed kept my spirits as high as my anxiety level. Securing my comfort in Los Angeles, my West Coast base of operations, were Dawn and Thomas Hollier, and Dave Schreiber and Carol Stutz. When I was in Atlanta, Jane and Ben Chance not only made me feel at home, but shook me up and down, took me out, and reminded me that Atlanta, in fact, is my home.

Last, there were four people without whose confidence this project never would have gotten off the ground. The first two were David Black and Dave Larabell, my ambassadors of *kwan* (as Rod Tidwell would say). The next was my editor, Marty Beiser. He recognized immediately the aim and the value of this project, and his belief in it never wavered. (Or, if it did, he was nice enough not to let me know it.) At any rate, his patience with this first-time author bordered on the saintly.

At this project's toughest hours, I always knew there was one person I could unfailingly count on for support. To paraphrase a great poet: Where there is no trust, there's always faith. And when there is no faith, there's always hope. And when there is no hope, there's always . . . Mom. Thanks, Mom.

INDEX

ABOUT THE AUTHOR

Chris Lewis began covering golf at the dawn of the Tiger Era and has contributed to all the game's major U.S. publications. He now works almost exclusively as a golf correspondent for *Sports Illustrated*. A New York native, he attended Columbia University and then migrated to Southern California, where he earned an M.A. in Comparative Literature at the University of California, Irvine. He now lives in Atlanta. His SI.com columns twice earned honorable mentions in the Best Daily Column category from the Golf Writers Association of America.